gay&
lesbian
online
4th edition

gay&
lesbian
online

4th edition

jeff dawson

alyson books
los angeles | new york

MANUFACTURED IN THE UNITED STATES OF AMERICA.

THIS TRADE PAPERBACK ORIGINAL IS PUBLISHED BY ALYSON PUBLICATIONS,
P.O. BOX 4371, LOS ANGELES, CALIFORNIA 90078-4371.
DISTRIBUTION IN THE UNITED KINGDOM BY TURNAROUND PUBLISHER SERVICES LTD.,
UNIT 3, OLYMPIA TRADING ESTATE, COBURG ROAD, WOOD GREEN,
LONDON N22 6TZ ENGLAND.

FIRST PUBLISHED BY PEACHPIT PRESS: MAY 1996
FIRST ALYSON EDITION (THIRD EDITION): DECEMBER 1998
FOURTH EDITION: NOVEMBER 2000

00 01 02 03 04 05 **a** 10 9 8 7 6 5 4 3 2 1

ISBN 1-55583-581-3
(PREVIOUSLY PUBLISHED WITH ISBN 0-201-68861-1 BY PEACHPIT PRESS.)

LIBRARY OF CONGRESS CATALOGING-IN-PUBLICATION DATA
  DAWSON, JEFF, 1958–
    GAY AND LESBIAN ONLINE : YOUR INDISPENSABLE GUIDE TO CRUISING
  THE QUEER WEB / JEFF DAWSON. 4TH ED.
      1. GAY MEN—COMPUTER NETWORK RESOURCES. 2. LESBIANS—COMPUTER
  NETWORK RESOURCES. 3. HOMOSEXUALITY—COMPUTER NETWORK RESOURCES.
  4. INTERNET (COMPUTER NETWORK). I. TITLE.
  HQ76.25.D37 2000
  025.04'086'64—DC21

For Bob Young

CONTENTS

Foreword

The extraordinary power of the Internet to link, inform, and inspire provides gay and lesbian individuals and organizations with a remarkable tool for personal growth and political activism, encouraging cooperation and solidarity throughout America and around the world. Jeff Dawson's research and well-written commentary chart the exploding queer presence in cyberspace in an easy-to-use and often hilarious manual for people at all levels of computer skill.

Encyclopedic in scope, *Gay & Lesbian Online* describes an ever-growing digital world, allowing you to gain access to the extraordinary archive of documents available on the web as well as instant connections to other gay and lesbian people who share your personal and political interests.

Gay & Lesbian Online is a great resource and a reminder of the importance of defending our First Amendment rights to freedom of speech. Our communities worldwide have much to gain from the free and unrestricted use of communications technology and much to lose if it is abridged.

Cleve Jones
Founder
The Names Project
AIDS Memorial Quilt

Introduction

When historians chart the rise of gay culture, they'll plot the tipping point as right now, at the turn of the century. And they will credit the Web and online technology as its locus. Every subject—whether history, activism, finance or simply finding one another—has reached a critical mass in a startling array of Web sites.

Where before you had to fumble through a techno-maze looking for our culture's key words, now the domain names are achieving a certain logic. Gay.com, Lesbiannation.com, Hatewatch.org—Web addresses are as straightforward as a headline. Our community's largest search engine is Rainbowquery.com, a name that is not only logical, but retains a sort of fey exactitude.

With the new transparency has come something close to universal access. Gay Latinos in Los Angeles, Gen X Bears in the Northeast, Queer Muslims in Arabia, lesbian drummers, it's hard to find a group that has not leapt the technical barriers to claim a place at the techno table.

What you have in front of you is an attempt to describe and map this amazing reflection of our individuality in the communications mosaic of the Web. From the acid frolics of filmmaker Bruce LaBruce to the joys of organic gardening on Ruralgays.com, you'll find that the best of the pages are always questioning, pushing for answers, and charting a new course. Whether it's in chat rooms discussing the dilemmas of miracle AIDS therapies or your dream trick's latest incarnation, queer Web pages are providing us not so much a new voice as a new method and manner of making ourselves heard. And it all takes place so often! Every second of the day, there are a couple hundred thousand of us rubbing technical antennae across every separating strata of our economic, racial, and sexual diversity.

What you'll find here on the queer Web is us, in all our variety—committed activists, campmeisters, and cruise masters, from the silvered pioneers of the movement to the café kid with coffee breath, a slow smile, and a quick way with a mouse. We take on heart-of-the-matter issues like activism, domestic partners, and sex, as well as lesser urgencies, such as how to wear stiletto heels on formal occasions. All you need is a modem and curiosity—no clearance pass required. Think of this book as a map for your journeys.

Although I've reached for a sort of Bible approach—casting the net around the world and throughout the subject index, with so many sites that, if you visit them, all your friends and house mates may begin to sing the computer widow blues, this book is meant to launch, rather than proctor, your cybervoyaging. The point is not to enslave yourself, but to explore this new and exciting territory where gay men and lesbians are a natural majority. Forget the technology; it's only a tool. Just be curious about the people. Take your information, absorb it, then contribute to the dialogue. (If you discover some great stuff, E-mail me at jdawson@sonic.net.)

One word of caution: All this communication is a strong cocktail. And this one is as pink as hell. You may be...modified. Cheers to queers.

COMPREHENSIVE INFORMATION

The Menu

For a taste of the world mix of *Gay & Lesbian Online*, take a look at the table of contents. There are resources for AIDS, activism, Asian-Americans and African-Americans, books, dating, erotica, gardening, gender, queer families, leather, lesbian resources, movies, politics, sex, seniors, travel, and youth. Destinations range from the eminently useful (financial advice) to the brilliantly silly (a '90s guy prescribing cure-alls for bad hair days). The C's, for example, contain everything from City Guides to CU-SeeMe and Cooking. Elsewhere you'll meet Max at the Fat Girl home page "for fat dykes and the women who want them." And you'll come across the nun whose collection of AIDS information is larger than the one at the Centers for Disease Control and Prevention. Then there's Hein in Amsterdam with his awesome list of links, Lady Bunny of Wigstock fame, and a group of wonderfully talented Web trailblazers like Amy Goodloe, Bob Skepsis, M.J. O'Neill, and David Casti. Of course, there's also the flock of overachievers at the Queer Resources Directory—a vast archive of queerology that's so large that any attempts to describe it fall short. It's been around so long that the new generation tends to knock it.

And, yes, the queer Web is international. Paris, Sydney, London, Tokyo, and Ipanema are rife with queerness. You'll find "the culture" in some less traveled but delicious spots like Majorca and Barcelona and down in Zimbabwe as well as up in Finland. As Christopher Isherwood said in mock shock, "Homosexuals. We're everywhere!" Language is not a problem. English, for better or worse, is the international tongue. Even the French are shrugging off the language wars, so their *Gai et Lesbienne* pages are mostly translated.

Why Queer Only?

Does the queer focus of *Gay & Lesbian Online* open the book to charges of ghettoization? No. Exploring ourselves is not separatism. It's natural curiosity with a big dose of convenience. There are distinct differences to being queer in this world. Think for a short second of leaving it: How do you write a will that protects your lover from being booted out of your home, the hospital room, or the funeral? While straight parents interested in adoption must jump through stringent legal hoops, only gay men and lesbians would want a list of whom to contact in various states for same-sex couples adoption. Who else would pore over the transcripts of judicial reports on gays in the military, hate-crimes bills, and domestic partners? What about hot bars and gay bed-and-breakfasts, the pros and cons of growth hormone, or breast cancer studies for lesbians? The answer is: us. As a multi-dimensional mosaic of the best of our culture, the Web subverts the once high barriers of geography, race and religion.

Easy Tour Guaranteed!

Gay & Lesbian Online is easy to use. You can take your time browsing the text descriptions of online sites and subjects, marking discoveries for a visit later on. These reviews are wholly subjective, sometimes quirky cherry pickings of all that's available. For subjects that contain vast resources (such as AIDS, Books, and Leather), there are a few orientation paragraphs so that you'll have a sense of the big picture and where to begin.

Mixed in with the large categories are descriptions of key sites, write-ups that concentrate on a single extraordinarily well-done home page. Larry Bob's Generic Queer Home Page is described in all its glory, as is Adult Children of Heterosexuals. And because subjects are cross-referenced, you can read about the Digital Queers under Activism, for example, or flip to page 207 and get a fuller picture of the organization and its work. You may even want to order a Digital Queers T-shirt (*très* chic!).

If you're itching to get on the Web, you can use this book as a straight (pardon the expression) reference book. Thousands of Web pages are listed immediately following the write-ups, so you're bound to find your cup of tea.

Warning! Dead Spots Ahead

The online world is a living thing, so naturally it can also be a dying thing. Sometimes you'll punch in an address and be greeted by a blank screen. Don't mourn; that's life online. The personal home pages are especially fragile. Their existence is supported only by the passion of digital monks willing to spend long hours and rare bucks on something they think is important. Eventually, passions flame out or a forwarding address gets lost.

I've tried to avoid potential URL graves by reviewing only those pages that have strong vital signs. Most of the time each chapter highlights a site (or sites) that has the deepest reach into its subject. For example, you'll be referred to Steve Sanders's Gay and Lesbian Politics in the Politics chapter, Lesbian.org in the chapter on Lesbian Resources, The Bears Resource List under Bears, and so on.

MAIL LISTS

E-mail is an essential glue of our age. Listed below are various queer and queer-related lists to which you can subscribe. To subscribe to a list, do the following:

1) E-mail a message to: majordomo@(list name and address).(domain—i.e., *com* or *net* or *edu* etc.)
2) Don't enter anything in the subject line
3) In the body of the message, and without the parentheses, write subscribe <list name> <your email address>
4) Send the message

The same procedure can be used to unsubscribing to lists by replacing subscribe with unsubscribe.

To find the list you want, use the search engines offered by DejaNews, QueerNet, Reference.Com and Usenet Information Center. Simply enter your issue and the relevant discussion thread will pop up.

The largest indexes are kept by Liszt, Topica, DejaNews or ONE List (which swallowed Egroups). Of the gay and lesbian mail lists, the best are found at Queernet, David Casti's List of Lists and The Sappho List. You can find discussions on domestic partners, lesbian rights, military policy, international human rights, immigration, the queer punk scene, and more. Queerlaw is all about legal theory and application of law. QueerPolitics is devoted to the discussion and analysis of the politics of the gay rights movement. Right Wing Watch Online is compiled by People for the American Way. There are also links and addresses of international, national, regional, and local rights organizations and gender-exclusive lists as well as state-by-state updates on antigay ordinances.

☐ *DejaNews*
http://www.dejanews.com

☐ *List of Lists*
http://www.tcp.com:8000/qrd/

☐ *Liszt.com*
http://www.liszt.com/select/Culture/Gay/

☐ One List
http://www.onelist.com

☐ Queernet
http://www.queernet.org/

☐ Queer Parenting
http://www.geocities.com/westhollywood/3372.email.html

☐ Reference.com
http://www.reference.com

☐ Sappho Mailing List
http://www.apocalypse.org/pub/sappho/

Newsgroups

Usenet Information Center
http://sunsite.unc.edu/usenet-i/

- ☐ alt.homosexual
- ☐ bit.listserv.gaynet
- ☐ uk.gay-lesbian-bi
- ☐ alt.feminism
- ☐ alt.journalism.gay-press
- ☐ alt.politics.homosexuality
- ☐ alt.politics.sex
- ☐ sci.med.aids
- ☐ soc.feminism
- ☐ soc.motss
- ☐ soc.women.lesbian-and-bit

SEARCH AND REFERENCE TOOLS

Up until recently, the solely queer search engines were rather limited, and Yahoo!'s links were indispensable, particularly in the arts, entertainment, and sociology categories. That's all changed now. As gay and lesbian sites have proliferated, our indexes have kept pace and become much deeper than the general list databases. Rainbow Query, NetQueery, HomoRama, QMondo, GayScape, the Mining Company, Gay Agenda, M.J. O'Neill's Web Links, and others are becoming less the alternative tool and more the first choice.

Another approach to finding particular subjects is to check out the links list of the relevant chapter's top sites: Critpath for AIDS, LeatherPage for Leather, Bear Networks for bears, and so on. These pages are specialists in their fields. Some more general favorites are *The Advocate*'s community resource links; DataLounge's high-quality selection; Amazon Online, for lesbians and bisexual women; Freedom.co.uk, "the gay search site"; Human Rights Campaign's links; National Gay and Lesbian Task Force's links; SomaBoy; and U Report ("poop for the modern homosexual"). All these and many more have partisans.

If it seems like there's a ocean of mainstreamy gay stuff on-line, try the Queer Hotlist. As it says in the introduction, "You won't find any links to the Log Cabin Republicans here." This list is oriented toward stringent criteria: Is it new? Does it question the status quo? Is it sexy? That's why you'll find academic treatises on genetic causes of sexuality alongside sites dealing with hankie codes and lost of stuff on young gay energy in music and 'zines.

Award Sites

Another good method of sifting the Web is to check out the award sites. Athena's Goddess of Wisdom Awards are bestowed only upon Web sites with strong content and impact for lesbians. The Queer Living Family Choice Award s selects for fine Web design and quality the whole family can enjoy. The Rainbow Award is one of the longest-running awards groups, choosing recommended sites for exceptional content, design, creativity, presentation, concept, and benefit to the community; its familiar logo is a rainbow earth and a pink triangle. Wit's End Literary Cyberzine gives its imprimatur to a an often brilliant batch of entertaining Web sites with good writing, presentation, and creativity. The crème de la crème!

Women's Indexes

In the last year women's indexes have exploded. At Phenomenal Women of the Web, Spyder gives out her seal to women's pages of excellence and honor, over 700 so far. A beautiful site that "will empower women and scare the crap out of most men!" Cybergrrl! has an incredible links list and Diva Great Sites for Girls features the G-Spot award. Perhaps the largest women's index is to be found at WWW Women, a comprehensive, searchable directory of women and women's resources. It's packed with pages on the arts, diversity, entertainment, government, health, history, media, civil rights, religion, and more—all lesbian, all the time. Since it has joined with Lesbian.org, it has become deeper and broader, rivaling Yahoo! in many categories and surpassing it for pages on lesbian poetry, fiction, and meeting places (such as chat lines and message boards). The home page list? No contest.

Web Rings

If you're just browsing, but want your journeys to remain within a theme, try a spin on a Web ring—an interconnected group of Web pages with a similar topic. Perhaps the largest network of rings is found at the Queer Ring, with Web pages linked together thematically on everything from cigars to youth and women loving women and motorcycling. The great thing about the Queer Ring is that it is rearranged once every week so that sites with little traffic are put after sites with high traffic. Among other rings is Bear Ring, one of the largest with hundreds of sites on every variation of ursine culture. Another vast LGBT ring, with about 300 sites at last count, is Gay S&M. Piglet, your host, takes you on a totally non-vanilla tour of S/M-oriented pages, including Leather, Rubber, Bondage, WaterSports, and "Sex Magik." Global TransGenderRing is "a group of Web sites focusing on all aspects of the Transgender experience, from cross-dressing to postoperative transsexuality...and all points between." The Out & Proud links pages about coming out with lots of resources both for your and your family and friends. Rainbow Spirituality Ring has a plethora of lesbian, gay, bisexual, and LGB-friendly spirituality, transgender and cross-dressing communities. Among the best women's rings are; WebWomyn Ring, a "guided tour of personal Web pages and IRC channel home pages featuring all kinds of women....lesbians, straight, bi, married, outrageous flirts, brave, crazy, sensitive, brash, sane, creative, intellectual, goofy...you name it..." The Women Loving Women Web ring is full of lesbians, dykes, Sapphos, butchies, and SassyFemmes.

Tips

This is not an exact science, so don't be surprised if you get a list of pages on one search engine that is different from those returned from another. One strategy is to make yourself familiar with each index's capabilities, which are all slightly different. In traditional search engines such as AltaVista, Yahoo!, and Excite you're searching on a particular word in the Web site title, and you don't have many options. A good alternative is

Ask Jeeves, which allows you to phrase your search question in plain English rather than just typing in a series of words or trying to use connectors like *and, or, not*. It can answer upwards of 8 million questions, so you stand a good chance of finding what you want without translating it into "searchese." Tip: If you're looking for information on the Metropolitan Community Church, try the subject name as well as gay/religion and gay/spirituality. Also take care with your spelling and play with variations like "queer-punk" or "Queerpunk."

Google

Google is a traditional search engine with a very effective twist. Unlike Yahoo! and Excite, which return pages with no discrimination other than alphabetical, Google pulls up pages to match your request by rank of how often they are linked to similar pages. In other words, it relies on the connections made by the Web masters (whom one assumes know the best pages) and sorts the return listings according to the highest link rates. And its database is huge. A search on "gay leather," for example, showed approximately 31,300 Web sites, and took 0.27 seconds. A search on "lesbian music" found 80,300 in 0.10 seconds. One of the great things about Google is that, even if a Web site has gone down, Google gives you the image of its former incarnation, very often containing the new address. Sometimes a search is in the right area but gives too many results. To narrow the results down, you might want to do a new search that searches only within the URLs returned by the too-broad search query. This is often called "narrowing a search" or "searching within the current search results." Google makes this process easy. Since Google only returns Web pages that contain all the words in your query, to narrow a search all you need to do is add more words to the end of your query. This gives you a new query that will return a subset of the pages returned by the too-broad query. You can also exclude a word by putting the "-" operator immediately in front of the undesirable term. Free of the advertisements that muck up most search engine portals, Google is an efficient, effective treat.

NET GUIDES AND GURUS

Along with all those Web pages there are mysterious (and easily mastered) things such as IRC, Cu-Seeme, mail lists, and news-groups. These receive cursory explanations from your service provider, and how-to books abound. Very often the FAQs will answer your questions, but if you prefer a more conversational instruction, what do you do? Jump on the Web and see your friendly queer Web mentor!

Perhaps the best coach in all things net is Amy Goodloe's Lesbian.org. After a general introduction, the guide goes on to discuss some of the key concepts and terms, and to recommend resources for further learning. The next section covers each of the main Internet tools—E-mail, newsgroups, mail lists, and the Web—from the point of view of a user rather than a techie. More than just tutoring, these provide site addresses for the tool described. For more information, you can also browse Lesbian.org's New Users and Netiquette sections. These are followed by a long list of links for learning about the Net. Among them are many women-specific sites—the most famous of which is the ADA Project. Although the goal of the ADA Project is much wider than just teaching Web usage (the creators aim to establish a universal clearinghouse for information and resources relating to women and computing), this centralized location includes information on conferences, projects, discussion groups, and organizations. You'll find what you need among its many links.

Whatever way you learn about the Net, realize that you're a budding activist. Just zipping around and adding numbers to queer site registers is strengthening the viability of our network. What an easy way to contribute.

WEB GUIDES & GURUS

☐ *Digital Diversity*
http://www.diversity.org.uk

☐ *Digital Queers*
http://www.dq.org/

☐ *Electronic Frontier Foundation Internet Guide*
http://www.eff.org/

☐ *International Guild of Gay Webmasters*
http://www.iggw.org/

☐ *Lesbian.Org Internet Guide*
http://www.lesbian.org/internet-guide/guide.html

☐ *Rainbow Guide.com*
http://www.rainbowguide.com

☐ *Tactics for Survival in a Homophobic Culture*
http://www.fas.harvard.edu/~saran/tactics.html

☐ *Techno Dyke Headquarters*
http://www.technodyke.com/

☐ *Webgrrls Internaitonal*
http://www.webgrrls.com/

☐ *Wise Women of the Web*
http://www.neosoft.com/~acoustic/www.html

INDEXES & SEARCH INDEXES

☐ *The ADA Project: Resources for Women in Computing*
http://www.cs.yale.edu/HTML/YALE/CS/HyPlans/tap/tap.html

☐ *Advocate Community Links*
http://www.advocate.com/html/gaylinks/resources.html

☐ *All-in-One Search Page*
http://www.allonesearch.com

☐ *AltaVista*
http://www.altavista.com/

☐ *Amazon City*
http://www.amazoncity.com/

☐ *Amazon Online*
http://www.amazon.org/

☐ *Ask Jeeves*
http://www.askjeeves.com/

☐ *Athena's Goddess of Wisdom Award*
http://www.qworld.org/staff/athena

☐ *BGLAD Online*
http://www.bglad.com

☐ *Bear Networks*
http://www.bear.net

☐ *Carleton Freenet*
http://www.ncf.carleton.ca/freeport/sigs/life/gay/menu

☐ *Caryl's Lesbian Links*
http://www.sirius.com/~caryls/

☐ *Clearinghouse*
http://www.clearinghouse.net/

☐ *Collected Queer Information*
http://www.cs.cmu.edu/People/mjw/Queer/MainPage.html

☐ *Cyber-Design's Best of the Lesbian and Gay Internet*
http://www.cyber-designs.com/pride

☐ *Cybergrrl!*
http://www.cybergrrl.com/netscape.htm

☐ *CyberQueer Australia*
http://www.cyberqueer.rainbow.net.au

☐ *CyberSocket*
http://www.cybersocket.com/

☐ *DejaNews*
http://www.dejanews.com/

☐ *Diva Great Sites — G-Spot award*
http://www.cyberwomen.com/

☐ *DivaNet*
http://www.zoom.com/divanet/

☐ *Femina Web Search for Women*
http://www.cybergrr.com

☐ *Feminist.com*
http://www.feminist.com/

☐ *Gay Agenda*
http://www.gayagenda.com/

☐ *Gay America*
http://www.gayamerica.com/

☐ *Gay Café*
http://www.gaycafe.com/links

☐ *Gay Europe*
http://www.gayeuro.com

☐ *Gay World*
http://www.gay.net

☐ *GayZoo*
http://www.gayzoo.com/

☐ *GLOLIS (Gay & Lesbian On-Line Information Systems)*
http://www.glolis.com/

☐ *Google*
http://www.google.com/

☐ *Hein's Ultimate Gay Links*
http://www.xs4all.nl/~heinv/dqrd

☐ *Homo De (Germany)*
http://www.homo.de

☐ *Homorama*
http://www.homorama.com/

☐ *Homosexual Agenda*
http://www.ouragenda.com/

☐ *Lavender Links*
http://www.lavenderlinks.com/

☐ *Lesbian.Org*
http://www.lesbian.org/

☐ *Lesbigay Pages*
http://www.actwin.com/queerindex.html

☐ *M.J. O'Neills Web Pages*
http://www.webcommunity.com/mjoneill

☐ *MiningCo*
http://gaylife.miningco.com/
http://www.gaylesissues.miningco.com/
http://lesbianlife.miningco.com/

☐ *Net Queery*
http://www.planetout.com/pno/netqueery/

☐ *The Other Queer Page*
http://www.qworld.org/friends/toqp/

☐ *OutBox*
http://www.outbox.com/

☐ *Phenomenal Women of the Web*
http://www.phenomenalwomen.com/

☐ *Pride Link*
http://www.pridelink.com/

☐ *Planet Amazon*
http://www.planetamazon.com

☐ *Pridelinks.com*
http://www.pridelinks.com/

☐ *QueerAmerica*
http://www.queer.com/queeramerica/

☐ *Queer InfoServer*
http://www.infoqueer.org/queer/qis/

☐ *Queer Living Family Choice Award*
http://www.geocities.com/~neurotaz

☐ *Queer Net*
http://www.queernet.org/

☐ *Queer Resources Directory*
http://www.qrd.org/qrd/

☐ *Queery.com*
http://www.queery.com/

☐ *QPlanet*
http://www.qplanet.com/

☐ *QWorld*
http://www.qworld.org/

☐ *Q-Zone*
http://www.lifestyle.com/qzone/

☐ *Rainbow Query*
http://www.rainbowquery.com/

☐ *Safier's Queer Information*
http://www.cs.cmu.edu/afs/cs.cmu.edu/user/scotts/bulgarians/main

☐ *Sex, Men and Queers (SMAQ)*
http://www.smaq.com

☐ *Skepsis GBLO Resource Page*
http://www.skepsis.com/.gblo/

☐ *Sonoma Zone*
http://www.sonomazone.com/

☐ *Stacey's Lesbian Links*
http://www.goodnet.com/~stacey/leslinks.html

☐ *Stanford Queer Resources*
http://www-leland.stanford.edu/group/QR/

☐ *Temenos*
http://www.temenos.net

☐ *Women Online Worldwide*
http://www.wowwomen.com/

☐ *Women's Web*
http://www.womweb.com/index.html

☐ *Women's Web Links (Europe)*
http://www.euronet..nl./~fullmoon/women.html

☐ *Womyn.org*
http://www.womyn.org

☐ *World Power Systems (punk)*
http://www.wps.com/#INDEX

☐ *World Gay Directory*
http://www.creative.net/~davidmc/company.html

☐ *WWWomen*
http://www.women.com

☐ *Yahoo! Gay, Lesbian, and Bisexual Resources*
http://www.yahoo.com/Society_and_Culture/Lesbians_Gays_and_Bi

QUEER WEB RINGS

☐ *Bear Ring*
http://www.geocities.com/WestHollywood/2301/bearring.html

☐ *Gay S&M Ring*
http://www.geocities.com/WestHollywood/6941/

☐ *Global TransGender Ring*
http://www.echonyc.com/~degrey/LCove/tgring.html

☐ *Latino Ring*
http://www.webring.org/cgi-bin/webring?ring=latino;list

☐ *Leather Ring*
http://www.geocities.com/WestHollywood/3322/

☐ *Out & Proud*
http://www.calweb.com/~darkmoon/lesbigay/

☐ *Queer Ring*
http://www.iesd.auc.dk/~zennaro/queerring.html

☐ *Queer Youth Webring*
   http://www.youthresource.com/

☐ *Spirituality Ring*
   http://www.geocities.com/WestHollywood/3528/rainbow.html

☐ *WebWomyn Ring*
   http://www.geocities.com/WestHollywood/4322/

Activism for Civil Rights

The battlefield has moved. If queer activism was defined by street action in the 1970s and 1980s, today the hotbed of advocacy is online—where hundreds of groups coordinate strategy and discuss policy, and where new bodies are recruited and old warriors deployed.

We are now organizing politically so that our power equals other minorities and moving on homophobia with reason and truly progressive methods. Individually and in groups we are expressing on the Web the hallmarks of a true culture with verifiable power at the voting booth as well as in day-to-day policy decisions. From the response to Matthew Shepard's murder to the controversy over gay marriage, queers have become one of the most organized groups in the world by using high-tech tools. In group after group, from national organizations such as the Human Rights Campaign, the Gay and Lesbian Alliance Against Defamation, and the National Black Gay and Lesbian Leadership Forum, to your local civil rights groups' home pages and E-mail campaigns of every sort and size, queers around the nation have organized their efforts at tremendous speed and with amazing coherence around every outgrowth of the fundamental desire to be ourselves. Whether you want to send a check or join the front lines, the growing cyberworld offers every one of us an easy entrée to make life better.

In fact, it's hard not to rub up against some form of activism. Most Web pages are enlivened by a social conscience and contain a number of links to gay and lesbian activist groups. Even primarily sex-oriented sites, particularly those of the leather and bear communities, regularly promote freedom of speech groups and AIDS activist resources. Everyone, it seems, believes that the personal is indeed political.

Top Guides to Rights Organizations

The two best-organized and most comprehensive indexes to activist political sites are Mike Silverman's TurnOut and Steve Sander's Gay and Lesbian Politics: WWW and Internet Resources. Both are amazingly comprehensive, with descriptions of all the groups listed under civil rights (both national, state, and local), marriage, military, immigration, health, workplace, violence, and youth. TurnOut (sponsored by TurnLeft, a general-rights group) includes a roster of all gay officeholders in the United States, many with Web pages.

GL Politics is perhaps the largest (*Out* calls it "mind-bogglingly thorough") and along with the subjects listed above also indexes sites on the debate over the origins of orientation, history of the gay political movement, religion, transgendered, media, and academic resources. The section on same-sex marriage is particularly deep, reflecting the author's special interest. Sanders also gives explanations of political newsgroups, mail lists and other search engines (which he rates)—a leg up for Web novices and experts alike.

United We Stand

Pages focused on specific advocacy agendas (for example, gay African-Americans, same-sex marriage, or transgender rights) often also contain addresses of like-minded activist groups. Lesbian.com has links to many lesbian organizations, as well as to the HRC, the National Gay and Lesbian Task Force and others. (See also Amazon Online, the International Lesbian Information Service, the Mining Company, the National Lesbian Political Action Committee, and Feminist.com (which, although not specifically queer, contains a long list of activist organizations with overlapping missions). For domestic-partnership issues, the Partners Task Force Home Page and the Same-Sex Marriage

Page give excellent information on the history and current state of this issue and also include links to other organizations such as the National Black Gay and Lesbian Leadership Forum, which in turn has links to transgender sites, among others.

Search Sites

General indexes bristling with political links include: Rainbow Query (probably the most current political links), Outbox, QWorld, QueerAmerica (youth organizations, centers, and support groups, searchable by zip code or area code), GayScape, and Gay Resources and Research, a new site with annotated links and a search engine for most every category including activists and activism. Of the lesbian indexes, WWWomen is the largest and most complete and has the added benefit of a terrific FAQ section (affiliated with Lesbian.org).

QRD Guide to Activist Groups

Preceding them all is the Queer Resources Directory (it began in the mid '80s by Ron Buckmire as an archive for Queer Nation). As the queer world's historic clearinghouse for online activism, the QRD sponsors hundreds of on-site groups (Jewish Activist Gays and Lesbians, Veterans for Human Rights, Wall Street Project, etc.) and maintains links to many more, from ACT UP to Forgotten Scouts, among others. It's rather stark (no pretty pictures or advertising banners) but well-organized, and you'll quickly become adept at deciphering the alphabet soup of GLOBE, LGIRTF:L/G, NGLTF, PFLAG, TRIKONE, and WHO. Once you've entered the QRD, you can move on to other off-QRD sites (including satellite QRDs in other countries) by clicking on the links. The Lesbian Avengers London Chapter, for example, has lots of links to European groups on its home page. So if you're searching for an organization in Cannes, France—or Kathmandu, Nepal, for that matter—just start clicking. Or return to the QRD and sift through the list of community-based organizations and local alerts. From well-financed national groups with plenty of political savvy to splinter cells of in-your-face digital warriors, they're all here.

NATIONAL ADVOCACY ORGANIZATIONS

Human Rights Campaign

The HRC, begun in 1980 and now 300,000 members strong, is the largest LGBT political organization in America and works toward building "an America where lesbian and gay people are ensured of their basic equal rights—and can be open, honest and safe at home, at work, and in the community." This site contains much of the same information and resources that the HRC uses to lobby members of Congress and educate the public toward ending workplace discrimination, combating hate crimes, fighting HIV and AIDS, working for better lesbian health, and protecting our families. Like its director, Elizabeth Birch, the HRC is sophisticated and scrappy, able to debate homophobes like Rep. Bob Barr (R-Ga.), author of the Defense of Marriage Act one night and subtly urge Clinton to greater support the next. HRC is our "insider" organization, a major player in Beltway politics. The site is good-looking, easy to navigate and includes news, press releases, resources, issue analyses, congressional scorecards, an "action center" for contacting politicians, and more.

Gay and Lesbian Alliance Against Defamation

Since 1985 this media watchdog has worked with extraordinary success to stamp out homophobia in the media. In addition to describing its past record and current campaigns, the GLAAD Web page is a collection point for alerts. If you see queers mistreated in the media (in anything from talk radio to major films or local advertisements), you can report the problem and alert the organization. GLAAD will then get to work applying pressure through a variety of means—ranging from write-in campaigns to direct confrontation with the offenders. An example of this was the "Do's and Don'ts of Reporting," a resource to media professionals on covering Andrew Cunanan. Using a carrot-and-stick approach, GLAAD regularly honors organizations and individuals for fair treatment of gay men and lesbians. Recent recipients include HBO, Miramax Films, Cher, and Ellen DeGeneres.

National Gay and Lesbian Task Force

NGLTF has supported grassroots organizing and advocacy since 1973. Probably the edgiest national organization, it has helped "combat antigay violence, antigay legislative and ballot measures, job discrimination, and has fought for the repeal of sodomy laws, an effective governmental response to HIV, reform of the health care system," and much more. Its "Fight the Right Action Kit" has become a manual for turning back the far right. With articles by men and women who have waged successful campaigns, this page explains the hows and whys of organizing—from enlisting volunteers to shaping an effective message. "The NGLTF is a national resource center for lesbian, gay, bisexual, and transgender organizations facing a variety of battles at the state and local level."

Gay and Lesbian National Hotline

GLNH offers free and anonymous access to a national database of more than 13,000 listings of groups and organizations of every imaginable type—political, religious, caregiving, HIV support, housing, and so on. It also offers information on gay-friendly businesses, restaurants, hotels, and clubs, as well as doctors, lawyers, therapists, and peer-counseling services. Callers can talk with "trained volunteers able to explain AIDS information and education and deal with the stress and anxiety affecting both the HIV-positive and -negative in a gay-averse world."

National Latina/o Lesbian, Gay, Bisexual & Transgender Organization (LLEGO)

The National Latina/o Lesbian, Gay, Bisexual and Transgender Organization is the national nonprofit organization representing Lesbian, Gay, Bisexual and Transgender (LGBT) Latinas/os. LLEGO's purpose is the organization of LGBT Latina/o communities from grass roots to national levels through mobilization and networking in a culturally sensitive environment in order to overcome social, health, and political barriers faced due to sexual orientation and ethnicity.

Digital Queers

Digital Queers is one of the most effective engines behind the Webification of activism. It has been instrumental in setting up online programs for the NGLTF, National Center for Lesbian Rights, Black Gay and Lesbian Leadership Forum, Asian Lesbians of the East Coast, the Latina/o National Lesbian and Gay Organization, Frameline International Gay and Lesbian Film Festival, and community centers in San Francisco, New York, Los Angeles, and Minneapolis, as well as Parents, Families and Friends of Lesbians and Gays, GLAAD, and Lambda Legal Defense. As a techno-helpmate to queer organizations, Digital Queers works mainly behind the scenes. Nevertheless, its tri-annual parties for selected organizations have been extremely effective in raising funds to "bring your favorite lesbian and gay rights groups the power to compete in the information game of the '90s by providing the silicon horsepower necessary to organize and communicate more effectively."

Parents, Families, and Friends of Lesbians and Gays

Although PFLAG is not a gay organization, its work on the front lines has garnered it a place of respect and admiration from almost every queer point of view. Importantly, it has spearheaded outreach to queer youths, a brave and necessary response to this minefield of a subject. PFLAG "promotes the health and well-being of gay, lesbian, and bisexual persons, their families, and friends through: support, to cope with an adverse society; education, to enlighten an ill-informed public; and advocacy, to end discrimination and to secure equal civil rights." One of the first organizations to reach beyond the queer community, PFLAG continues to grow and now has chapters around the country.

And Justice for All

AJA, along with PFLAG, is in a sense protecting our flank by reaching out to the straight community for support, particularly on university campuses and at public events such as pride marches. "Founded in mid 1995 to fight for equality for everyone without regard to sexual orientation, AJA seeks to achieve this goal by increasing the visibility and participation of heterosexuals in the lesbian, gay, bisexual, and transgender rights movement."

The National Body of the Black Men's Xchange (NBBMX)

NBBMX is a national organization that bases its philosophy on the idea of integrating the gay and straight aspects of the African-American community. Seeing great misunderstandings on both sides, it works to demystify the many different ways of "living, loving, making love and being loved." For an exciting example of the group working to connect and reconnect Black gays and lesbians to the Black community, see the Web site for a transcript of Cleo Manago's debate with Dr. Afrika (representing the Nation of Islam) on the origins of homosexuality in the black community. BMX has conducted numerous similar national and local retreats and conferences and publishes the magazine *Brothers On The Move*.

National Lesbian Political Action Committee

The first national political action committee to use the word *lesbian* in its title, NLPAC is a politically savvy group focused on influencing policy changes at a national level by making contributions to candidates who support lesbians through their positions

on several key issues: the Employment Non-Discrimination Act, adoption and custody issues affecting lesbians, inclusion of sexual orientation in hate crimes legislation, lesbian health issues, domestic partnership, and same-sex marriage. Though new on the scene, it's well-connected and highly effective.
(See the table of contents for chapters on major rights subjects: African-American, AIDS & HIV, Law & Legal Issues, Lesbian Resources, Politics, and Radical Religious Right)

Gay and Lesbian Victory Fund

GLVF provides money, advice, and training to qualified out gay and lesbian political candidates.

Gay, Lesbian and Straight Education Network

"The largest organization of teachers and community members dedicated to ensuring that all students are valued and respected, regardless of sexual orientation."

International Association of Lesbian/Gay Pride Coordinators

"A international organization made up of many cities producing gay and lesbian pride events worldwide."

International Lesbian and Gay Association

"A worldwide federation of national and local groups dedicated to achieving equal rights for lesbians and gay men everywhere."

☐ *ACLU Gay and Lesbian Rights*
http://www.aclu.org/issues/gay/hmgl.html

☐ *And Justice For All*
http://www.ajfa.org/

☐ *AllTogether.com*
http://www.alltogether.com

☐ *Anti-Violence Council*
http://www.powerup.com.au/~avc/

☐ *Black Gay and Lesbian Leadership Foundation*
http://www.nblglf.org/

☐ *Campaign to End Homophobia*
http://www.endhomophobia.org

☐ *Citizens Against Homophobia*
http://www.actwin.com/cahp/index.htm

☐ *Citizens Against Discrimination.com*
http://www.gay-discrimination.com

☐ *Community United Against Violence*
http://www.xq.com/cuav/index.html

☐ *Creating Safe Schools for Lesbian and Gay Students*
http://members.tripod.com/~twood/guide.html
A guide.

☐ *Defense of Marriage Act*
http://www.hrcusa.org/issues/leg/doma/billtext.html
Fact sheet: http://www.hrcusa.org/issues/leg/doma/factshet.html
Poll: http://www.hrcusa.org/feature1/marpoll.html

☐ *Digital Queers*
http://www.dq.org/

☐ *EGALE (legal rights, Canada)*
http://www.egale.ca

☐ *E-mail Lists of Organizations*
http://www.qrd.org/qrd/electronic/e-mail/#links

☐ *Employment Non-Discrimination Act (ENDA)*
http://www.religioustolerance.org/hom_empl.htm

☐ *ENDA: List of Cosponsors*
http://www.igc.apc.org/lbg/enda.html

☐ *ENDA: Briefing From the Human Rights Campaign*
http://www.hrc.org/issues/leg/enda/index.html

☐ *E-The People*
http://www.e-thepeople.com

☐ *Federal Register Online (Official publication for presidential documents and executive orders as well as notices, rules, and proposed rules of federal agencies)*
http://www.access.gpo.gov/su_docs/aces/aces140.html

☐ *Feminist Activist Resources on the Net*
http://www.igc.apc.org/women/feminist.html

☐ *Gay/Lesbian Issues Resource and Information Guide (Mining Co.)*
http://gaylesissues.miningco.com

☐ *Gay and Lesbian Activists Alliance*
http://www.glaa.org/

☐ *Gay and Lesbian National Hotline*
http://www.glnh.org/

☐ *Gay and Lesbian Parents Coalition International*
http://www.glpci.org

☐ *Gay and Lesbian Politics: WWW and Internet Resources (Steve Sanders)*
http://www.indiana.edu/~glbtpol

☐ *Gay and Lesbian Victory Fund*
http://www.victoryfund.org/

☐ *Gay and Lesbian Web Alliance*
http://colossus.net/glwa/glwa

☐ *Gay, Lesbian and Straight Education Network*
http://www.glsn.org/

☐ *Gay Liberation Front*
http://www.geocities.com/westhollywood/stonewall/5835/

☐ *Gay Male S/M Activists*
http://www.gmsma.org/

☐ *Gay Workplace Issues*
http://www.nyu.edu/pages/sls/gaywork/gaywkpl.html

☐ *Gay and Lesbian Alliance Against Defamation*
http://www.glaad.org/

☐ *GLB Veterans of America*
http://www.glbva.org/

☐ *Gay and Lesbian Political Action Support Groups*
http://www.glpasg.org/

☐ *Gay Men of African Descent*
http://www.GMAD.org/

☐ *Gender Pac*
http://www.gpac.org/

☐ *GuideStar:searchable database of US nonprofits*
http://www.guidestar.org/index.html

☐ *Hollywood Supports*
http://www.hsupports.org/hsupports/guide.html

☐ *The Human Rights Campaign*
http://www.hrcusa.org

☐ *Institute for Gay and Lesbian Strategic Studies*
http://www.iglss.org/

☐ *International Association of L/G Pride Coordinators*
http://www.interpride.org/

☐ *International G & L Human Rights Commission*
http://www.iglhrc.org/

☐ *International Lesbian and Gay Association*
http://www..ilga.org/

☐ *International Network of Lesbian and Gay Officials*
http://www.geocities.com/WestHollywood/2663/inlgo.html

☐ *It's Time America*
http://www.tgender.stargate.com/ita/

☐ *LAMBDA Legal Defense and Education Fund*
http://www.lldef.org

☐ *Leadership Conference on Civil Rights*
http://www.civilrights.org/

☐ *Lesbian and Gay Association of Lawyers*
http://www.le-gal.org/

☐ *Lesbian Avengers*
http://www.lesbianavengers.org/

☐ *Lesbian.org*
http://www.lesbian.org/

☐ *LesBiGay Directory at IGC*
http://www.igc.apc.org/lbg

☐ *Lesbigay Resources From the Carleton Freenet*
http://www.ncf.carleton.ca/freeport/sigs/life/gay/les/menu

☐ *Mining Company's Gay/Lesbian Resources*
http://gaylesissues.miningco.com

☐ *National Association of People with AIDS*
http://www.thecure.org/

☐ *National Black Gay and Lesbian Leadership Forum*
http://www.nbgllf.org/

☐ *The National Body of the Black Men's Xchange*
http://www.earthlink.net/~blkembrace/nbbmx.htm

☐ *National Center for Lesbian Rights*
http://www.nclrights.org/

☐ *National Gay and Lesbian Task Force*
http://www.ngltf.org/

☐ *National Gay Lobby*
http://www.nationalgaylobby.org/

☐ *The National Lesbian and Gay Latina/o Lesbian, Gay, Bisexual & Transgender Organization*
http://www.llego.org/

☐ *National Lesbian & Gay Journalists Assoc.*
http://www.nlgja.org/

☐ *National Lesbian Political Action Committee*
http://www.lesbian.org/nlpac/

☐ *National Organization for Women—(NOW)Lesbian Rights*
http://www.now.org/issues/lgbi/index.html

☐ *OutProud, the National Coalition for Gay, Lesbian and Bisexual Youth*
http://www.cyberspaces.com/outproud/

☐ *Out Rage!*
http://www.outrage.cygnet.co.uk

☐ *People For the American Way*
http://www.pfaw.org/

☐ *PFLAG*
http://www.pflag.org/

☐ *PlanetOut*
http://www.planetout.com/

☐ *Pride At Work*
http://www.prideatwork.org/

☐ *Queer Infoservers*
http://www.infoqueer.org/queer/qis/

☐ *Queer Legal Resources*
http://www.qrd.org/qrd/www/legal/

☐ *Queer Nation*
http://www.cs.cmu.edu/Web/People/mjw/Queer/MainPage.html

☐ *Queer Organizations*
http://www.qrd.org/qrd/orgs/

☐ *Queer Resources Directory*
http://www.qrd.org/qrd/

☐ *Radical Faeries*
http://www.eskimo.com/~davidk/faeries/faeries.html

☐ *Radical Religious Right Pages*
http://www.casti.com/QRD/www/RRR/rrrpage.html

☐ *Rainbow Alliance for the Deaf*
http://www.rad.org

☐ *Romania Action for Gays, Lesbians and Bisexuals*
http://www.raglb.org/uk

☐ *Gay and Lesbian Alliance Against Defamation*
http://www.glaad.org/

☐ *Roy Radow's List of Gay and Lesbian Organizations*
http://www.qrd.org/QRD/browse/north.american.glb.resources

☐ *Safier's Queer Information*
http://www.cs.cmu.edu/afs/cs.cmu.edu/user/scotts/bulgarians/

☐ *Servicemembers Legal Defense Network*
http://www.sldn.org

☐ *Sisters of Perpetual Indulgence, Inc.*
http://www.thesisters.org/

☐ *Skepsis GBLO Resource Page*
http://www.skepsis.com/.gblo/

☐ *Stop Abuse For Everyone*
http://www.dgp.toronto.edu/~jade/safe/

☐ *TurnOut*
http://www.turnleft.com/out/
Guide to gay and lesbian politics on the Web.

☐ *We can always call them Bulgarians*
http://www.cs.cmu.edu/afs/cs/user/scotts/ftp/bulgarians/mainpage.
html

☐ *WebActive's GLBT activist index*
http://www.webactive.com/webactive/cgi-bin/wniadirsearch?Bisexu
al,+Gay,+and+Lesbian

☐ *Yahoo!'s List of LGBOrganizations*
http://www.yahoo.com/Society_and_Culture/Lesbians_Gays_and_Bi

Adult Children of Heterosexuals

With so many dead-serious sites on the Net, it's always a perspective-restoring exercise to visit this page. Created by veterans of a "cabaret/political-theater rock band," some of whom are "'putergeeks," it's ironic, blunt, and cheeky: "If you have no sense of humor—or are offended by the glorious colorful musings of bisexuals, transsexuals, dykes, fags, and freaks—we strongly advise that you stop viewing this right now! (There's so much else you could be doing.)"

Once you've passed the product labeling, Adults goes on to an irreverent, sex-positive sampling of the Web. In the first section you get short reviews of three top sites. One week readers were pointed to Susie Bright's Homepage, a place Adults characterizes as "hard to describe it's so fabulous. Skateboard freaks on acid. Funny writing." Play "Lesbian or German Lady"; "Carrie vs. Angel."

Other sections are titled Queer Music Review, Queer Resource Links, Bisexual Hell, Girl Stuff, and Transgender Madness. Each is a model of editing, a sort of cream-of-the-crop list of links taking you from general information sites that everybody should know (such as the Queer Resources Directory) to more narrowly focused destinations (such as the Pink Pages for a taste of gay Amsterdam or the Pinkboard for a tour of queer Australia). Usually these links receive a capsule description. For example, the Radical Religious Right page is described as a place to "keep track of our friends (who want us dead...)." Immediately following is a link to Digital Queers: "God bless 'em. Aren't we all...?"

Although the selections are well-chosen, ranging from the obvious to the obscure, you could find this information all over the Web. There are no pretensions or claims that Adults is comprehensive. It is casually and simply just the informed musings of a fellow Web traveler, albeit one with a wicked sense of humor. And that's the charm of this ironically titled page. It has no agenda and no mission to accomplish other than simply sharing a few online jewels. The illustrations are playful too—especially a picture from *The Wizard of Oz* showing Dorothy and the gang skipping though the poppy fields on the way to the Emerald City. Drop by for the digital equivalent of a chat with a friend.

☐ *Adult Children of Heterosexuals*
   http://www.tiac.net/users/danam/acoh.HTML

Whether the heat comes from politics or sex, a sense of recapturing lost history or a reach for the future, you'll find resonant issues addressed at their most passionate pitch in today's black Web sites.

black church vs. the black GLBT community, being out versus being on the DL, queens versus "real men," "black" versus "African-American"—all the schisms that are elsewhere glided over as part of the queerscape are confronted here head-on. It makes for a hot mix that flowers powerfully in the personal sites like the "Raw Poetry" page of Charles Harvey as well as in the huge and incredibly vital Web sites of BlackStripe and NBBMX. Threaded through each page, large or small, is the call to come home, that the divisions only make finding connections more crucial. In the words of Chocolate City, life is "phat and full of flavor!"

Blackmen.com

One of the most interesting pages is Blackmen.com (formerly Da Site). The opening image is always telling—a gym-toned, sweat-glistening torso of a man holding his dick like a weapon, or more recently, a cropped torso shot of a chiseled guy pumping iron. Whatever the visual, this site is sexy and has a purpose. Matching ultrasophisticated graphics with fiction, poetry, and forums on health and AIDS, it reflects a real world with aggressive sensuality that's right on target with its audience of young black urban gay men (personals are black only). Both in the photo galleries and the writing you'll enter a frank (not pornographic) world with its own language and culture. "Do you enjoy reading hot stories about fine black intelligent men having sex and loving one another? Or maybe stories about lost loves, struggling to overcome obstacles, or stories about the first time having sex with another man, then the Black Stories Section is for you!" Always, whether in the poetry or advice on health and safe sex, the author is a teacher, guiding his audience to follow the site's motto, "Reach for the Future."

Eloquent Fury

This is a collection of writings by Alicia Banks, an out lesbian radio producer and disc jockey for KPFA. The columns are raw and hard-hitting—slamming bigotry wherever it raises its head. "I am no less African because I am a lesbian. I am no less revolutionary because I am not an incubator, a maid, or a baby-sitter. I am no less afro-centric because my reality is absent from gay media." Taking themes from the headlines, she measures today's events and news-makers on the very stringent scale set by heroes such as Martin Luther King Jr. and Cornel West. All the source quotes remain, sadly, revolutionary. Huey Newton: "We must relate to the homo-sexual movement because it is a very real thing."

Black Stripe

The Black Stripe is on everyone's bookmarks. From the first days of the Web, it has been a rich, erudite space for and about "Les-bians, Gay Men, Bisexuals and Transgendered People of African Descent." It takes polls, such as "Is the church a welcoming envi-ronment for sexual minorities of African descent?" (14% yes, 78 % no) and articles ("AIDS in the Gospel Choir," "Profile of Black Gay Writer Essex Hemphill"), a book list, discussion groups, a film list, and information about queer African-American resources and or-ganizations. Is it political and inclusive? Yes. The home page opens with a quote by Audre Lorde testifying how it feels to be an out mi-nority. "When I picketed for welfare mothers' rights, and against the enforced sterilization of young black girls, when I fought institu-tionalized racism in the New York City schools, I was a black les-bian. But you did not know it because we did not identify ourselves, so now you can say that black lesbians and gay men have nothing to do with the struggles of the black nation." Point made. And then

Black Stripe goes on to page after page of debate and link-filled resources, further deepening the queer African-American voice. As Black Stripe's motto has it, "Africa is the center of my rainbow." Also check out the "Black List," the largest, most detailed, and constantly growing list of queers of African descent who've made and are making a difference. You'll find lots of recognizable names here, such as Alvin Ailey and Angela Davis. But there are also brief histories of lesser knowns such as Larry Duplechan, author of *Eight Days a Week*, *Blackbird*, and *Captain Swing*, and Herbert Evans, former pastor of the Metropolitan Community Church in Philadelphia, the AIDS National Interfaith Network, and the Ecumenical AIDS Committee. "While honoring those on this list, take a moment to reflect on how you, too, are making history."

BLK Homie Page

With a pair of guys and a pair of girls kissing on the opening page, you might think BLK is about sex. And it is, partly. The personals section covers each state in the nation, with detailed ads for every kind of fetish and foible. Men Unplugged and Women Unplugged "where the 'sex' in homosexual takes center stage" connects you to erotic messages and photos. (Men's listings are much larger than women's, mostly BM looking for other BM with a typical age range being 35 to 45 years—see Personals, page 410). And the Adult listings have knowing asides such as a warning that many of the newsgroup pictures of women, purportedly for lesbian women, are actually blaxploitation.

But the editor of these pages has a much more ambitious agenda than sex or even selling BLK publications (*Black Lace*, *BMaxx*, etc.). The National Calendar of Events for Black People in the Life lets you know the what, when, and where of happenings in the national black lesbian and gay community—from talks at Harvard University and A Different Light's Los Angeles store to a safe-sex party in Durham, N.C. There's also a large links page divided up into categories: Health and AIDS, Political and Social, Publications and Literary Groups, and Religion. On the lighter side, read DeWann's alerts of upcoming events (he knows Patti

LaBelle's schedule by heart) or check out the Party Places listings—a worldwide directory of places to party that includes bars, discos, bathhouses and sex clubs that are black-owned or have black clientele.

Black HIV Men Meeting Place

This club was created for HIV-positive men of African descent to share information and promote positive relationships within the community. An average of 80 members a day talk among themselves in a supportive, intimate, and honest conversation about how they're handling the virus, what meds they're on, how they deal with family and work and love. "I have dealt with this situation completely alone and have told not one soul and feel this is the only avenue I have… Is there anyone else in the same situation or know of the same situation?"

Gay-Lesbian-Bisexual People of Color

If you want to join an international dialogue on queer African-American topics ("Homosexuality and Religion," "European Decadence as the Cause of Black Homosexuality"), join the conversation. GLBPOC is a long-running forum in which "issues of race and sexual orientation can be discussed in a supportive and nonthreatening manner." The theme is one of self-discovery: "Who are we? How do we define ourselves? Which symbols do we choose? Do we choose symbols drawn from the struggles of Europeans? Do we create symbols rooted in our African heritage, or does our double consciousness—as described by W.E.B. DuBois—cause us to create a synthesis between our African and American identities?"

National Body of the Black Men's Xchange

NBBMX is a impassioned site on fire with the mission of providing a place where "black homosexual and bisexual men can affirm and address issues relevant to their lives as black same-gender-loving men." The founder, Cleo Manago, felt it was important that "we stop riding the disrespectful, racist apron strings of the white/gay community and acknowledge that we have a unique history and legacy that is black in essence, not German (via the pink triangle) or white (via the rainbow flag)." Independent and challenging, BMX moves toward its goal through a collection of articles such as "The Black Gay Movement and Its Relationship to the AIDS Epidemic," "Black SGL Men Who Prefer Not to Love Other Black Men. Does It Matter?" and "Homophobia in the Black Community! Fact or Fiction?" And NBBMX does more than talk. It has chapters around the country, marches in parades, and takes the fight into mainstream media with appearances on television shows such as Oprah Winfrey's. And check out the transcript of Cleo Manago's debate with Dr. Afrika (representing the Nation of Islam) on the origins of homosexuality in the black community. "There is no closet space in BMX, but ample room for self-discovery, reconnecting, embracing, and cradling our connection to each other."

Nubian Web

This is a very glossy and sexy commercial site that is all about living life to the fullest—whether that's on the chat lines, in the personals, in bars, or at the beach (they work with with ATBLA, the largest black beach party in the world). Along with all the sex (links to the "best" black sex sites and a question-and-answer section with Dr. Dick), there's more sex in galleries and HookUp, which has more than 1,000 ads with photos.

ATBLA

ATBLA (At The Beach Los Angeles) began in the summer of 1988 when a group of friends got together for a day at the beach. Today, more than 8,000 men and women, primarily from the African lesbian and gay community gather from across the country as well as many foreign countries such as Nigeria, Ghana, Mexico, Venezuela, France, and England on the Fourth of July, Independence Day weekend, over four days. Along with a lot of fun, the events provide a networking forum for the African American Same Gender Loving People.

SBC Magazine

The online version of this "Afrocentric Homosexual Publication" is just as hot and immediate as the monthly paper version. Along with columns, articles ("From Top to Bottom, to Bottom to Top"), new fiction, and links, SBC prints its always-fascinating interviews with notable black gay men, such as a recent dialogue between James Earl Hardy and E. Lynn Harris. "E. Lynn Harris and James Earl Hardy have taken black-on-black love out of the revolutionary stigma promoted by media hell-bent on objectifying black, same-gender–loving Americans…and have lit the sparks that show the way of real black-on-black love. Not as a revolutionary act, but as an act of God, an act of nature, an act of coming to terms with oneself within the beauty of the black community, where heterosexuals and homosexuals have always coexisted, sometimes uneasily, often condescendingly, routinely clandestine, but always as family."

☐ *Adodi*
   http://members.aol.com/amassictr/index.htm

☐ *African American AIDS Institute*
   http://www.against.org/

☐ *African Studies WWW Links*
   http://www.sas.upenn.edu/African_Studies/Home_Page/WWW_Link

☐ *Afrikan American Gay Women's Associaton*
   http://www.aagwa.com/mission.html

☐ *African-American Lesbian Gay Alliance*
   http://ourworld.compuserve.com/homepages/AALGA/

☐ *AMASSI*
http://www.amassi.com/

☐ *ATBLA (At The Beach, LA)*
http://www.atbla.com/

☐ *Bay Drum*
http://www.tomato.com/~baydrum/

☐ *(Taylor) Beckford*
http://www.brothas4ya.com/beckford/index.html

☐ *BGM Pages*
http://home.aol.com/BGMPages

☐ *BlkTrianGurl*
http://members.aol.com/blktrngurl/homepage.html

☐ *Black and White Men Together*
http://www.studsnet.com/bwmen.htm

☐ *Black Boyz*
http://www.BlackBoyz.com/

☐ *Black Gay and Lesbian Leadership Forum*
http://abacus.math.oxy.edu/QRD/orgs/BGLLF/

☐ *Black HIV Men Meeting Place*
http://clubs.yahoo.com/clubs/blackhivmenmeetingplace

☐ *Black Is...Black Ain't*
http://www.itvs.org/programs/BIBA/index.html

☐ *Blacklines*
http://www.suba.com/~outlines/

☐ *Black Lesbian Support Group*
http://www.blsg.com/

☐ *BlackLight Magazine Online*
http://www.blacklightonline.com/

☐ *The Blacklist*
http://www.blackstripe.com/blacklist/

☐ *Black Lesbian Support Group*
http://www.blsg.com/

☐ *Black Girl*
http://www.blackgirl.org/

☐ *Blackmen.com (formerly Da Site)*
http://www.blackmen.com/

☐ *Black Men n2 Black Men's Feet*
http://www.web-orion.com/blkfeet/

☐ *Black Lesbian Support Group*
http://www.blsg.com

☐ *Black Pride*
http://users.aol.com/blgpd/pride.htm

☐ *Black Stripe*
http://www.blackstripe.com

☐ *BlackWorld Links Directory*
http://www.blackworld.com/art/gay_les.htm

☐ *BLK Homie Page*
http://www.blk.com/

☐ *BMX*
http://home.earthlink.net/~blkembrace/bmx.htm

☐ *Brutha Man's Club*
http://clubs.yahoo.com/clubs/thebruthamansclub

☐ *Catch's Place*
http://www.catchsplace.com

☐ *Chocolate City*
http://www.chocolatecityusa.com/

☐ *Clikque Magazine*
http://www.clikque.com/

☐ *Ebony Male*
http://www.ebonymale.com/

☐ *Essex Hemphill Tribute*
http://www.qrd.org/qrd/www/culture/black/essex/tribute.html

☐ *Everything Black*
http://www.everythingblack.com

☐ *Eloquent Fury*
http://www.geocities.com/CapitolHill/Lobby/5224/

☐ *E. Lynn Harris*
http:www.elynnharris.com/

☐ *For Love of Alice (Walker)*
http://www.luminarium.org/contemporary/alicew/

☐ *Free my heart so my soul may fly*
www.freemyheartsomysoulmayfly.atfreeweb.com/free%20my%20
heart/enter%20my%20world.htm/

☐ *Gay Black Men (Dating service)*
http://www.gayblackmen.com/

☐ *GLBPOC*
http://www.qrd.org/QRD/electronic/e-mail/glbpoc

☐ *GLAAS(Gay and Lesbian African-American Salon)*
http://www.glaas.com

☐ *Gay Men of African Descent*
http://www.gmad.org/

☐ *Hardy, James Earl*
http://www.geocities.com/SoHo/Studios/3702/

☐ *Interracial Voice*
http://www.webcom.com/~intvoice

☐ *John Keene*
http://pages.nyu.edu/~jrk3150/

☐ *Like Breathing (Ricc Rollins)*
http://www.likebreathing.com/

☐ *Mosaic Books*
http://www.mosaicbooks.com

☐ *National Association of Black and White Men Together*
http://www.nabwmt.com/

☐ *National Body of the Black Men's Xchange*
http://home.earthlink.net/~blkembrace/nbbmx.htm

☐ *National Black Lesbian and Gay Leadership Forum*
http://www.nblglf.org

☐ *NetNoir—The Soul of Cyberspace*
http://www.netnoir.com/index.html

☐ *Nubian Web*
http://nubian.webspot.net/main.html

☐ *Other Countries*
http://www.artswire.org/ocountry/index.htm
Collective of gay and lesbian artists and writers.

☐ *Outlines/Black Lines*
http://www.suba.com/~outlines

☐ *Queer Resources Directory*
http://www.qrd.org/qrd

☐ *Raw Poetry Charles Harvey*
http://www.geocities.com/SoHo/Cafe/7480

☐ *Respecting the Soul (Keith Boykin)*
http://hometown.aol.com/boykink/kb/RTS.htm

☐ *Sapphic Sisters*
http://www.geocities.com/WestHollywood/Park/2535/

☐ *SBC Online*
http://www.sbc-online.com

☐ *Shade*
http://www.glyphmedia.com/host/shade/

☐ *S and J's Homebase*
http://www.geocities.com/WestHollywood/1243/

☐ *SistahScape*
http://www.sisterscape.com/

☐ *ULOAH*
http://www.uloah.com

☐ *Ursa Noir (Bears)*
http://members.xoom.com/ursanoir/

☐ *Venus Magazine*
http://venusmagazine.com/

☐ *Vibe Magazine*
http://www.vibe.com

☐ *(Denzel) Washington*
http://eden.simplenet.com/guys/denzel/index.html

☐ *Women in the Life*
http://www.womeninthelife.com

☐ *Womyn of Zami*
http://www.geocities.com/WestHollywood/9005/

General Information Sites

☐ *AfroNet*
http://www.afronet.com

☐ *Black Voices*
http://www.blackvoices.com

☐ *BlackWorld Links Directory*
http://www.blackworld.com/art/gay_les.htm

☐ *Urban Biz*
http://www.urbanbiz.com

Search Engines

☐ *AfriSearch*
http://www.afrisearch.com

☐ *Blackseek*
http://www.blackseek.com/

☐ *Black Web sites*
http://www.blackweb sites.com

☐ *Drum Links*
http://drum.ncat.edu/

☐ *Everything Black*
http://www.everythingblack.com

☐ *Soul Search*
http://www.soulsearch.com

AIDS & HIV

There is probably no other subject on the Internet with so many resources of such high quality—a heartening sign of the queer community's sustained energy in understanding and defeating the epidemic.

Where do you start? With treatments, case studies, or chat lines? There's no road map, no all-encompassing site with answers and instructions on every facet of this hydra-headed disease, but there is a sort of path of information you can follow.

HIV Chat Groups

One of the most popular and effective methods to orient and inform yourself is on the chat lines. Michael Staley's AIDSmeds.com has an excellent list of discussions, including the University of California, San Francisco's HIV Insite, the Johns Hopkins Patient Forum and The Body—Insight From Experts. You can get a quick picture of discussion topics by browsing the headlines of various postings ranging from complex "salvage" treatment to basic guidelines on when to begin treatment, each with an expert's answers.

Some of the friendliest and best chat rooms can be found at OnQ. Originally the Gay and Lesbian Community Forum on AOL, onQ has its own Web site now and hosts a variety of groups. Some chat groups are open and others meet in private rooms and are "facilitated," meaning there is a moderator who controls the debate so everyone gets heard. More chat groups can be found at Michael Davon's Web-Depot.com, which hosts many HIV/AIDS-related support groups, such as "HIV-Support" and "GayPoz." For a good set of instructions and links list, see the Chat section at Marty

Howard's Web site, where you'll also get directions to IRC, Usenet and Undernet chat sites.

COMPREHENSIVE AIDS INFORMATION SITES

If you start with the large sites, you can familiarize yourself with all that's available today and how it applies to you. Working through topics—ranging from new treatments to service groups—allows an overview, a kind of survey course in AIDS. The AIDS Treatment Data Network and the Critical Path Project, for instance, cover immense amounts of territory. From the most recent antiviral studies to drug interactions and simpler everyday concerns over getting a flu shot, each has reams of detailed information within a central framework.

AIDSmed.com is a new, large, and terrifically sensible and user-friendly site. Though it has sections on everything from when to begin treatment, to forums where long term survivors discuss drug interactions, it retains the patient's focus throughout. For example, in the Check My Meds section, you can learn how the drugs you are taking interact with each other, or interact with a certain food, and cause a bad reaction in your body. And rather than doling out vague recommendations, the advice offered is specific and workable. And you can almost always follow links to the studies and reports informing the advice.

Sites devoted to a single topic tend to provide the deepest intelligence on the title subject. For example, the AIDS Clinical Trials Information Service not only has a comprehensive nationwide listing of drug trials and excellent descriptive information, but it also contains a handbook explaining all the scientific lingo—such as the difference between Phase One, Two, and Three trials and what a "log" refers to in viral load tests. It also gives excellent advice, warning patients to pay attention to the length of the study (particularly those that run the risk of being eclipsed by newer research). By heeding this bit of wisdom, you can make sure you're not a guinea pig confirming already-solid research merely to satisfy some grant requirement.

Whichever sources you settle on as most suited to your needs, it's advisable to consult other similar pages. Along with a quick confirmation of the quality of information you're getting, a second or third guide keeps you abreast of sometimes unexpected developments. The ACT UP chapters in New York, Philadelphia, and San Francisco are excellent cross-references for early alerts, as are Project Inform (San Francisco), Gay Men's Health Crisis (New York), Philadelphia FIGHT, HIV InfoWeb (New England), ARIC (Baltimore), and AIDS Project Los Angeles.

Queer Resources Directory

The QRD has thousands of resources on AIDS and an immense documents file. Included are links to AIDS organizations, mailing lists, and newsletters and the addresses of newsgroups and chat lines discussing the epidemic. The search engine is rather a blunt tool for sifting this mountainous pile, but with some patience you can access a broader compilation of resources than with any other page. The QRD has encyclopedic references to online trials information and support groups and there are pointers to a wealth of related areas like Positive Planet ("the world's only Gay and HIV dating magazine") and since the QRD was begun by Queer Nation, you'll find most every AIDS activist site in the world.

The Critical Path AIDS Project

If there is an alpha and omega of AIDS information on the Net, this is it. It's huge, incredibly complete, and infused with the sort of urgency appropriate to its mission: "Critical Path was founded by persons with AIDS (PWAs) to provide treatment, resource, and prevention information in wide-ranging levels of detail—for researchers, service providers, [and] treatment activists, but first and foremost, for other PWAs who often find themselves in urgent need of information quickly and painlessly." The chapter headings are: Late-Breaking News, Prevention, Research, Clinical Trials, Treatment, Publications, Alternative Treatments, Organizations, Regional Services, Technical Support, and Index/Search. Every chapter is updated monthly with a rigor and completeness other resources can only attempt to emulate.

The introductory text for each heading gives you an orientation to the topic and evaluates the information in light of recent changes. Under Treatment, for example, the federal Centers for Disease Control and Prevention's AIDS standard of care is listed—with the implied proviso that a better protocol can be found at ACT UP Philadelphia. This same sort of eminently sane irreverence is constant throughout this site. Under Alternative Treatments, you'll find the largest, most seriously considered library of complementary and unconventional approaches to HIV treatment, along with "information which will help protect PWAs from quackery." Another unusual aspect to this site is that although it has a vast and comprehensive listing of Web pages and uses the latest Internet technology in its search engine, it also gives a full accounting of other resources—from BBSs, newsgroups, and FTP sites to phone numbers and street addresses. In short, everything that moves toward a cure is given its due. Go see, read, and act on the wonderful usefulness of this page.

AIDS Resource List

Though this links list is nowhere near as long as what you'll find at the above sites, every organization mentioned is an excellent one. Along with such mainstays of Web site information as the CDC home page, Yahoo!'s list of AIDS/HIV information, the QRD, and the AIDS Virtual Library, the AIDS Resource List provides a good selection of valuable information scattered elsewhere on the Internet. You can find Usenet addresses for the newsgroups sci.med.aids, clari.tw.health.aids., misc.health.aids, and misc.health.aids.home page, along with FTP sites for answers to common AIDS questions and addresses for newsletters such as "AIDS Weekly."

CDC National AIDS Clearinghouse

This is the home of the Centers for Disease Control and Prevention, the government's umbrella organization for a host of AIDS

studies programs. Although you might expect institutional dull-
ness, you'd be wrong. Since a recent face-lift, this page looks terrific and is much more user-friendly. Along with a long list of
AIDS links (weighted heavily toward university programs), you
can find a complete rundown of governmental educational outreach programs, a huge compilation of mailing lists, and pointers to the AIDS Clinical Trials Information Service and the
HIV/AIDS Treatment Information Service. The newsletters catalogue is perhaps the largest available, including: "AIDS Informa-
tion Newsletter," "Being Alive Newsletter," "Body Positive
Newsletter," "Bulletin of Experimental Treatments for AIDS,"
"Centers for Disease Control–Daily Reports," "Community AIDS
Treatment Information Exchange," "FOCUS: A Guide to AIDS
Research and Counseling," "Gay Men's Health Crisis Treatment
Information Newsletter," and "Morbidity and Mortality Weekly
Report." AIDS-related newsgroups are also inventoried and de-
scribed, with profiles like the following for misc.health.aids:
"This newsgroup is the only worldwide forum dedicated to a
free and open exchange of ideas about AIDS. There are more
than 42,000 readers of misc.health.aids worldwide."

Marty Howard's HIV/AIDS Home Page

Although Marty Howard is straight, he's otherwise close to perfect. His page is a long list of AIDS links. Maneuvering through
the lists is quite easy because he's divided everything into sections: HIV/AIDS-related education, mailing lists and support
groups, news and information, Usenet newsgroups, and clinical
trials and medications. There is also a sub-page for HIV/AIDS
regional service organizations providing food, legal support,
and other assistance. Refreshingly, his page is very personal. It
opens not with a dry title followed by chapter headings, but a
message of the day, a survey/questionnaire, and an article such
as "Protective Immunity Against HIV Infection: Has Nature
Done the Experiment for Us?" Since this is Marty's home page,
he's included a personal profile and is not afraid to give his own
opinion. IRC channels recently came in for a well-deserved
blast for rudeness to newcomers.

Aegis

If you choose only one AIDS information newsgroup, sign up for Aegis. You'll be kept abreast of the latest developments in AIDS medicine and informed on the specific topics that concern you most personally. Additionally, you can sift back through the Aegis library of more than 300,000 AIDS-related documents which are stored in five areas (including an enormous cache of journals such as AidsLine, AIDS Information Newsletter, AIDS Treatment Data Network, Being Alive Los Angeles, BETA, and more), the CDC's AIDS Daily Summary, and the Prevention Newsline (HIV-related articles from the major wire services and newspapers across the United States). The Aegis search engine also lets you hunt through scientific abstracts from the National Library of Medicine (AIDSLINE), as well as tens of thousands of other documents. It's a dazzling achievement made more singular by its creator: Sister Mary Elizabeth, who operates it along with her fellow Sisters of St. Elizabeth of Hungary in San Juan Capistrano, Calif. The range of information available is so vast and its quality so dependable that national and international organizations routinely log onto the system to converse or download clinical information or late-breaking news.

GMHC (Gay Mens Health Crisis)

From its founding in the early '80s, GMHC has been at the forefront not only of treatment issues but in helping patients take a practical, rounded approach to living with HIV. Today the site is an excellent resource no matter how familiar or unfamiliar you are with meds, studies, insurance, qualifying for ADAP, and the million and one facets of dealing with AIDS. There's a glossary, nutrition guide, help in navigating your way though combination therapies, and reports on the latest treatments written from a patient's point of view. The site is also available in Spanish, and the hotline, when you need someone to talk to, is available 24 hours daily.

The Body

The Body is a far-reaching and popular reference for online AIDS resources that is communicated in an open, jargon-free manner. You'll find a wide range of information, from AIDS basics such as a pamphlet for people who've just learned they are positive to reports on drug resistance, advice on diet, nutrition, and financial, spiritual, and legal issues. There is a chat group, an interactive question-and-answer forum on treatment issues by Dr. Joel Gallant of Johns Hopkins University, and a preset message area where you can monitor—and add your voice to—the efforts of AIDS Action Council to refine governmental AIDS policy. There is also a large pool of articles from the leading treatment newsletters and AIDS advocacy organizations. For questions of faith and AIDS, the religion section has the wonderful counseling of the Rev. A. Stephen Pieters (see the Religion and Spirituality chapter for more information on his work).

TREATMENT NEWS AND DRUG TRIALS

Critical Path Treatment and Drug Trials

For a critical accounting of drug trials and related information found in journals and treatment activist sites, the Treatment and Clinical Trials sections in Critical Path offer the most complete guide. Particularly important today, when many patients feel themselves informed enough to read and interpret testing results, there are pointers to sites containing trials data. You can use this site, which is frequently updated, to compare and contrast your options in both conventional and unconventional research. Some of us, for example, put more faith in using the existing immune system to fight the virus, which goes somewhat against the general direction of attacking HIV via synthetic drugs. Critical Path offers information about a variety of trials outside the mainstream, from herbal therapies to the immune system–based augmentation studies. You can also find links and descriptions of activist AIDS treatment organizations such as Project Inform, Treatment Action Group, and the Field Initiating Group for HIV Trials. Each of these groups has been instrumental in securing early release of effective therapies and alerting the community to overlooked strategies—reminding the medical community that trials are (or should be) about making people well, not simply a cautious gathering of data points. Very sympathetic to self-advocacy, Critical Path's treatment section also has pointers to other resources for the involved patient, such as expanded access programs, accelerated approval, parallel tracks, and the new "lotteries," as well as information on each state's AIDS Drug Assistance Program.

AIDS Clinical Trials Information Service

Unlike Critical Path or Project Inform, ACTIS has no point of view; nevertheless, it is the most complete accounting of federally and privately sponsored AIDS clinical trials. The descriptions include the purpose of each study, whether it is open to enrollment, study locations, eligibility requirements and exclusion criteria, names and telephone numbers of contact people, and descriptions of drugs being studied. ACTIS is a public health service project sponsored by the Centers for Disease Control and Prevention, the National Institute of Allergy and Infectious Diseases, the Food and Drug Administration, and the National Library of Medicine.

AIDS Treatment Data Network

This national not-for-profit group rivals Critical Path in its ease of use and depth of information. In addition to extensive, up-to-date databases about AIDS treatments, research studies, services, and accessing care, it has a trials directory where you can scan early-bird results and a glossary of drugs, treatments, opportunistic infections, and conditions. (Most of the information is also available in Spanish.) Of significant interest to anyone considering joining a research study is the handbook "Should I Join an AIDS Drug Trial?" It is a must-read guide for those willing to put their life on the line. You'll learn the basics of what drug trials are, their purpose, what it's like being in a trial, why you should pay strict attention to the consent agreement, what questions to ask before signing up, and how and when to leave enrollment. The site is also a good place to read up on personal experiences with alternative treatments like herbs and acupuncture, cat's claw, garlic, and SPV-30. The aptly named "Simple Facts Sheets" describes protease inhibitors, 3TC, fungal infections, steroids, oral ganciclovir, and so on. Check out the news section, a catchall for research and treatment articles from journals, newsletters, newspapers, and the Internet.

ACT UP

Along with news on "zaps"—street actions calling attention to hurtful AIDS policies (against drug pricing, for example)—ACT UP chapters in New York, San Francisco, and Philadelphia offer cutting-edge treatment information on  their Web pages. The New York branch has "Real Treatments for Real People," an overview of current helpful treatments that includes reports on studies both within and outside of the Food and Drug Administration's sanctions. ACT UP Philadelphia has a focus on "Women's Standard of Care" that seeks to redress the lack of research on HIV-positive women. Why a separate study? "Not only because their bodies are different than men's, but also because their lives are different.... The women's standard of care includes: the latest treatment regimen for gynecological diseases, including vaginitis, PID, menstrual irregularities, HPV, cervical cancer, and common HIV and OI treatments' interactions with drugs such as oral contraceptives, street drugs, and antidepressants."

Project Inform

For sheer everyday usefulness of information targeted to laypeople, Project Inform offers the most readable updates on AIDS treatment for everything from antivirals to CMV, immune system restoration, skin problems, and lipodystrophy. In addition to medication appraisals, PI is packed with background information (such as a glossary explaining cross-resistance and why you should care). You can learn about drug absorption rates (how eating various foods will affect a drug's efficacy) and side effects (along with how to deal with them), as well as who the manufacturers are and how their distribution policies affect access. "Hot" therapies always receive timely and lengthy coverage. PI was one of the first groups to push for immune restoration therapies months before the national media had realized it was the logical next step after the protease inhibitor breakthrough. Strikingly, PI targets not only the HIV-positive audience, but also the government officials and policy makers whose decisions affect our lives. PI was the first AIDS advocacy group to begin working with the FDA on speeding drug approval and has since worked with many other agencies in tailoring better treatments and making them affordable. Spanish translations are available.

CenterWatch

This group supplies much of the same drug trials information available in more complete form on ACTIS. Still, it does have the unique service of patient notification for upcoming trials. If you'd like to be notified by E-mail of future postings to this site in a particular therapeutic area, you can sign up easily and confidentially. There is also an E-mail service, which you can customize to areas of interest, about drugs that have been newly approved by the FDA.

Local Trials Sources

Some large metropolitan areas have organizations devoted to listing and describing area clinical trials. Many of these are also activist groups urging faster implementation of proven newer therapies, including GMHC in New York, APLA in Los Angeles, Project Inform in San Francisco, ARIC in Baltimore, and FIGHT in Philadelphia (see ACTIS for the full list). It's only practical to visit the pages of your neighborhood watchdog—all have contact numbers, and the information can be printed out easily to inform (or wake up) your primary caregiver as to what's available. Fight's page, created by a consortium of people with AIDS and doctors, is an especially good example. It not only details the trials, but it also gives background on the treatments.

PUBLICATIONS

Because all AIDS treatment information quickly becomes obsolete, one of the best ways to stay informed is through online editions of newsletters. Usually these provide monthly (and sometimes weekly) updates on research, anecdotal information, and breakthroughs. Though governmental publications (such as daily reports offered by the CDC) are important, many of the most searching and least convention-bound analyses can be found in the newsletters of community-based AIDS organizations and activist groups. The following sites are all excellent, but they are only a small portion of those available. For a complete list of AIDS publications, see the lists of publications offered by the CDC, Critical Path, and Aegis.

AIDS Treatment News

As its title suggests, this newsletter searches out news on treatments, all of it extremely up-to-date. For instance, coverage of the International Congress on Drug Therapy in HIV Infection comes online within a week of the event. The newsletter is good at giving a context for its reports. In the piece on the third congress, it gave a brief background on the finding that blood and lymph tissues' viral loads match, reminding readers that "undetectable HIV viral load in the lymph nodes does NOT mean that the virus has been eradicated—only that it is not actively reproducing." On a subject of particular interest to many study patients, it went on to point out that HIV levels can be gauged by taking biopsies of tonsils, a much less drastic procedure than removing an entire lymph gland.

AIDS Weekly Plus

"AIDS Weekly Plus" draws its articles from a broad selection of high-profile events. It's a mix of social-barometer articles (Clinton officials attending an AIDS lab dedication, how the autobiography of Ryan White has been placed back on library shelves at a Pennsylvania school) and research findings. These are often unfiltered, leaving readers unfamiliar with medical terms rather stumped by passages like "RNA decoys are short oligonucleotides which correspond to the Rev-responsive element (RRE) or to…"

Dirt on AIDS

The "Dirt On AIDS" is the newsletter put out by ARIC, a Baltimore-based AIDS service group. Though its editorials quite rightly focus on local issues, the articles are of use to everyone. Jargon-free pieces regularly emphasize new treatments (the editor described one issue as a delight for "trial geeks").

BETA

"BETA" is one of oldest and most respected newsletters. It assumes a rather educated audience, but is still one of the best reporters of breakthroughs, particularly in treatments and clinical trials. Based at the University of California, San Francisco, the regional slant is still applicable wherever you live.

Consumer News

"Consumer News" reports, practical, real-life information for people with AIDS and caregivers in the daily struggle against the disease. This includes stories on governmental initiatives (such as projected effects of Medicaid reform) and workplace, housing, and nutrition issues, along with monthly columns on books and profiles on people with AIDS. The newsletter is especially good at covering the struggle of women and children.

GMHC Treatment Issues

"GMHC Treatment Issues" covers its territory with a wide range of articles from an analytic perspective, reporting on opportunistic diseases like yeast and fungal infections and giving advice on overcoming the constraints of managed care. There are also monthly features giving a historical appraisal of where we are now. A recent piece was titled "The New Giddy Optimism Meets the Old Hard Realities."

Positive Living

"Positive Living," the newsletter of AIDS Project Los Angeles, has a magazine feel with letters, features, and departments on health, politics, clinical trials, community efforts, women, legal and insurance issues, and treatment news. It is written for an informed but not professional readership.

TAGlines

Treatment Action Group has a monthly paper of three to four articles that fairly burn off the screen. The sarcasm could melt metal, but if you're looking for a densely written insider's report on the latest in treatment research, this is where to come for compelling, rigorously informed news that is mercilessly focused on finding a cure. Note: Straighten up your collar and tuck in your shirt before checking out the star-studded supporter list — it's all A-list.

AIDS SERVICE ORGANIZATIONS

ASOs are the backbone of the AIDS movement, providing day-to-day support for people with AIDS grappling with the social, financial, and legal consequences of the epidemic. As community-based organizations, they're often the first place we turn to for help (and we just as frequently receive it). Today, however, they're moving on to the Web in such increasing numbers that the list below is only a small sample. If your area's  service organization is not listed, see the index at the end of this chapter or go to the pages of Stop AIDS and the Colorado AIDS Organization for a complete links list.

Los Angeles

AIDS Project Los Angeles, one of the first and largest AIDS service organizations, began its client work in 1983 when early volunteers began visiting patients at their hospital beds. This was the beginning of the "buddy program," which continues today along with programs for food distribution, medical transportation, home health care, and counseling on mental health, legal, insurance, and public-benefits issues. Its efforts on education, public policy, and AIDS funding remain the model for many groups across the country.

New England

AIDS Action is New England's oldest and largest provider of AIDS services, education, and advocacy. It offers free advice and counseling on housing, legal, financial, and insurance questions. Volunteers assist with transportation, delivery of meals, housecleaning, shopping, or moving. Other services include a buddy program, the AIDS Action Hotline at 1-800-235-2331, and the HIV Resource Library for up-to-date information on medical treatments.

Texas

AIDS Foundation Houston provides nurse-practitioner services, rent, and utility assistance, a food program that also dispenses free personal hygiene items, housing, and an HIV/AIDS hotline.

Colorado

The mission of the Colorado AIDS Project is to "improve lives affected by HIV/AIDS and to prevent HIV infection." Client services include everything from advice on insurance and legal issues to housing, medical referral, and education. Its Web page, one of the most sophisticated around, includes HIV/AIDS terminology, links to other AIDS organizations on the Web, and hotline numbers.

Michigan

The Detroit Community AIDS Library Web page contains contact numbers and descriptions of area service organizations. Among the groups specifically targeting people with AIDS is Caregivers/AIDS Home Support, which provides personal care, housekeepers, and maintenance personnel. It also lists many health and well-being organizations, from the Red Cross to Cabrini Clinic.

New York

Gay Men's Health Crisis, founded by volunteers in 1981, is the nation's oldest and largest not-for-profit AIDS organization. It offers medical, legal, financial, and insurance support to 7,300 men, women, and children with AIDS in New York City, as well as education and advocacy services. The GMHC page is one of the most handsome and useful on the Web, offering straightforward advice on joining the fight as well as caring for yourself and friends. The newsletter and "Useful Facts" sheet are filled with quality, up-to-date tips and news.

San Francisco

The Stop AIDS Project is a specialized service organization that quite literally grabs gay men by the collar and invites them to join a discussion group on AIDS, its effects, safe sex, and community. By funneling people into peer groups (young men, couples, men over 50) it enables members to talk and act on issues such as sex, monogamy, and feelings of vulnerability. Rather than supply the usual range of services, it refers people with AIDS to the appropriate local agencies, each of which is listed on site.

Baltimore

Though ARIC has a guide to local ASOs offering other forms of assistance (legal, housing, and so forth), its mission is "patient empowerment through information." Among its publications are the encyclopedic AIDS Medical Glossary and a quarterly newsletter ("The Dirt on AIDS"), an AIDS Information Library (a collection of documents explaining the human immune system's parts), and a PWA Resource Guide (index), and a large collection of documents containing information of immediate practical use to the person living with HIV/AIDS taken from the six informational appendixes of the AIDS Medical Glossary. The site also has a list of links to other informational sources on the Web.

DICTIONARIES, GLOSSARIES, AND FREQUENTLY ASKED QUESTIONS

A major dilemma in dealing with AIDS is the language. Without fluency in AIDS terminology, you may find it difficult to understand what your doctor is saying, let alone take control of your health. To help make yourself familiar with the lingo, most all of the large AIDS pages have definitions lists, including The Body, Critical Path, and the AIDS Treatment Data Network. Another resource is the HIV/AIDS Frequently Asked Questions site. In addition to definitions it has a good sampling of common questions about topics such as the dispute over the cause of AIDS: Is the virus a hoax? Was it caused by too much partying? This site lines up the major arguments on both sides and lists documented information for you to evaluate. It's not scintillating reading, but it will help clear the clouds of misinformation.

Most of the AIDS information sites mentioned above have search tools—use them. As the databases become increasingly large and detailed, you may easily overlook pertinent files if you simply browse tables of contents. The search engine in Critical Path is especially exact and actually has three sets: one for searching files and Web links, another for searching newsletters, and yet another for sifting through newsgroups. The CDC and QRD also have searchable Usenet newsgroups and AIDS organization lists.

CHAT LINES

☐ *Gay Poz Web Site*
http://www.gaypoz.com

☐ *HIV Support Web Site*
http://www.hiv-support.com/

☐ *Marty Howard's Online Support Groups*
http://www.smartlink.net/~martinjh/aolonqgone.htm

☐ *Michael Davon's Web-Depot.com*
http://www.web-depot.com/

☐ *On Q*
http://www.onq.com

RESOURCES

☐ *ACT UP New York*
http://www.actupny.org/

☐ *ACT UP Philadelphia*
http://www.critpath.org/actup

☐ *Acupuncture*
http://www.acupuncture.com/

☐ *Aegis*
http://www.aegis.com

☐ *AIDS Action Organization*
http://www.aidsaction.org/

☐ *AIDS BBS List (Norman Brown's)*
http://www.qrd.org/QRD/aids/aids.bbs.list

☐ *AIDS Benefit Calendar*
http://jeffpalmer.com/~jpalmer/AIDSBenefitCalendar.html

☐ *AIDS Clinical Trials Information Service*
http://www.actis.org/

☐ *AIDS Foundation Houston*
http://www.powersource.com/afh/

☐ *AIDS and HIV (Einet Search Engine)*
http://galaxy.einet.net/GJ/health.html

☐ *AIDS HIV Resources Page*
http://itec.sfsu.edu/aids/aids.html

☐ *AIDS Infoweb*
http://www.jri.org/infoweb/

☐ *AIDS Legal Referral Panel*
http://www.lyb.com/high-brow/alrp-hp.html

☐ *AIDS Links*
http://www.aidsnyc.org/links.html

☐ *AIDSmed.com*
http://www.aidsmed.com

☐ *AIDS Nat'l InterFaith Network*
http://www.thebody.com/anin/aninpage.html

☐ *AIDS Project Los Angeles (APLA)*
http://www.apla.org/

☐ *AIDS Treatment Data Network*
http://www.aidsinfonyc.org/network/

☐ *AIDS Treatment News*
http://www.immunet

☐ *AIDS Virtual Library at Planet Q*
http://planetq.com/aidsvl/index.html

☐ *AIDS Weekly*
http://www.newsfile.com/x1a.htm

☐ *AIDS Resource Information Center (ARIC)*
http://www.critpath.org/aric

☐ *AmFar*
http://www.amfar.org/

☐ *Being Alive*
http://www.beingalive.org/

☐ *BETA*
http://www.sfaf.org/beta.html

☐ *The Body*
http://www.thebody.com/

☐ *Caregivers Support Network*
http://www.wolfenet.com/~acsn/

☐ *Community AIDS Treatment Information Exchange*
http://www.catie.ca/

☐ *Centers for Disease Control and Prevention*
http://www.cdc.gov/cdc.html

☐ *CDC AIDS Daily News*
gopher://cdcnpin.org/news/prevnews/htm

☐ *CDC National AIDS Clearinghouse*
http://www.cdcnpin.org/

☐ *Centerwatch Clinical Trials*
http://www.centerwatch.com

☐ *Chronic Ill Net (AIDS)*
http://www.chronicillnet.org/aids/

☐ *Colorado AIDS Project*
http://www.coloaids.org/

☐ *Critical Path Project*
http://www.critpath.org/

☐ *Consumer News*
http://aidsnyc.org/cnews/

☐ *Detroit Community AIDS Library*
http://www.libraries.wayne.edu/dcal/aids.html

☐ *Diet and Nutrition HIV (The Body)*
http://www.thebody.com/dietnut.html

☐ *Elton John AIDS foundation*
http://www.ejaf.org/

☐ *GENA Mailing List Archives*
http://gopher.hivnet.org:70/1/newsgroups

☐ *Gay Men's Health Crisis*
http://www.gmhc.org/

☐ *GMHC's Living with HIV or AIDS*
http://www.gmhc.org/living/living.html

☐ *Herbal Resources*
http://www.crl.com/~robbee/herbal.html

☐ *HIV Electronic Information Media Review*
http://florey.biosci.uq.oz.au/hiv/HIV_EMIR.html

☐ *HIV Insite*
http://hivinsite.ucsf.edu

☐ *HIV Infoweb*
http://www.infoweb.org/

☐ *HIV/AIDS Information Outreach Project*
http://www.aidsnyc.org/about.html

☐ *HIV Medication Guide*
http://www.jag.on.ca/asp_bin/main.asp

☐ *HIV Plus magazine*
http://www.hivplusmag.com/

☐ *HIV Sequence Database WWW Home Page*
http://hiv-web.lanl.gov/

☐ *HIVNET/GENA Information Server*
http://www.hivnet.org

☐ *HIV Standard of Care ACT UP Philadelphia,*
Critical Path
http://www.critpath.org/stcare8.htm

☐ *HIV Treatment Information Service*
http://www.hivatis.org/

☐ *Immunet*
http://www.immunet.org/

☐ *InfoWeb*
http://www.infoweb.org/

☐ *JAMA HIV/AIDS Information Center*
http://www.ama-assn.org/special/hiv/hivhome.htm

☐ *Just Say Yes*
http://www.positive.org/justsayyes/index.htm

☐ *Johns Hopkins AIDS Service*
http://www.hopkins-aids.edu/

☐ *Lambda Pages*
http://www.lambdapages.com

☐ *Marty Howard's HIV/AIDS Home page*
http://www.smartlink.net/~martinjh/

☐ *Names Project (AIDS Memorial Quilt)*
http://www.aidsquilt.org/

☐ *NAPWA*
http://www.napwa.org

☐ *National AIDS Treatment Advocates Project*
http://www.natap.org/

☐ *Nutrition (Positively HIV)*
http://www.hivnalive.org/

☐ *OUTline (Treatment Activism)*
http://www.out.org/

☐ *Oral Sex Risk*
http://www.tht.org.uk/pubs/oralsex.htm

☐ *Philadelphia FIGHT*
http://www.libertynet.org:80/~fight/

☐ *Poz magazine*
http://www.poz.com

☐ *Project Inform*
http://www.projinform.org/

☐ *Project Open Hand (HIV/AIDS Support)*
http://www.openhand.org/

☐ *Queer InfoServer/AIDS and HIV*
http://www.infoqueer.org/queer/qis/health.html

☐ *Queer Resources Directory: AIDS*
http://www.qrd.org/qrd/aids/

☐ *Safer Sex Page/AIDS Resources*
http://safersex.org/

☐ *SSA Handbook on Benefits for PWAs*
http://www.ssa.gov/pubs/10020.html

☐ *Stop AIDS*
http://www.stopaids.org/

☐ *TAGline*
http://www.aidsnyc.org/network/tag/tag.html

☐ *Treatment Action Network*
http://www.aidsnyc.org/network/tag/

☐ *Treatment Newsletters*
http://www.jri.org/infoweb/treatment/library/readlist.htm

☐ *UNAIDS (formerly WHO Global Program)*
http://www.unaids.org/

☐ *The Underground*
http://www.healthsites.com/AIDS/

☐ *Women Alive Newsletter*
http://www.the body.com/wa/wapage.html

☐ *World Wide Web Virtual Library: AIDS*
http://planetq.com/aidsvl/index.html/

☐ *Yahoo! AIDS/HIV Organizations*
http://www.yahoo.com/Health/Diseases_and_Conditions/AIDS_HIV/

The AIDS Memorial Quilt

The official Names Project AIDS Memorial Quilt home page is beautifully designed. The main image is a bird's-eye view of the quilt on the Mall in Washington, D.C., as it rolls up to the Capitol dome. The resolution is low, but you can just make out surrounding monuments and thousands of figures wandering about in stooped positions, reading about the men and women (both gay and straight) whose lives are memorialized on the acres of cloth-covered ground.

By clicking on the rather stark titles arranged on either side of the image, you can find out all about the quilt, where it will be displayed, and the costly difficulties of maintaining the fragile panels. There is a donation page, a newsletter, and a guide to AIDS information resources.

Among the linked pages are remarks delivered on World AIDS Day by the quilt's founder, Cleve Jones: "I am what is called a long-term survivor of AIDS. It is a bittersweet experience: I have lived longer than I expected—long enough to watch many friends die; long enough to watch three presidents fail to lead the nation forward against the epidemic; certainly long enough to know despair. But while despair about AIDS is hardly surprising, it is a luxury none of us can afford." He goes on to talk about how the quilt began, what it means today, and what it must not become. "We must be very clear that the only way to stop World AIDS Day from becoming a permanent fixture on our calendars—and to prevent quilt displays from having an emotional impact equal to holiday broadcasts of *It's a Wonderful Life*—is to demand that government step up its research efforts and clinical trials programs.... Before we make a donation, walk a precinct, or cast a ballot, we must ask ourselves: Will this dollar, this hour, this vote, bring us any closer to a cure for AIDS?"

Check out Memories of the Quilt by Barbara Milton, a mom. Her son Chuck died of AIDS in January 1994 and October 1996 was her first chance to see Chuck's panel displayed with the rest of the quilt. The page is her account of the experience.

Other quilt-inspired sites on the Web are the AIDS Mosaic and the Virtual Quilt. Both mirror the cloth quilt, offering templates to illustrate and return, and incorporating these designs with others to form a huge digital quilt. Like the Names Project, design recommendations are completely open—a brief biography, a piece of poetry, or anything you feel is fitting. This material is linked to the main page.

The quilt is growing. Still.

☐ *AIDS Memorial Quilt*
  http://www.aidsquilt.org/

☐ *AIDS Memorial Sculpture*
  http://www.artandarcht.org/AIDSMemorialSculpture/

☐ *Canadian AIDS Memorial Quilt*
  http://www.quilt.ca/

☐ *Estate Project for Artists with AIDS*
  http://www.artistswithaids.org/

☐ *Memories from the Quilt, D.C. '96*
  http://www.web-arts.com/milton/bmquilt.htm

☐ *National AIDS Memorial Grove*
  http://www.aidsmemorial.org

America Online

Who isn't an alum or current member of America Online? Unlike Prodigy or CompuServe, it has always been a queer-friendly commercial service. At one time more than 20% of all AOLers were gay men or lesbians, and our presence was reflected by a wide variety of forums on everything from travel to AIDS, books, news, and politics. There are signs, though, of AOL's gay slippage. The designation of a chat room as "gay lifestyle" seems more appropriate for a less politically sensitive company. OnQ's AIDS information is no longer under the big tent and, once in, you'll find that Planet Out is shouldering most of the work. Just as it has with Ivillage for women's content and Net Noir for Blacks, AOL has shifted gay and lesbian content over to a specialist. This seems reasonable because PNO is a talented group and its excellent site has expanded all that was previously offered, including an advice column by Betty DeGeneres ("Ellen's Mom," as we are told).

Even today you can find member chat rooms on most any subject and a limited PNO-sponsored number on fringier topics (there's one on leather and a "Bear Cave.") The simple fact that such forums exist proves AOL's commitment to diversity. AOL is also brave enough to include a variety of queer youth chats and organizations—despite threats from the religious right, it has always supported and defended those groups. And the buddy lists and instant messaging are as hot as ever.

And yet there's a distinct smell of antiseptic in the air. You see it in the multiple warnings from moderators that distasteful comments will be deleted, in top-of-the page admonitions that "personal ads" are inappropriate, and the fact that it now takes three navigational turns to get to the gay and lesbian sections.

A couple of highly publicized blunders have added weight to the impression of AOL's retreat. The first and most damaging was the illegal turnover of AOL member Lieutenant Timothy McVeigh's chat room postings to the Navy—a breach of the company's privacy agreements which AOL has since made up for in an undisclosed settlement as well as public apologies. This head-snapper (which resulted in McVeigh's firing) was further aggravated when it was discovered that AOL's online edition of Merriam-Webster's thesaurus listed "homosexuality" to mean slurs such as "fag" and "pansy." But together, these buffers amount to a none-too-subtle message that gay men and lesbians, while welcome, need to conform to AOL's standards—they're a "family" kind of place.

After visiting the more freewheeling World Wide Web, you may prefer this paternal approach and be reassured by the structured environment. For example, before entering very specifically age- and sex-demarcated chats (gay men in their 20s or 30s) you'll see a sign for "Rules and Schedule." They are very much as your camp counselor gave out when you wore Keds: Don't be rude, let others speak, and if you are having problems make sure and only complain to the moderator. (But don't get impatient if you don't get an answer quickly: "They are doing the best they can!"

And perhaps that sense of measured tolerance within the boundaries of AOL shouldn't be underestimated. This is a club, and members have a sense of camaraderie that is perhaps as important as breadth of coverage. It's a relentlessly tolerant atmosphere. If you can abide the constraints, or are more comfortable within them, AOL remains a good value.

 Art

Queer art. How do you define that? By the subject or by the artist? Must you be queer to get it? Lesbian to appreciate lesbian art? Is it activism or is it art? Even legendary gay artist Robert Rauschenberg is coy when asked about homoerotic elements in his work, and others, like Jasper Johns, call their lawyers when definitions are used. Because queer art is such a semantic and threatening mess of a term, finding it is like watching for shooting stars. Every now and then a dazzling exhibition will streak across the horizon, such as "Goodbye to Berlin?," OutArt's yearly shows, "World's Women Online!" or the stellar shows by Queer Arts Resource. And slowly, very slowly, modern-learning museums such as the Whitney in New York City are curating shows of out artists like Paul Cadmus and even putting them on the Web—paced as always by the Andy Warhol Museum.

Queer Arts Resource

The best starting place is Queer Arts Resource's home page. It's a terrifically smart, good-looking page that offers exhibitions, forums, a bookshop, and the highest-caliber queer arts links anywhere. The glory of this page is in the exhibitions and archives of past shows, which range from retrospectives of Hubert Stowitts and George Platt Lynes to showings of contemporary artists such as Robert Flynt, Kim Anno, and Elizabeth Stevens. The accompanying pictures are crisp and nicely sized and the curator's remarks are thoughtful and succinct. For example, QA says, "David Wojnarowicz is recognized as one of the most potent voices of his generation, and his singular artistic achievements place him firmly within a long-standing American tradition of the artist as visionary, rebel and public figure. Often overlapping text, paint, collaged elements, and photography, and sometimes organizing them in quadrants or comic strip–like frames, Wojnarowicz created provocative narratives and historical allegories dealing with dialectical themes of order and disorder, birth and death. Advertisements are transformed into visions of horror, as in his supermarket ad series. *Untitled [Sirloin Steaks]* (1983), is a fusion of eroticism and death, a powerful indication of the rage he felt at how much more attention society gave to killing men rather than loving them."

The Stowitts show is particularly interesting as his rediscovery parallels the emerging validity of homosexual art. Contrary to the prevailing refusal to acknowledge gay content, Queer Art Resource "believe(s) that a focus on queer art as such contributes to a deeper understanding of art, of our community, and of the universal artistic impulse." Great site.

The Andy Warhol Museum

"I paint pictures to…I guess, yeah, to remind myself that I am still around." Warhol is still very much alive in his museum's Web site, where images and text tour you through the works and world of the "most influential artist of the last 50 years of the 20th century." It's appropriately mundane/chic, complete with a floor plan of the coat check as well as the gold-plated benefactor list. There are only a few images—*Self-Portrait* (1986), *Man* (1950s), *Electric Chair* (1965), *Jackie* (1964), *Marilyn—Three Times* (1962), and *Shoe* (1950s)—but the notes accompanying the wide-angle photos of galleries on each of the four floors are models of their kind, giving the works a clear, eye-opening context. The "oxidation paintings" (1978), we're told, were "made by the artist and others urinating on canvases prepared with copper and bronze metallic pigments which oxidized as the painting dried. The "oxidations" are metaphors for transubstantiation, the transformation of base materials into precious objects. They also refer to Jackson Pollock's paintings of the 1940s, made by dripping paint onto a horizontal canvas, and to Yves Klein's blue and gold paintings, which were imprinted by nude bodies."

Haring/Kahlo

You will often see a devotee put up a site dedicated to a dead painter. Like love notes or flowers on graves, these sites are intensely personal, sweetly obsessive moments. For example, Keith Haring had a shrine by the Orange Room. The URL has gone black, but another has appeared. That's part of the Web's charm: A page pops up, makes a gesture, and is gone—and replaced by another, named appropriately enough, "haring.com." There's also the Francis Bacon Image Gallery and an homage to lesbian artist Romaine Brooks. One artist whose followers show no sign of fading is Frida Kahlo, whose fans offer nearly 20 pages to her memory as a painter and lesbian icon. For an apostle's view, check out the World of Frida Kahlo— and buckle your seat belt as you read of her operatic cremation: "Frida's lips appeared to break into a seductive grin just as the doors closed shut." There's lots more "stuff on Frida," including links to "Kahloism," a new "religion that worships Frida Kahlo as the one true God."

For an exhibition of a more inclusive passion, visit the "El Museo de Gayo." Its creator has taken it upon himself to create the largest museum on the Web devoted to gay art. It's a curious mix of old world and new, with Leonardo da Vinci side by side with modern-day artists like David Hockney and Francis Bacon.

Goodbye to Berlin?

This blockbuster site opens with a close-up of a shapely pink butt tattooed with a red heart circled with a banner asking, "Goodbye to Berlin?" This is the landmark exhibit by the Gay Museum Berlin documenting 100 years of struggle for gay and lesbian liberation. Hundreds of photographs illustrate the story that begins in the early 1900s, continues through the gay liberation movement's flowering in the Weimar Republic and eventual purging during World War II, and highlights the movement's rebirth in the '70s. The story ends today, when the curators see activism as atrophied by prosperity. Many links (most in German) to related sites are included.

Day With(out) Art—Visual AIDS

Day Without Art (DWA) began in 1989 as the national day of action and mourning in response to the AIDS crisis. To raise awareness and inspire positive action, some 800 U.S. art and AIDS groups participated in the first Day Without Art, shutting down museums, sending staff to volunteer at AIDS services, or sponsoring special exhibitions of work about AIDS. Since then, Day With(out) Art has grown into a collaborative project in which an estimated 8,000 museums, galleries, art centers, AIDS Service Organizations, libraries, high schools, and colleges take part on both the national and international levels. In the past Visual AIDS has initiated public actions and programs, published an annual poster and copyright-free broadsides, and acted as press coordinator and clearinghouse for projects for Day Without Art/World AIDS Day. In 1997 Day Without Art become a Day *with* Art, to recognize and promote increased programming of cultural events that draw attention to the continuing pandemic: "We added parentheses to the program title to highlight the pro-active programming of art projects by artists living with HIV/AIDS and art about AIDS that was taking place across the country. It had become clear that active interventions within the annual program were far more effective than actions to negate or reduce the programs of cultural centers."

The Web site features an introduction to the program, a historical overview, a national listing of events, examples from past years and an archive containing copyright-free images of posters, broadsides, postcards and PSAs you can download and reproduce for your own use.

The World's Women Online!

Originally presented at the United Nations' Fourth World Conference on Women in Beijing, this site has hundreds of digitized images of abstract and figurative art by painters such as Etal Adnan (Lebanon) and sculptors such as Liz Maxwell's (United States) bronze nude holding flowers. There's scant help to learn more about the artist, and no annotation to help guide you through the alphabetized lists, but the sample pictures are large, and at no other place in reality or cyberspace can you survey so many female artists.

Tom of Finland/Robert Mapplethorpe/Paul Cadmus

Between the three of them, Tom of Finland, Robert Mapplethorpe, and Cadmus have in a sense defined the debate over pornography and "real" art. You can decide for yourself by visiting sites devoted to each artist's work as inseparable from the political context. The Tom of Finland Foundation's opening page takes a strong position on "the value of erotic art and [it is] working to see it eventually accepted and respected as a valid and important part of artistic expression." Next to the text is a Tom of Finland drawing: a hunk in gloves and leather cap with the signature hypermasculine body. The sample catalogue is for sale, as are prints and originals of other artists' work: a farmhand and a devil disrobing and a color pencil drawing of two young guys—one black, one white—hugely, fantastically erect.

The Mapplethorpe site is especially generous, with large images of *Lisa Lyon, Self Portraits, Posterior View of Black Man,* and *Two Nude Men Embracing.* Background notes are interesting. "In the late '70s, photographs of nude men embracing sparked wild hysteria. These two embracing bodies, captured under perfect studio conditions, tantalize viewers with slivers of excitement from Mapplethorpe's life—well-formed muscles, lights and shadows on perfect human forms, blacks and whites. Mapplethorpe's photography perpetuates the classical idea of the human form. He photographs men and women as they would appear in the eye of Rodin."

Paul Cadmus's work and career are covered in a variety of sites, ranging from a list of museums displaying his work at Artcyclopedia to a fascinating interview from PBS's *Frontline,* "Paul Cadmus: enfant terrible at 80."

Guerrilla Girls

The arts are the breath of activism and are nowhere more effective than in work by the artists known as the Guerrilla Girls, "the conscience of the art world." One example of their scholarly wit is a slightly modified painting from ancient Turkey—men and women in hand-to-hand combat, and the women, gorilla masks in place, are winning! "We declare ourselves feminist

counterparts to the mostly male tradition of anonymous do-gooders like Robin Hood, Batman, and the Lone Ranger." The Guerrilla Girls use humor to focus on the issues rather than the personalities and also to "show that feminists can be funny." How popular are they? They've been in the *New Yorker*, and one collector tried to sell a portfolio of their work at Sotheby's Auction house for big bucks. (GG was angry, and the group picketed. Sotheby's buckled. GG notched up another victory and rode off into the sunset. In the last decade they've created more than 70 posters, artworks, and street actions, and show most of them here along with a calendar of action events across the nation.)

Penis Project and Pier 45

Some of the most interesting and powerful exhibitions you'll find on the Web are the sites artists have put up themselves. Try the Penis Project (an Israeli artist exploring the boundaries of art and pornography) or the ButchDick Collection and himself.com where works range from "hi-tech to supra-natural, abstract and revisionist expressionism to works of in-your-face homoerotica." Along with the sites of such well-known artists as Gilbert and George or Trevor Southey's retrospective of the artist's paintings and drawings called "Reconciliation: Africa/Family/Mormon/Gay," there is Richard Renaldi's "Pier 45." " 'Pier 45' is a collection of images I have photographed in the area of Manhattan adjacent to the Hudson waterfront in the West Village, an area known simply as "the Piers" to its habitués. I have long been attracted to the openness and wide horizons along this particular stretch of the Hudson; one feels as though they were on the remote edges of the city. It is here where people go to find solitude, friends, and recreate from the fast pace of New York life. It is a landscape composed of water, concrete, fence, and sky, where the changing quality of the light is reflected throughout each day in its reflections on the buildings lining the Jersey shore opposite and on the shimmering surface of New York harbor in the distance. My intention throughout this project has been to convey the unique character of this urban space as well as the faces which populate it: dog walkers and joggers, drag queens and dropouts, muscle boys on roller blades, homeless veterans, Stonewall survivors, elderly couples out for a Sunday stroll, sunbathers, and curious tourists—black and white, rich and poor, gay and straight, and every category in between".

Starving Artists

"All artists are starving artists/Hungry for the creative/No matter how great their success/Eternally longing for the creative spark/That ignites passion for the work." These lines constitute the first paragraph a visitor sees upon arriving at this site. Serious and searching, this is an absorbing page with an Eastern influence. An ever-changing gallery, often of photographs (not always queer), it presents artists such as Jim Omtatoo, one of whose photographs is a still life of objects of violence and vanity: brass knuckles, handcuffs, and guns jumbled with a make-up brush, lipstick, and a compact with the reflection of a woman painting her lips. There is a links page as well as brief introductions to the artists.

Isle of Lesbos—Lesbian Images in Art

With more than 65 works from 40 artists, this page is a survey of art going back to the year 1500. "The images were chosen because they have a lesbian appeal to them, depicting emotional or romantic interaction between women. Some are clearly sexual; others are not. In some cases you could say the women pictured are friends or sisters, but they could just as well be lovers too… This means that images that show the broader range of

lesbian experience (tender interaction between female partners, companionship, and so on) might not be recognized as reflecting more than friendship between women.... You'll note
that this site features only a few women artists, such as Marie
Laurencin, Tamara de Lempicka, and Ida Teichmann. Recent
works are excluded 'out of respect for the artist's livelihoods.' "

University exhibitions:
In a Different Light

Another art-rich area is the university exhibition. Although
scheduled exhibitions are hard to come by, regular visits to the
University of California, Berkeley, Carnegie Mellon University,
Stanford University, and New York University are rewarded with
smartly curated exhibitions. University Art Museum/Pacific Film
Archive's "In a Different Light" has been up for three years now,
and its popularity seems to assure many more. "The initial inspiration for the exhibition was the dynamism and innovation evi-
dent in the work of the contemporary generation of young gay
and lesbian artists. Remarkably, these artists, living in a generally hostile social climate—amidst the constant threat of 'gay bash-
ings,' proscriptive legislative initiatives, and surrounded by the
tragedy of AIDS—not only persist in making art, but do so in a
spirit of humor, generosity, and flamboyance." The online images
represent a sampling of the groups titled Void, Self, Drag, Other,
Couple, Family, Orgy, World, and Utopia.

Web Art Archives & Indexes

Among the Web art archives, (Artscape, Art on the Net, Internet for the Fine Arts, the Web Museum, World Wide Arts Resource), Artcyclopedia and Art In Context seem to be the easiest place to find an overall guide to queer artists' recent and
past exhibitions. Just go to the search function and type, for
example, Lari Pittman or David Hockney.

☐ *Alternative Creations*
  http://www.alternative-creations.com

☐ *Andy Warhol Museum*
http://www.warhol.org/warhol/warhol.html

☐ *ArtAIDS*
http://www.artaids.org/

☐ *Artcyclopedia*
http://www.artcyclopedia.com/

☐ *Art In Context*
http://www.artincontext.org/

☐ *Art of Desire (Kinsey Inst.'s 50th)*
http://www.fa.indiana.edu/~sofa/feat/index.html

☐ *Art on the Net*
http://www.art.net/

☐ *Artscape*
http://www.artscape.com/

☐ *(Francis) Bacon*
http://www.cable.lime.tm/coil/bacon.html
http://home3.pacific.net.sg/~danny.chaplin/

☐ *Berkeley Art Museum/Pacific Film Archive*
http://www.bampfa.berkeley.edu/

☐ *(Richard) Bolingbroke*
http://www.rbolingbroke.com/

☐ *A Brief History of the Male Nude in the
United States (Physique Magazine)*
http://models.badpuppy.com/archive/davem/dave1.htm

☐ *Bronzino's Portrait of a Young Man*
http://www.walrus.com/~jonnonyc/bronzino/

☐ *(Romaine) Brooks*
http://www.geocities.com/Vienna/8616/romfot1.htm

☐ *Butch Dick*
http://www.lorenarts.com/

☐ *(Paul) Cadmus*
http://www.artcyclopedia.com/artists/cadmus_paul.html

☐ *(Paul) Cadmus—Enfant Terrible at 80*
http://www.pbs.org/wgbh/pages/frontline/shows/farmerswife/dave/cadmus.html

☐ *Carlos & Billy*
http://www.geocities.com/WestHollywood/Village/1783/

☐ *(Howard) Cruse*
http://www.skyhouse.org/howard

☐ *Crazy-Gay Berlin*
http://members.tripod.de/crazygay_berlin/

☐ *Daimonix*
http://www.daimonix.com

☐ *Day With (out) Art [Visual AIDS]*
http://www.visualaids.org/

☐ *Demuth, Charles*
http://www.artincontext.com/listings/pages/artist/x/531zv7px/menu.htm

☐ *For Lesbians: Art and Poetry of Women*
http://www.goodnet.com/~stacey/staceys_other.html

☐ *Gilbert and George*
http://www.gilbertandgeorge.co.uk/

☐ *(Wilhelm von) Gloeden*
http://web.ukonline.co.uk/richard.wykes/gloeden/gloeden01.html

☐ *Goddesses for the New Millennium*
http://www.netdreams.com/registry/corinne/

☐ *Goodbye to Berlin?*
http://www.gayactivism.com/chooselang.html

☐ *Guerrilla Girls*
http://www.guerillagirls.com

☐ *Haring, Keith*
http://www.haring.com/

☐ *Himself.com*
http://ragingzone.com/ragecam.htm

☐ *In a Different Light Exhibition Home Page*
http://www.bampfa.berkeley.edu/exhibits/idl/dlhome.html

☐ *Internet for the Fine Arts*
http://www.fine-art.com

☐ *Isle of Lesbos*
http://www.sappho.com/

☐ *Kahlo, Frida*
http://www.cascade.net/kahlo.html

☐ *(Chris) Komater [male nudes]*
http://www.chriskomater.com

☐ *Lawrence Grecco Photography*
http://www.grecco.com/

☐ *LarvaLand: The Way-Out Web-World of Luz de Korum*
http://www.sirius.com/~larva/

☐ *Leonardo Gallery*
http://www.leonardo.net/museum/main.html

☐ *Lesbian Images in Art*
http://www.sappho.com/

☐ *Lesbian Photography on the US West Coast: 1972-1997*
http://www.sla.purdue.edu/waaw/Corinne

☐ *Leslie-Lohman Gay Art Foundation*
http://www.leslie-lohman.org/

☐ *(J.C.) Leyendecker*
http://www.geocities.com/WestHollywood/Heights/8255/leyendecker.html

☐ *Michelangelo*
http://www.michelangelo.com/buonarroti.html

☐ *OutSmart Magazine (Robert Rauschenberg)*
http://www.outsmartmagazine.com

☐ *Penis Project*
http://come.to/tpp

☐ *Pier 45 by photographer Richard Renaldi*
http://www.renaldi.com/portfolio/pier1.html

☐ *Queer Arts Resource*
http://www.queer-arts.org/

☐ *Queer Cultural Center of SF*
http://www.queerculturalcenter.org/

☐ *Q-U-E-E-R-S-I-G-H-T*
http://www.newfestival.com/queersight/

☐ *Rage Cam*
http://ragingzone.com/cam.htm

☐ *Robert Mapplethorpe Retrospective*
http://www.ocaiw.com/mapple.htm

☐ *Saint Sebastian*
http://www.geocities.com/WestHollywood/1718

☐ *Trevor Southey—Reconciliation: Africa/Family/Mor
mon/Gay*
http://www.trevorsouthey.com

☐ *Starving Artists*
http://www.starvingartists.com/

☐ *The Stowitts Museum and Library*
http://www.stowitts.com/index.htm

☐ *Tom of Finland*
http://www.eroticarts.inter.net/foundation/welcome.html

☐ *Utopia Gallery*
http://www.freakography.com/gal.htm

☐ *Wojnarowicz, David*
http://www.artincontext.org/artist/w/david_wojnarowicz/

☐ *Women's Artist Archive*
http://libweb.sonoma.edu/

☐ *Women's Studio Workshop*
http://www.webmark.com/wsw/wswhome.htm

☐ *The World's Women Online*
http://wwol.inre.asu.edu/artists.html

☐ *Worldwide Arts Resource*
http://wwar.com/

☐ *Yahoo!*
http://www.yahoo.com/yahoo/Art/

To collapse the variety and depth of Asian-American sites into one chapter is impossible. This vast subject covers sites such as Gay Muslims, a mailing list for gay and lesbian Muslims who believe being homosexual and practicing Islam are not mutually exclusive, to *Bombay Dost*, India's only gay and lesbian magazine, and the pages of the Long Yang Club, a social organization supporting the gay Asian-American community .

There are hundreds of wonderful pages, but perhaps the best place to start piecing together the gay scene in Asia is at Utopia. A comprehensive yet very personal site, Utopia has descriptions of gay life in all of Asia: Australia, Burma/Myanmar, Cambodia, China/Hong Kong, Indonesia, Japan, Korea, Laos, Malaysia, North America, New Zealand, Philippines, Singapore, South Asia, South Korea, Taiwan, Thailand, and Vietnam.

Broken down country by country into sections, the information is generally focused on travelers' perceptions and begins with a first-hand description of gay life. Often, as in the case of Cambodia, you get a real flavor of being there: "The night scene is quite different from Manila or Bangkok—like stepping back 20 years. We visited the pleasant bar called The Heart of Darkness, run by Samsang , a friendly and campy Khmer chap... The legacy of the Khmer Rouge still hangs heavily over this sad land—most people have lost a family member or even their entire families in the "Killing Fields." But the country has its wondrous Angkor temples and if you want the experiences seen in movies like *Indochine, The Lover*, and *The Scent of Green Papaya*—you'll find it here."

The write-ups on Japan put it at the leading edge of modern gay Asian life. There's a long section on the leading magazines with descriptions of many such as Badu, the hippest gay publication for young male Japan. It has a "broad range of model types, manga, nude sports club initiations, hidden camera pictures, kink, Japanese erotic fiction and personals."

Among the many insightful cultural tips is an explanation of the seeming exclusivity of Japanese gay clubs. Here's advice on finding your way: "Locate venues that feature your 'type' and you will be welcomed into a cozy and secluded world where other patrons are prematched to your tastes. This is simply the result of hundreds of years of specialization within the shadow world and an economic reality of limited space and prohibitive rents."

Utopia is very good about updating their huge collection of links which covers everything from bars to home pages, expatriate clubs, AIDS/HIV, art, magazines—the gamut.

KEANOO'S

Another comprehensive page, that is more focused on Asian-American sites is Keanoo's, a home page by Duc Nguyen. He left Vietnam in 1975 and now lives in Canada. Aside from a brief personal résumé, his page's main goal is to provide a "collection of all the available Internet sites of interest to gay and lesbian Asians and their friends." Though the links concentrate on North American sites, they also include those around the world. And the lists are annotated, usually with satisfyingly long descriptions. You'll find very long Asian-American sources for AIDS, entertainment (books and movies), magazines, organizations, news, and home pages. The home pages are especially good, containing brief introductions by the authors.

Keanoo's annotated list to Asian-American organizations is also impressive. You'll find write-ups and links, including Asians and Friends chapters, Gay Asian Pacific Alliance, Long Yang association, Pacific Friends, and more.

TRIKONE

Trikone ("tri" as in trim, "kone" as in cone—Sanskrit for triangle), is both a news center for this rights/social organization's members and "an important community resource for queer (lesbian/gay/bisexual /transgender) people of South Asian descent." In this it resembles most of the other Asian American organizations around the globe, such as Pacific Friends and the Long Yang clubs. It contains articles, interviews, poetry, personal stories, art, essays, classifieds, personal ads, and resource listings as well as schedules of club events such as dinners and pride dates.

Distinctively, Trikone has articles tackling a broad range of subjects that have included coming out, queer Asian film, Hinduism, and homosexuality. The crisp writing is by people who have lived the subject. In one issue devoted to Pakistan there are fascinating pieces on growing up gay in Karachi, case studies of hijras and zenanas, and a reflection on the effects of British colonization by a exiled Pakistani gay man. The links list (for men and women) to publications, organizations, mail lists, and queer-related subjects is amazingly complete and current.

MAGAZINES

OG, Dragun and Threelip are slick, under-30 modern magazines that combine photo spreads of Asian men along with serious editorial. Like hip versions of *XY,* there is often poetry as well as works of fiction as they showcase fashion and youth interests alongside features about gay Asians living in Asia and in the West..

Queer Korean News is both a rights and news magazine. News articles have included an analysis of the Korean government's policies on homosexuality. There's also a message board through which Korean-American queers can make friends.

Kabaklaan Queer Webzine is a lifestyle magazine for lesbians with sections on the state of lesbian liberation in Philippines, book reviews, short stories, poetry, and jokes. The writing is lively and engaging, particularly in the editor's column. Addressing the subject of gay marriage, she says, "Why is it that two of the plaintiffs who sued the state of Hawaii for the right to marry their own gender are Filipinos?... Here we are, Filipinos in this strange land, always looking for Filipino role models who are making it in the American mainstream—well, here are two excellent examples of Filipino role models—two once-ordinary Filipino-Americans, who have made history for all of us."

☐ *AIDS services in Asian Communities (Philadelphia)*
http://www.critpath.org/asiac

☐ *ALBA (Asian Lesbian Bisexual Alliance)*
http://www.alba.org/

☐ *Aqua (youth)*
http://www.aquanet.org/

☐ *Asian Avenue (Community site)*
http://www.asianavenu.com/

☐ *Asians & Friends—New York (plus many others in North America)*
http://www.afny.com

☐ *Asians & Friends—Ottawa*
http://www.cyberus.ca/~afo/

☐ *Asians & Friends—Pittsburgh*
http://ftp.tcp.com/qrd/www/orgs/afpgh/rof.html

☐ *Asians & Friends—Washington*
http://members.aol.com/afwash/afw.htm

☐ *Asian Pacific Alliance of New York (APANY)*
http://members.aol.com/apany/index.html

☐ *Asian and Pacific Islander Wellness Center*
http://www.apiwellness.org/

☐ *Asian Resources*
http://www.best.com/~utopia/

☐ *Asian Queers*
http://www.reg.uci.edu/UCI/LGBRC/asian.html

☐ *Badi Magazine*
http://www.best.com/~ashop/magmisc.htm#badi

☐ *Bombay Dost Magazine*
http://www.bombay-dost.com

☐ *Buddah Lounge*
http://www.buddahlounge.com/

☐ *Cyber-Japan*
http://www.so-net.ne.jp/CYBERJAPAN/

☐ *Dragoncastle's Gay Asia Thai Site*
http://www.dragoncastle.net/

☐ *Dragun Magazine*
http://www.dragunmagazine.com

☐ *Gay & Lesbian Hong Kong*
http://sqzm14.ust.hk/hkgay/

☐ *Gay Muslims*
http://queernet.org/lists/gay-muslims.html

☐ *Gay China*
http://www.gaychina.com/home.hts

☐ *Gay Net Japan*
http://www.gnj.or.jp/welcome.html

☐ *GAPA (Gay Asian Pacific Alliance)*
http://www.gapa.org/

☐ *Gay Vietnamese Alliance*
http://www.gva.org/

☐ *Gay Tokyo*
http://www.geocities.com/WestHollywood/4248/

☐ *Grinding Tofu*
http://www.geocities.com/Tokyo/Towers/4289/

☐ *Han Queerean Korean*
http://www.otherwise.net/HanQ/

☐ *Kabaklaan Queer Webzine*
http://www.hain.org/badaf6/

☐ *Kakasarian—queer resources for Filipinos*
http://www.tribo.org/bakla/bakla.html

☐ *Keanoo's Gay Asian Links*
http://www.x-cite.web.com/kgal/

☐ *Khush Net*
http://www.khushnet.com

☐ *Long Yang Clubs (Boston, Montreal, Holland, New York, Sao Paolo, San Diego, Toronto, Thailand, Vancouver)*
http://www.longyangclub.com/silklink/

☐ *Mt. Fuji*
http://hello.to/mtfuji/

☐ *OG Magazine*
http://www.ogusa.com

☐ *Pacific Friends*
http://www.PacificFriends.org

☐ *Queer and Asian*
http://www.drizzle.com/~qasian/

☐ *Queer Korean News*
http://homepage.interaccess.com/~jasini/

☐ *Samalinga Writings*
http://www.geocities.com/WestHollywood/5838/

☐ *Sequin Queen (Hong Kong)*
http://www.sequinqueen.com/

☐ *Thai Scene*
http://www.thaiscene.com/

☐ *Threelip Magazine*
http://i.am/threelip/

☐ *Trikone: Lesbian and Gay South Asians*
http://www.trikone.org/

☐ *Utopia*
http://www.utopia-asia.com/

☐ *Vietnamese Gay/Lesbian/Bi Friends*
http://neptune.netimages.com/~gallery/vn-gblf/

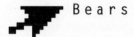 Bears

Why are bears so cheerful? Sure they can growl and cuff you hard—but it's all in play, which, to judge from the hundreds of on-line caves, is a main activity of bears from Amsterdam to Motor City and all furry spots in between.

Bear pages run the gamut from history (the Bear History Project) with archives, research papers, art exhibits focusing on gay bear culture, community and masculinity to the Filthy Grizzly's Smut Show. Two of the hottest sites are MuscleBears and Beefy-Boyz. Musclebears is packed with exactly what its name suggests: big, usually furry, always muscular guys. It's a sort of national gallery of the kind of guys who demand an appreciative *woof!* when you see them. The index is broken down state by state and by weight so you can find a 300-pounder in Texas or a 250-pound Californian in a few seconds. There's also a gallery of less furry musclemen like "Bigpec-sny", a.k.a. Carl, who is "prowling for muscle bottoms to play with."

Beefy Guys

Beefy Boyz is both a gallery of big hot men and the home page of Jim and Bob: "Bob sez Jim is the stuff that dreams are made of...Jim sez that the stars he reaches for can only be seen in Bob's eyes." So there's a nice (but rough) personal touch to this page which includes a section on bear events around the world like the International Bear Rendezvous, Desert Bear in Palm Springs. And don't miss Bare Beefy Boyz—a constantly updated page of some serious prime beef.

Among popular bear events sites, one of the best is is hosted by Castrobear, describing the festivities taking place north of San Francisco over the fabled Lazy Bear Weekend; four days in which 2,000 guys converge on the beautiful redwood tree–covered area of Guerneville up at the Russian River in Northern California's Sonoma County. Four hot days and nights when the big and furry have lots of fun and raise thousands for AIDS charities.

If you're looking for a comprehensive page to begin exploring all aspects of the ursine world, the place to start is the Bears Resources List, also known as NetBears. Since its beginning in 1994 it's grown so much that it regularly receives over 2 million hits a month. Amazing. Through it bears worldwide maintain connections among themselves. There's a terrific list of links to services on the net, a mailing list, clip art, and a semiserious list of bears in movies, and tons of bear clubs, each with descriptions of upcoming gatherings (dinners, beer busts, and benefits) and links to member home pages.

You'll find a huge index of bear clubs, including perhaps the premier bear club: Bears of San Francisco (B.O.S.F.), which hosts the International Bear Rendezvous. Check out "Bear Scratchings," the newsletter of B.O.S.F. for more about how this charitable organization and its members.

Woof!

Of course, there are rogue bears too. To meet a gruff one go to Wolf's CyberDen. (A wolf is a bear, but not every bear is a wolf. It's something to do with aggression.) The main image of this very sophisticated site is a black wolf howling against a blood-red sunset. Among the various pages he offers is a detailed profile of his sexual side. "I am rather aggressive and outgoing (as if you couldn't guess from my home page) with a demented sense of humor (bet you couldn't have guessed that either—grin) and I have been told that I am disgustingly optimistic as I will always try to find the 'bright side' to any situation. Sexually, I have probably tried it all at some time during my life and consider myself VERY open-minded. I can go from 'mild to wild' and truly enjoy everything—from intimate romantic times with someone special to pretty wild (and sometimes even kinky) fantasy sessions." After declaring himself "99.5% top," he runs down a list from Romance ("Yup—a lot!") to Heavy S/M ("NOPE!") to more penetrating endeavors ("Yup—a lot!").

One of the things that will strike you about the bear scene is how diverse it is. Along with thousands of home pages and club listings scattered around the world, you'll find bear-friendly businesses such as Pete's Tours, a travel agency specializing in ursine vacation packages to the California gold country or exotic getaways like Tahiti. BrushCreek Media has a roster of magazines and *Classic Bear* videos. Gen X Bears is a new organization with chapters in more than 15 cities and towns all over the world. There's even a site identifying movie bears, Fur on Film Bears.

LoneStar Saloon

Known as "the dome of the rock," for its revered status as the birthplace of the bear movement, the Lonestar Saloon in San Francisco has one of the best of the bear bar pages. It's great-looking and funny too: "We're committed to our community—OK, some of the staff have been briefly committed and later released!" Along with a calendar of events and a general store with everything from baseball caps to boxer shorts, they have a large listing of Web sites and a recipe page of bear grub (Don't bother counting the calories!).

Bars

Because bears come in all shapes and sizes and have different sexual proclivities, you might want to read the unofficial classification guide in Net Bears. It's amazing. The beard length descriptions go from "5 o'clock shadow" to "belt-buckle-grazing long beards." You'll find codes for height, fatness, "the daddy factor," and cub quotient. But wherever you fall in the grading, the basic requirement is being comfortable in your

own skin. As Bears Resources says, bearishness "is often defined as more of an attitude than anything else—a sense of
comfort with our natural masculinity and bodies that is not
slavish to the vogues of male attractiveness that is so common
in gay circles and the culture at large." Growl!

*Thanks to Jimmy Stemple of the Lonstar for his help.

☐ *Adams, Jim*
http://members.iglou.com/artbear/

☐ *AZDadBear*
http://gcwp.com/azdad/

☐ *BackWoods Bears*
http://www.primenet.com/~rstbear/bwbears.html

☐ *Beach Bears*
http://www.geocities.com/WestHollywood/2000/

☐ *BearButt's Homepage*
http://www.geocities.com/WestHollywood/3103/

☐ *Bear Date Page*
http://www.bearbudfl.com/bears/page.html

☐ *Bear History Project*
http://www.bearhistory.com

☐ *Bear Networks*
http://www.bear.net/

☐ *Bear Youth*
http://www.bearyouth.org

☐ *Bear Press*
http://www.bearpress.com/

☐ *Bear Ring*
http://www.bearring.org/admin.html

☐ *Bears of San Francisco (B.O.S.F.)*
http://www.bosf.com

☐ *Bears Resources List (Resources for Bears)*
http://www.skepsis.com/.gblo/bears/

☐ *Bear Land*
http://www.bearland.com/index.html

☐ *Bear Networks*
http://www.bear.net.

☐ *Beefy Boyz*
http://www.beefyboyz.com/

☐ *Bigpecsny*
http://members.aol.com/bigpecsny/

☐ *Brush Creek Media*
http://www.brushcreek.com/

☐ *CyberCub's Home Page*
http://www.cybernw.com/~cybercub/

☐ *Donald "Wolf" Tombe (Wolf's CyberDen)*
http://www.wolfe.com/

☐ *Filthy Grizzly's Smut Page*
http://www.odyline.com/~grizzly

☐ *Gen X Bears*
http://www.genxbears.org/

☐ *Hairy Chest Page*
http://www.creative.net/~hcp/

☐ *The Harry Bears Page*
http://www.creative.net/~thepark/wilderness/

☐ *Howeth, Mike*
http://rampages.onramp.net/~tmike/

☐ *International Bear Calendar*
http://www.zoom.com/personal/aberno/calendar.shtml

☐ *IRC #Bearcave Address*
http://www.skepsis.com/gblo/BEARS/OFFSITE/irc_bearcave.html

☐ *Lazy Bear Weekend*
http://members.aol.com/LazyB2000/

☐ *Lonestar Saloon*
http://www.lonestar-saloon.com

☐ *MarcoStuds*
http://www.marcostuds.com/

☐ *Muscle Bears*
http://www.musclebears.com/

☐ *Net Bear*
http://users.aol.com/netbearmag/

☐ *Northwest Bears*
http://www.nwbears.org/

☐ *The Powerlifting Bears Clube*
http://members.aol.com/plbearclub/

☐ *TopBear Entertainment*
http://www.topbear.com/

☐ *TopCub's Little Corner*
http://www.topcub.com/

☐ *UrSir's Digital Den*
http://www.magna.com.au/~asclarke/home.html

☐ *Wolf's CyberDen (Donald "Wolf" Tombe)*
http://www.wolfe.com/

☐ *XLarge Homepage*
http://www.xlarge.ch/

Books & Poetry

To judge by the explosion of queer literary sites on the Web, we are experiencing a renaissance of gay and lesbian literature. New writers are published, small houses are getting much wider exposure, and book lovers of every disposition are creating their own sites and finding audiences of a similar passion. There is everything from the official Clive Barker Web site to Lesbian Pulp Fiction and the African-American Literature Book Club— literally hundreds of new sites recovering and discovering all the varying facets of gay literature. Whatever your taste, even if you feel that separating out the gay and lesbian writing is a dubious business, the Web, as never before, is bringing to light many books and authors whose experience is close to our own.

All the community sites—QWorld, PlanetOut, Shescape, Da Brotherhood—have some sort of books page and are increasingly linked with online booksellers such as Barnes and Noble or Amazon.com.

And there are magazines like *Girlfriends*, *A Gay Place* (where you can publish fiction and poetry), *Blair*, and *SBC*, which has satisfying, long interviews with black writers like E. Lynn Harris and James Earl Hardy (who describes the queer writing renaissance as a white-only phenomenon). Then there are hip monthlies like *OutSmart* and *Genre* for buffed, up-to-the-minute short stories à la *Esquire*.

Setting the quality bar for all new gay and lesbian fiction on the Web is the phenomenal Blithe House Quarterly. It's awash in awards, and rightly so. Of all gay and lesbian sites, Blithe House is the golden child, the one to be entered in the Literature

Olympics. None of the stories needs special cosseting as *our* fiction. Be skeptical and go see the site!

For a taste of the best of the print literary magazines visit *The Gay and Lesbian Review* (formerly the *Harvard Gay and Lesbian Review*) and *Lambda Literary Foundation*, which also publishes the monthly *Lambda Book Report*, the quarterly gay men's literary magazine, and *The James White Review*, which sponsors the annual Lambda Literary Awards.

Authors Pages

For the largest resources of links to author-specific pages try Google.com, Yahoo!, or BookWire. You'll find pages about contemporary writers such as Tony Kushner, Audre Lorde, and Kathy Acker, as well as to the gods of gay literature like Truman Capote, Jean Cocteau, James Baldwin, Jean Genet, Michel Foucault, and Tennessee Williams. Yes, the goddesses are also ensconced—Sappho and Gertrude Stein, along with default-goddess Radclyffe Hall. And there's more, including home pages by people who pour their passion for a particular writer into excellent Web sites. For example, there is a tribute to the life and literature of John Rechy and an appreciation page called Gertrude Stein Online. Anniina's Alice Walker Page opens with a biography, additional links, and continues on in what amounts to a short book on this prolific author.

Another way to get to know authors better is to visit Literary Locales, a fascinating site with links to the places that figure in the lives of famous authors. There are many surprises: Henry James's home was, contrary to most of his characters' baronial mansions, a modest country cottage far from the cosmopolitan world.

Quote Links is a wonderful page of links to sites that contain collections of quotes from the worlds of literature, poetry, art, sports—you name it. Annotations guide your choices. So if you're looking for what Tennessee Williams said to Gore Vidal on finding a lover in 1955 Rome, you'll probably find it. Pugzine also has links to great authors. Not all are gay, but you'll find most of the legends: Yukio Mishima, Marguerite Yourcenour, and Jean Genet—often in original language—plus links to further sites.

Although the occurrence is rarer you can sometimes find an author's own page. Larry Townsend, the "father of leather," has a terrific page (check out the interview), and there are many more. Katherine V. Forrest, author of *Curious Wine, Daughters of a Coral Dawn, An Emergence of Green, Dreams*, and *Flashpoint*, along with the wildly popular Kate Delafield mysteries, maintains her own Web page. It's a modest effort with a bibliography, an E-mail address, and a nice personal note: "She lives with her partner, Jo Hercus, as well as a ferocious tabby cat and a mild-mannered German shepherd, in San Francisco, California." Some books, like *Shade* (an anthology of short fiction by writers of African descent) have a page that combines both the commercial aspect and the larger purpose of giving an expanded voice to their audience. Anne Rice, whose queer following is huge, has a newsletter maintained by a devoted fan under the (strict!) guidance of Madame Rice herself. Among others there is a page on Willa Cather with a list of quotations such as this one from *O Pioneers*: "Isn't it queer; there are only two or three human stories, and they go on repeating themselves as fiercely as if they had never happened before; like the larks in this county, that have been singing the same five notes over and over for thousands of years."

Finding Authors

Pages on writers not in vogue are rarer but not impossible to find. If an author search in Google, BookWire, and Womyn Books comes up blank, you can often ferret out overlooked or forgotten writers in offerings by rare book repositories like Bibliophile.com, Priapian Tomes, or Everglades Book Company. Tomes is an antiquarian's dream where you'll find early editions of perennially rediscovered authors like E.F. Benson (of the Miss Mapp series) and, for the true fanatic, even his darkly brilliant mentor, Baron Corvo (whose 19th-century novel of a gay pope makes him kin to Gore Vidal's incendiary imaginings). Not all the Queer Resources Directory author listings have Web pages, but enough do so that you can review catalogs on the screen. Most have at least an E-mail address.

For astute, opinionated reviews of queer-themed books published by small and avant-garde publishers, go straight to the Queer Book Review section at Holy Titclamps. You'll find everything from science fiction to the memoirs of English performance artist Michael Atavar and a book of essays titled *Toward the New Degeneracy* by Bruce Benderson. Mega-authors such as Clive Barker and Patricia Nell Warren have pages—press-release style if they're put out by a publisher, and highly personal and biographical if a fan maintains them. Less known but arguably more weighty writers like Perry Brass and Frank O'Hara are on fans and publishers pages. And Everglades Book Company has stacks of unballyhooed treasures as well as reviews that help place them in a historical context.

Bookstores

The search for queer titles is most amply rewarded in the gay and lesbian bookstore catalogs. One of the best is put up by A Different Light bookstore. Thousands of titles and authors from James Purdy to Mae Sarton and Andrew Sullivan are cataloged, and you'll come across everything from best-sellers to obscure staff favorites. New writers published by small houses are given particular attention. Sifting through title listings is easy. Just click through folders of increasing specificity. If you're looking for *Maurice*, start at Fiction, move to Gay Men, then scroll down to E.M. Forster—and you're there. The options are immense. In addition to a list of links to other sources, there's a schedule of book signings at each of the three stores (in Los Angeles, New York, and San Francisco).

Giovanni's Room (some of the best capsule reviews), Sisters and Brothers, Lambda Rising, People Like Us, and others are very fine, and together they're somehow surviving the onslaught of the book chains and continuing to turn up authors in the surprisingly deep "gay niche market." One measure of our new place in publishing is the guest list at Lambda Rising's annual awards, the Lammies, attended by editors from the big houses in New York and mavericks like Cleis Press. (See the list of winners at Lambda Rising.)

Lesbian Literature

Once in the world of books online, you'll find that women writers and readers are extraordinarily well-served. Sapphisticate, for the "dykescriminating reader," is an excellent source with features on every aspect of lesbian literature, from authors to publishers like Cleis Press. Deborah Levinson's page at the Mining Company has forums and a quality-only links list pointing you to Sapphic Inc., Women's Books and the books section of the *Washington Blade*. There's also a bunch of links to queer-themed children's books with brief, sometimes sharp appraisals.

Q*Ink! Lesbigaytrans Writers is a wonderfully useful page for writers, with a huge listing of current submission calls from publishers as well as lots and lots of links to all aspects of the writerly world. Womyn Books is a comprehensive directory of lesbian bookstores and titles. WWWomen: Arts and Literature has a vast links to writers and poets. Sapphic Ink, Sappho.com, and the Lesbian Writers Homepage offer reviews, discussions, interviews, and excerpts. The Writing Pad sorts through current pick of lesbian writers and serves up work by such authors as Paula Martinac with excerpts and an annotated bibliography. CyberZine has features on Leslie Feinberg, Minnie Bruce Pratt, and Kate Bornstein. Women's poetry is eloquently championed and represented in sites like The Isle of Lesbos and Lesbian Poetry (this is an amazing site containing an archive going back from 1922 to Sappho with poems and biographical material). Among the lesbian community sites, Shescape is continuing its excellence with an expanded book-review section. Cynical Dog Lesbian Book Salon has poetry and fiction. And lesbian writers can find loads of useful information at Grrlz Wrrld, The Lesbian-Writers Homepage, The Lesbian Writer's Guild, and Bearlife. The passion in all these pages is amazing; and judging by the numerous forums, there's a hunger for dialogue here that you don't find among gay men. Is a portion of the male fine arts energy siphoned off into the more quickly fed appetite for pornography or for politics? This is a good question that will only be asked on the women's forums.

Book Lovers Home Pages

Personal home pages are a rich source of information. The greatest of them all is Richard Norton's Queer History and Literature. It's a mammoth site with a number of Norton's essays, beginning with "The Homosexual Pastoral Tradition" (Edmund Spenser and his coterie) and a consideration of sex ads, "Young Hung Stud Seeks Same: The Myths Behind the Wanton Ads." The links list is huge and annotated. Gay Literati is wonderful, especially if you're just discovering the riches of gay literature. There are reviews of current works along with a primer on the classics of E.M. Forster, André Gide, Thomas Mann, Yukio Mishima, and Oscar Wilde along with contemporary stars like Michael Cunningham, David Leavitt, Armistead Maupin, and Joe Orton. Also worth checking out are Gay Lit Now—with more than 30 reviews of some of the best-selling gay men's fiction along with a links list to related sites—and Gay Literature, with reviews of fiction, nonfiction, and must-reads such as Reynolds Price, Marguerite Yourcenour, and Larry Kramer. Kenneth Harrison's Home Page promises excerpts from his own erotic fiction writer and delivers a small but savvy list of writers' links.

Publishing Houses

Smaller presses (Alyson, Cleis, Naiad, Red Hen and Blackwattle) are especially worth a visit not only to take advantage of price discounts but also to possibly discover another author that speaks your language, since they tend to publish works of like spirit. Among these independent gay publishers, Gay Sunshine Press is the oldest and hosts the most interesting site, not so much because of the length of its book roster but the depth of history. Visit it not only to check out titles such as *Gay Dharma*, but to learn of its crucial place in gay liberation as attested to by contributors over the last 30 years. New York writer Richard Hall (*The Butterscotch Prince*) writes: "I first became aware of *Gay Sunshine* around 1971, when I passed three young men hawking copies on Christopher Street. I stopped dead in my tracks. 'Did you say "sunshine"?' 'Yessir. Sunshine' As I stood there on the greasy pavements of this overbuilt city, something stirred in me. The hippie movement had gone gay. How wonderful. And it could only have happened in California. A closer took at the three salesmen confirmed this. They were wearing batik and angelic smiles. California—definitely. I bought a copy and took it home. It had the dirtiest poetry I had ever read. Forests of cocks exploded with awesome regularity. There seemed to be one orgasm per column inch. California again. I loved it…. The cocks are still exploding, along with a great many new ideas."

Of the large houses—Random, Doubleday, Crown, Simon & Schuster, etc.—St. Martin's Press is a sort of favorite son—its Stonewall Inn imprint having been founded by the legendary Michael Denneny as the first gay and lesbian division of a major books company. It's a surprisingly personal site that adheres to its original mission. "It is important that we do not forget what it is like to stumble upon gay and lesbian books and see them as something unique and special. When you become too complacent with their existence, that is exactly when they will be ripped from the hands of those who need them," says then-associate editor Mikel Wadewitz. You can find all the classics by Randy Shilts (*And the Band Played On*), Paul Monette (*Love Alone*), and Edmund White (*Nocturnes for the King of Naples*) as well as new works of fiction, nonfiction, and the most complete and updated list of queer bookstores on the Web. It even has the bookstore in my tiny hometown, population 1,200!

Sources

Though they've unquestionably hurt the independent book stores new books sales, the superstores such as Borders, Amazon and Barnes and Noble are nevertheless a terrific resource for gay and lesbian writing and field a much larger and more varied sampling than any other gay and lesbian literature site. They feature robust write-ups, synopses and reviews, author interviews, and staff recommendations of both new and backlist books. Gay readers can cruise through best-seller rankings as well as a read of classics and out-of-print books. No online gay book resource has been able to keep up with the new offerings.

Other sources include the large search indexes—Yahoo!, AltaVista, and Bookwire—and in the list of links put up by books pages such as the Lesbian-Writers Internet Resource List. Another course is to look under title and author in large directories such as Writers, the Ultimate Book List, Writers Page, and Urban Desires.

Public institutions like the New York Public Library and university libraries are also good sources. The University of Maryland has vast bibliographies of books, critical works, and every author who has ever lived or commented on queer life.

☐ *A Different Light*
http://www.adlbooks.com

☐ *African American Literature Book Club (AALBC)*
http://aalbc.com/books1.htm

☐ *Afterwords Books*
http://www.afterwords.com/

☐ *AK Press*
http://www.akpress.org/mainmenu.html

☐ *Allison, Dorothy*
http://www.fatso.com/fatgirl/dorothy.html

☐ *Alyson Books*
http://www.alyson.com

☐ *Amazon Books*
http://www.amazon.com

☐ *And the Flag Was Still There*
http://www.angelfire.com/ca/theflag/

☐ *Anniina's Alice Walker Page*
http://www.alchemyweb.com/~alchemy/alicew/

☐ *Antinous*
http://www.netscorp.net/~hadrian/

☐ *Ascaridata Alternative Story Page*
http://members.aol.com/K4584767/index.html

☐ *Author's Calendar*
http://www.kirjasto.sci.fi/calendar.htm

☐ *Author Links*
http://www.wessexbooks.com/authors.htm

☐ *Baldwin, James*
http://www.bridgesweb.com/baldwin.html
http://www.kirjasto.sci.fi/jbaldwin.htm
www.artswire.org/ocountry/baldwin.htm

☐ *Banned Books*
http://www.cs.cmu.edu/Web/People/spok/banned-books.html

☐ *Barker, Clive*
http://www.clivebarker.com/

☐ *Black Writers Club*
http://clubs.yahoo.com/clubs/blacklesbigaywriters

☐ *Blackwattle Press*
http://www.pinkboard.com.au/~blackwattle/

☐ *Blair Magazine*
http://www.blairmag.com/

☐ *Blithe House Quarterly*
http://www.blithe.com/

☐ *Bookwire Index*
http://www.bookwire.com/

☐ *Boston Review*
http://www-polisci.mit.edu/bostonreview/br19.6/lesbian.html

☐ *Bright, Susie*
http://www.susiebright.com/

☐ *Brass, Perry*
http://www.perrybrass.com/

☐ *Brother's Touch Bookstore*
http://www.brotherstouch.com

☐ *Capote, Truman*
http://members.gnn.com/jkb12/capote.htm
http://www.ansoniadesign.com/capote/

☐ *Cather, Willa*
http://icg.harvard.edu/~cather/

☐ *Chicano & Latino G&L Bibliography*
http://icg.harvard.edu/~cather/

☐ *Church-Wellesley Review*
http://www.xtra.ca/cwr/

☐ *Cleis Press*
http://www.cleispress.com/

☐ *Cocteau, Jean*
http://www.kirjasto.sci.fi/cocteau.htm

☐ *Crane, Hart*
http://unr.edu/homepage/brad/hart/crane.html

☐ *Creative Visions Bookstore*
http://www.hedda.com/creative-visions/

☐ *Creative-Women.Com Web Ring*
http://www.creative-women.com

☐ *CrossRoads Bookstore*
http://www.crossmarket.com/welcome/

☐ *A Crystal Diary by Frankie Hucklenbroich.*
http://www.mindspring.com/~honorine/Crystal_diary.html

☐ *Curzon-Brown, Daniel*
http://home.pacbell.net/curzon/

☐ *Cynical Dog Lesbian Book Salon*
http://www.cynicaldog.com/

☐ *Delaney R., Samuel*
http://www.uic.edu/depts/quic/history/samuel_delaney.html

☐ *Dickinson, Emily*
http://www.colorado.edu/EDIS/

☐ *Different Drummer Bookstore*
http://www.ccweb.com/ddbooks/

☐ *Everglades Book Company*
http://www.evergladesbookcompany.com/

☐ *FeMiNa*
http://www.femina.com/

☐ *Feminist Bookstores*
http://www.geocities.com/WestHollywood/1027/

☐ *Forrest, Katherine V.*
http://www.art-with-attitude.com/forrest/forrest.html

☐ *Foucault, Michel*
http://www.stg.brown.edu/projects/hypertext/landow/SSPCluster/Fou

☐ *French Language/Literature*
http://humanities.uchicago.edu/ARTFL/ARTFL.html

☐ *Gay Antiquarian Books*
http://www.erols.com/priapean/index.html

☐ *Gay Asian Literature*
http://www.geocities.com/WestHollywood/3821/

☐ *Gay and Lesbian Bookstores Directory*
http://www.qrd.org/QRD/www/media/print/bookstores/glbwnets.html

☐ *Gay and Lesbian Presence in American Literature*
http://www.georgetown.edu/tamlit/essays/gay_les.html

☐ *Gay & Lesbian Review(formerly "Harvard G&L R)*
http://www.hglc.org/hglc/review.htm

☐ *Gay and Lesbian Themes in Children's Books*
http://www.armory.com/~web/gaybooks.html

☐ *Gay Heroes*
http://www.gayheroes.com

☐ *Gay Literati*
http://www.geocities.com/WestHollywood/3705/books.html

☐ *Gay Lit Now*
http://glweb.com/gaylitnow/

☐ *Gay Literature*
http://www.gayliterature.com

☐ *Gay Readers Book Club*
http://www.gayreaders.com/

☐ *Gay Place*
http://www.gayplace.com/pages/fiction/fiction/fiction.html

☐ *Gay Poetry*
http://www.gaypoetry.com/

☐ *Gay Sunshine Press*
http://www.gaysunshine.com

☐ *GayWired Reviews*
http://www.gaywired.com/books.htm

☐ *Genet, Jean*
http://www.sirius.com/~plezbert/genet/genet.htm

☐ *Genre Magazine*
http://www.genremagazine.com

☐ *Gertrude Stein*
http://www.uta.fi/~trkisa/literature/stein.html

☐ *Gertrude Stein & Sherwood Anderson*
http://www.geocities.com/WestHollywood/Heights/7439/Stein.html

☐ *Gide, Andre*
http://www.lm.com/~kalin/gide.html

☐ *Gidlow, Elsa*
http://www.sappho.com/poetry/e_gidlow.htm
http://www.geocities.com/~wildheartranch/index10.html

☐ *Ginsberg, Allen*
http://ezinfo.ucs.indiana.edu/~avigdor/poetry/ginsberg.html

☐ *Giovanni's Room Bookstore*
http://www.giovannisroom.com

☐ *Girlfriends Bookstore and Café*
http://www.girlscafe.com/girlfriends/

☐ *Girlfriends Magazine*
http://www.gfriends.com

☐ *Glad Day Bookshop*
http://www.gladday.com/

☐ *GLINN Publishing*
http://www.glinn.com/books/gpc1.htm

☐ *Griffth, Nicola*
http://www.sff.net/people/Nicola

☐ *Handbook on Living Together as a Same-Sex Couple*
http://www.geocities.com/CollegePark/Library/1049/index.htm

☐ *Hardy, James Earl*
http://www.geocities.com/SoHo/Studios/3702

☐ *Haworth Press*
http://www.haworthpressinc.com

☐ *Hemphill, Essex*
http://www.qrd.org/qrd/www/culture/black/essex/tribute.html

☐ *Holy Titclamps*
http://www.io.com/~larrybob/

☐ *Homosexual Writers Project*
http://www.geocities.com/WestHollywood/5139/hwp.html

☐ *Hoss*
http://www.hossmag.com/

☐ *Isle of Lesbos*
http://www.sappho.com/poetry

☐ *Jewish Lesbian Reading List*
http://www.nyu.edu/pages/sls/jewish/jewles.html

☐ *Karla Jay*
http://www.karlajay.com/

☐ *Kitchen, Abel*
http://www.abel-kitchen.com/

☐ *Kushner, Tony*
http://www.mojones.com/MOTHER_JONES/JA95/bernstein.html

☐ *Lambda Literary Foundation/Lambda Book Report/ James White Review*
http://www.lambdalit.org/

☐ *Lavender Salon*
http://www.athenet.net/~lavsalon/

☐ *Lesbian Literature—Books For and By Womyn*
http://www.onestopcom.net/llit/

☐ *Lesbian Plays*
http://www.monitor.net/~carolyn

☐ *Lesbian Pulp Fiction*
http://www.evergladesbookcompany.com/bibliozz-lesbianpulp fiction.htm

☐ *Lesbian Poetry*
http://www.sappho.com/poetry/

☐ *Lesbian Reading Group*
http://members.aol.com/rosecyrus/bookgrp.htm

☐ *Lesbian-Writers*
http://www.lesbian.org/lesbian-writers/index.html

☐ *Lesbian Writer's Guild*
http://members.aol.com/lezbnlit/lwg

☐ *The Lesbian-Writers Homepage*
http://www.lesbian.org/lesbian-writers/index.html

☐ *LGBT Bookstores List*
http://www.bookweb.org/directory/

☐ *Literary Locales*
http://www.sjsu.edu/depts/english/places.htm

☐ *Little Sisters Books and Art Emporium*
http://www.lsisters.com/default.htm

☐ *Mishima, Yukio*
http://www.injapan.net/members/tokyojon/cjourn.htm

☐ *Naiad Press*
http://www.naiadpress.com

☐ *NewTown Writers*
http://www.newtownwriters.org/

☐ *New York Public Library, Gay and Lesbian Studies*
http://www.nypl.org/research/chss/grd/resguides/gay.html

☐ *Nifty Erotic Stories Archive*
http://www.nifty.org/

☐ *Nolo Press*
http://www.nolo.com/

☐ *OBS Search Request Form*
http://www.obs-us.com:80/obs/english/finder/searchf3.htm

☐ *Oscar Wilde Bookstore*
http://www.oscarwildebooks.com/

☐ *Oscariana*
http://www.jonno.com/oscariana/

☐ *Out Books*
http://www.outbooks.com/

☐ *Out-Write*
http://www.geocities.com/SoHo/Studios/7361

☐ *Paris Green*
http://home.earthlink.net/~tobgar

☐ *Pictures of Djuna Barnes, Colette, Oscar Wilde,
Edna St. Vincent Millay*
http://info.umd.edu:80/Pictures/Sexual_Orientation/

☐ *Pink Triangles and Purple Jacks Bookstore*
http://www.duff.net/trijax

☐ *PlanetOut*
http://www.planetout.com/

☐ *Pugzine*
http://www.pugzine.com/linkage.html

☐ *Priapean Tomes*
http://www.erols.com/priapean/

☐ *Premier Gay Books*
http://www.gaybook.co.uk

☐ *QRD Books*
http://www.qrd.org/qrd/media/books/

☐ *Queer Chicano Fiction*
http://www2.ucsc.edu/people/ktrion/jotas.html

☐ *Queer Frontiers*
http://www.usc.edu/archives/queerfrontiers/

☐ *Quote Links*
http://www.starlingtech.com/quotes/links.html

☐ *QWorld*
http://www.qworld.org/

☐ *Radclyffe Hall*
http://www.net-link.net/~smootsg/hallbib.html

☐ *Rainbow Room*
http://www.loft.com

☐ *Rechy, John*
http://www.johnrechy.com

☐ *Red Hen Press*
http://www.redhen.org/

☐ *Rice, Anne*
http://www.anne-rice.inter.net/

☐ *Rich, Adrienne*
http://herbie.ucs.indiana.edu/~rtompkin/rich/rich.html

☐ *Rimbaud (Arthur)*
http://members.tripod.com/~roadside6/

☐ *Rita Mae Brown*
http://www.ritamaebrown.com

☐ *S&M Non-fiction*
http://www.barnsdle.demon.co.uk/span/nonfic.html

☐ *San Francisco Public Library G&L Cntr.*
http://sfpl.lib.ca.us/glcenter/home.htm

☐ *Sapphic Ink*
http://www.lesbian.org/sapphic-ink/

☐ *Sapphisticate Books*
http://www.sapphisticate.com

☐ *Sappho*
http://www.earthlight.co.nz/users/spock/sapphoi.html

☐ *SBC Online*
http://www.sbc-online.com/

☐ *Seal Press*
http://www.sealpress.com

☐ *Serpent's Tail Press*
http://www.serpentstail.com/

☐ *Shade*
http://www.glyphmedia.com/host/shade/bios.html

☐ *Signorile, Michael*
http://www.signorile.com/

☐ *Sisters & Brothers Bookstore*
http://www.sistersandbrothers.com

☐ *Sisterspirit Bookstore and Coffee House*
http://www.elf.net/sisterspirit/

☐ *Sonoma Zone*
http://www.sonomazone.com/

☐ *Stacey's Place for Readers and Writers of Lesbian Fiction*
http://www.goodnet.com/~stacey/staceys_place.html

☐ *Stein, Gertrude*
http://www.tenderbuttons.com/index_2.html

☐ *Stonewall Inn/St. Martin's Press*
http://www.stonewallinn.com/

☐ *Susie Bright*
http://www.susiebright.com/

☐ *Townsend, Larry (Father of Leather)*
http://www.larrytownsend.com/

☐ *Trilogy Books*
http://www.trilogybooks.com/

☐ *University of Maryland, Bibliography*
http://www.inform.umd.edu:8080/EdRes/Topic/Diversity/Specific/

☐ *Vidal, Gore*
http://www.randomhouse.com/atr/fall95/vidal.html

☐ *Walker, Alice*
http://wwwvms.utexas.edu/~melindaj/alice.html

☐ *Walt Whitman*
http://www.infopt.demon.co.uk/whitman.htm

☐ *Web of the Spider Woman (Feminist Bookstore List)*
http://www.geocities.com/WestHollywood/1027/

☐ *White, Edmund*
A Farewell Symphony
http://www.nytimes.com/books/first/w/white-farewell.html
Collected Reviews
http://www.nytimes.com/books/97/09/14/reviews/970914.14benfeyt.html#

☐ *Whitman, Walt*
http://jefferson.village.Virginia.EDU/whitman/
http://www.infopt.demon.co/uk/whitman.htm/

☐ *Wildcat Press/Patricia Nell Warren*
http://www.gaywired.com/wildcat/

☐ *Wilde, Oscar*
http://web.lsmsa.edu/~chad/literature/oscar_wilde/oscar.html

☐ *Williams (Tennessee)*
http://www.lacollege.edu/depart/ejl/south/williams.html

☐ *Wit's End*
http://www.geocities.com/WestHollywood/4128/
☐ *White Crane Journal*
http://www.whitecranejournal.com/

☐ *Women's Review of Books*
http://www.wellesley.edu/WomensReview/

☐ *Womyn Books*
http://www.qworld.org/womyn/books/index.html

☐ *XXX Fruit*
http://www.echonyc.com/~xxxfruit/

☐ *Yahoo!'s gay and lesbian lit links.*
http://www.yahoo.com/Business_and_Economy/Companies/
Lesbian__Gay_and_Bisexual/Magazines/

☐ *Zeeland, Steven*
http://www.stevenzeeland

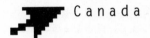 Canada

Although Canada has a landmass larger than that of the United States, its gay and lesbian network has the sort of clubbishness more typically found in European countries. Far more than in the States, there's a sense that everyone knows everybody else—and all of them like each other. You can see this in the generous sharing of links among sites that in the United States would consider themselves competitors. Another difference is the strong support for the queer business community. Even personal home pages will include a local bookshop or gay-owned travel company in their hot links.

New on the block are Queer Canada and My Gay Canada. Both are aiming for a comprehensive picture and have links lists to clubs, social groups, and businesses. The three Web sites that have long offered some of the best starting points to all things Canadian are: Groovy Annie's, Life on Brian's Beat, and GayCanada.com. Each is very large and reflects its name, with the two home pages being more personal and Canada.com being rather buttoned-up, almost corporate. Still, among these three you can find everything from bar life to support groups, the political, social, legal, sexual, travel items, and almost everything else imaginable.

Groovy Annie's is the work of a true Web enthusiast with a particular interest in film and writing. It has a serious ballast too, with links to queer news and political stuff (including polls) as well as lesbian forums and chat lines. There are lots of sections, such as: Advocacy, Bookstores, Diversity, Music and Musicians, Shopping, and Writing, each of which gets a long list of links. In a change from the normally gay-centric orientation of most large home pages, there's a definite tilt toward lesbian point of view in the links, which reach across the border to America. Here's the author on why she built and maintains this ad-free page: "I feel it is very important for lesbians, feminists, people of colour, and gay men to get hooked up to the net and make their own Web pages to network to counterbalance the present situation.... Forget picketing (although I must say I do picketing as well)—the Internet is the new battleground. People look for all kinds of information when they are anonymous. They will ask questions they wouldn't dare ask in person or on the phone. They will take bigger risks.... It's also a way for me to contribute to the lesbian and gay community, ease my guilty conscience, and stay at home. (End of sanctimonious speech.)" GA is that rare combination: both political and funny.

Life on Brian's Beat

This is a large, intelligent page that is by turns exhausting and exhilarating. You'll find many Canadian links here, but to hem in this page under any nation's boundaries is a disservice. It ranges about like a restless Renaissance man's mind, settling on everything from news and books to shopping and justice, both legal and social, to facts of life such as AIDS, getting older, and cooking a good meal. You'll get pointers to the best of the primary sites and the related sites as well. Under "Homostory," for example, there are pages for the most respected queer history sites on the Web, as well as the unexpected such as two on Allan Turing or Glenn Gould (and, yes, you should know who they are). The quotes are dated and credited—everything is precise on Brian's Beat. Sometimes cranky like all missionaries, he's a mix of seeming contradictions: he loves Garth Brooks as well as Quentin Crisp; he never uses the word "queer," but he is chromosomally averse to fakery.

Canada.com

GayCanada.com is billed as Canada's largest online resource, and the contents match the claim. The business directory contains more than 500 listings of queer and queer-friendly businesses, including those with same-sex benefits. The city directory, covering metropolitan areas around the country, gives profiles and tourist-related information on bars and restaurants. Click on Toronto, for example, and find links to Community Groups and Organizations; University and College Gay and Lesbian Organizations; Accommodations and Other Lodgings; Bars, Nightclubs, and Other Entertainment, Restaurants; and more. You can use this as an all-in-one site to find dating services and a classified-ads section that covers the gamut from cottages for rent to "Union/Marriage" announcements.

Tides of Men

Tides of Men: The Lives of Gay Men in British Columbia is part history, part biography, part social commentary. It's a documentary drawn from the collected the stories of Canadian men from all walks of life and many backgrounds talking about what it has been like to grow up and grow old(er) in one of the most beautiful places in the world. These special stories detail a facet of history that has gone largely unnoticed.

Gay Toronto

Gay Toronto is the largest of Canada's online magazines and covers its city's beat in a lively style with features and write-ups on local bars, restaurants, and bathhouses. There are plenty of political issues here too. The magazine also reports regularly on the Catholic Church's position on same-sex relationships.

Queers Online

This is a new biweekly magazine with stories on Canadian queers. The interviews and movie and book reviews are especially good. There are event listings from across Canada as well as chat rooms, classifieds, and E-mail postcards designed by gay artists. News, features, listings, links, stories, interviews, film reviews, and book reviews are also listed.

The Lambda Educational Research Foundation

This foundation "promotes research into lesbian and gay issues and lifestyles for the purpose of public education." If their mission sounds carefully worded and nonconfrontational, that's because it is. By working within institutional boundaries, they take on homophobia through community seminars and workshops and the distribution of pamphlets to libraries around the country.

Equality for Gays and Lesbians Everywhere

This is an activist group "committed to the advancement of equality and justice for lesbians, gays, and bisexuals in Canada." EGALE was instrumental in holding the government to its commitment to add "sexual orientation" to the Canadian constitution, successfully lobbied for federal hate-crimes laws to protect lesbians and gay men from gay-bashing, and intervened before the supreme court of Canada in support of same-sex relationship recognition. It's an effective, exciting organization at work in many areas, such as representing Canadian gay men and lesbians at international conferences, including the Beijing Women's Conference and the Vienna United Nations Conference on Human Rights.

Indexes that include Canadian listings: GayScape, Gay Web, Lesbian Org, Queers Online Gay Guide, Queer Resources Directory, Rainbow Query, and The Other Queer Page.

☐ *Black Eagle, Toronto*
http://www.blackeagle.com

☐ *Canadian Gay, Lesbian, and Bisexual Resource*
http://www.gaycanada.com

☐ *Canadian Gay and Lesbian Archives*
http://www.web.net/~queeries/index.htm

☐ *Canada Pink Pages (Pink Umbrella)*
http://www.gayvictoria.com/pinkpages/

☐ *Capitol Q Online*
http://www.capitalq.com.au/

☐ *Clue, Canada*
http://www.canuck.com/clue/

☐ *Cool Canadian Space Station*
http://www.geocities.com/Paris/LeftBank/3730

☐ *Egale Canada*
http://www.egale.ca/

☐ *Fab Magazine*
http://www.propowr.com/rainbow/fab/toronto/

☐ *Gaibec Quebec*
http://www.gaibec.com/

☐ *GayBlade Canada*
http://www.blade.com/

☐ *Gay Toronto*
http://www.gaytoronto.com/

☐ *GLOWWW Canada*
http://www.glowww.com/

☐ *Groovy Annie's*
http://www.interlog.com/~meow/

☐ *Haven't Got a Clue?*
http://www.canuck.com/clue/

☐ *Lambda Educational Research Foundation*
http://www.ualberta.ca/~cbidwell/cmb/lambda.htm

☐ *Lambda North (Prince Albert)*
http://www.citylightsnews.com/palambda.htm

☐ *Life on Brian's Beat*
http://www.web.apc.org/~jharnick/brians.html

☐ *Little Sister's Book & Art Emporium*
http://www.lsisters.com/

☐ *My Gay Canada.com*
http://www.mygaycanada.com/

☐ *Ms. Purdy's Women's Club*
http://www.pangea.ca/~buzz

☐ *Net@Finder.Com-Canada's GLB Web Magazine*
http://www.netfinder.com/surfwest/welcome.html

☐ *OutLooks (Alberta)*
http://www.greatwest.ca/ffwd/

☐ *Quebec Gay Archives*
http://www.agq.qc.ca/

☐ *Queer InfoServer Canada*
http://www.infoqueer.org/queer/qis/canada.html

☐ *Queers Online*
http://www.queersonline.com/welcome.html

☐ *Rainbow BC*
http://www.netidea.com/~bnilsen/queer/rbbc.html

☐ *Steve Allen's Dance Links*
http://syborg.ucolick.org/~sla/dance/dance.html

☐ *Tides of Men*
http://www.lesbigay.com/tides/

Catalogs & Shopping

L.L. Bean in the fall, Neiman Marcus for the holidays, and Saks Fifth Avenue in the spring. For many years catalog lovers had to exercise a trick of the mind to envision these exclusively straight books as part of queer life. Today you don't have to change the sex of the models as you pore over the new breed of lushly colored dream books. The photography is beautiful, the scenes are styled to a tee, and same-sex relationships are depicted as they should be.

Along with a confident new style, queer catalogs have graduated far beyond the level of rainbow schlock, even among the novelty catalogs. Don't Panic Virtual Retail Store has all kinds of (non-sexual) gay-themed merchandise from T-shirts to socks (with the motto "Fuck My Socks Off") and some of the most current dance CDs with circuit party mixes. Faboo is a hybrid catalog/community site with stuff like liquid chocolate to spray on your partner, and a Nancy Reagan shrine where you can find out if she got ever her china in order and Ron's skid marks off his underwear. Mr. Ray's Wig World is a hoot—hair pieces to transform you into Cher, Shaft, or Roseanne Roseannadanna. And of course there's always *International Male* with its signature sexy designs and dreamboat models in come-hither poses.

If you haven't dropped by in a while, you'll be surprised at other things too, such as convenience. It's standard now for online catalogs to have a nifty computerized shopping "cart"—which means that you can order anything from the page where it's displayed by placing it in your cart with a click of the mouse. When you've finished, proceed to the order form. The last step will take you to a secure server so that your credit card numbers will be transmitted safely.

Tzabaco, 2xist

At the top of the style heap are the catalogs by Tzabaco and 2xist. Much like its paper version, Tzabaco is attractively photographed and shockingly natural—men and women are unquestionably gay and as casually appealing as their surroundings—most often a relaxed country home atmosphere. There's a nostalgic air to the pages, and the models are beautiful but approachable. They smile and always seem caught mid conversation as if you're joining friendly hosts on a lazy Sunday. It's almost rude not to accept their offer of fluffy flannels, T-shirts, caps, and cookie jars—along with more pricey items like leather jackets and furniture.

Tza·ba·co \za-bäh-kö\ n:[orig: Gay, Lesbian. Pomo Indian, Portuguese, all-American] 1: Queer America's premiere catalog 2: cool, casual 3: the place for everything; from the essential to the exceptional 4: your source for the brands you want 5: a "how-to" guide for the relaxed life 6: service you rely on 7: absolute shopping confidence with a «GUARANTEED FOREVER» policy. 8: partners in the community. Sharing resources and supporting organizations that promote civil rights for gay and lesbian Americans 9: POMO INDIAN PLACE name of the 250-year-old Spanish land grant named after a Pomo Indian chief in Northern California. Same area where the original Tzabaco store and catalog were founded 10: [Port deriv. of tzabaco] COUNTRY DWELLING

2(x)ist takes a much less domestic approach. The models (some of whom you may recognize as porn stars) are bathed in a caressing light and arranged as if their bodies were sculptures and the underwear haute couture. They are selling a dream, yes, but such a silky, seductive one! The cut and materials are nothing like JCPenney and would make Tommy Hilfiger blush.

That's another interesting thing about the catalogs. The fewer products sold, the more sophisticated the presentation. Boots Plus is so wild for its subject (the photo galleries go on forever) that you can easily forget it's a catalog. Coach Ron's site concentrates on wrestling singlets and he's so enamored of his subject that his pages contain a history of when the design was conceived and why. When you're among these specialists, you're treated like a VIP. RawHides, for example, reassures viewers of its custom-made leather wear. "We can adjust for any body type, so don't let our models intimidate you!" And the tone always fits the merchandise. Scarred Rubber, a custom shop for the serious bondage rubber crowd, has a comprehensive line of full bodysuits, pod suits, bags, and gas masks. There are pages describing the quality of its vinyl and an incredibly detailed set of instructions for taking measurements.

Distinctive Postcards

For a greeting card catalog that has absolutely no relation to Hall-mark's, go to Daimonix. When you open the page there's a teardrop–shaped figure looking out with fearful eyes. The candy colors are bright so that you don't worry too much, but then…ouch! The title races across and, in a spray of blood drops, slices our hostess's head off. What is this? Click on one of the remaining heads and you're whisked to one of about 50 cards, each "a bitter little cartoon to spice up your dharma." For Rude Gays Only has a picture of a shaved-headed coffeehouse type on his knees in front of a glory hole, grinning diabolically. The caption reads: "There are those moments—whether you're tugging a pubic hair off your tongue or lubricating a new toy—when Mama's affirmation isn't what you hold uppermost. You don't care. At its worst, gay life is the best. In the back room you don't have to pretend it's anything better." An acid bath.

An Online Trip to the Mall

The more conventional catalogs don't have the visual flair or personalized touch, but they've grown into true emporiums. GayWeb used to be a funky yet tasteful neighborhood store you might find in the Castro district or in the Village—full of affordable tchotchkes like posters, mugs, stuffed animals, candy, skin-care products, and removable tattoos. You can still find all the cozy stuff, but now there's lots more to choose from, much of it having to do with sexy men. There are erotic CD-ROMs, a calendar ("new dicks every day!"), and even a screen-saver hunk or hot gal (there's loads of stuff for women too). Other additions include music, books, art, and photography.

Catalogue X has also grown and now has general merchandise along with a greatly expanded sex toys section. "Enlargers" alone has 20 different products to expand penises and nipples. Even if you don't buy anything, you learn so much—such as that a typical snakebite kit contains very effective rubber cups. Works great, so the ad says. "Check out a typical hunter's nipples!"

Although Southern California Gay Wired is much more than a catalog (it has magazine sections that include short bits on what's hot locally, feature stories, and classified ads), its Gay Shopping area certainly qualifies. It has a wide inventory on par with GayWeb, including dress shirts, slacks, and sport coats, along with a wine rack, food, flowers, and art by gay and lesbian artists. All items are found on individual pages, sort of like shops within the Gay Wired mall. Some are nationally known purveyors, but most are local, and all will deliver internationally.

For a general list of catalogs, go to the Internet Mall Listings. You'll find thousands of catalogs, from Eddie Bauer to Urban Outfitters.

☐ *2(x)ist Underwear*
http://www.2xist.com/

☐ *Batteries Not Included*
http://www.batteriesnotincluded.com

☐ *Blowfish*
http://www.blowfish.com/

☐ *Big Black Boots*
http://www.boot.com/

☐ *Bill's Wetware Emporium*
http://www.io.com/~casper

☐ *Billy Doll*
http://www.thebillydoll.com/

☐ *Black Iris Home Page*
http://www.blackiris.com/

☐ *Bodyworship*
http://www.bodyworship.com/

☐ *Bondage Gear by Fetishwerks*
http://www.Fetishwerks.com

☐ *BootsPlus "Bootopia!"*
http://www.bootsplus.com

☐ *Boy Toy*
http://www.boytoy.com/

☐ *California Muscle*
http://www.briefs.com/calmuscle/

☐ *Catalog X*
http://cataloguex.com/

☐ *Club Studios*
http://www.gay-art.com/

☐ *Coach Ron*
http://www.chroma.net/singlet/index.html

☐ *Codpiece International*
http://www.teleport.com/~codpiece

☐ *Condom Sense Various*
http://www.webcom.com/condomz/welcome.html

☐ *Da Boiz Toys*
http://www.gayweb.com/151/shirts.html

☐ *Daimonix Greeting Cards*
http://www.daimonix.com/

☐ *DivaNet (fetish)*
http://www.divaweb.com/

☐ *Doc's Leathers*
http://www.asgo.net/Docs/

☐ *Don't Panic*
http://www.dont-panic.com

☐ *Everything for Gays*
http://www.gays.com/

☐ *Faboo*
http://www.faboo.com/

☐ *Flamingo Park*
http://www.flamingopark.com/

☐ *Gay Biz (surfers)*
http://www.gaybiz.com/

☐ *Gay Holland*
http://www.gayholland.com/

☐ *Gay Mart*
http://www.gaymart.com/

☐ *Gay Men's Mall*
http://www.gaymensmall.com/

☐ *Gay Pride Pages*
http://www.gaypride.com/

☐ *Gays and Lesbians on the World Wide Web*
http://www.glowww.com/

☐ *GaySpace Online*
http://www.gayspace.com/

☐ *GayWeb*
http://www.gayweb.com/

☐ *Gay Wired*
http://www.gaywired.com/unity/index.html

☐ *Jockstrap Heaven*
http://www.bentbar.com/jockstrap.html

☐ *International Male*
http://www.intmale.com/

☐ *Male Posters*
http://Posters.com/

☐ *Mr. B Leather*
http://neturl.nl/mrb/

☐ *Mr. S Leather and Fetters*
http://www.dnai.com/sex-bondage/

☐ *N2N BodyWear Exotic Wear for Men*
http://www.toga.org/N2N/

☐ *Outerwear Leather*
http://www.furs.com/FUR/OuterwearLeather.html

☐ *Picky Women Sportswear and Accessories*
http://www.pridewear.com/

☐ *Pride Company*
http://www.blackiris.com/pride/

☐ *Pride Productions*
http://www.prideproductions.com

☐ *Pridelink*
http://www.pridelink.com

☐ *Q-Mall*
http://www.qmall.com/

☐ *Rainbow Mall*
http://www.rainbow-mall.com/
☐ *RawHides Custom Leatherwear*
http://www.rawhides.com/

☐ *Romantasy*
http://www.romantasy.com/

☐ *Saffo TeeZ*
http://www.art-with-attitude.com/saffo/teez.html

☐ *Scarred Rubber*
http://www.scarred.com/

☐ *Sexy Boyz*
http://www.sexyboyz.com

☐ *Skinz*
http://www.gayweb.com/418/418home.html

☐ *Tom of Finland*
http://www.eroticarts.inter.net/

☐ *Underwear.de*
http://www.underwear.de/

☐ *University of Dyke*
http://www.dykewear.com/

☐ *Urban Outfitters*
http://www.outnow.com/63/camper.html

☐ *U.S. Cavalry*
http://www.gc.net/cavalry/cavalry.html

☐ *Woman's Touch*
http://www.a-womans-touch.com

☐ *Zebra'z Boutique*
http://www.zebraz.com/

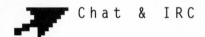 Chat & IRC

A search on Google for "gay chat" will give you upwards of 12,000 sites to choose from. Everyone, it seems, wants to talk, and especially now that the larger companies have entered the markets, the options are huge and varied. Yahoo! has 60 GLBT clubs, each with over 500 members. What is all the chattering about? Subjects are all over the board and range from guys into underwear to bears into baseball to women into each other. Even the ubiquitous Michelangelo Signorile has a forum where you can match (or try to), the wide range of his interests and opinions.

Gay.com

 Of all the community, Gay.com and PlanetOut are the largest, deepest repositories of chat areas. People are talking, arguing and socializing there 24 hours a day on nearly innumerable topics in a conversation among half a hundred countries and at least seven languages.

PlanetOut has partnered with Yahoo! and hosts ongoing chat areas as well as set chat times on specific subjects, known as as "net events." At 8 A.M. it's Gay Books, where there is chat about your favorite books and other gay publications. At 10 A.M. it's time for Queer Professionals to gather, and at 1 P.M. the subject is Gay Spirituality, and later Gay Seniors. At these and tens of other net events, people gather and talk.

The largest most varied collection of chat rooms around is Gay.com. More than just an index of hundreds of groups discussing various topics, Gay.com has become a full-rounded community site with sections on arts and entertainment, food and wine, travel, sports, and positive living. In addition to relevant chat rooms, each section is rich in Web-only features such as polling, message boards, and topical news feeds. In the finance section for example, you can join in a round table on guidelines for investing in an initial public offering as well as read articles on everything from coming out in the workplace to writing your will and saving for your children's education

And the days of empty chat rooms are over. Even during work hours there are more than upwards of 7,000 people talking about any of a couple hundred different subjects. Like all the newer chat rooms, once you pick a room a screen will display what everyone is saying. On the side is a list of those in attendance. Say you're interested in "Buffboy." Click on the name and you'll get a profile. To join in, just type in the message area. It really is as simple as that.

Tip: Remember that this is live chat. Although most of the sex rooms are always going, there are prescheduled chats also. The key here is to review the schedule for discussion times.

Women

Women visiting Gay.com can look in on an equal number of discussions. Lesbian Dinner Party is a round table about women's issues, coming out, and "lots of fun stuff." Single and Looking is exactly what it says—women talking about their interests, girlfriends, family, etc. Professional Networking is for making business contacts, and Dykes on Bikes is for motorhead gals.

Sex

Of course, the most common subject (as in their cousins, the personal forums) is sex: What are you like? What do you like? The pickup lines are distinctly familiar, if perhaps a little more blunt than what you hear at the corner cruise bar. The larger chat sites, Gay.net (now part of Gay.com) for instance, are intentionally broadly named. Almost everything a queer would be interested in has a particular chat room. But smaller groups often tip you off to their style by their name. Female Dungeon, Gay Punk, and Leather 'N Lace are obvious. Badpuppy, one of the most popular on the Web, is indeed mostly for and about young guys from 18 to 20-something. Badpuppy offers a sizzling smorgasbord of more than 20 subject rooms, including Alone in the Dorm, Bathroom, Foot Fetish, and Young and Horny. The most popular rooms are for guys.

IRC or Webtalk?

Until quite recently most chat rooms were in Internet Relay Chat. You had to download the software and learn the rather arcane commands in order to participate. Nowadays the newest browsers allow you to skip the IRC language. This in part explains Gay.com's popularity—Netscape and Microsoft's browsers give you a seamless connection.

Still, IRC channels are flourishing. One terrific Web page that hosts an IRC channel and also has a good introduction to its usage is #gaySoCalif on the Undernet. There are sections on terminology, commands, and a links list to other sites as well as a calendar of chat events. Here's their explanation of their form of chat: "IRC is similar to the chat rooms found on AOL, Compuserve, and bulletin board systems. Users log into an IRC network and join one or more channels of interest (a channel is just like a "room" on AOL). The two biggest IRC networks, the Undernet and EFnet, have thousands of channels from which to choose. Most channels are temporary in nature but some, like #gaySoCalif, are permanent channels, open 24 hours per day. For newcomers to IRC, the Undernet is a "kinder, gentler" network; as the newer of the big two, the Undernet was planned with the idea of being more organized and user-friendly than EFnet."

A good collection of IRC chat groups for women is over at Grrltalk, among them Indigo, Lasha, and Lesbos. Most listings come with a short description. Jaggedpill, for example, has the name and E-mail address of its founder along with this explanation: "Jaggedpill is an open chat channel to all genders. Chat mainly consists of lost loves and whatever is bothering you at the moment. (Note: Founder is a lesbian.)"

Badpuppy has a particularly easy-to-follow menu of Windows, Macintosh, and Unix software links—just click a button and the program is transferred to your hard drive. Very few chat hosts, though, offer instructions on how to use the program. For these you need to look within the program's Help file or go to one of the IRC Guide pages listed below.

☐ *Above & Beyond Gender Resources*
   http://www.abgender.com

☐ *After Glow (women only)*
   http://www.geocities.com/WestHollywood/2213/index.html

☐ *BackDoor*
   http://www.backdoor.com/welcomeframes.html

☐ *Badpuppy*
   http://badpuppy.com/

☐ *Bear Cave*
   http://www.skepsis.com/.gblo/bears/OFFSITE/irc_bearcave.html

☐ *Black Stripe*
   http://www.blackstripe.com/

☐ *CyberGrrl*
   http://www.cybergrrl.com/explorer.htm

☐ *Butch-Femme.Com*
   http://www.butch-femme.com/

☐ *Deaf Queer Chat*
   http://www.deafqueer.org/

☐ *Dragworld*
   http://www.dragworld.com

☐ *Female Dungeon*
http://www.geocities.com/WestHollywood/1925/

☐ *Gay Christians.org*
http://www.gaychristians.org/

☐ *Gay.com Chat House*
http://www.gay.com/

☐ *Gay Cyber Geeks*
http://www.gaycybergeeks.com/

☐ *Gay Chat*
http://www.gay-chat.com/

☐ *Gay Teen Christians*
http://www.geocities.com/westhollywood/7322/

☐ *Gay Washington D.C.*
http://www.mcr.net/damone/gaydc/

☐ *Girl Bar*
http://www.girlbar.com/

☐ *GLB Latino/Hablamos tu mismo*
http://www.glblatino.com/

☐ *Grrltalk*
http://www.geocities.com/WestHollywood/1123/grrl.html

☐ *HIV Positive*
http://www.hiv-positive.com

☐ *Khush Net*
http://www.khushnet.com

☐ *Leather 'N Lace*
http://www.geocities.com/WestHollywood/1925/

☐ *LesbianLes.Com (women only)*
http://www.lesbianles.com

☐ *Lesbian's Zone*
http://home.earthlink.net/~medicg/

☐ *Lesbo*
http://www.geocities.com/WestHollywood/1478/lesbopg.html

☐ *LesChat*
http://www.spiritone.com/~sappho/leschat/

☐ *Positive Network*
http://www.poz.org

☐ *QNet*
http://www.irc.q.net/

☐ *Qworld*
http://www.qworld.org

☐ *Rainbow Network*
http://www.rainbownetwork.com

☐ *Rural Gay.com*
http://ruralgay.com

☐ *SACWN (women only)*
http://www.cwo.com/~sacwn/webchat.html

☐ *Techno Dyke*
http://technodyke.com

☐ *Women Online Worldwide*
http://www.wowwomen.com/

☐ *Womyn's Nation*
http://www.geocities.com/WestHollywood/1655/

Reference:

☐ *Frequently Asked Questions*
http://www.kei.com/irc.html

☐ *ichat!*
http://www.ichat.com

☐ *IRC at NetPro*
http://www.teleport.com/~netpro/irc_nets.htm

☐ *Lowe's IRC Information*
http://www2.undernet.org:8080/~cs93jtl/IRC.html

☐ *IRC Help!*
http://www.irchelp.org/

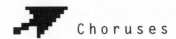 Choruses

Choruses are not often considered very hip; they're one of the last refuges for old Cole Porter tunes and Stephen Sondheim romps. Even so, some choruses are unquestionably modern. "Hidden Lega-cies" by Gay Men's Chorus of Los Angeles and Turtle Creek's "When We No Longer Touch" speak direct-ly (yet differently) about AIDS in our community. Neither *Details* nor *Vanity Fair* will be doing a feature on choruses any time soon, but for lesbians and gay men, they are in-credibly important. Is it the memories that a song can so quickly re-call, or is it the image of men and women on risers, innocent and vul-nerable yet wonderfully strong? Attend any concert and you'll see an emotion unlike any other.

Much of the passion of choruses comes from their roots in gay lib-eration. The San Francisco Gay Men's Chorus, for example, first ap-peared singing a memorial hymn on the steps of the San Francisco City Hall in November 1978, on the evening Harvey Milk was as-sassinated. Today there are gay and lesbian choral groups around the world and the song lists range from classical to pop.

Hailed this year by the *Los Angeles Times* as "one of the last im-portant links to a glorious tradition in music," the Gay Men's Cho-rus of Los Angeles has been singing for 20 years. Formed in 1979 as a completely volunteer effort of 99 gay men from every area of Los Angeles, GMCLA became the first gay U.S. Chorus to tour central Europe in 1991, giving performances in Budapest, Prague, Berlin, Vienna, and Copenhagen.

For information on gay and lesbian choruses all around the world, go to the GALA Choruses home page. More than 135 groups from North America, Europe, and Australia are listed with schedules, recordings, and (if you join) lists of members. You'll learn that choruses in general, and GALA members in particular, have commissioned new music by queer composers like Ysaye Barnwell, Roger Bourland, David Conte, Joseph Jennings, Erika Luckett, and Gwyneth Walker. Recently, GALA has come out from the concert stage to work with other international gay and lesbian organizations, including the Gay Games and the National Gay and Lesbian Task Force.

Whether you join a local chorus or want to attend a concert, take a moment to read a few of the clubs' mission statements. They're vows of devotion. Time and again you will read of striving for "musical excellence" and enhancing gay pride. Old-fashioned? Perhaps. Easily lampooned? Any commitment is. But these groups have power. As one reviewer wrote of the Central Pennsylvania Womyn's Chorus, "What left me speechless was the precision, wit, and charm with which the Womyn's Chorus began the second half of the show.... This was the breath of our community at its finest."

Gay Men's Chorus of Los Angeles describes itself as "an ensemble dedicated to excellence in the performance and advancement of the broad range of men's choral music. GMCLA builds a sense of community and positive self-image among gay men and lesbians and provides important bridges of understanding to the public at large."

Harmony Colorado Chorale in Denver offers a similar mission: "We are women and men who enjoy working together and singing together. From our base in the gay and lesbian community we reach out to include our families and friends. Through our commitment to musical and personal excellence we seek to empower ourselves and all who hear us."

☐ *Alamo City Men's Chorale*
  http://www.acmc-texas.org

☐ *Bay City Chorus*
http://www.freedomweb.com/baycity-chorus/index.html

☐ *Boston Gay Men's Chorus*
http://www.bgmc.org

☐ *Capital City Men's Chorus*
http://www.io.com/~ccmcaus/

☐ *Chicago Gay Men's Chorus*
http://www.enteract.com/~cjrowl/cgmc

☐ *Cincinnati Men's Chorus*
http://www.cincinnati.com/cmchorus

☐ *Columbus Gay Men's Chorus*
http://www.cgmc.com

☐ *Crescendo: The Tampa Bay Womyn's Chorus*
http://www.tampabayarts.com/crescendo/

☐ *Denver Gay Men's Chorus*
http://www.tde.com/~dgmc/

☐ *Denver Women's Chorus, The*
http://www.tde.com/~dwc/

☐ *GALA Bears*
http://www.csun.edu/~dlt/gala/GALA_Bears.html

☐ *GALA Choruses*
http://www.galachoruses.org/

☐ *Gay Men's Chorus of Houston*
http://www.gmch.org

☐ *Gay Men's Chorus of Los Angeles*
http://www.gmcla.org

☐ *Gay Men's Chorus of San Diego*
http://www.gmcsd.org

☐ *Golden Gate Men's Chorus (SF)*
http://www.ggmc.org

☐ *Gay Men's Chorus of Washington, D.C.*
http://www.gmcw.org/

☐ *Harmony: A Colorado Chorale*
http://www.tde.com/~harmony/

☐ *Heartland Men's Chorus, The*
http://www.kcnet.com/~hmckc/

☐ *Lesbian/Gay Chorus of San Francisco*
http://www.lgac.org/lgcsf/chorus.html

☐ *New Orleans Gay Men's Chorus*
http://members.aol.com/nogmc/index.htm

☐ *New York City Gay Men's Chorus*
http://virtualscape.com/nycgmc/

☐ *One Voice Charlotte Mixed Chorus*
http://www.geocities.com/WestHollywood/2897/

☐ *San Francisco Gay Men's Chorus*
http://www.sfgmc.org

☐ *Seattle Lesbian and Gay Chorus*
http://www.geocities.com/WestHollywood/Village/2289

☐ *Sydney Gay and Lesbian Choir*
http://maya.eagles.bbs.net.au/~sglc/

☐ *Triangle Gay Men's Chorus*
http://www.geocities.com/~tgmc

☐ *Turtle Creek Chorale*
http://www.turtlecreek.org

☐ *Twin Cities Gay Men's Chorus*
http://www1.minn.net/~lancesch/tcgmc.html

☐ *Voices: Bay Area Lesbian Choral Ensemble*
http://www.lesbian.org/voices/

☐ *Women's Chorus of Dallas*
http://dc.smu.edu/twcd/

Circuit Parties

You can almost feel the heat steaming off the shirtless, dance-crazed bodies at Parties.com and Circuit Noize. These pages capture the pulse of male tribal dance events around the country like Sundance, The White Party, and the D.C. Black Party. They're all about "The Circuit," a network of parties all over North America where thousands of gay men gather for music and dance marathons lasting three and sometimes four days of testosterone, rhythm, and confidence—modern day bacchanalias.

Parties.com is one of the largest guides, a nearly comprehensive hub where the drumbeat of this cultural phenomenon is taking place. It's full of gossip about past parties and the buzz on the next one. There's a terrific links list to all the various elements, such as promoters, DJs, music styles, fashion, and, of course, there are travel links to special deals with airlines to get you there and the hotels to house you. Always dreamed of being a go-go boy? Check out the link to Dance One, a contest whose winners get the chance to dance in a club for a night (on a box) and for life (on tape).

Circuit Noize is another picture-filled page that throbs to the beat of the scene. It's got a neat search engine that allows you to find your next party by filling in the city, date and even DJ of your ideal party. House, industrial, electronic, hand-bag, fluffy, hi-NRG, ambient—take your pick of music. You can also consult a party ratings chart and get reviews of past events by visiting the forum. And if you're still unsure there's always the advice offered by the "Circuit Sage."

Among the links you'll find is one to San Francisco's most prominent circuit party impresario, Gus Presents. The page opens with a young guy in a sarong (or indian print towel?), a big floppy hat and white shell necklace. He's smiling, of course, looking cute and innocent—in an experienced sort of way. Next come scenes from the event-studded year: Colossus in spring, Sundance in summer, Mass all year long. But no matter the season, the guys are always smiling and dancing joyously as they take part in what Circuit Noize calls an "altered world where friendship, dancing, love, spirituality, and self-expression are celebrated."

☐ *Circuit Noize*
http://www.circuitnoize.com

☐ *Circuit Parties*
http://www.circuitparies.com

☐ *Jeffrey Sanker Presents*
http://www.jeffreysanker.com

☐ *Gus Presents*
http://www.guspresents.com

☐ *Parties.com*
http://www.parties.com

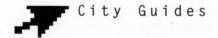 City Guides

The first thing most queer travelers do upon arrival in a new city is to scour the weekly gay and lesbian tabloids. In them you can always find a list of the hot spots, gauge the queer-friendly quotient, and generally begin to know where you are. Locals turn to them for a look in the mirror, checking community politics, nightlife, events, and, of course, the sex ads.

Today, city-based papers have jumped on the Web with a vengeance. Even the smallest paper offers a rundown of bars and restaurants, while the best complement hot lists with tours of the city that give you a true sense of the local flavor. New Orleans's *Ambush 2000*, for example, introduces you to the Big Easy with a picture-filled guide by local legend Becky Allen. She takes you up and down Bourbon Street and into the bars and eateries with a native's eye: "In New Orleans you can go out, party all night, get drunk, fall into the gutter and the next day all your friends still talk to you! In other cities you wind up in rehab." How true! There's even a bluesy sound track to get you in the mood.

Of course, not every city has such dramatic material as the French Quarter, but that's the great charm of most city guides. Natives, at least the ones who write about their town, usually have an incurable pride of place. They think their personal hangouts (bars, restaurants, and parks) and friends are the most wonderful, unique, and worthwhile combination in the world. And in a miracle of persuasion, they prove it nine times out of ten.

Town Life

Phoenix's *Echo* covers the local life particularly well, giving a sense of political goings-on between gay and straight community developers. *Out* presents Pittsburgh's gay news and nightlife and has an advice column by Dr. Dick. Like many of the smaller circulation papers on the Web, the *Wisconsin Light* makes up for bulk of the big city counterparts, with just the kind of things you'd want to know if you're moving there or traveling through.

Big Apple Plus

As you might expect, the largest cities have more numerous weeklies. The very unbuttoned Boston has *Bay Windows*, one of the best arts-oriented weeklies, with a calendar of events and links reaching to lesbians and gays all over New England. New York weighs in with *HX*, *the NY Blade*, *Gay NYC.Net*, *MetroBeat*—and that's not including the home pages packed with insider news or the many clubs and organizations that contain a more tailored list for subgroups (like drag, leather, activists, and club kids). San Francisco has both *Frontiers Newsmagazine*'s Northern California edition, a well-designed site with lots of pictures, and an article archive, as well as the *Bay Area Reporter*. The *B.A.R.* is graphics-poor, but has an average of more than 100 pages on San Francisco news, events, arts, obits, and one of the largest classifieds in the country. All the columns (obits, Mr. Marcus, Sweet Lips) are there along with more than 200 masseurs and models. Along with local news, *Seattle Gay News* has totally revamped its pages and now has the best links list to the Northwest.

Two of the best all-round city papers are the *Philadelphia Gay News* and *The Washington Blade* with clean, easy-loading graphics, lots of current stories, and archives of past editions. And both reflect their cities while reporting local and national news. *The Washington Blade* is highly political and *the Philadelphia Gay News* is quite literate and serious without being stodgy. Its book section is especially good, with a large roster of reviewers and terrific interviews and essays by local and national writers.

International

Foreign cities are equally well-reported. There's the *Dublin Pink Pages*, *Outrageous Tokyo*, the *Copenhagen Gay Pages*, *Pol Gay*, on the emerging scene in Poland, and *Pothos* for the word on queer Greece. And then there's that Goliath of queer Web activity, Australia. Here's a few of the city papers from Down Under: *BrotherSister*, *Capitol Q*, *Lemon*, *Melbourne Star Observer*, *Queer News*, and the *Sydney Star Observer* (the biggest of all). The *Sydney Star Observer* is everything a full-fledged newspaper should be, with features, departments, gossip columns, and classifieds all focusing on gay and lesbian life. The mix is a heady blend of politics (they seem to have a version of Newt in their government who is always roiling a radical right agenda), health (updates on HIV and hepatitis), and dish about the latest happenings in Sydney's hopping bar scene.

Amsterdam's *Pink Pages* is a terrific resource for the scoop on Amsterdam, a "multicultural international village with a long history of tolerance." There is concise historical background information and a list of coffee shops, restaurants, and bars— everything that Amsterdam is famous and infamous for. Like other online sites it is advertiser supported. Bars, restaurants, and hotels are the most frequent advertisers, yielding loads of information for tourists. Clix.net also has links to dating services, leather groups, and club listings. Among the many off-site pointers is GayLinc, which provides information on events and parties throughout the Netherlands.

Gay and Lesbian Times and *Diva* magazine work together for a great guide to London and all of the United Kingdom. Divided into two sections, for "screaming pansies" or "complete dykes," it has the latest news and features, reports on the arts and entertainment, polls, chat lines, and a compressive review of the queer bar and restaurant scene. The guide to London alone has 249 entries over ten pages.

Comprehensive Guides

Beyond city orientation offered by local weeklies, you can also visit Rainbow Query's City Guide section as well as web based indices such as GayGuide.net. But don't hesitate to guess the obvious address and just type in www.gay(city name).com. You'll find hundreds of gay city guides from Gay Tulsa to Gay Knoxville and Gay Key West.

Amsterdam

☐ *Dutch Queer Resources*
http://www.xs4all.n.~heinv/dqrd

☐ *Gay Amsterdam On-Line*
http://www.gayamsterdam.com/

☐ *Gay News Amsterdam*
http://www.Gaynews.nl/

☐ *Gay Ronald's Gay Amsterdam*
http://www.tip.nl/users/r.bekkie/

☐ *Pink Channel, The*
http://clix.net/clix/pinkpages/

☐ *GayLinc (Netherlands)*
http://www.dds.nl/~gaylinc/agenda.html

Arizona

☐ *Echo (Phoenix)*
http://www.echomag.com/

Atlanta

☐ *Atlanta Gay & Lesbian Visitor's Center*
http://www.atlgaylesvisit.w1.com/

☐ *ETC Magazine*
http://www.etcmag.com/

☐ *Gay Atlanta*
http://www.gayatl.org/

☐ *The Guide to Gay Atlanta*
http://www.gayguides.com/atlanta/

Australia

☐ *The Australian Gay Leather Directory*
http://www.geocities.com/WestHollywood/Heights/6771/

☐ *Capitol Q (Melbourne, Australia)*
http://www.capitalq.com.au/

☐ *Cyberqueer Australia*
http://cyberqueer.rainbow.net.au/

☐ *Gay Australia-Sydney*
http://www.magna.com.au/~gismith/gayaust1.htm

☐ *Gay Melbourne*
http://www.ozemail.com.au/%7Eprees/gaymelb.html

☐ *Links to the Australian Gay & Lesbian Community*
http://www.tma.com.au/gaylinks.html

☐ *Melbourne Star Observer*
http://www.bluestone.com.au/mso/

☐ *Queer Perth*
http://www.iinet.net.au/~lezderin/

☐ *Sydney sex venues*
http://cyberqueer.rainbow.net.au/sydney_s.html

☐ *Sydney Star Observer*
http://sso.rainbow.net.au/

☐ *Austrian Lesbian & Gay Homepage*
http://www.oeh.uni-linz.ac.at:8001/homo/

Baltimore

☐ *Baltimore Alternative*
http://www.baltalt.com

Berlin

☐ *Berlin*
http://www.informatik.hu-berlin.de:80/~holz/privat/

☐ *Homo De*
http://www.homo.de

Boston

☐ *Bay Windows*
http://www.baywindows.com/

☐ *The Boston Phoenix*
http://www.bostonphoenix.com/

☐ *Gay Boston*
http://www.gayboston.com/

Budapest

☐ *Budapest, Hungary*
http://www.gayguide.net

Canada

☐ *Montreal*
http://www.mcs.net/~hcarter/

☐ *RG (Quebec)*
http://www.gaibec.com/rg/

☐ *Toronto*
http://www.gaytoronto.com/

☐ *Vancouver*
http://gayvancouver.bc.ca

Chicago

☐ *FAG!*
http://huitzilo.tezcat.com/~scheie/

☐ *Out Chicago*
http://www.outchicago.org/

☐ *OUTlines*
http://www.suba.com/~outlines/

Colorado

☐ *Gay Colorado.com*
http://www.gaycolorado.com/

☐ *Aspen*
http://www.rof/yp/aspengay

Copenhagen

☐ *Copenhagen Gay Pages*
http://store.cybercity.dk/cgh/gayhome.htm

Dublin

☐ *Dublin Pink Pages*
http://qrd.tcp.com/qrd/www/world/europe/ireland/orient.html

Florida

☐ *Florida Lesbian and Gay Guide*
http://flagg.net/

☐ *Gay Miami*
http://www.ecko.com/~gaymiami/

☐ *Gay Tampa Bay*
http://www.gaytampa.com/gaytampa/welcome.html

☐ *Tampa Bay*
http://www.bayfriendly.com/

☐ *Scoop*
http://www.scoopmag.com/

☐ *Southern Exposure (Key West)*
http://www.kwest.com/

Gothenberg

☐ *Kinky Gothenberg*
http://www.algonet.se/~levin/kinkyguide.gbg.html

Greece

☐ *O Pothos*
http://www.geocities.com/westhollywood/heights/2958

☐ *Gayly Oklahoman*
http://www.gayly.com/

☐ *Inside Out (Cleveland)*
http://members.aol.com/insideout.html

Hawaii

☐ *Island Life (Honolulu)*
http://www.tnight.com/ilm/

Ipanema

☐ *Ipanema (Brazil)*
http://www.ipanema.com

London

☐ *QX Magazine*
http://www.qxmag.co.uk

☐ *Gay Times and Diva (London)*
http://www.gaytimes.co.uk/

☐ *UK Gay*
http://www.demon.co.uk/world/ukgay/ukg0001.html

Los Angeles

☐ *Gay Asian Pages for Los Angeles and Orange County*
http://members.aol.com/APXRDS/gap.html

☐ *Gay Los Angeles*
http://www.gaylosangeles.com/

☐ *Frontiersweb Online News Magazine*
http://www.frontiersweb.com/

New Orleans

☐ *Ambush Magazine 2000*
http://www.ambushmag.com/

☐ *Gay New Orleans*
http://www.gayneworleans.com/

☐ *New Orleans Impact*
http://www.impactnews.com/

New York

☐ *Club NYC*
http://www.clubnyc.com

☐ *GayNYC.Net*
http://www.nyc.net

☐ *Gay Resources for NYC*
http://www.gaycenter.org/gaynyc/

☐ *New York Blade*
http://www.nyblade.com/

☐ *HX Magazine*
http://www.hx.com/

☐ *Kinky City Guides*
http://members.tripod.com/~pboots/cities.html

Ohio

☐ *Indianapolis*
http://www.gayindy.org/

☐ *Columbus*
http://www.outincolumbus.com

Palm Springs
☐ *Palm Springs*
http://www.palmspringsgay.com

Paris
☐ *Paris Pages*
http://www.paris.org/

Pennsylvania

☐ *Gay Philly*
http://www.gayphilly.com/

☐ *Out! Magazine*
http://www.outmagazine.com/

☐ *Philadelphia Gay News*
http://www.epgn.com

Poland

☐ *Pol Gay (Gay Poland)*
http://www.qrd.org/qrd/www/world/europe/poland/

Prague

☐ *Pragconnect.com*
http://www.pragconnect.com

Provincetown

☐ *Provincetown Village*
http://www.provincetown.com/

Puerto Vallarta

☐ *Provincetown Village*
http://www.discoveryvallarta.com/guide.html

Romania:

☐ *Romania Action for GLBs*
http://www.raglb.org/uk

☐ *Romainian Lesbigays*
http://www.geocities.com/westhollywood/1811

San Francisco:

☐ *Amazon Online*
http://www.amazon.org/

☐ *Castro Online*
http://www.castroonline.com

☐ *The Castro*
http://www.bpe.com/ports/sf/etc/castro.html

☐ *Folsom Street Fair*
http://www.folsomstreetfair.com/

☐ *GayGlobal San Francisco*
http://www.gayglobalsf.com/

☐ *Gaysf.com San Francisco's Gay Tourist Information Center*
http://www.gaysf.com/

☐ *Gus Presents*
http://www.guspresents.com/

☐ *Lavender Pages Online Business Directory*
http://www.lavenderpages.com/

☐ *Q San Francisco*
http://www.qsanfrancisco.com/

☐ *Q San Francisco Guide*
http://www.qsanfrancisco.com/qsf/guide/contents.html

☐ *Castro Street Live*
http://www.castrostreetlive.com

☐ *San Francisco Lesbian Gay Bisexual Transgender Pride*
http://www.sfpride.org/

☐ *Web Castro*
http://www.webcastro.com/

☐ *OutNow (San Jose)*
http://www.outnow.com/

☐ *The Slant (Northern Calif.)*
http://www.theslant.org

☐ *Sonoma Zone (Northern Calif.)*
http://www.sonomazone.com/

Sofia (Bulgaria)

☐ *Gay Life in Bulgaria*
http://www.bulgayria.com

St. Louis

☐ *Gay life in St. Louis*
http://www.gaystlouis.com/

☐ *Stevie's Gay Pages*
http://www.geocities.com/WestHollywood/Heights/6937/

Texas

☐ *Dallas Voice*
http://www.dallasvoice.com

☐ *Dallas Gay Page*
http://www.divanet.com/dallas/

☐ *Houston Gay Web*
http://HoustonGayWeb.com/

☐ *Houston Voice*
http://www.houstonvoice.com/

☐ *Texas Triangle*
http://www.outline.com/triangle/hp.html

Tokyo

☐ *Outrageous Tokyo*
http://www.geocities.com/westhollywood/4248/

Washington

☐ *Experience Seattle On The Web*
http://www.aa.net/~seaofblk/

☐ *Pacific Northwest Gay Pride Web Page*
http://members.aol.com/deanolywa/

☐ *Seattle Gay News Online*
http://useattle.uspan.com/

☐ *Seattle S/M Resources List*
http://www.halcyon.com/elf/seattle.html

Washington, D.C.

- ☐ *The D.C. Bitchy Bar Guide*
  http://www2.smart.net/~mikebilt/bars.html

- ☐ *Gay D.C.*
  http://www.gaydc.com/

- ☐ *Chocolate City*
  http://www.chocolatecityusa.com

- ☐ *The Washington Blade*
  http://www.washblade.com/

Zagreb

- ☐ *Zagreb Gay Life*
  http://www.geocities.com/westhollywood/heights/2040

Collectibles & Antiques

Is there something redundant in the term *gay decorator*? Or has the field of antiques and collectibles been so thoroughly infiltrated that labels are superfluous? Surprisingly there are no pages to famous queer decorators like Billy Baldwin. It's safe to say, though, that when you go to the auctions looking for collectibles, you'll be amongst like company. The fever for used sports uniforms is suspiciously queer, especially when jocks and sweatpants come up for bid! For a comprehensive list go to Internet Auction List or etour where you'll find Ebay, Yahoo! auctions, Sothebys.Amazon, Modern Auction and more.

Whether you're looking to buy or sell, the online world is an excellent resource. To make sure you know what you're doing, start out at Learn About Antiques ("Education about antiques and learning to deal effectively with dealers are the keys to successful antique collecting and trading"). Then visit Antiques and Arts Weekly—it's rather sparse as online magazines go, but you can read recent issues and get a feel for what's hot in the upscale market. Follow links provided by both these sites for pages put up by collectors talking about their fascinations. One, for example, writes a thorough introduction to Chinese porcelain complete with pictures, prices, and ordering information.

Art Channel

Art Channel is one of the largest directories. It has hundreds of sections you can sift through as well as a very good search engine that makes hunting for a specific item easy. For example, to find mahogany bookcases, search for "mahogany book." Another very helpful section has a long list of museum Web sites with descriptions slanted for the collector. About the Egyptian Museum in Cairo it says: "Although not obvious from the Web page, The Egyptian Museum of Cairo possesses the greatest collection of Egyptian antiquities on the planet.

Internet Antique Market is a new site that's also worth a visit. It has many categories and lots of images with links to the dealer for information on an item or availability of something similar.

World of Art and Antiques is another site aiming to be comprehensive and has a good search function enabling you to look for antiques by era. So if you're a Biedermeier fan, for instance, you won't have to slog through extraneous listings.

Antiques World has one of the largest directories of links to auctions and auctioneers, resources and references, and museums and exhibits. It also lists online shops and even provides pointers to repair and refinishing shops to help find a match for that broken finial on the back stair. You'll also find information on collectibles like comic books, dolls, and sports cards.

Collectibles

For curios try In One Era, Out the Next or Curioscape. Along with a finding a new piece of mercury glass or Fiestaware, you can write a about an antique that you can't identify. Or maybe you want to know the name of the manufacturer or when it was made. Just send a note and you'll get a reply from an expert. If you have no luck with these sites forums, try the huge discussion list—more than 150 ranging from autographs to woodworking.

Book collectors have a particularly fine source in Jack Cummins at Booknet. Just type in an author's name and up pops a listing of his antique books. There were four books each for both Somerset Maugham and Oscar Wilde and two of James Baldwin's books. A first edition of *Giovanni's Room,* described as a "fine copy in slightly faded dust jacket," was listed for $200.

There are also storefront home pages put up by antique shops often gathered in trade associations like the Art and Antique Dealers League of America. These are fun to visit and give you an especially good idea of prices for country homewares, quilts, etc.—in short, Martha Stewart–style housewares. If you're a confirmed flea-market browser, sift through the World-Wide Collectors Digest. You can find anything here from old china to dolls, coins, and sports memorabilia.

☐ *An Expert's Advice on Chinese Antique Porcelain*
http://www.hk.super.net/~joeyf/orientiq/feature.html

☐ *Antiques*
http://willow.internet-connections.net/web/antiques/

☐ *Antiques and Arts Weekly*
http://www.thebee.com/aweb/aa.htm

☐ *Antiques World*
http://www.antiquesworld.com/

☐ *Art and Antique Dealers League of America*
http://www.dir-dd.com/aadla.html/

☐ *Art Channel*
http://www.artchannel.com/

☐ *Booknet/James Cummins Bookseller*
http://www.abaa-booknet.com/catalogues/cummicat/58-7.html

☐ *Internet Antique Market*
http://www.househome.com/antique/

☐ *Learn About Antiques*
http://willow.internet-connections.net/web/antiques/

☐ *World-Wide Collectors Digest*
http://www.wwcd.com/

☐ *Yahoo! Collectibles/Antiques*
http://www.yahoo.com/Business_and_Economy/Companies/Hobbies

Auctions

☐ *Ebay*
http://www.ebay.com

☐ *etour*
http://www.etour.com

☐ *J.P(eterman) Marketplace*
http://www.auction1.jpeterman.com/marketplace.htm

☐ *Internet Auction List*
http://www.internetauctionlist.com

☐ *Modern Auction*
http://www.modernauction.com

☐ *Sotheby's.Amazon*
http://www.sothebys.amazon

☐ *Yahoo! Auctions*
http://www.auctions.yahoo.com

First of all, some orientation. How comfortable are you with being called *queer*? You'd better get used to it, because on campuses the term is used routinely as a nonpejorative designation for same-sex orientation. The smart, ambitious, and industrious kids at these schools are to a large degree the architects of cyberspace, so we'll all be following their language lead in the future. Gay is for guys, lesbian is for women, and we're all queer—as in "infoqueer" and "inqueery," two commonly used titles for campus information centers.

Just as language is being redefined, so are social freedoms. It seems as if every school has recognized the importance of computers and the Internet. From liberal California to the Bible Belt, student organizations have quickly taken to the new technology. And almost without exception the groups are digitized. The sheer normality of queerness on campus can be startling, particularly if you remember school as yet another closet. And these kids aren't shy; students active in setting up networks and maintaining queer sites list the experience on their résumés.

Perhaps the most comprehensive page on the LGBT college scene is Campus Links. There are links for queer campus groups across America and schedules for conferences as well as resources for legal and professional groups. There is also a "ring" of campus links, where a random tour will show you just how widespread and sophisticated gay groups have become.

Queer Berkeley is one of the most sophisticated university GLBT sites. It's page is a smoothly functioning guide to an amazingly complex queer campus life. First comes the Queer Council (a sort of directorial body) and the various resources under its purview: social and discussion groups such as CalDykes: a lesbian and bisexual women's group, and Fluid: For bisexuals, questioning students, and everyone who chooses to go without a label. Then there's Mantra Magazine: UC Berkeley's Queer Magazine, MOeBIUS: Non-denominational spiritual group as well T-Cal: Cal's first and only group for transgender students.

Along with many other groups, you'll find information on studying for an LGBT Minor and classes dealing with gender and sexuality. Then there's a schedule of upcoming lectures on campus dealing with queer issues such as Homosexuality and the Torah and Homosexuality in Modern China. There are also dances, social mixers—all in all an increasingly rich and varied queer campus culture in full, glorious display.

Info List

The best place to find out about queer activity on campuses across the nation is the LGBT Campus Resource Directors. Along with listing queer university sites, it's a resource for encouraging "higher education environments in which lesbian, gay, bisexual, and transgender students, faculty, staff, administrators, and alumni have equity in every respect." Begun in association with the National Gay and Lesbian Task Force, Campus Resource has a column on the climate for queer students, links to papers on the subject, financial aid, legal advice, and more.

Although the campus groups of today are primarily chartered to address serious student issues like harassment, peer pressure, and coming out, they're appropriately optimistic and often have a well-deserved silly side. Links lists almost always have a good sprinkling of gay comics pages, with "Dyke Street" being perhaps the most popular.

All have areas of support for coming out, against bashing, and for political expression. The overwhelming message is that it's not cool to insult or harass gay students anymore—they talk back!

☐ *Campus Links*
http://www.youthresource.com/campus/

☐ *LGBT Campus Resource Directors*
http://www.uic.edu/orgs/lgbt/

☐ *National Gay and Lesbian Task Force's LGBT CampusOrganizing: A Comprehensive Manual*
http://www.uic.edu/orgs/lgbt/ngltf_manual.html

Campus Groups

☐ *Allies Clubs—Penn State*
http://www.clubs.psu.edu/allies

☐ *Auburn University*
http://www.auburn.edu/~aglassn/

☐ *B-GLAD—East Carolina University.*
http://www.ecu.edu/org/bglad/

☐ *Ball State University*
http://bsuvc.bsu.edu/~d000lbgsa/index.html

☐ *Bath University*
http://www2.bath.ac.uk/~su4lgbs/

☐ *BiGALA—SUNY Oswego*
http://www.oswego.edu/~bigala/

☐ *Bisexual, Gay, and Lesbian Alliance of Northwestern University*
http://www.studorg.nwu.edu/bgala/

☐ *Bryant Pride Bryant College's GLBisexual Student Association*
http://www.bryant.edu/~pride/

☐ *Cal Poly Pomona Pride Center*
http://www.csupomona.edu/pride_center/

☐ *Caltech LesBiGay Union*
http://www.cco.caltech.edu/~clu/

☐ *CampusQ at the University of Washington*
http://weber.u.washington.edu/~lpjames/campusq.html

☐ *Carnegie Mellon University ALLIES*
http://www.contrib.andrew.cmu.edu/org/allies/

☐ *Carnegie Mellon University CMUout queer events,*
resources, and links
http://www.contrib.andrew.cmu.edu/org/out/

☐ *Colorado College Bisexual, Gay, and Lesbian*
Alliance Information
http://www.cc.colorado.edu/Students/BGALA/

☐ *Columbia's Lesbian Bisexual Gay Coalition*
http://www.columbia.edu/cu/lbgc/

☐ *Copper Country Gay Lesbian Bisexual Alliance,*
Michigan Tech
http://www.sos.mtu.edu/ccglba/

☐ *Cornell University LGB Resources*
http://cu-lbgt-www.cornell.edu/

☐ *Duke University's Queer Infoserver*
http://www.duke.edu/lgb/

☐ *Emory University's Office of Lesbian/Gay/*
Bisexual Life
http://www.emory.edu/LGBOFFICE/office.html

☐ *GLBT Programs Office, University of Minnesota*
http://www.umn.edu/glbt/

☐ *Gay Lesbian Bisexual Student Organization—*
University of North Carolina at Greensboro
http://www.uncg.edu/student.groups/glbsa/

☐ *Gay, Lesbian, and Bisexual Student Organization—University of Southern Mississippi*
http://www-org.usm.edu/~glbso

☐ *Gays and Lesbians—University of Saskatchewan*
http://duke.usask.ca/~ss_glus/

☐ *Southern Illinois University at Carbondale*
http://web1.siu.edu/~glbf/

☐ *George Washington University LGBA Home Page*
http://gwis2.circ.gwu.edu/~lgba/

☐ *Georgia Tech Gay and Lesbian Alliance*
http://cyberbuzz.gatech.edu/gala/

☐ *Harvard Gay and Lesbian Caucus*
http://WWW.ActWin.Com/hglc/

☐ *Knox College GLBCA*
http://knox.knox.edu:5718/~glbcawww/

☐ *LBGSA Home Page—University of Texas at Austin*
http://www.utexas.edu/students/lbgsa/

☐ *LGSU—The Univeristy of Utah's Lesbian and Gay Student Union*
http://www.gayut.com/lgsu/

☐ *Lesbian Gay Bisexual Coalition at Northern Illinois University*
http://www.geocities.com/WestHollywood/2222/

☐ *Lesbian, Gay and Bisexual Student Union of the University of Florida*
http://grove.ufl.edu/~lgbsu/

☐ *Middlebury Open Queer Alliance*
http://www.middlebury.edu/~moqa/

☐ *MIT Bisexual, Gay, and Lesbian Alumni/ae Association*
http://alumweb.mit.edu/groups/bgala/

☐ *MIT's GAMIT*
http://web.mit.edu/gamit/www/index.html

☐ *McGill University Lesbian, Bisexual, Gay and Transgender Students*
http://vub.mcgill.ca/clubs/lbgtm/index.html

☐ *Oberlin Lambda Alumni Homepage Web site*
http://www.oberlin.edu/~alumassc/OLA

☐ *Ohio University Open Doors*
http://oak.cats.ohiou.edu/~opendoor/

☐ *Princeton University Lesbian/Gay/Bisexual Alliance*
http://www.princeton.edu/~lgba/index.html

☐ *QUIC—University of Illinois at Chicago*
http://www.uic.edu/depts/quic/

☐ *Quiver: A Queer Student's Literary Companion from the University of Colorado*
http://www.colorado.edu/StudentGroups/Quiver/index.html

☐ *Rainbow Alliance at Pitt*
http://www.pitt.edu/~rainbo/

☐ *Rensselaer Polytechnic Institute Gay/Lesbian/Bisexual Association*
http://www.rpi.edu/dept/union/glba/public_html/index.html

☐ *Stanford Masque (a queer literary and art magazine)*
http://www-leland.stanford.edu/group/masque/1/index.shtml

☐ *Stanford University's Queer Resources*
http://www-leland.stanford.edu/group/QR/

☐ *Swarthmore College's Sager Committee*
http://www.sccs.swarthmore.edu/org/sager/

☐ *The Other 10% (Ha'asiron Ha'acher)—The Hebrew
University*
http://www.ma.huji.ac.il/~dafid/asiron.html

☐ *The Purdue University LesBiGay Network*
http://expert.cc.purdue.edu/~triangle/

☐ *University of California, Davis, LGB Resource
Center*
http://lgbcenter.ucdavis.edu

☐ *University of California, San Diego, Lesbian Gay
Bisexual Association*
http://sdcc13.ucsd.edu/~ucsdlgba/

☐ *University of Georgia LGBSU*
http://www.uga.edu/~lgbsu/

☐ *University of Illinois at Chicago, Office of GLB
Concerns*
http://www.uic.edu/depts/quic/oglbc/

☐ *University of Massachusetts-Lowell Bi-GaLA*
http://www.geocities.com/WestHollywood/2085/

☐ *University of Wisconsin-Eau Claire GLOBE*
http://www.uwec.edu/Student/Globe/globe.htm

☐ *University of Alabama Gay Lesbian
Bisexual Alliance*
http://ua1vm.ua.edu/~glba/glba.html

☐ *University of Arizona Bisexual, Gay,*
and Lesbian Association
http://www.azstarnet.com/~fission/bgala.html

☐ *University of Connecticut's Bisexual, Gay, Lesbian*
and Ally Alliance
http://www.ucc.uconn.edu/~bigala

☐ *University of Kansas Queers and Allies KU Queers*
and Allies
http://www.ukans.edu/~qanda/

☐ *University of Oregon Lesbian, Gay and Bisexual*
Resources
http://www-vms.uoregon.edu/~jallen/

☐ *University of South Dakota Gay Lesbian Bisexual*
Alliance
http://www.usd.edu/student-life/orgs/glba/

☐ *University of Virginia Lesbian Gay Bisexual Union*
http://scs.student.virginia.edu/~lambda1/

☐ *University of Wisconsin Ten Percent Society*
http://tps.stdorg.wisc.edu/TPS/

☐ *Washington University in St. Louis—Lambda*
Online
http://pear.wustl.edu/~lambda/

☐ *Western Illinois University's BGLFA*
http://www.wiu.edu/users/mibglf/

☐ *Yale Lesbian, Gay, Bisexual Cooperative*
http://www.yale.edu/lgb/

Comics Strips & Characters

With the Lambda-radiated superheroes of Queer Nation (the hottest full-color queer comic strip on the Web) and all the wonderful super and everyday heroes created by Alison Bechdel, Roberta Gregory, and Howard Cruse, it might seem we've always had a wide choice of queer comics. Good for a quick laugh, a bit of nostalgic sentiment, we tend to dismiss them as an amusing look in the fun house mirror of our teenage dreamscape. But as you'll begin to discover while sifting through the queer comics on the Web, these renegades are true artists and the story of how they've reached today's level of acceptance and brilliance parallels that of gay liberation itself.

Gays in Comics

Look to Gays In Comics for the fascinating history, going back to the 1930s, when characters were closeted, up until today when even mainstream publishers like DC and Marvel have out characters. (In the 1950s Batman and Robin were castigated for promoting perversity!) GIC also has a list of gay and lesbian characters and characters whose homosexuality has been "fixed," from various publishers such as DC, Marvel, Image, and Milestone. Just click on any name for a history of specific characters and where they are now. It also contains links to the Queer Comics message board where you can research gay and lesbian characters in mainstream comics.

Queer Nation

To get a taste of tomorrow's comic hall of fame, go to Queer Nation to see what the *New York Blade*, *Washington Blade*, *HX*, and *XY* are raving about. There are two strips here, Tales of the Closet (the trials and tribulations of a tough kid in a Queens, New York high school) and Queer Nation, the only full-color gay superhero comic on the Web. QN's story so far: A strange comet shoots across the skies, radiating lambda rays from the comet's tail that imbue queers with incredible powers, often at the most unexpected moments. Check it out to meet the cast of fascinating characters: Lucifer, the winged avenger who takes violent and sometimes murderous action against gay bashers. Is he the Gay Devil or Gay Deliverance? With just a snap of his newly empowered fingers, Laminette LaForge can instantly alter his clothes, hairstyle, makeup, and accessories to suit whatever strikes his flamboyant imagination— thus giving birth to more costume changes than a Diana Ross concert. Bille Barlowe was in the middle of kinky sex with her girlfriend Amy when the Great Vanishing made all lesbians worldwide disappear—all except Billie! Now she's on a quest to find her lost sisters, with her Glock and Uzi blazing!

Beek's Books

Beek's Books' gay and lesbian section is another treasure for queer comics lovers into the heroic genre. It's filled with reviews of comic books, comics, graphic novels, and sample illustrations such as: Steven's Comics #3 by David Kelly (the bittersweet life of a gay kid); Bull's Balls by Ralf König (outside temptations spell trouble for a committed gay couple); Coley Running Wild by John Blackburn (a seductive male model's adventures); The Enchanters by Steven Gellman (a team of magical gay/lesbian superheroes); Dancin' Nekkid with the Angels by Howard Cruse (underground comix by a veteran gay cartoonist); Handjobs by Julius (erotic fiction featuring "daddy" and "son" types with lots of sex); Heroes by Matt Wayne, ChrisCross, and Prentis Rollins (Milestone's first "public" superhero team); Chiaroscuro by McGreal, Rawson, and Truog (speculative biography of Leonardo da Vinci and his ward Salai); Glitch #1 by Timothy Piotrowski (slice-of-life from a mainstream-alternative gay perspective); What They Did to Princess Paragon by Robert Rodi (what if DC made Wonder Woman a lesbian?); Cyber-Zone #1-7 by Jimmie Robinson (future adventures of a street-tough woman and her sentient Gunn); Hardthrob by John Blackburn (a seductive male model upsets the life of a young man and his sister); Leatherboy by Craig Maynard (a gay sex-toy superhero fights a super-powered-sex menace); Seven Miles A Second by Wojnarowicz and Romberger (autobiography of former child prostitute with AIDS); and many more. GayComix has pictures of gay and lesbian comic book heroes and heroines. The panel of "Hero" (a member of the "Ravers") shows him coming out. He stands in tight blue jeans, flannel shirt, goatee, and a military haircut. His bubble caption reads, "Well mostly I mean 'Homosexual!' "

Jitterbug Press

If there's a smarter or funnier bunch of queer writers and illustrators than those at Jitterbug Press, they're not yet on the Web. The Jitterbug folks haven't won any awards yet, but as the publisher says in the introductory page, "Who needs awards?... Someone we know read the first chapter of Buffalo Girls and laughed so hard that milk came out of her nose." This site gives you samples of Jitterbug's best work, including Allysa (The Untamed), an illustrated fantasy novel in the bad-girl-with-a-sword genre. "Sure, Conan hung out with Red Sonja and John Carter tied the knot with Dejah Thoris, but isn't it about time the woman occupied center stage and the guy was the sidekick?"

Open Prairie/Comicazee

The Open Prairie Syndicate, also known as the Comicazee Alternative Comics Collection, is a huge collection of queer-themed strips including Roberta Gregory's "Bitchy Bitch," Alison Bechdel's "Dykes To Watch Out For," Robert Kirby's "Curbside," Jennifer Camper's "SubGURLZ," and John D. Anderson's "Honestly Ethel." Joe Hoover's strip, "The Open Prairie," has a selection of drawings targeting the nastiest senator around, Jesse Helms. With his beady eyes and pursed lips, he's a hilarious subject that Hoover takes to task in panels such as Helms on the NEA, Nightmare on Helms Street, and Closet Masturbators.

Fags In Space

Fags In Space, "a completely queer cosmic comic," is deceptively simple. The illustrated panels portray a future in which genetic warfare designed to kill homosexuals makes earth uninhabitable, forcing an exodus to planet-based biosphere colonies like QM4—which fags call home. "QM4 is an orderly, peaceful place, governed by the wisdom of the 'Big Queen.' A vogueing contest is held every two years in the 'Big Bubble' to determine who the Big Queen will be for the upcoming term...." In the first adventure our heroes Steve (a cyberpilot) and Ron (his spouse) must deal with Ron's discontent. Concerned, Steve says, "A beautiful home, friends who love us. What more could you want?" He feels "empty." Steve is puzzled. "But we have Glob!" (Glob is a pet grown in a petri dish, a gooey quivering green ball). Ron wants...more. "Are you saying what I think you're saying?" asks Steve. "Yes," says Steve. "I want a family!" But their joy is short-lived. Glob runs away! Depressed he goes to the Big Queen for answers.... How will it go with Steve and Ron, with poor lonely Glob,? Will the Big Queen's wisdom solve things or are other forces about to intervene? There's a war on, you know!

Such Is Life

A gentler, more traditionally drawn character is Buckminster Duck, "a gay duck on the path of self-discovery," from the Such Is Life page. This Web page (no pun intended) has weekly panels chronicling the absurdities of politics, love and romance, spirituality, and societal attitudes. And since Mr. Duck waddles around the movie capital of the world, he's frequently quacking about Hollywood gossip with whimsical satire.

Lesbian Comics

Lesbian comics and cartoon characters are particularly well-represented. Cyberdyke's Cartoon-corner has Katrin Kremmler and Lesbian Sex From A-Z, a collage of Kremmler's drawn figures interacting with usually heroically posed women. There's also Hothead Paisan for anyone who wants to "read about a homicidal lesbian terrorist who likes to kill straight men." Naughty Bits is a lesbian comic book series with a hilariously bitchy edge. The site gives samples of the legendary "cucumber scene," the story of "Midge's abortion, with an educational aside on how a D&C is done," and how the main character Bitchy turns 40 "and uses her mom's birthday check to buy a high-tech vibrator."

Hear me out

Laura Jimenez's column is a text-only "small dose of lesbian humor for the whole human race." Her themes revolve around the tribulations of fulfilling professional bliss and dealing with the guilt of her "genetic" coding as her lover's housewife. "It's a wonder I haven't killed thousands by now."

Whichever of these artist renegades you're most interested in, you'll find this field is much deeper than commonly imagined. Though the large indexes are often useful, the best way to find similar work is to check the links list on your favorites page.

☐ *Adam & Andy*
　 http://www.crosswinds.net/~adamandy/home.html

☐ *Beek's Books*
　 http://www.simplecom.net/verbeek/books/rainbow.html

☐ *Black Boy Fantasy*
http://www.blackboy.virtualslave.net/index.htm

☐ *Comicazee Alternative Online Colletion*
http://www.comicazee.com

☐ *Comics Sites Alliance*
http://www.comicsites.com

☐ *Chelsea Boys*
http://chelseaboys.com

☐ *Cybergrrl*
http://www.cybergrrl.com/

☐ *Cyberdyke's Cartooncorner*
http://www.qworld.org/DykesWorld/Cartooncorner.html

☐ *Doggie Style*
http://www.members.aol.com/toonzville/doggistyle.html

☐ *Drag Strip*
http://www.thedragstrip.com/default.html

☐ *DYKES ON DYKES!*
http://www.qworld.org/DykesWorld/DykesonDykes1.html

☐ *Dykes to Watch Out For*
http://www.visi.com/~oprairie/bechdel/bechdel.html

☐ *Fanny*
http://www.pavilion.co.uk/cartoonet/network/fanny/fanny.htm

☐ *Fatgirl Comics*
http://www.fatgirl.com/fatgirl/

☐ *GayComix*
http://members.aol.com/GayComix/

☐ *Gays in Comics*
http://members.aol.com/GayOLeague/gaycharacters.html

☐ *Gay Comix*
http://www.skyhouse.org/robert/gay.htm

☐ *Gay Toons Syndicate*
http://www.gaytoons.com

☐ *HIV & Me*
http://members.aol.com/hivnme

☐ *Howard Cruse Central*
http://www.howardcruse.com

☐ *Jane's World*
http://www.reuben.org/janesworld/

☐ *Jitterbug Press*
http://www.jitterbug.com/

☐ *Joe Hoover*
http://www.visi.com/~oprairie/hoover/hoover.html

☐ *Jonah Weiland's Comic Book Resources*
http://comics.envisionww.com/

☐ *Kyle's Bed & Breakfast*
http://www.members.aol.com/kylesBnB/index.html

☐ *Junkie Boy*
http://www.geocities.com/Paris/arc/9257/

☐ *Midtown Court (881)*
http://www.members.aol.com/chrisco57/881_midtown_court.html

☐ *Mostly Unfabulous Life of Ethan Green*
http://www.stonewallinn.com/Ethan/index.html

☐ *Nick Fitton's Home Page*
http://artemis.earth.monash.edu.au/~fitton/

☐ *OutNow! Editorial Cartoons*
http://www.outnow.com/

☐ *Open Prairie Syndicate*
http://www.visi.com/~oprarie/

☐ *Pussy Rules*
http://www.dykesworld.de/dod2/dod2framed.html

☐ *Queer Nation*
http://www.queernation.com/

☐ *Queerview Magazine*
http://www.queerview.com/qv02/qv980228.htm

☐ *Ralf König*
http://tau.uab.es/~viktor/ralf/

☐ *Robert Kirby*
http://www.visi.com/~oprairie/kirby/kirby.html

☐ *Roberta Gregory*
http://www.robertagregory.com

☐ *Spray Liz Homepage*
http://www3.vega.it/sprayliz/

☐ *Such Is Life*
http://www.gaywired.com/~unity/quack/suchlife.htm

☐ *Wonder Woman Homepage*
http://wonderwoman.simplenet.com/

 Cooking

Is cooking a queer thing? Sneak into any of the top ten catering companies in America, peek under a lid, and an indignant queen will smack you with his toque. If the guy next to you in line at the grocery store has balsamic vinegar in his basket, you know he's gay. And vegetarians? All dykes. All right, the reasoning here is specious—still, cooking and good nutrition are community watchwords. Perhaps it's all that waitering. Regardless, the online universe is full of cooking hints and culinary wisdom.

For the online equivalent to a queer cook's kitchen confab, go to Gay.com's food and wine channel. You'll find menus for every occasion, from romance to comfort food to specialty diets and nutrition. There's even a discussion of etiquette and how to brew your own beers. One of the most interesting threads is on aphrodisiacs—chocolate, oysters, truffles—and how to fit these sexual boosters into your favorite recipes.

Perhaps the sexiest food site is Gay Cooking, a German/English page that is as delectably designed as the recipes it provides. The recipes, created by master chef Heinrich Röder, are a satyr's feast for the eye and tongue. Each recipe is presented by one of five handsome bodies, each model being responsible for one culinary area. A cookbook binder is available in five different jacket covers (steel, leather, or latex as well as in jeans and uniform design) and contains 30 erotic recipes.

Chef Gregory's Home Page features menus of the month—including all recipes and any directions specific to the preparation of those menus. He also has listed his favorite desserts, entrées, and hors d'oeuvres with recipes. His intent is to help you in the kitchen so that you can impress that special man or woman without all the headache. He also has some fun things and a few photos in the site—there is a section for him to ramble on any topic that comes to mind—and he also provides professional menu planning for that special event.

There are times when cooking is something you'd rather not do. In that case, the Web offers tons of lazy luxury sites. Most every gourmet deli/market now has a delivery service that lets you order up everything from the perfect pasta to a champagne brunch. Check out the amazing list of cheeses at Dean and DeLuccaor the full selection of appetizers, breads, side dishes, entrées and desserts at Balducci's page of Italian specialties (Catalogo del Buongustaio). Delivery may take a few days and cost a bit, but hey—you won't have to clean the oven!

Elsewhere on the Net, a bunch of Web pages have been put up by national brands and chains. Godiva has a luscious order form with lots of gold and chocolate-colored accents. And, of course, there's Welcome to PizzaNet! served up by Pizza Hut. (This page definitely needs a dose of queer styling.)

Queer Cooks

If you're looking for the recipes of well-known gay cooks like James Beard or Craig Claiborne, the best approach is to use the AltaVista Search engine. Beard's foundation has nary a queer note, but there's plenty of subtext simmering beneath the surface. Entering Claiborne's name will get you about 100 different mentions of this out author and critic. Most, though not all, contain either recipes or pointers to sites for such dishes as snail pizza (!), corn bread, various stir-fry dishes, and more. Among the listings are lots of foodie haunts like GourmetBytes Home Page and the Happy Eater.

Custom Diets

Special diets for AIDS and cancer patients can be found among the vast holdings of information at the Centers for Disease Control and Prevention as well as the larger AIDS treatment organizations (search under nutrition). For articles on specific interactions of HIV drugs with diet, see newsletters from Alive 'N Kicking, Gay Men's Health Crisis, AIDS Treatment News, and Critical Path or search on "nutrition." WWWomen has a good selection of vegetarian links like Veggies Unite! and Whole Foods online. For other particularized regimens—say, for macrobiotics or muscle builders—try Yahoo!, Lycos, and AltaVista.

Bulk Builders

For big portions and lots of calories, go to the Bear Grub page of the Lonestar Saloon. Billed as "man-pleasing," some of the recent recipes included Ursa Major-Alarm Chili, Texas Greenhorn Salsa Verde, and Rio Grande Salad with Lime Dressing. The text walks you through preparations and gives advice even notoriously near-sighted bears can follow. Of course there's heavy ladling of real butter and lard ("not Crisco!"), but that's half the point. For those who enjoy romping in the mud and playing with their food, Redbear's Mudpit helps you explore the joys of this fetish.

☐ *Amy Gale's Recipe Archive Index*
   http://www.cs.cmu.edu/~mjw/recipes/

☐ *Centers for Disease Control and Prevention*
   http://www.cdc.gov/

☐ *Chef Gregory's Home Page*
   http://members.tripod.com/chefgregory/

☐ *Chefs Susan Feniger and Mary Sue Milliken's Page*
   http://starchefs.com/Tamales/recipes.html

☐ *Chile Page*
   http://neptune.netimages.com/~chile/

☐ *Chocolate Lovers' Page*
   http://bc.emanon.net/chocolate/

☐ *Gay Cooking*
http://www.gaycooking.com

☐ *Gay.com food and wine channel*
http://www.gay.net/community/channel_food.html

☐ *Gay Goodies*
http://www.gayweb.com/125/candy.html

☐ *Godiva Online Home Page*
http://www.godiva.com/

☐ *GourmetBytes*
http://www.gourmetbytes.com/

☐ *Happy Eater*
http://detnews.com/menu/stories/24186.htm

☐ *Lesbian/Gay/Bi/Queer Vegetarian Page*
http://www.alumni.caltech.edu/~brett/qveg.html

☐ *Lonestar Saloon*
http://www.slip.net/~lonestar/

☐ *Nutrition for Life*
http://www.csun.edu/~hbbio016/nfl.html

☐ *Redbear's Mudpit (Fetish)*
http://users.why.net/redbear/gay/mud/index.html

☐ *PizzaNet*
http://www.pizzanet.net/

☐ *Vegetarians Unite!*
http://www.vegwb.com/

☐ *Whole Foods online*
http://www.wholefoods.com/wf.html

Cowboys & Cowgirls & Rural Gays

As the Web increasingly connects all facets of gay life, so are rural gays and lesbians lassoeing an active part of the queerscape. The largest network and community space for gay or lesbian farmers, cowboys, truckers, hunters, eco-activists, ranchers, artists or just folks who like life in the country, is Ruralgay.com.

It's a rich and varied site with chat rooms, personals, home page lists, forums, recipe boards, an organic gardening and sustainable living column, and the very popular, Tim's Tales From the Road—true stories of a long-haul trucker/cowboy. You'll also find dozens of out-of-the-way inns, guest houses and campgrounds run by rural gay folk as well as links to gay and lesbian artists, musicians and more. The events calendar, lists gay rodeos and events and the Help Wanteds is the place to look for ranch hands.

Gay Rodeo

In 1975 the first gay rodeo struggled to life in a makeshift arena just outside Reno, Nev., but still made a few thousand dollars for charity. Among the problems to surmount was finding enough livestock—ranchers weren't keen on loaning steers to gays. Today the event has evolved into a national organization with 21 hugely successful rodeos. These are sponsored by the International Gay Rodeo Association, which represents 27 states, the District of Columbia, and two Canadian provinces. Over the years the chapters have given more than $1 million to benefit of community charities. Needless to say, finding good beef is no longer a problem, and with sponsors like Miller Beer and United Airlines, rodeos are held in professional arenas.

To read about and perhaps join these cowboys and cowgirls, mosey on over to the IGRA home page or one of the chapter Web sites. The Greater Los Angeles Chapter of the Golden State Gay Rodeo Association, for instance, will give you an idea of what's going on. In addition to its annual rodeo, the Los Angeles area chapter offers a variety of events and information on its own chapter and all the others around the nation. Locally you can sign up for training in rodeo events, dances, and beer busts, with hotel specials for attendees.

You'll also see that IGRA events are sensitive to animal rights groups, going so far as to have a single page full of their strict animal treatment guidelines.

Golden State Gay Rodeo Association

If you're interested, test yourself by going to the photographs page of the Golden State Gay Rodeo Association, which includes lots of hot cowboys roping, bull riding, dancing and just passing time at a rodeo for "our family." Whether or not you decide to go western, don't miss the history of IGRA. It's an amazing story of how a couple of guys pyramided their love of Western traditions into a series of events including barrel racing, calf roping, a mounted drill team, and enough big, sexy belt buckles to gild the western skies.

☐ *Arlen's Stompin' Ground (Gay Cowby Ring)*
  http://www.geocities.com/westhollywood/6075/

☐ *Cowboys*
  http://www.perfectmen.mansclub.com

☐ *Cowboys and Cowgirls*
  http://cyberrodeo.com/guysgals/index.html

☐ *Cowboystuds*
http://205.134.188.51/stable.index.html

☐ *Dallas Cowboys*
http://nflhome.com/teams/cowboys/cowboys.html

☐ *Gay Cowboy Resources on Rural Gay.com*
http://www.ruralgay.com/gay-cowboys.asp

☐ *Hot Naked Cowboys*
http://www.velvetspike.com/cowboys/index.htm

☐ *Golden State Gay Rodeo Association (Los Angeles)*
http://users.aol.com/gsgraglac/rodeo.html

☐ *International Gay Rodeo Association*
http://www.igra.com/

☐ *Round-Up 45*
http://www.gayimage.com/roundup/index.html

☐ *Rural Gay.com*
http://www.ruralgay.com

☐ *South Eastern Gay Rodeo Association*
http://www.lambda.net/~segra

CU-SeeMe & Web Cams

With prices for a black-and-white video camera down to $100 and software about $70, CU-SeeMe, online chat with simultaneous visual feedback has exploded. What's got the queer world going is the sex angle. You can cruise the net by words but also by appearance. Of course this cuts both ways, and having a nickname like "muscleboy" means you've got to deliver.

You meet in two ways. The first is in a reflector (or "ref"), which is a public cyber room where you list your nickname as well as profile. Along with this you have the option of attaching your picture. The idea is to advertise yourself and your interests, so you'll want to arrange yourself attractively. Some guys are naked, others just showing a bit of chest or whatever.

The second step, "going one on one (1:1)," takes it to a different level. This is a private connection where you and another guy do or say everything short of touching and smelling. You start by clicking on another guy's nickname and sending him a note or by messaging the whole group. "Anybody want to see me shoot?" is a popular line. When a visitor drops by, you'll hear a sound like a camera clicking and there he is, hand on the trigger, as it were.

Stats?

Be prepared for aggressive conversation. The preliminaries can be as simple as: "Want a show?" A good reply might be: "Stats?" Also, because cameras are crude you may want to see some movement in your partner's picture—a magazine centerfold in front of the camera looks live, unless of course there's a tree or a finger on the edge!

Web Cam Diaries

One of the most interesting aspects of CU-SeeMe are the video diariy Cam sites especially popular with 20-somethings. Much as early home pages had an insouciant charm because of their simplicity and lack of artifice, so the recent wave of cam pages fascinate by their authenticity. Here's the intro to "1 On 1 boys": We are 21- and 23-year-old boyfriends who love to be watched. This Webcam is an ultimate fantasy for both of us. We get off knowing thousands of people are watching. Watch us, chat with us, hang out with us, follow us around. Bedroom cam, bathroom cam, shower cam, kitchen cam, hot tub cam. JO a few times a day...."

Keith.cam opens with the enticing remark, "it's warm and real at keithcam.com." He then goes on to say, "This is a view into my world, not a gay sex cam site. You'll see me shirtless often, and even some of Davis's 'tasteful nude pics' (grin), but this site is about life, warmth and sensuality, not sex." This is written in sky blue text across from a "foto" of Keith himself, a young guy with an old-fashioned air lent by the hair parted in the middle and made slightly aggressive by the dog tags dangling on his thin, hairless chest. The main feature is a cam diary that follows him throughout the day, one day hunting for apartments, another having coffee with a friend whom he later spanks. The cam follows him to the bathroom, the hallway, out on the streets—various points in the day of a seemingly regular young man living in San Francisco at the turn of the century. And somehow, despite the mundaneness of it all, it's fascinating—part voyeurism, part anthropology, and wholly representative of a new queer openness. It's a sexy, private version of MTV's *The Real World.*

Sources

For a guide try the Gay CU-SeeMe Page. It's full of information on the technical and social ins and outs. There're also links to reflectors (both heavily used and new ones).

Thanks to Greg Seiler of GizmoSoft (http://www.gizmosoft.com/) and Edward Martinez for their crucial help on this chapter.

☐ *1 On 1 Boys*
http://www.1on1boys.com/

☐ *AZ BOY*
http://www.azboy.com

☐ *Cockpit*
http://www.cockpit.com/video.html

☐ *CU-See-Me Info Page*
http://www.geocities.com/WestHollywood/9785/

☐ *BioMan's List of Gay/Bi Reflectors*
http://users.abac.com/Bioman/

☐ *Eroscan Index: Gay CU-See-Me*
http://www.eroscan.com/links/pva/pvav/pvavcusm/pvavcusmg/

☐ *Gay Cams*
http://www.gaycams.org/

☐ *Gay CU-See-Me*
http://www.gaycuseeme.com

☐ *Gay Watch CU-SeeMe*
http://www.gaywatch.com

☐ *GregPa's Web Site*
http://darkknight.net/~sirsson/newestreflist_4_23_98.html

☐ *Keith Cam*
http://www.keithcam.com

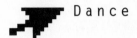 Dance

Nowhere among the arts are sex and sexuality as elusive as in dance. It's there in ballet and flamenco, of course (what's sexier than bodies moving in rhythm?), and yet it's not there. The same is true of dance as it appears on the Web. You won't find a page of dancing homos—perhaps because, as Jennifer Dunning said in her biography of Alvin Ailey, "the dance world has always been entirely open." The categories just don't break down that way, divided instead into all the various styles and schools of dance.

This isn't to say that you can't discover the gays and lesbians of the dance world. Out dancer-choreographers such as Merce Cunningham, Mark Morris, Paul Taylor, and Bill T. Jones, for example, all have pages. Jones's famous "Still/Here," in part about his personal battle with AIDS, is written up on ArtsWire: "In Still/Here, choreographer-poet Bill T. Jones expresses the aspect of pain and healing that are beyond the scope of words alone. Meeting with survivors of serious illnesses, Jones choreographed coping strategies through a grammar of motion…translated individual resiliency into a celebration of courage." And the Paul Taylor Dance company has a wonderfully full and long series of pages detailing the history of his company, its dancers, and its current schedule. But you'll find these pages listed under the artists' professional qualifications. Sexual orientation doesn't seem to matter.

Dance Pages

Among the comprehensive dance pages, the Dance section of the World Wide Web Virtual Library (co-maintained by ArtsWire and DanceUSA), is unquestionably the largest. Whether you want to read up on dance or individual dancers, join a troupe, find a schedule of events, browse a list of companies around the world, log onto newsgroups, join mailing lists, consult a schedule, buy tickets, or explore an assortment of links, it's all exhaustively here. The index is broken down into the categories of Dance Schools, College and University Dance Programs, and Dance Pages Organized by Type. Types are further divided into 25 headings from Ballet to Break Dancing, Flamenco to Irish, and Renaissance to World Dance. Of these, the Ballet section is the largest.

CyberDance focuses on Web resources. The Ballet section alone has more than 2,000 links connecting you to Events, Research and FAQs, Newsgroups, Bulletin Boards and Chat Lines, Articles, Reviews, and Magazines. This is a researcher's paradise. The Events page, for instance, even maintains links for old performances so that you can look up what went on, for example, at the Kennedy Center last year. The list of magazine links is the largest available, with 20 online publications (from *Dancing on a Line* to *The Muse* and *Theater* magazine).

Cyberdance also has a long links list to dancers like Alvin Ailey, Rudolph Nureyev, Vaslav Nijinsky and Mark Morris. These are brief career sketches. For a more in-depth look at particular artists, search alt.culture (named "cool site of the day" by MTV) for contemporary figures such as Mark Morris.

Other comprehensive dance sites include Arts USA, A Dancer's Page, Arts online's In Motion, and Dance Links. These offer document archives, competition schedules, calendars, and more. In Motion has one of the largest collections of international dance links, including Prajwal, Tantric Buddhist Dance of Nepal, Kamala Cesar, Bharata Natyam (South Indian Dance), and Potri Ranka Manis, Tribal Dances of the Philippines.

Dance Links

Dance surf addicts beware, Dance Links has a tremendous collection of dance links—over 3,000—as well as a new way to keep up on what's happening. Their News of the Dance World section has notes on current topics such as the 45th Anniversary celebration of Paul Taylor Dance Company at City Center and Artswire's report that the Bill T. Jones/Arnie Zane Dance Company will not perform at Spoleto Festival USA in Charleston, S.C., in order to support a boycott of the South Carolina tourism industry initiated by National Association for Colored People (NAACP) protesting the flying of the Confederate Battle Flag at the South Carolina Statehouse.

Culture Finder

The centerpiece of CultureFinder is a searchable database of over 350,000 cultural events including dance, theater, music, and visual arts, in 1,500 cities throughout the United States. In addition, the "Learn More About..." section provides a crash course in dance via short informative articles and a dance dictionary.

Company Sites

Of all the company sites, none is more beautiful and roomy than the New York City Ballet's, which is a balletomane's feast. Here you can find not only schedules and company history but also all the details of every dance, from "Tzigane" to "Stars and Stripes." The write-up on "The Four Temperaments" has notes on the music, the premiere date, and a brief on why this ballet has assumed its seminal place among Balanchine's works.

This page is also generous with dancers' biographies. Principal dancer Jock Soto is profiled in detail, both professionally (the various dances in which he performs leading roles) to more personal elements, such as the charities he works with (God's Love We Deliver, which provides hot meals for bedridden individuals throughout Manhattan; participation in the March of Dimes Gourmet Gala, which features the creations of celebrity chefs; and his active fundraising for AIDS research.")

For a general update on available sources, it's always a good idea to browse Yahoo!'s dance links.

Note: The only specifically "gay" dances on the Web are found in pages put up by jiggle bars. The Corner Pocket in New Orleans, for example, has a really gaudy, quintessentially Bourbon Street come-on: "Boys Dancing! New Meat!" And there are pictures! One shows a hunky guy in a leopard-print jock (stuffed with money) dancing on top of the bar as customers paw at his body. *Laissez les bonne temps rouler* (Let the good times roll)—this is dance too.

☐ *Alt.culture*
http://www.alt.culture.com

☐ *Arts online*
http://www.arts-online.com/

☐ *ArtsUSA*
http://www.artsusa.org/

☐ *ArtsWire*
http://www.artswire.org/Artswire/www/dance/dance.html

☐ *Balanchine, George*
http://www.http://www.www.ids.net/picpal/mrb-home.html
http://www.ens-lyon.fr/~exouche/danse/balan.html

☐ *Cunningham Dance Foundaton*
http://www.merce.org/

☐ *Corner Pocket*
http://www.gayneworleans.com/The_Pocket

☐ *Culture Finder*
http://www.culturefinder.com

☐ *Dancer Links*
http://www.danceronline.com

☐ *Dance Millennium*
http://www.arts-online.com/dance/dance2.htm

☐ *Dance Pages Directory*
http://emporium.turnpike.net~dpd/index.html

☐ *Dance Resources*
http://www.cs.fsu.edu/projects/summer94/group4/dance.html

☐ *A Dancer's Page*
http://www.phantom.com/~netrunnr/dance.html

☐ *Dancing online*
http://www.danceonline.com/

☐ *Duncan, Isadora*
http://www.kqed.org/fromkqed/cell/calhist/duncan.html

☐ *Estelle Souche's Dance Page*
http://www.ens-lyons.fr/~esouche/danse/dance.html

☐ *Farrell, Suzanne*
http://www.kuwayama.com/farrell

☐ *Fokine, Michael*
http://www.ens-lyon.fr/~esouche/danse/fokin.html

☐ *Graham, Martha*
http://www.ens-lyon.fr/~esouche/danse/graham.html

☐ *Jones, Bill T.*
http://www.pbs.org/ktca/alive/prodbios.html#bill
http://www.pbs.org/ktca/alive/Stillhere.html

☐ *Mark Morris*
http://www.mmdg.org
http://www.altculture.com/site/entries-text/morrisxm.html

☐ *New York City Ballet*
   http://www.nycballet.com/

☐ *Nijinsky, Vaslav*
   http://www.www.dance.hoio-state.edu/files/dance_history/connec-tion/people/nijinsky-vaslav.html

☐ *Soto, Jock*
   http://www.nycballet.com/bios/sotobio.html

☐ *Steve Allen's Dance Index*
   http://syborg.ucolick.org/~sla/dance/dance.html

☐ *Taylor, Paul*
   http://www.ptdc.org/

☐ *Tudor, Anthony*
   http://www.ens-lyon.fr/~esouche/dance/tudor.html

☐ *World Events Database*
   http://www.ipworld.com/EVENTS/HOMEPAGE.HTM

☐ *WWW Virtual Library-Dance*
   http://www.artswire.org/Artswire/www/dance/dance.html

☐ *Yahoo! Dance Links*
   http://www.yahoo.com/Arts/Performing_Arts/Dance/

Digital Queers

When historians sit down to write the history of gay liberation in the 1990s, one of the early chapters will be devoted to the Digital Queers. Even though their work is behind the scenes, you see its benefits all around you. Quietly, yet with great speed, they're building a worldwide cyberscaffold of gay and lesbian organizations on the Internet. Among the many queer rights organizations they've helped are the National Gay and Lesbian Task Force, National Center for Lesbian Rights, National Black Lesbian and Gay Leadership Forum, Asian Lesbians of the East Coast, the Latina/o Lesbian, Gay, Bisexual and  Transgendered Organization, Frameline International Gay and Lesbian Film Festival, and community centers in San Francisco, New York, Los Angeles, and Minneapolis, as well as PFLAG, GLAAD, and Lambda Legal Defense.

Whether your organization needs help getting online or you're interested in contributing to the cause (donors receive terrific T-shirts), see the Digital Queers home page. It's a simple design, with only a few discreet icons for illustration; DQ's energies are focused on evangelizing the Net.

But don't despair that this is yet another dour rights organization. DQ is fun. They have a sense of humor and a queenly, ironic tone that enlivens even the FAQ list. For example, why does DQ use the word queer? They answer: "Which do you prefer: Digital Gays, Bisexuals, Lesbians and Transgender, i.e. Digital GiBLeTs? Or Digital Queers?" Pronounce GiBLeTs out loud and you'll get the full effect. Subsequent pages walk you through a tour of DQ activities, the requirements for membership, and a list of local chapters, including those serving Atlanta, Boston, Los Angeles, San Francisco, the Pacific Northwest, Texas, Florida, and Australia.

There's also a schedule of legendary DQ fund-raising parties given by the local chapters. Why are the parties legendary? These puckish guys and gals have figured out that a bit of glamour helps the cause. Mrs. Doubtfire made a surprise appearance one year and other famous and near-famous partygoers have included Herbie · Hancock, Todd Rundgren, Lea DeLaria, and Marilyn Pittman.

As I said, these are fun queers with a wicked sense of humor and a passionate devotion to gay rights. They're even ready to help you meet that special someone, sort of: "In all modesty, we like to think that we've facilitated some new technology transfers and offline alliances that got their start at DQ parties."

☐ *Digital Queers*
   http://www.dq.org/

Domestic Partners
& Same-Sex Marriage

Among the documents collected in the Queer Resources Directory's Domestic Partners folder is a copy of "Tom and Walter's Marriage," a short piece that ran in the *New Yorker*. It's the narrative of two men preparing for and finally exchanging vows. "Tom Stoddard and Walter Rieman went shopping at Tiffany's last month. The salesman was polite but distant. After asking him dozens of questions, after trying on this one and then that, they decided to buy what Tom had wanted from the start: two plain gold bands." Later, Tom says that same-sex marriage is going to be "the next big battle."

It turns out Tom was right, way back in 1994 when the article was written. Today the Web is alive with rights activity. Large activist organizations such as the Human Rights Campaign and the National Gay and Lesbian Task Force are marriage rights veterans, and they've been joined by new groups dedicated solely to this issue. Freedom to Marry has the complete text of Judge Kevin Chang's decision in Hawaii upholding our right to marry. FORM has a preaddressed E-mail form. Fill in your message, and the group will forward it on to congress. Partners Task Force lists 14 organizations (including the American Civil Liberties Union) that are working to equalize marriage law. And that's just for starters. There is a new group of pages ready to help you raise a family with same-sex parents, even to find a sperm bank for same-sex partner (see the chapter on Family).

There are also hundreds of pages with advice for couples making do with the laws on adoption, custody issues, and other family-related topics for gays and lesbians raising or planning

a family. You'll find resources for both custodial and noncustodial parents. Gay Law Net is a great site with information about and links to a wide variety of legal issues affecting same-sex couples. Financial Planning for Unmarried Couples is a short page listing off the key steps to financial protection for unmarried couples. Unmarried Couples' Issues is a California lawyer's site with special legal and financial sections for unmarried couples on taxes, insurance, adoption, agreements, etc. The site contains extended excerpts from his handbook about estate planning for unmarried couples in California.

You can even educate straight friends by sending them to Are You Planning a Wedding? This site is for people who are getting married and want their wedding to be sensitive to lesbian, gay, bisexual, and transgendered people in attendance.

Partners Task Force

Partners Task Force for Gay and Lesbian Couples is the largest and most detailed compilation of information on the subject. Contents include notes on recent developments, surveys, legal marriage essays, marriage data, information from the United States and around the world, tips on safeguarding your relationship, and lots of resource links as well as articles from *The New York Times*, *Newsweek*, *10%*, and the *Harvard Gay and Lesbian Review*. In "Marriage, What's it to You?" the *San Francisco Examiner* explains the practical dollars-and-cents side of the issue, such as the imbalances for gay men and lesbians relating to insurance, social security, pensions, and more. And these are just the benefits related to the workplace—other money is lost in inheritance, house and car insurance, frequent-flyer miles, and taxes. Partners also has a connection to newsgroups and forums discussing the issue, including the Domestic Partnership mailing list, Queer Immigration, Queer-Parents, Gaydads, and Moms (women only).

Freedom to Marry

The appropriately named group Freedom to Marry is a same-sex rights organization with a comprehensive arsenal of arguments for its position, including a state-by-state report on marriage laws. You'll find that the United States is a crazy quilt of laws and precedents: Wyoming dismisses gay and lesbian marriage outright while the District of Columbia funds seminars for queer family adoptions.

FORM is a Boston-based grassroots group offering educational and activist information on the right to same-sex marriages. The group has a list of resources ranging from an overview of the issue's social and legal evolution to a sample wedding announcement. There is also an accounting of Senate and House voting records on DOMA and the Employment Non-Discrimination Act.

Online Chat Groups

To subscribe to a great mail list source of information and support about domestic partner benefits, send a message saying "subscribe domestic [your e-mail address]" to majordomo@queernet.org. Unmarried Partners is a bulletin board for online discussion about the experience of being a parent without marriage. Prospective Queer Parents has good resources for considering parenthood in general, especially if you're lesbian, gay, bisexual or transgendered. Couples Place is an interactive site supporting all couple relationships. They provide information, skills training and networking services. This page has an incredible resource list and some great free discussion forums.

News & Developments

The Same-Sex Marriage Home Page is more of a news center that contains many links and lists of resources, news from states, lobbying groups, and general information. Check the FAQ for discussions of the current status of domestic partnership initiatives and their ramifications for tax law, costs, and how adoption and child-bearing are affected. One strategic point mentioned by gay tax experts is that no matter how progressive your company is, IRS policy determines taxes, and to change that will require an act of Congress. One more nudge toward the voting booth.

☐ *ACLU Gay Marriage*
http://www.aclu.org/issues/gay/gaymar.html

☐ *Are You Planning a Wedding?*
http://www.staff.uiuc.edu/~roswald

☐ *Couples Place*
http://www.couplesplace.com/

☐ *Domestic Partner Benefits*
http://www.bayscenes.com/np/progress/dpb.htm
http://www.ngtlf.org/pubs/dp_pub.html
http://www.hrc.org/issues/workplace/data.html
http://www.nlgja.org/

☐ *Domestic Partnerships and Same-Sex Marriages*
http://www.cs.cmu.edu/afs/cs.cmu.edu/user/scotts/domestic-part

☐ *Estate Planning*
http://www.nolo.com/nest/1f.html

☐ *Family Matters and Seniors*
http://www.nolo.com/category/family.html

☐ *FORM*
http://www.calico-company.com/formboston/

☐ *Freedom to Marry*
http://www.ftm.org/

☐ *Lavender Collar*
http://www.lavendercollar.com

☐ *HRC*
http://www.hrc.org/

☐ *Marriage: The Ultimate Perk (Patricia Nell Warren)*
http://www.mindspring.com/%7esagecomm/whosoever/warren.html

☐ *Mining Company*
http://gaylesissues.miningco.com/

☐ *Partners Task Force Home Page*
http://www.buddybuddy.com/

☐ *Queer Resources Directory*
http://www.qrd.org/qrd/www/legal.html

☐ *Queer Wedding Webring Homepage*
http://www.angelfire.com/me/queer-wedding

☐ *Relationship LLC*
http://www.relationshipllc.com/

☐ *Same-Sex Marriage Home Page*
http://starbulletin.com/specials/samesex.html

☐ *Unmarried Couples' Issues*
http://www.unmarried.org/

☐ *Unmarried Partners as Parents Bulletin Board*
http://boards.parentsplace.com/messages/get/ppunmarriedpart-
ners4.html

 Family

Insemination, surrogates, disapproving schools, a churlish legal system—all the many hurdles to creating a family might seem impossibly daunting, but they're not. In fact, after reading some of the personal histories of the many gay and lesbian parents now available on the Web, you'll find that becoming a parent can turn out as naturally as it is surely meant to be.

As recently as 1997 there were only a few sparse resources for queers interested in parenting. Now, thankfully, there are many pages discussing the questions you (and your partner, if you have one) will have to answer before you begin your family. How important is it for the child to be genetically linked to (one of) you? If one of the biological parenting options is not available to you, are you willing to adopt a child who is not an infant? Who is disabled in some way? Who is of mixed racial heritage or a different race from yourself (or your partner)?

There are various organizations that are supportive of queer families, information on support groups, books and articles for adults and kids, fun links for kids, and legal information.

Family Pride Coalition

Family Pride Coalition (formerly Gay and Lesbian Parents Coalition International) began in 1979 as group of gay dads, the Gay Fathers Coalition. This group later became Gay and Lesbian Parents Coalition International (GLPCI), a grassroots organization whose primary purpose was to connect with and support local gay and lesbian parenting groups. Today, it has a full-time staff and a Web site covering topics such as second parent adoption, surrogacy and insemination information, facts about GLBT parents, coming out to children, education issues in schools, a national newsletter, and a parenting group listserv.

Family Diversity Projects has wonderful photo-text exhibits and books on topics like lesbian, gay, bisexual, and transgender families, multiracial families, mental illness in the family, adoptive and foster families, single-parent families, immigrant families, and more.

Lesbian Moms

Lesbian Moms addresses the more specific concerns of lesbian mothers. Unlike Family Q, Lesbian Moms doesn't set itself up as an expert. If you need professional advice, the author, Debbie Ranard, says, see a lawyer or a doctor. But "if you are looking for the wisdom and life experiences of other lesbian moms...read on." That's the charm and useful distinction of this page—whatever the topic, the text is straight from the writer's life. And the topics are exhaustive. There's a lesbian mom discussion group, a state-by-state list of doctors and sperm banks, an essay on the positive and negative aspects of anonymous donors, insemination information, answers to insurance and legal questions, and an evaluation of the "unique issues for lesbian families."

The Family Diversity Project

The Family Diversity Project has wonderful photo-text exhibits and books on topics like lesbian, gay, bisexual, and transgender families, multiracial families, mental illness in the family, adoptive and foster families, single parent families, immigrant families, and more. Or, you can take advantage of the comprehensive and excellent advice.

Gaydads

Gaydads, like Lesbian Moms, has the added impact of personal history. Its well-informed author, Richard Jasper, came out in 1993 to his wife, children, in-laws, parents, siblings, and coworkers. It was messy but necessary. His guide is designed "first and foremost to be a resource for any married gaydad who is contemplating coming out or who is in the process of doing so. It includes a rather detailed description (My Story) of what led me to marry and what prompted me to come out; a list of resources (paper, electronic, and in real life) that I have found useful in my journey; and a list of Frequently Asked Questions—asked of me, that is!" Informal and extensive—it includes an essay on coming out to children—Gaydads is a heartfelt and encouraging page for "any gaydad, gay stepdad, or gaydad wannabe, regardless of whether they have been married, regardless of whether they are in or out of the closet."

Another page gay fathers might want to read is Alan and Steve's page. Though the fathering section is only a part of this huge home page (which also features lots of bear talk), it provides a great example of how two men raise a son from age seven until the time he's able to tell his father "that he will someday marry a woman, and he would only be interested in the kind of woman who had comfort and ease with gay people."

Love Makes a Family is a traveling exhibition of pictures and text of a diverse group of families with gay or lesbian moms or dads, grandparents, or teenagers and young adults. "At the most basic level, it combats homophobia by breaking silence and making the invisible visible." The exhibit has been endorsed by many national organizations: NGLTF, GLPCI, COLAGE, GLSEN, PFLAG, and others. The site offers wonderful stills and text from the exhibition and information on bringing the video to your school or organization.

Alternative Family Magazine

AFM is a terrific magazine for GLBT parents and their children and takes on many of the subjects that other parenting magazines cover: health, nutrition, and child development issues. However, it also covers issues most mainstream and GLBT magazines don't cover. Things like what being "out" as parents means to your children, how to negotiate your way through the sometimes hostile institutions important to your children's lives, and how parents can claim their place in gay community events like pride festivals. As well as articles you'll find AFM is an excellent source for features on the subject from around the world.

Check out the QRD for other Web sites along with articles such as "Children's Insight into Gay Love," "Gay Parenting" (*Time*), "Gay Parents" (*The New York Times*), "Girls Fare Better in Gay Households," and "Gay Parenting—Statistics."

For practical information on writing a will, check out the Nolo Press home page. Among the books in their catalog is *A Legal Guide for Gay and Lesbian Couples*. For less than $20 you can learn how to write living-together contracts, plan for medical emergencies, secure estates, handle domestic-partner benefits, and learn about legal aspects of having and raising children. It's all pro-family.

☐ *Action for Gay Marriage*
  http://www.mediabass.co.nz/agm/agm.html

☐ *Adoption Resources*
  http://www.adopting.org/gaystate.html

☐ *AllTogether.com*
  http://www.alltogether.com

☐ *American Psychological Association regarding gay and lesbian parents*
  http://www.apa.org/pi/parent.html

☐ *Adoption FAQ*
  http://www.dimensional.com/~tennco/faq.htm

☐ *Alan & Steve's page*
  http://www.geocities.com/WestHollywood/1001/

☐ *Alternative Family Magazine*
http://www.altfammag.com

☐ *Alternative Family Project*
http://www.queer.org/afp/

☐ *Baby Dancing*
http://www.tor-pq1.netcom.ca/~lnalor/baby.html

☐ *Camp Lavender Hill*
http://www.pw1.netcom.com/~ksf/me/camp.html

☐ *Child Welfare Services for lgbt youth*
http://www.casmt.on.ca/lgby1.html

☐ *COLAGE (Children of L's & G's Everywhere)*
http://www.colage.org

☐ *Coming Out to Children*
http://world.std.com/~ewk/outchil.html

☐ *Couples National Network*
http://www.couples-national.org/

☐ *Co-Parent Adoption*
http://www.inet.net/adopt/gay/gay2.html

☐ *Family Pride Coalition (formerly GLPCI)*
http://www.familypride.org/

☐ *Gay Dads-UK*
http://www.gaydads.co.uk

☐ *Gay & Lesbian Adoption*
http://www.adopting.org/gaystate.html

☐ *Gay Parent Magazine*
http://www.gayparenting.com

☐ *Gay Themes in Children's Books*
http://www.armoury.com/~web/gaybooks.html

☐ *LeGaL's Home Page (Lesbian and Gay Lawyers)*
http://www.interport.net/~le-gal/

☐ *Lesbian Moms' Guide*
http://www.lesbianmoms.org/

☐ *Lesbian Mother's Support Society*
http://www.lesbian.org/lesbian-moms/

☐ *Love Makes a Family: Lesbian and Gay Families*
http://www.familyties.org/

☐ *Nolo Press*
http://www.nolo.com/

☐ *Parent Perspective*
http://www.FlamingoPark.com/Perspective/

☐ *Partners Task Force for Lesbian & Gay Couples*
http://www.buddybuddy.com/

☐ *PFLAG*
http://www.pflag.org/

☐ *Prospective Queer Parents*
http://www.geocities.com/WestHollywood/3373/

☐ *Queer Living*
http://www.queerliving.com

☐ *Rainbow Families*
http://www.lesbianmoms.org/rainbofamily/index.html

Fat Girl

Exploding through the air like a superhero with her fist held high, hairy armpit in your face, and big belly aquiver, the Fat Girl logo that illustrates this home page says it all: This is the place for fat dykes and the women who want them. With lists of related organizations, along with poetry, stories, and calls to action (a hit list of diet centers to harass by dialing their 800 numbers), Fat Girl is fun, colorful, and does that miraculous Internet thing—it gives a minority a voice heard 'round the world.

And what a voice it is. The poetry has featured such titles as "Clean Satisfaction" by Hannah R. Thigpen. It opens with the lines, "236 pounds/and today I would date myself,/that's how good I look./Levi's and flannel/(damn I love winter)...." Stories include "Queer Punks Chew the Fat," "Fat and Bi, No Excuses," and "The Fat Truth" by Max Airborne, creator of this site.

Not long ago the Fat Girl page was essentially a subscription tease for the full-scale 72-page 'zine. But it has grown into a complete online magazine with editorials, cartoons, and a store selling T-shirts along with the famous Fat Girl toilet paper: "High-quality, two-ply, 500-sheet roll imprinted with size-positive messages. Great for guerrilla activism! When you're feeling feisty, find a public restroom and wrap this inspirational paper around the stall's existing loo roll. Try airports, museums, even your place of work.... Free the ass and the mind will follow!"

Jolly fatsos? Not really. The creators of this page are on a mission to break down stereotypes and promote acceptance. And they use humor, as well as in-your-face tactics. Under the heading of Action! (strategies for the activist fat girl), you can learn how to make an FG cocktail: "Drink a quart of red juice and top it off with a cup of ipecac. Then quickly position yourself in front of the target, say a Jenny Craig franchise, aim, open mouth, and fire."

You'll find practical advice here too about clothing, health and hygiene, and legal services. For the lovelorn query Aunt Agony, who offered this advice to a sad sack upset about size shyness: "GET A GRIP ON YOURSELF!! Some people may see being fat as a liability, but we do have our advantages. For example, we make terrific pillows and even better float toys. Extra insulation also makes us great bed warmers."

The links page is huge, with roughly 50 sites for resources on fat women, general women's sites, and size-related information. And be sure to check out Fat!So? (Fat Girl's sister publication), another great page "for people who don't apologize for their size." The opening image depicts 12 big and beautiful butts, each of which can be clicked to display the dozen points of the Fat!So? manifesto. "The revolution starts with a simple question: You're fat! So what? There's nothing wrong with being fat. Just like there's nothing wrong with being short or tall or black or brown. These are facts of identity that cannot and should not be changed. They are birthright. They're beyond aesthetics. They provide the diversity we need to survive.... Large, big-boned, heavy, overweight, chubby, zaftig, voluptuous, Rubenesque, plump, and obese are all synonyms for fear."

☐ *About Fat Acceptance*
   http://www.bayarea.net/~stef/fat.html

☐ *Amazon's Arena*
   http://www.globalmark.com/globalmark/amarena.html

☐ *Anvil Dungeon*
   http://www.anvildungeon.com/

☐ *Big Difference*
http://www.kaiwan.com/~bigdiff/

☐ *Fat Girl*
http://www.fatgirl.com/fatgirl/

☐ *Fat!So?*
http://www.fatso.com/

☐ *Largesse, The Network for Size Esteem*
http://www.fatgirl.com/fatgirl/largesse/

☐ *National Organization to Advance Fat Acceptance*
http://naafa.org/

☐ *Queer 'Zine Explosion*
http://www.qrd.org/qrd/www/media/print/queerzine.explosion/new.

☐ *Yahoo! Fat Acceptance Directory*
http://www.yahoo.com/Society_and_Culture/Size_Issues/Fat_Accep

Gardening

Gay or straight, all of the most interesting people have some connection with gardening—whether it's a suburban plot, an urban window box, or an oh-so-chic orchid on the mantel. Plants are pretty, therapeutic, civilized, and practical. And there's a bumper crop of information about them online.

For queer gardeners, one place to start is Gay Gardens and Gay Gardeners, where you'll find a (growing) links list to green-thumbed gays and lesbians. It opens with nicely ironic graphics, big fat lavender pansies, and along with information on the club activities around Amsterdam, it will point you to FOTE (Fruits of the Earth) and other American sites such as Alex and Jeff's home page, which has a picture-filled section on their semitropical garden in Florida. Chase-Cross Garden is a very literate gardeners' page with a beautifully written history of how Messrs. Chase and Cross created an award-winning garden from "a pile of rubble and a rickety picket fence" in Nova Scotia. Chris and Stephen's Garden page is a sort of cyberwalk through a beautiful garden in Northern California. Den of Dreams is Rand B. Lee's page; he's coeditor and cofounder of *The American Cottage Gardener*, so you can imagine the knowledge to be gained.

Lesbian Gardens

Lesbian gardens? "Now there's a name to conjure up some interesting mental images. Everybody knows what to expect when they visit a rose garden, herb garden or vegetable garden, but what might we expect to find in a lesbian garden?" LG is a wonderful site humorous site with gardening links, potting shed chat, "witches' potions" and lots more, including the home pages of the lesbian gardens mailing list.

Gay & Organic!

To find an organic gay gardening page is almost to much to wish for but there are two great ones. Scut's Garden is the most detailed gay gardening page of all, with pictures, tips on everything from pests to finding seeds and reaching the goal of an all-organic garden. The range of links is pretty amazing (even one for disabled gardeners) and though the text is often geared to his area (the Pacific Northwest), there's plenty for gardeners in any climate. Another excellent choice is on Ruralgay.Com by Zintis, a professional gardener in New York state who gives weekly updates on what's happening throughout the growing season and talks about seeds and catalogs off-season. He's a cautious gardener and frugal in his methods (he saves seeds up to two years and gives tips on all sorts of things, including how to check seed viability) but he's extravagant with gardening advice on how he's shaped his own cut-flower business into a thriving one.

Garden Spider's Web

Though the author's sexual orientation is unmentioned, one of the friendliest, best-informed sites is the Garden Spider's Web. The general tone is one you'd expect from a calm, rather talkative dirt-digging plant lover. It's as if your neighbor, the one with the enviable garden, decided to peel off her gloves and give you some advice.

The contents include the Cyber-Plantsman, an online magazine for the serious gardener that lets you in on some of the more interesting—though less-heard-from—plants, people, books, events and organizations. The GardenWeb Forums allow you to tap the collective wisdom of this page's readers; you can post queries on plant care and sources or initiate a discussion on a particular topic. Garden Tips from Sesbania Tripeti answers specific questions on watering, pest management, soil composition, and starting seeds. Wild-Flowers offers a wealth of information about what's available, both online and off, and a handy state index makes it easy to see which places and events can be found in your area. The site also has two forums for wildflower enthusiasts, one on meadows and prairies and another on woodlands.

The Garden Exchange is a place where gardeners can post requests for seeds and plants as well as offers of items for trade. This is the place to try to find that unusual tomato hybrid or maybe that night-blooming daylily you've heard about but never seen.

Next are lists and links of solid horticulture information, most supplied by the many universities online. Here you can find the cure for what's bugging your garden or how to grow a scent border. You'll also come across links to magazines, books, catalogs, and a wealth of newsgroups discussing those plants that are particular to your climate.

The Garden Gate has a similar across-the-back-fence tone. This is a commercial site that provides serious information on related links and offers gardeners a well-organized, incredibly deep library of botanical news—from tips on dealing with cyclamen mites to the regal history of roses. There are also guides to newsgroups where people talk and share information on their gardening passions.

These two sites are terrifically extensive, but you might also want to check out What's Coming Into Bloom? and the Yahoo! Guide. And the Web page of *Hortus* magazine can't be recommended too highly. *Hortus* is quirky, obsessive, and very English. Its writers resolutely avoid personal chitchat, unlike the French magazines. And contrary to American magazines, you'll never be patronized. *Hortus* is unique, and it's a very chic addition to your bookmarks. Anyone who knows the difference between a geranium and a pelargonium will be impressed.

☐ *American Horticultural Society*
   http://eMall.com/ahs/ahs.html

☐ *The Chase-Cross Garden*
http://is.dal.ca/~chase/dgarden.html

☐ *Cool Owl's Page*
http://dovenetq.net.au/~coolowl/

☐ *Daisy in Donnybrook*
http://www.iinet.net.au/~daisy

☐ *Den of Dreams*
http://www.geocities.com/WestHollywood/2903/

☐ *Federation of Gay Gardeners*
http://members.aol.com/gardenfed/index.html

☐ *Fruits of the Earth (FOTE)*
http://www.geocities.com/WestHollywood/Heights/3824/

☐ *Garden Gate*
http://www.prairienet.org/garden-gate/

☐ *Garden Kathe*
http://members.aol.com/gardkath/page1.html

☐ *Gardening Hotline*
http://www.deltanet.com/allstar/garden.htm

☐ *Gardening List WWW*
http://www.cog.brown.edu:80/gardening/

☐ *GardenNet*
http://www.trine.com/GardenNet/

☐ *Garden Spider's Web*
http://www.gardenweb.com/spdrsweb/

☐ *Gardening.Com*
http://www.gardening.com

☐ *The Gay Garden Club*
http://www.gardenweb.com/directory/ggc2/

☐ *Glenda's Lovely Cottage Garden*
http://www.mindspring.com/~honorine/garden/invasive.html

☐ *Hortus*
www.hortus.co.uk

☐ *Internet Garden*
http://www.internetgarden.co.uk/index.htm

☐ *Lesbian Gardens*
http://www.algonet.se/~davies/

☐ *Lesbian Gardeners*
http://www.gaycanada.com/womonspace/may99.html

☐ *The NY Lesbian & Gay Community Center Garden*
http://www.gaycenter.org/garden.html

☐ *Puget Sound Gay Gardeners*
http://weber.u.washington.edu/~bbeer/gaygard.html

☐ *Queer Living Gardening Corner*
http://www.geocities.com/WestHollywood/Heights/3000/garden.html

☐ *Ruralgay.com Gardening*
http://www.ruralgay.com/zintis.asp

☐ *Scut's Garden*
http://www.teleport.com/~scut/garden.htm

☐ *What's Coming Into Bloom?*
http://www.prairienet.org/garden-gate/whatsnew.htm

☐ *Yahoo!: Recreation: Home and Garden: Gardening*
http://www.yahoo.com/Recreation/Home_and_Garden/Gardening/

Generation X

Yes, *Generation X* is a sorry name for those born in the 1970s, but *baby boomers* isn't much better. To meet your peers, or to just keep up, there are a number of interesting sites, none of which fall neatly within the usually pejorative Generation X characterization of "slacker." Thousands of questions are answered, analyzed, and occasionally mocked at one of the world's great Gen X hangouts: www.lonelyplanet.com. It's mixed sexually (that's part of being modern) and is itself a branch of a huge electronic bulletin board called the Thorn Tree which receives 2 million hits and 6,000 posts a month. Subjects range from obscure travel questions on bus schedules in South America to "Slack Girls" to dealing with a "Peggy Lee moment (Is that all there is?)."

As you browse around you'll find that 20-something gay men and lesbians are not scuttling off into separate spaces; they're operatives in all of the activist groups and online magazines, and they have built some of the most interesting digital spaces. They're also responsible for a disproportionately large chunk of home pages that typically urge the less digitally adept (read: older generation) to get online. Sure, TV and pop iconography are ubiquitous, but the online gay youth quake is not creating a community outside the mainstream of gay and lesbian interests.

X-Zines

If there's one area where Generation X'ers seem most thickly concentrated, it's among 'zines, that new hive of the publishing world. It makes sense that they would gravitate to this high-tech business since they're the first generation with computer skills. Among 'zine links, the largest is Queer Zine Explosion, followed closely by Ezine Listings and online Zines. What will you find? Odd-sounding publications like *MUZ*, *Gurl*, and others with willfully playful titles like *Happy Gay Place*, *Sassy Femme*, and *Queer Nasty*.

Queer Nasty

Queer Nasty is a lot of things, the first of which is idealistic. "*Queer Nasty* is a 'zine dedicated to radical thought and intelligent humor. We are tired of being forced to conform to an image of how others think we should be. This includes religious freaks and breeders, as well as those in the 'lesbigay' community who think that we are 'harming' them  by our actions.... *Queer Nasty* is devoted to ending homophobia, queer-phobia, bi-phobia, and tranny-phobia within the so-called gay community." But don't laugh or smile patronizingly; they have a plan and a 'zine that can compete with any other.

So what's on the menu? Lots of terrific stuff—like a guide to being a gay man in the 1990s, an exposé about sex with straight men, a proclamation of basic sexual rights, and an article on the state of queer activism today. For an excellent list of hot links on the youth list, *Queer Nasty*'s is the best. There's also humor, such as a collection of naughty nursery rhymes: "Jack be nimble, Jack be quick, Jack me off and suck my dick." Not quite genius caliber, but clever and subversive (or just sane?) like the entire 'zine.

Sometimes the laughs in Generation X sites are coal-black, such as the links list at Killer Klicks to a page that includes "proof" of Bert's (*Sesame Street*) friendship with Jeffrey Dahmer. Bert cheerfully asks, "How's the meat this season?" Don't look for respect in these 'zines or even much tolerance. The venerable Queer Resources Directory is dismissed as "tired." Instead you'll find a fascination with music, computers, tools, and philosophies freed from the deadweight of previous generations' foul-ups.

Cyber Grrls & Gen-X Bears

Less ironic, but equally in tune with the zeitgeist are CyberGrrls and Gen-X Bears. CG is an all-modern, all-grrl community site with tips and guidance for getting the most from the Web. Gen-X Bears reflects polls showing that this generation is one of the more spiritually-minded to come along this century. Their mission is inclusive: "Gen-X Bears shall not be discriminatory based on age, race, religion, national origin, physical or mental ability, physical stature, sex, sexual orientation, sexual identification, or any other classification which can act as a precedent to divide people."

Naturally enough, some of the best sources of Generation X information are the gay and lesbian university and college organizations. Most concentrate on student life, with articles on issues like censorship, politics, coming out, money, and career choice (see page 166, Colleges and Universities).

☐ *Blair, The Mag for Modern Fags*
http://www.blairmag.com/

☐ *Boys2Men*
http://www.boys2men.com/

☐ *Brave New Tick*
http://www.tickcentral.com/

☐ *CGX: Conservative Generation X*
http://www.cgx.com/

☐ *Ezine Listings*
http://www.meer.net/~johnl/e-zine-list/

☐ *FAQ*
http://www.youth.org/ssyglb/ssyglb-faq.html

☐ *Gender, Sex, and Sexuality*
http://www.ccnet.com/~lafond/sex.htm

☐ *GenX Bears*
  http://www.genxbears.org/

☐ *Happy Gay Place Lead or Leave*
  http://www.cs.caltech.edu/~adam/lead.html

☐ *H2Homo*
  http://www.indword.com/H2oMO/h2omo.html

☐ *MUZ (Queerpunk)*
  http://www.jett.com/

☐ *Mayhem.net*
  http://www.mayhem.net/mendoza.html

☐ *Online Zines*
  http://www.etext.org/Zines/

☐ *OutRight*
  http://outright.com

☐ *The Other Queer Page*
  http://www.qworld.org/friends/toqp/

☐ *PFLAG*
  http://abacus.oxy.edu/QRD/orgs/PFLAG/

☐ *OUTREACH*
  http://www.also.org.au/outreach/

☐ *Planet SOMA*
  http://www.best.com/~dgwynn/

☐ *Queer InfoServers*
  http://www.infoqueer.org/queer/qis/

☐ *QIS—College and University Gay and Lesbian Information List*
http://www.infoqueer.org/queer/qis/college.html

☐ *Q Planet*
http://qplanet.com

☐ *QRD—College and University Organizations List*
http://www.qrd.org/qrd/orgs/glb.campus.worldwide

☐ *Queer Nasty*
http://www.tripnet.com/q-nasty

☐ *Queer Zine Explosion*
http://www.io.com/~larrybob/hotlist.html

☐ *SassyFemme*
http://www.txdirect.net/~sassyfem

☐ *SheScape*
http://www.shescape.com/

☐ *Slack Girls Live*
http://www.girlspace.com/

☐ *Slacker Stories*
http://www.ice.net/~nehring/slacker/1.htm

☐ *Stanford Queer Resources*
http://www-leland.stanford.edu/group/QR/

☐ *Student Pride USA*
http://www.studentalliance.org/PrideUSA.htm

☐ *Tight Bluejeans*
http://members.gnn.com/ratpye/denim.htm

☐ *U Report*
http://www.ureport.com/ureport

☐ *Welcome to CAM*
http://hwbbs.gbgm-umc.org/

☐ *XY Magazine*
http://www.xy.com

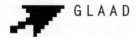 GLAAD

Quietly, but with tremendous force, the Gay and Lesbian Alliance Against Defamation has worked wonders since its founding in 1985. Its victories include persuading Hallmark Cards to delete "lesbian" from its list of offensive words, convincing NYNEX and Pacific Bell Yellow Pages to agree to include a new Gay and Lesbian Organizations section, pressuring ABC to let Ellen "out," and challenging InterNIC for allowing the registration of the domain name "godhatesfags.com." The list goes on and on, with a concentration on raising awareness of the general media to obvious and subtle forms of homophobia..

Based on the belief that culture and media carry hugely important messages, GLAAD has accomplished these feats of sanity without pressing a single lawsuit, endorsing candidates, or arranging lobbying trips to various seats of power. They're shoulder-to-shoulder with the shouters, but they have a different attack method.

GLAAD has expanded its reach to the World Wide Web with a home page explaining its mission and current efforts. The graphics are spartan, but that's not the point. GLAAD is using the high profile provided by the Web to redouble its efforts to "keep contacting those individuals and companies that are helping to shape the attitudes and form the ideas in our country. There is a need for continual gay and lesbian reaction to the events that are shaping our lives and our future. Communication is one of our most effective tools."

The page has lots of alerts to homophobia in media across the country, whether they be in newspapers, on television and movies, or in judicial decisions. These can be sent in by anyone through filling out a simple form. Are you watching a news report on television or reading an article in your newspaper and are angered by homophobic coverage? Did your favorite television show have a gay character on it? Has the Radical Right placed an article in your local newspaper? Alert GLAAD!

There's also a list of alerts to such things as celebrities coming out, to articles on teaching tolerance in schools, and antigay bills in Congress as well as a persistent coverage of "don't ask, don't tell." You can sign up for the mail list providing these as well as join the online opinion forum for members to discuss media representations of the lesbian, gay, bisexual, and transgendered community.

So who are these cultural watchdogs? As the late Craig Davidson, the first executive director of GLAAD's chapter in New York, said, "GLAAD was founded in 1985 to fight the defamation of lesbians and gays and their enforced invisibility in the popular culture." Read, join, and inform yourself.

For a little activist stardust, don't miss the alerts to upcoming films and TV shows with gay and lesbian themes or featuring gay and lesbian characters.

☐ *GLAAD*
  http://www.glaad.org/

☐ *Exploiting Media Opportunities—How To Make Sure Lavender News is Black & White and Read All Over*
  http://www.glaad.org/glaad/electronic/online-resources.html

☐ *Queer Infoserver's Media Page*
  http://www.infoqueer.org/queer/qis/media.html

☐ *Queer Resources Directory's Media Page*
  http://www.qrd.org/qrd/media

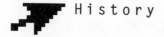 History

"Looking at any history textbook one would think that never has a society praised the love of man for man, never has a painter or poet or pope shared his bed and his heart with another male. Such evidence is quietly ignored, as with the Greco-Roman period, or quickly destroyed, as Europeans have done since the early days of the invasion with Inca and Mayan art depicting homoerotic themes." This excerpt from the introduction of the Androphile site is typical of the new vigor of gay and lesbian history Web pages—queers are rediscovering their past and unearthing historical facts and documents that prove we've shaped every facet of society and loved each other since the beginning. It's exciting and bold and for perhaps no other subject has the "Web effect" been as powerful.

You can experience Greenwich Village and the Castro in the '70s as well as read the unabridged truth about queer life in Greece, medieval times or the Victorian days, when the first activists began speaking out. "We're here, we're queer, get used to it" suddenly has an antique ring when you visit the Androphile page and click on any area of the globe to see an ancient fresco of two men embracing and read a translation of their love poems from the original Mayan, Chinese, or African languages. An entire multigenerational, multigeographical society of same-sex–loving men and women are emerging from the traditional heterosexist chronicle. Even "God's word" is coming in for revision in the Calendar of Lesbian, Gay, Bisexual, and Transgender Saints: "History involves an excavation and reading of what the past means for us today. Thus, while we have virtually no knowledge about St. Sebastian, he has been the subject of a homoerotic cult for so many centuries that it would be absurd to omit him."

If there is one place to begin, it's with Paul Halsall's People With A History. It's a combination of narrative and links on queer history from the Ancient Mediterranean, Medieval Worlds, Europe to World War I, Europe Since World War I, Africa, Asia, Latin America, Oceania, and North America. Each section is divided into subsets and given an introduction; so if you're interested in Native Americans, for example, you can read about the tradition allowing children to choose their gender. "A male child who chose female clothes, for instance, would be raised as a female, and would marry a man." Wherever you land you'll come across similarly fascinating information written in a clear, energetic style. And always, there's an extensive bibliography for further inquiry.

Whether the history page you're reading has a tight focus (gays in the Holocaust, Lesbians in the 17th century, Daughters of Bilitis, Weimar Germany, Gay Youth in '20s Miami) or ranges over the centuries, there's an urgency in all the writing, a distinct lack of arid noninvolvement. Some of this is in reaction to our previous invisibility and a rebuttal to the virulence of modern homophobia. For example, though he's as careful to cite resources as the most scrupulous academic, Halsall is not of the "objective" school of historians, particularly as he draws nearer recent times. About ACT UP he writes, "For all the toughness, for all the beatings its members received from the police, no ACT UP member resorted to violence. But more, in the 1980s, an age when college kids around the United States asserted that their highest goal was 'to join a financial planning corporation,' ACT UP members demonstrated again and again that there is meaning in human lives."

Gay Games

The fire in most gay history pages is not always so overt. In the story of the Gay Games, for instance, WebCastro simply lays out the facts and lets the outrage speak for itself. In 1992 the United States Olympic Committee obtained an injunction in federal court prohibiting the use of the word "Olympic." The USOC had ignored the use of the ancient word by Special Olympics, Police Olympics, Nude Olympics, Dog Olympics, and others."

Modern History

Among the many excellent history sites are New York City, a gay history which details bar history from Chelsea to Harlem;

1970s Lesbian Feminism, which gives an overview of that exciting period; the Gay Liberation Front is described at Anglefire (as are many other aspects of gay history) and there are many more fascinating pages, including excellent studies on John Addington Symonds and Karl Ullrichs. Ullrichs coined the term "Uranism" and was the first to claim homosexuality was "normal." The site is packed with Ullrichs's writings, his biography, and a timeline as well as other information on the pioneers of gay history including Magnus Hirschfeld.

Timelines

Gayhistory.com is an introduction to the stories and the people of modern gay history from 1700 to 1973. Among other things you'll see the pendulum of acceptance swing from the tolerance of the late 18th century, when Pennsylvania dropped the death penalty and France decriminalized pederasty, to a slow move to restriction over the next century as doctors begin to medicalize sex.

For another overview, try Frank Bruni's Timeline, which measures the increasing visibility of gays in modern times. He tells, among other things, how Massachusetts Congressman Barney Frank was outed, when the nation's largest union came out for gay rights, and of that startling night when Torch Song won the Tony and the producer thanked his gay lover. For more recent victories see a compilation of last year's progress at the GLBT Accomplishments page with examples of the slow but steady diminution of homophobia: Over 200 state and local governments (representing one third of the US population) now have laws banning antigay discrimination.

Religious History

The history of gays and lesbians within a religious context is inextricably tied to homophobia (many of the history pages have links to radical religious homophobes). You can find sites on Pope John Paul II's "war" on homosexuals, a fascinating article on the black clergy's resistance to gay rights (an article by Henry Louis Gates in the New Yorker) as well as a long list of the struggles of the Metropolitan Community Church, Baptists, and Episcopalians. Recently debuting on the Web is Johnny Abush's Jewish GLB Archives. It's a fascinating and huge compilation of material that Abush began after an AIDS diagnosis prompted him to reconsider his origins as a member of two persecuted minorities. Contents include profiles of gay rabbis, a newsletter and mailing lists, and a guide to biographies and memoirs—as well as the light side of things on the Joke Page.

Lesbian History

Doubly hidden by homophobia and a patriarchal society, lesbian history pages are finally coming to light. The Lesbian History Project ambitiously attempts to tell the full story of lesbians from ancient to modern times. Both a researcher's tool and a public fact sheet, the list of notable lesbians is huge and contains many links to women of note from Midge Costanza (a White House aide in the Carter administration) to Frida Kahlo. There's also an archive of oral histories, articles and interviews, quotations, and a long list of links to other lists, people, and resources related to lesbian history.

Swade's Tribal Voice has a similar list of lesbian heroines, from Sappho to Judith, Queen of Falasha, to Ma Rainey along with notes on events like that of 1896, when two actresses first kissed on an American stage—with ushers standing ready to douse shocked patrons back to consciousness. The June L. Mazer Collection, though bereft of images, tells about fascinating collections of personal letters and scrapbooks, lesbian artwork, manuscripts, books, records, newspapers, magazines, photographs, videotapes, fliers, papers of lesbian organizations, private papers, and even clothing, such as softball uniforms from the 1940s and '50s. The Lesbian Herstory Archives of New York City, the largest and oldest Lesbian archive in the world, has one of the deepest collections of obscure lesbian and feminist periodicals and books. Chances are they've got that illusive issue you've been looking for. Diotoma and Joan Korenman's pages are scholarly sites packed with the history of women and gender with links to many online articles, book reviews, databases, and images.

Archives

There are many other academic archives and libraries of gay and lesbian history. New York Public Library Gay and Lesbian Studies has been collecting materials about lesbian and gay populations since 1911. The ONE Institute International Gay and Lesbian Archives (ONE/IGLA) houses one of the world's largest research libraries on gay, lesbian, bisexual, and transgendered concerns. The Human Sexuality Collection at Cornell University Library is a collection of texts, films, artwork, erotica, legal briefs, private correspondence, and diaries concerned with gay life and significant events in the American gay rights movement since World War II. The James C. Hormel Gay and Lesbian Center and Collections documents lesbian and gay history and culture by collecting, preserving, and providing material on all aspects of the lesbian, gay, bisexual, and transgendered experience.

The Kinsey Report

With 1998 the 50th anniversary of the Kinsey Report's volcanic finding that ten percent of the world's people were gay or lesbian, it seems appropriate to drop in. You won't be able to do much except look through the digital gates. There are only a few images from the archives and just tantalizing descriptions of what may be the largest collection of queer history in the world: over 7,000 works of art, 75,000 photographs, 80,000 books, journals, and scientific articles, 6,500 reels of film and the 18,000 interviews. The institute's founder, Alfred Kinsey, once said, "We are recorders and reporters of facts—not judges of the behavior we describe."

Ancient History

Jumping back a few thousand years, visit Queer Mummies! to read about the discovery of an Egyptian burial chamber that contained the remains of two gay lovers. The pictures are at once ancient and modern. Two men (slaves to a pharoah, it is supposed), drawn in the Egyptian style of single-eye profile, embrace in poses that recall their love three millennia ago.

Another view of the historical past is Homosexuality in Ancient Greece, a paper that explains its subject's importance for modern-day queers: "Ancient Greek culture accepted same-sex love as an integral part of military, athletic, and ceremonial life. Our exploration of same-sex sexuality in a social historical context empowers the lesbian and gay communities as the debate surrounding service in the military, protection against discrimination, adoption rights, and legalized same-sex marriages continues."

History of Origins

If you're interested in the latest studies on genetic and behaviorist factors, go to Queer Frontiers. This academic organization hosts studies on queer origins. Other sites that deal with the current and past perceptions of origins are the Nature Vs. Nurture page and the Gerber/Hart Library and Archives. To find books on gay history or gay language, see Gregory Ward's bibliography page. Titles include Dyke Diction: The Language of Lesbians, Kinks and Queens, Terminology for Gays, and A Glossary of Homosexuality.

Culture

For literally hundreds of other papers on queer origins and culture, see the QRD. Titles include "Born That Way," "Gay Sheep—Gay Brains," "Homosexuality and Genetics," and the famous Kinsey scale that first reported that ten percent of the population is homosexual. As you browse the QRD storehouse, you'll come across surprising findings. In the Yankelovich survey of gays in the United States, studies show that (among many misconceptions) the idea that demographically, queers are the richest group, is false. There's also a pointer to the entire text of *With Down Cast Gays*, a privately printed book from England in 1972 which was one of the first widely read critiques of gay life by gays. It's described as "seminal" by the QRD and is very much of the *Boys In the Band* period, but at the time it gave voice to a gagged world.

International Sites

Histories of gays and lesbians are not limited to American sites by any means. The National Women's History Project has an exhaustive list on links to sites in all the European countries along with Japan, Poland, the United States, Canada, and Mexico. Make sure and see "Goodbye to Berlin? 100 years of Gay Activism" in Germany. England is by far the richest repository. Along with comprehensive sites such as the Hall Carpenter Archives there're lots of links to extraordinary minutiae; at least eight links to studies of "Polari," a gay slang language, which has now almost died out. Read the definitions list for nostalgia—you'll recognize the vocabulary of an older, forcibly secretive generation, many borrowed from Italian and French.

Famous Queers

There are at least five Web pages naming famous queers in history: the Blacklist, Out List, Famous Queers Index, Lesbian History Project, and Reclaiming History. All the usual suspects are here (Homer, Sappho, Leonardo da Vinci, Oscar Wilde), along with living exemplars like Edward Albee, John Rechy, and James Earl Hardy.

Queers in History is the most scholarly list of who "Was...Might have been...Probably was...Could have...and Certainly appears to have been Gay in the last 5,000 years." Reclaiming History has pictures along with short biographies not only of avowed homos but some who we claim by circumstantial evidence. The biography on Francis Bacon includes stories of his love of young Welsh houseboys and the essay on Emily Dickinson, points out that many of her poems exist in two versions—with alternate sets of pronouns.

One of the most interesting historical figure pages is on John Addington Symonds, the first modern historian of (male) homosexuality, and the first advocate of gay liberation in Britain. Rictor Norton's site is a fascinating compilation of his memoirs, criticism, and poetry.

Harvey Milk

Ten years after publication, Randy Shilts's book *The Mayor of Castro Street* remains a best-seller. To see why, visit the sites dedicated to Harvey Milk. The Forgotten Populist gives a short biography of Milk, emphasizing his political achievements. The Mayor of Castro Street covers the short but dramatic arc of Milk's life through contemporary photos and text. I Remember Harvey is the personal reminiscence of Ron Williams, who gives a wonderfully evocative picture of the era—and whose memories of Milk are filtered through his own life as a gay man. "I remember the hair, pony tail, strong eyes and friendly handshake. I was very apathetic toward politics; my interests were in sex, drugs, and rock 'n' roll, and I thought Harvey was just another political radical exploiting the gay vote." This page contains excerpts from four of Milk's speeches, in addition to a transcript of a tape marked "Play only in the event of assassination."

Rainbow Flag

No history of gays and lesbians would be worth its spangles without mention of the rainbow flag. Steven W. Anderson's article in *Gaze* magazine, reprinted at the Rainbow Flag site, is one of the best: "The first Rainbow Flag was designed in 1978 by Gilbert Baker, a San Francisco artist, who created the flag in response to a local activist's call for a community symbol. (This was before the pink triangle was popularly used as a symbol of pride.)...In November 1978, San Francisco's gay community was stunned when the city's first openly gay supervisor, Harvey Milk, was assassinated....Wishing to demonstrate the gay community's strength and solidarity in the aftermath of this tragedy, the 1979 Pride Parade Committee decided to use Baker's flag....The Rainbow Flag reminds us that ours is a diverse community—composed of people with a variety of individual tastes of which we should all be proud."

Gay & Lesbian History Month

Perhaps the most public project working to lift the shroud over queer history is found at the Lesbian and Gay History Month site, which is collating the histories of many activist groups and academics (including GLAAD, HRCF, GLA, Project 10, Project 21, and the American Historical Association Committee on Lesbian and Gay History). Read the essay by Vicki L. Eaklor: "Moving forward may demand a closer look at where we have been...without visibility there is no history and no movement.... History can offer examples from which to draw strength, to imitate, or avoid.... Is this history an agenda? Of course. Knowledge always serves someone's agenda, and for too long it has served those few already in power, already with a voice. Now that we have heard and seen, let's not just learn our history, but learn how to be part of it. It's there. It's ours. We deserve it."

☐ *African Same Sex Love*
http://www-rci.rutgers.edu/~lcrew/africa.html

☐ *AIDS History Project Collection*
http://www.library.ucsf.edu/sc/ahp/

☐ *Alan Turing*
http://www.wadham.ox.ac.uk/~ahodges/Turing.html

☐ *Although it was hot from the late '52 on...*
http://www.conterra.com/jsears/writjew.htm

☐ *Ancient Spirituality of Gallae and Amazons
(Transgender History)*
http://www.azstarnet.com/~gallae/gallae.htm

☐ *Aphra Behn*
http://www.sappho.com/poetry/historical/a_behn.html
http://wwwprometheus.cc.emory.edu/behn/index.html

☐ *Archives Gaies Du Quebec*
http://www.er.uqam.ca/nobel/c2220/agq.html

☐ *Audre Lourde*
http://www.lamda.net/~maximum/lourde.html

☐ *Austin Lesbian Activists of the '70s Herstory
Project (ALA)*
http://m2.monsterbit.com/water/ala.html

☐ *Bear History Project*
http://www.tiac.net/users/codybear/bear.htm

☐ *Bibliography of Studies of Gay and Lesbian
Language*
http://www.ling.nwu.edu/~ward/gaybib.html

☐ *Blacklist*
http://www.udel.edu/nero/lists/blacklist.html

☐ *Canadian Lesbian and Gay Archives*
http://www.web.net/archives/

☐ *Castro Sweep*
http://members.aol.com/sfpdriot/sweep.html

☐ *Clan Blue Feather*
http://www.locksley.com/locksley/hh/bluef.htm#contact

☐ *Famous Homos*
http://www.panix.com/~glyph/cb/famhomos.htm

☐ *Famous Homosexuals ThroughOUT Herstory*
http://www.panix.com/~glyph/cb/FamHomos.htm

☐ *Famous Queers, Queens, and Dykes*
http://www.efn.org/~mastrait/famousqueers.html

☐ *FBI Files: J. Edgar Hoover*
http://www.thesmokinggun.com/archive/hoover1.html

☐ *France: Memorial for Homosexual Deportation*
http://www.france.qrd.org/fqrd/assocs/mdh/mdh.html

☐ *Frank Bruni's Timeline*
http://www.tcp.com:8000/qrd/culture/queer.timeline-FRANK.BRUNI

☐ *FTMs in History*
http://www.geocities.com/westhollywood/village/5855

☐ *Gay Culture and History*
http://www.qrd.org/qrd/culture

☐ *The Gay Film List*
http://www.cs.cmu.edu/afs/andrew.cmu.edu/usr/out/public/Filmlist

☐ *GayHistory.com*
http://www.gayhistory.com

☐ *Gay in America: 1996*
http://www.sfgate.com/examiner/special/gia/1996/part-1/

☐ *Gay and Lesbian Historical Society of Northern California*
http://www.glhs.org

☐ *Gay & Les Themes in Hispanic Literature*
http://wanda.pond.com/~stevecap/la000001.htm

☐ *GLBT Library/Archives of Philadelphia*
http://wanda.pond.com/~stevecap/la000001.htm

☐ *Gays, Lesbians and Bisexuals in History*
http://www.cs.cmu.edu/afs/cs.cmu.edu/user/scotts/bulgarians/history-pg.html

☐ *Gay and Lesbian Archives of the Pacific Northwest*
http://www.teleport.com/~caliburn/glapn/

☐ *Gay and Lesbian Historical Society of Northern California*
http://www.glhs.org/

☐ *Gay & Lesbian Language*
http://www.ling.nwu.edu/~ward/gaybib.html

☐ *Gay Liberation Front*
http://www.angelfire.com/on2glf2000/

☐ *Gay Medieval History*
http://www.qrd.org/qrd/culture/gay.medieval.history

☐ *Gay & Lesbian Milestones on TV*
http://www.religioustolerance.org/hom_0042.htm

☐ *Gay and Lesbian Regional History (especially the American South)*
http://www.jtsears.com/history.htm

☐ *Gay and Lesbian Themes in Hispanic Literature and Cultures*
http://www.cc.columbia.edu/cu/libraries/events/sw25/case9.html

☐ *Gay Milestones in Entertainment History*
http://www.as.wvu.edu/~thumm/milestones.html

☐ *Gerber/Hart Library and Archives*
http://www.gerberhart.org/

☐ *GLBT History Quiz*
http://www.datalounge.com/trudy-cgi-bin/glaad-history.pl

☐ *Goodbey to Berlin? 100 Years of Gay Activism*
http://www.gayactivism.com/

☐ *Gregory Ward's LGB Bibliography*
http://www.ling.nwu.edu/~ward/gaybib.html

☐ *Hall-Carpenter Archives*
http://www.lse.ac.uk/blpes/archives/hallpag.htm
http://www.adpa.mdx.ac.uk/services/ilrs/hca/presscut.htm

☐ *Harvey Milk*
http://www.echonyc.com/~xxxfruit/

☐ *Harvey Milk*
http://www.kqed.org/cell/neighborhoods/castro/harveymilk.html

☐ *Harvey Milk, Hero and Martyr*
http://www.kqed.org/Cell/neighborhoods/castro/harveymilk.html

☐ *HM (Execution of Justice)*
http://www.randy.com/executionofjustice/

☐ *HM (Forgotten Populist)*
http://www.hicom.net/~oedipus/milk.html

☐ *HM (I Remember Harvey)*
http://webcastro.com/harvey.htm

☐ *HM (Mayor of Castro Street)*
http://www.best.com/~dgwynn/sf1970/scene/harvey.html

☐ *Halsall, Paul (homepage)*
http://www.bway.net/~halsall/home.html

☐ *Herstory: Lesbians in the Arts*
http://www.geocities.com/soho/suite/9048/herstory1.html

☐ *High Points in Lesbian History*
http://www.mindspring.com/~swade/les_hist.htm

☐ *Historic Lesbian Couples*
http://www.geocities.com/woodyandpat

☐ *Historical Lesbian Couples*
http://www.mindspring.com/~swade/les_hist.htm

☐ *History of the Gay Bath Houses*
http://www.geocities.com/westhollywood/cafe/8767/

☐ *History of the Gay Games*
http://www.backdoor.com/CASTRO/Gaygames.html

☐ *History of Homosexuality*
http://www.qrd.org/qrd/culture/history.of.homosexuality

☐ *History of Homosexuality History*
http://www.cc.columbia.edu/cu/libraries/events/sw25/case5.html

☐ *History of the Transgender Forum on AOL*
http://members.aol.com/onqgwen/history.html

☐ *History/Herstory*
http://www.im1ru12.org/TOQP/hisherstory.html

☐ *Homodok [The Netherlands]*
http://www.dds.nl/~gldocu/hdkeng.htm

☐ *Homosexuality in Ancient Greece*
http://www.well.com/user/assaf/HiAG.html

☐ *Homosexuals in Government*
http://www.english.upenn.edu/~afilreis/50s/gays-in-govt.html

☐ *Human Sexuality Collection, Cornell University Library*
http://rmc.library.cornell.edu/Division-Info/rmc-hsc/rmc-hsc.html

☐ *Human Sexuality Library, University of Washington*
http://weber.u.washington.edu/~sfpse/ftpsite.html

☐ *Inventing Queer Space*
http://www.eagles.bbs.net.au/~marcg/Queer-pl.html

☐ *Jewish GLBT Archives Online*
http://www.magic.ca/~faygelah/Index.html

☐ *James C. Hormel Gay and Lesbian Center*
http://nick.sfpl.lib.ca.us/glcenter/homeonly.htm

☐ *Joan Korenman (Diotoma)*
http://www-unix.umbc.edu/~korenman/wmst/links.html

☐ *John Addington Symonds*
http://www.infopt.demon.co.uk/symfram1.htm

☐ *June L. Mazer Lesbian Collection*
http://www.lesbian.org/mazer/index.html

☐ *Karl Heinrich Ulrichs (Celebration 2000)*
http://www.angelfire.com/f13/celebration2000

☐ *Kinsey Institute*
http://www.indiana.edu/~kinsey

☐ *Leyland Publication (Sunshine Press)*
http://www.gaysunshine.com/article_leyland.html

☐ *Lesbian Archive and Information Centre*
http://www.quine.org.uk/resources/glasgow_womens_library/

☐ *Lesbian Avengers in Action*
http://summit.stanford.edu/~rory/lesbians.txt

☐ *Lesbian & Gay History Month*
http://www.glaad.org/glaad/history-month/

☐ *Lesbian History Archives*
http://wwwdatalounge.net/network/pages.lha

☐ *Lesbian History Project*
http://www-lib.usc.edu/~retter/main.html

☐ *Lesbian Tribal Voice Swade's History*
http://www.swade.net/swadepages/les_hist.htm

☐ *Los Angeles Lesbian History 1970-1990*
http://www-lib.usc.edu/~retter/chrono.html

☐ *Magnus Hirschfield*
http://www.angelfire.com/f13/celecbration2000/

☐ *Martin Duberman Papers [At NYPL]*
http://web.nypl.org/research/chss/spe/rbk/faids/dubmain.html

☐ *Marvel Library of Congress GLB Resources*
gopher://marvel.loc.gov/11/global/socsci/area/gay

☐ *Mining Co. Gay/Lesbian Issues/ History*
http://gaylesissues.miningco.com/

☐ *Most Frequently Banned Books in the '90s*
http://www.cs.cmu.edu/%7Espok/most-banned.html

☐ *National Deaf Lesbian, Gay & Bisexual Archives*
http://www.deafqueer.org/

☐ *National Museum and Archive of Lesbian and Gay*
History [US]
http://www.panix.com:80/~dhuppert/gay/center/culture.htm#
museum

☐ *National Women's History Project*
http://www.uky.edu/ArtsSciences/Classics/whither.html

☐ *Nazi Persecution of Homosexxuals*
http://members.aol.com/dalembert/lgbt_history/nazi_biblio.html

☐ *Never Again: The Pink Triangle Pages*
http://www.cs.cmu.edu/afs/cs/user/scotts/bulgarians/pink.html

☐ *New York Public Library Gay and Lesbian Studies*
http://www.nypl.org/research/chss/grd/resguides/gay.html

☐ *Notable Lesbians*
http://www-lib.usc.edu/~retter/database.html/

☐ *Ohio Lesbian Archives*
http://www-lib.usc.edu/~retter/ohiomain.html

☐ *ONE Institute International Gay & Lesbian*
Archives (ONE/IGLA)
http://www.usc.edu/Library/oneigla/

☐ *Out List*
http://www.mps.org/~rainbow/Words/OutList.html

☐ *People with a History (Paul Halsall)*
http://pwh.base.org

☐ *Photos From Queer History*
http://carnap.umd.edu:90/queer/picture_gallery/history.html

☐ *Pink Triangle Pages*
http://www.cs.cmu.edu/afs/cs/user/scotts/bulgarians/pink.html

☐ *Polari*
http://nz.com/NZ/Queer/Polari/

☐ *Qhistory*
http://www.psn.net/~martyn

☐ *Queer Archives & Libraries Around the World*
http://www.outline.com/saa/archives.hp.html

☐ *Queer Frontiers: Queer Theory and Studies*
http://www.usc.edu/Library/QF/

☐ *Queers In History*
http://quistory.clever.net/qih/index.html

☐ *Queer Mummies!*
http://www.sirius.com/~reeder/niankh.html
http://www.egyptology.com/niankhkhnum_khnumhotep/

☐ *Queer Studies Bibliography*
http://www.duke.edu/web/SXL/biblio.html

☐ *Queer Teen Life in the 50's*
http://www.conterra.com/jsears/writjew.htm

☐ *Rainbow Flag*
http://www.cs.cmu.edu/afs/cs.cmu.edu/user/scotts/bulgarians/

☐ *Rainbow Query Index of History Sites*
http://www.glweb.com/RainbowQuery/Categories/Queer_
History.html

☐ *Reclaiming History*
http://www.uic.edu:80/depts/quic/history/reclaiming_history.html

☐ *Rowse History Centre*
http://www.sbu.ac.uk/~stafflag/history.html

☐ *St. Louis Lesbian and Gay Archives*
http://www.umsl.edu/~whmc/whmgay/whm0545.htm

☐ *Stonewall*
http://www2.netdoor.com/~richardd/stonhist.htm
http://www.columbia.edu/cu/libraries/events/sw25/index.html
http://www.umass.edu/stonewall/
http://www.qrd.org/QRD/www/Stonewall25.html
www.cs.cmu.edu/afs/cs.cmu.edu/user/scotts/bulgarians/stonewall.txt

☐ *Swade's History (Lesbian Tribal Voice)*
http://www.swade.net/swadepages/les_hist.htm

☐ *Twice Blessed: The Jewish GLBT Archives Online*
[At Magic.ca]
http://www.magic.ca/~faygelah/Index.html
http://www.usc.edu/isd/archives/oneigla/tb

☐ *With Downcast Gays: Gay Self-Oppression*
http://www.wadham.ox.ac.uk/~ahodges/wdg/intro.html

☐ *Wizard's Gay Slang Dictionary*
http://www.wadham.ox.ac.uk/~ahodges/wdg/intro.html

Hollywood Supports

The Web has its share of fear-mongering conspiracy theorists shooting darts at every gay and lesbian advance, but none of these groups has the star power and glamour of the Hollywood Supports home page. As its mission statement says, it "was launched to counter workplace fear and discrimination based on HIV status and sexual orientation. The prime objective is to ensure a safe working environment free of stigma, fear, and bigotry."

It's a star-studded counterbalance to the right, with a trustee list that amounts to a who's who of Hollywood. There are producers and directors like Aaron Spelling, Steven Spielberg, Dawn Steel, Oliver Stone, Steven Bochco, James L. Brooks, Barry Diller, Michael Douglas, Michael Eisner, Samuel Goldwyn Jr., and Sherry Lansing. Actors also lend their names, including Richard Dreyfuss, Tom Hanks, Goldie Hawn, Ron Howard, Jeffrey Katzenberg, Alan Ladd, Jr., Bette Midler, Jack Nicholson, Sylvester Stallone, Barbra Streisand, Elizabeth Taylor, Lily Tomlin—and these are just a few of the most recognizable backers.

Although the page has no articles or even an E-mail address, it does that wonderful Internet thing of spreading information—in this case, news of achievements in the entertainment industry that will have a ripple effect (or so it is hoped) in other less public professions.

These effects are detailed in a range of programs like the AIDS in the Workplace seminars, employee benefits counseling, and perhaps the most far-reaching Hollywood Supports effort, consulting assistance on portrayals of HIV and AIDS in film and television. Credit these guys for much of the truthfulness on TV and in movies like *An Early Frost* and *Philadelphia*.

Another of Hollywood Supports' influential contributions is a plan for group health benefits for employees' same-sex partners, which has now been adopted by yet another star-studded list: MCA/Universal, Viacom, HBO, Warner Bros., Time, Sony Pictures, Paramount Pictures, CAA, William Morris, TicketMaster, Lucas Films, E! Entertainment, and Capital Cities/ABC.

Do other companies, perhaps the one you work for, take their lead from the media? If so, Hollywood Supports is doing its job.

☐ *Hollywood Supports*
http://www.hsupports.org/

Home Pages

Home pages are just that—places where you'll find people at home. Like any dwelling, after a while they acquire the digital equivalent of that lived-in look. Most have bookcases (hot lists of links), bulging closets (pages of old enthusiasms), and comfy spots (biographical stuff). They even have addresses and mailboxes. Perhaps it's their personal nature that keeps them honest. You'll rarely find home pages titled with a fake handle; even Amy's Obsession and Robin "Girl Wonder" use their true first names.

Starting

The best place to start is with your own interest. Go through the chapters in this book and log on to a page whose subject gets your attention. The BLK page has African-Americans on the Web, CyberGrrl has loads of women, the cyberwoods are full of sociable bears, and so on. Pigmedia has loads of nasty and very horny men who like it rough and dirty. Or, if you want to mingle randomly, browse the list maintained by PlanetOut's NetQueery. Pages are indexed by country outside the United States, and by state inside our borders.

Most all the links listed under Canada contain home pages, as does the chapter on Australia. For Europe, try Clix.net. Though most home pages are for the Netherlands, especially Amsterdam, you'll come across guys and gals in Scandinavia, Germany, and even as far away as the Baltics.

One thing you know about all these pages is that whoever you punch in will have something to say; quite a few are net evangelists. Ron Buckmire, one of the founders of the QRD, has a list of home pages drawn from soc.motss members. If such a thing as an "A" list exists in cyberspace, his home page compendium is definitely a contender.

Favorites

Two favorites are Jonno's and Abel Kitchen. Jonno's is incredibly sophisticated graphics-wise and yet totally approachable. Abel Kitchen is a more abstract exploration of his work and life as a gay man living in Asia. Both pages give you the feeling of live theater— highly professional yet intimate, always compelling performances.

Jonno's page opens with a beguiling image, a photograph of the author with his face partly concealed behind an uplifted arm–the first clue of the revealing yet private nature of the pages to come. The only text are the simple words: LIFE, PROJECTS, LINKS, CONTACT and a motto that gives you a sense of the author's wit: visited often/ supports all ribbons/frames free/banner free/won't clog pores/kind to trees/all hail the walrus. This last is not a Beatles reference but an homage to an affordable Internet service provider whose logo is a pig with wings (there are lots of playful obscurities here in Jonno-land). If you click on Life, you get another picture of Jonno, partially effaced as was the first, but this time he's wearing what looks like a skin freshner facial masque. He supplies some "stats": DOB: 22 October 1967 (double Libra, moon in Gemini); residence(s): New York City and New Orleans, U.S.A.; height: 5 feet, 10 inches; weight: variable by season; his significant other is Richard. There's lots more information, all equally well displayed on other pages—a journal, notes on projects, and an image of Bronzino's *Portrait of a Young Man* accompanied by quotes on how we see art by Oscar Wilde and E.M. Forster. There's more, but you'll have to see for yourself. It's all simple and complex at the same time. And its very, very romantic. Here's a sample from his journal: "Richard and I live together in a sweet little house in New Orleans, not far from the French Quarter, with our hounds, Gaston and Kika, and our cat, Lolita. We celebrated our second anniversary in April 1999 and we're every bit as goofily in love with one another as we were when we first met. Watch this space for even more nauseatingly cute pictures of us being happy together."

Abel is 31, grew up in England, lives in Taipei, China, and is a poet. As his pages unfold, poems pass under a dancing figure— a young guy in shorts and T-shirt who capers around and tosses his head upwards every now and then with what seems like sheer joy in movement. The poetry is immediately accessible, full of images, and very sensual, of a kin to Frank O'Hara's work. Here's an excerpt: "ah/reach for the handsome/the man who keeps askin'/what I say when I'm sleeping/and what do I mean." The guest book is a journal of his thoughts on the "smell of China, the tang of subtropical Taipei," on boredom, Madonna's new album, a thunderstorm rattling his apartment's windows. The journal is a sort of open diary and many readers respond as if it and the entire page were an oasis in an unfeeling world. Abel also prints some of the attack mail. To "Stan," who ends his homophobic vitriol with "Fuck Off!" Abel suggests a glass of sweet wine ("You need it.") and a trip to the local truck stop where he (so Abel imagines) will find a "closeted truck driver, bearded, and wearing a baseball cap emblazoned with the epithet: GIVE ME HEAD TILL I'M DEAD. "Allow him to sodomize you in the men's toilet. You'll feel better. Really." By turns harsh and tender, Abel's page does that wonderful thing—makes you curious about the author as you would be of a friend. Also, thankfully, the page comes up quickly—despite all the graphic richness.

Not all home pages are so readable, but the best of them take you for a few minutes or an hour into another life. And when you add in the links to other sources, home pages are indispensable—like people-watching in an outdoor café—but better. You won't be caught staring unless you want to be. Every home page has a line asking for your feedback. Why not oblige?

☐ *Out on the Net*
   http://www.outonthenet.com

☐ *2fags.com*
http://www.2fags.com

☐ *Abel-Kicthen*
http://www.abel-kitchen.com

☐ *About Me*
http://ourworld.compuserve.com/homepages/sappho/about.htm

☐ *Amy's Obsession*
http://www.lesbian.org/home.html

☐ *Arrgh!!!*
http://www.aaarrgh.com

☐ *baby girl's playground*
http://www.geocities.comwellesley/garden/1479

☐ *Beverly's Place*
http://www.geocities.com/westhollywood/1769

☐ *BondageMaster*
http://www.bondagemaster.com

☐ *bzone*
http://www.bzone.com/l

☐ *Callen's Home Page*
http://www.geocities.com/westhollywood/4675

☐ *Chuck Tarvers*
http://www.udel.edu/ner/chuckt.html

☐ *Cris Williamson and Tret Fure*
http://www.cris-tret.com

☐ *Daniel Pittman's Kweer Com*
http://www.kweer.com

☐ *Donald's Page*
http://www.hkstud.com

☐ *DJ Dynasty*
http://www.djdynasty.com

☐ *Eric's Family Tree*
http://www.geocities.com/westhollywood/heights/2359

☐ *House of Love*
http://www.houseoflove.com

☐ *Houston Fister*
http://www.westom.com/fister

☐ *Joe Gallagher*
http://www.leathrpage.com

☐ *Jon & Gary*
http://www.users.dircon.co.uk/~inamorato/page1.html

☐ *Jon Jims Intro Page*
http://members.aol.com/jonjimct

☐ *The Other Queer Page*
http://www.im1ru12.org/toqp/people.html

☐ *That Fabulous Faghag*
http://www.geocities.com/southbeach/lounge/2493

☐ *PlanetOut*
http://www.plantetout.com/

☐ *Planet Soma*
http://www.planetsoma.com

☐ *Ron Buckmire*
http://abacus.oxy.edu/~ron/

- [ ] *Susie Bright*
  http://www.susiebright.com

- [ ] *United Kingdom Poof's List*
  http://uk-poofs.quipu.com

- [ ] *Where the Girls Are*
  http://www.eskimo.com/~susan/girls.htm

- [ ] *Wolfe's Cyber Den*
  http://www.wolfe.com

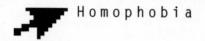 Homophobia

Gay murders. The Defense of Marriage Act. "Don't ask, don't tell." Simple name-calling—the particular battle points in the war against homophobia are depressingly many until you visit the vast array of Web sites devoted to overturning bigotry. In the last year especially ,the Web has reached a kind of critical mass and become the focal point of antibigot activism.

Over 750,000 people per year log on to Hatewatch.org., perhaps the most sophisticated and certainly one of the most forceful gay rights pages. Go here to read the latest news on the rights front and become informed on exactly where our rights are being attacked and learn how to respond—and it's all done in a progressive way that avoids mimicking the hate-filled tactics of the those spreading malice.

And it's not just alerts of the latest outrage. You'll get the full text of the offense as well as specific calls to action once you've informed yourself on chat lines, discussion centers, interviews, and probably the largest and most up-to-date links list to hate groups.

Major Rights Groups

All of the large rights groups (such as GLAAD, HRC, and NGLTF) have been on the Web for years, sounding the alert and pressing the political machine for change on both local and national levels. Each has specific sections dealing with homophobia in with respect to issues from family rights to same sex marriage and the workplace. You'll also find some frightening statistics on the rise of hate crimes as reported by the FBI and the progress—and lack of it—in passing stronger laws. The NGLTF has written what's become the online bible of countering bigotry in the Fight the Right Action Kit. All these organizations and many more are listed in the QRD and described more fully in the chapter on Activism.

Issue Groups

In the past few years, a number of smaller, more focused groups have begun to appear on the Web. Citizens Against Homophobia uses mass media campaigns to reduce homophobia. One print ad features the torsos of four men under the headline, "IF YOU GO OUT OF YOUR WAY TO PICK ON GAYS, PSYCHIATRISTS HAVE A NAME FOR YOU...LATENT HOMOSEXUAL." Beneath this are a few short lines, including the following: "These days, when you harass gay people, it just puts the spotlight of suspicion on you. So maybe you'd better mind your own business, unless you want others to think that homosexuality is your business!" Effective and highly targeted, these ads are free, the only exception being a $7 charge for digital audiotaped copies of the radio commercials. Queer By Choice is the ironic title of a group that offers information meant to dispel the underpinnings of homophobic beliefs. The page presents clear, accurate explanations of scientific research on sexual orientation, homophobia, crimes, and HIV/AIDS.

Schools & Medicine

Creating Safe Schools for Lesbian and Gay Students offers practical advice for teachers, administrators, and students on how to combat homophobia within schools. Jewish Activist Gays and Lesbians (JAGL) targets young gay, lesbian, and bisexual Jews struggling against homophobia in the Jewish community and anti-Semitism in the gay world. The Fair Report, though not solely devoted to homophobia, has articles that point out various examples of antigay bias in the media. The Gay and Lesbian Medical Association is an organization of 2,000 lesbian, gay, bisexual, and transgendered (LGBT) physicians, medical students, and their supporters in all 50 states and 12 countries. Founded in 1981, GLMA works to combat homophobia within the medical profession and in society at large.

Homophobia in the Military

The three best sites dealing with homophobia in the U.S. military are: Gays and Lesbians in the Military, Servicemembers Legal Defense Network, and Dave's Gay Military Site. Each is a solid, extremely intelligent call to action with statistics, profiles, and examples from other nations that have successfully integrated their militaries. Dave's in particular is packed with news, features, references, and Web links of interest to gay and bisexual military personnel, veterans, and their friends. Includes extensive references on the "don't ask, don't tell" policy, news for and about gay, lesbian, and bisexual military personnel, and the fight against official military antigay policies.

A Lover of Soldiers page is a different animal. Although its a sales page for Steven Zeeland's books on gay life in the army with reviews and synopses, its a terrifically powerful argument against homophobia on the simple grounds that an individual's sexuality exists apart from his ability to perform—that homophobia is just that—a phobia, a mind game.

Also see Timothy McVeigh's home page. He talks movingly about his case with the service, his reaction to AOL's violation of his privacy and the current situation with "don't ask, don't tell."

Worldview

Though Gay Law Net is a British site, it is worth visiting and emulating for American lawyers. Both a resource for finding a lawyer (should you be the victim of homophobia) and a quick way to answer general questions on your civil rights, the site takes queries on arrests, starting a business, property rights, wills, and death, and it promises to answer them within a day. Each topic receives an overview and an example situation.

For a worldview, check out International Gay and Lesbian Human

Rights Commission. It tracks gay rights violations around the world, from murder as part of "social cleansing" to electroshock "therapy," incarceration, forced psychiatric "treatment," torture, arbitrary arrest, forced marriage, immigration restrictions, and the revocation of parental rights.

Web Active

Another source that is chipping away at homophobia—often with a sledgehammer—is Web Active. It has an excellent set of antibigot links, along with pages of how-to advice for raising consciousness on the Internet. These include a page on Jesse Helms, pro and con mailing lists, and a list of newsgroups where homophobia is the highly flammable topic. WebActive also has a search engine that you can use to hunt homophobia around the world on the Internet.

If you're interested in going behind the lines of the Christian right, try the pages put up by Freedom Writer. These include investigative pieces by a writer who went inside far right meetings and reports on what participants really say before toning it down for the press release.

Snake Oil

Some jaded veterans of the homophobe wars may especially enjoy the shock treatment administered at Snake Oil, Your Guide to Kooky Kontemporary Kristian Kulture. The author has made it his business to track and expose the seamiest purveyors of hate from the pulpit; he's even attended jury trials of various "fallen angels." Each month he condenses his discoveries into a long article. Snake Oil also serves as a forum for its many readers. There are also cartoons, including one of Newt Gingrich morphed into—you guessed it—a wiggly newt. His head swivels, his eyes bug out, and then, zap—a Pepto-Bismol–colored tongue lashes out, forked, of course.

Although the indexes also have comprehensive listings of Web pages fighting homophobia, AltaVista is perhaps the best tool for researching antibigotry. Among the hundreds of sites it catalogs, it includes Gay Stories of Homophobia, Homophobia in Women's Sports, Family Values Hate Groups, and Citizens Against Homophobia Links to the World.

☐ *About the Right (PFAW)*
http://www.pfaw.org/issues/right/

☐ *ACLU*
http://www.aclu.org/issues/gay/argl.html

☐ *American Guardian*
http://www.thundernet.org/

☐ *And Justice For All*
http://www.aja.org/

☐ *Blue Ribbon Campaign*
http://www.eff.org//blueribbon/activism.html

☐ *Campaign to End Homophobia*
http://www.endhomophobia.org

☐ *Carleton Freenet*
http://www.ncf.carleton.ca/freeport/sigs/life/gay/homo/menu

☐ *Citizens Against Homophobia*
http://www.gay-discrimination.com

☐ *CyberQueer Lounge*
http://www.idowebs.com/GLAIDS/

☐ *Citizen's Project*
http://citproj.ppages.com/fwjun97.htm

☐ *Electronic Privacy Information Center*
http://www.epic.org

☐ *Family Values Hate Groups*
http://www.bibble.org/gay/phobia/hate_groups.html

☐ *Feminist Activist Resources on the Net*
http://www.igc.apc.org/women/feminist.html

☐ *Fight the Right Network*
http://www.critpath.org/ftrn/ftrn.html

☐ *Fight the Right Action Kit*
http://server.berkeley.edu/mblga/html/ftr/tblcntnt.html

☐ *Fred Phelps Resource Page*
http://members.tripod.com/~fredphelps/

☐ *Freedom Writer*
http://www.berkshire.net/~ifas/fw/

☐ *Gay Cybergeeks Pow-Wow Tribe*
http://www.interlog.com/~donaldb/gcg/gcg.html

☐ *Gay Law Net*
http://www.geocities.com/WestHollywood/3181/

☐ *Gay, Lesbian, & Straight Teachers Network Against Homophobia*
http://www.glstn.org/freedom/

☐ *Gay Stories of Homophobia*
http://www.bibble.org/gay/stories/phobia.html

☐ *GLAAD*
http://www.glaad.org/glaad/

☐ *Hands Off Washington! (Fighting Antigay Ballot Measures)*
http://www.eor.com/howhtml/how.htm

☐ *Hatecrimes Prevention Center*
http://www.civilrights.org/icef/hcpc/

☐ *Hatewatch.org*
http://www.hatewatch.org

☐ *Homophobia in Women's Sports*
http://www.lifetimetv.com/WoSport/TOPICS/HOMO/homo.htm

☐ *HRC*
http://www.hrc.org/

☐ *International G&L Human Rights Commission*
http://www.iglhrc.org/

☐ *It's Time*
http://www.gender.org/ita/

☐ *Keeping Watch*
http://205.162.178.160/KeepingWatch/index.html

☐ *Lesbian Avengers Handbook*
http://www.lesbian.org/chicago-avengers/avengerhandbook.html

☐ *Matthew's Place*
http://www.matthewsplace.com

☐ *Matthew Shepard Tribute Page*
http://www.mattshepard.org/

☐ *National Gay and Lesbian Federation of Gay and Lesbian Associations*
http://www.ecn.org/gayrage/azione/aoindex.htm

☐ *National Lesbian & Gay Journalists Assoc.*
http://www.nlgja.org/

☐ *Not in Our Town*
http://www.igc.org/an/niot/

☐ *Political Research Associates*
http://www.publiceye.org/

☐ *QRD (Queer Resources Directory)*
http://www.qrd.org/qrd/

☐ *Radical Religious Right*
http://www.casti.com/QRD/www/RRR/rrrpage.html

☐ *Reactionary Religious Right*
http://www.webcom.com/~albany/

☐ *Right to Pride*
http://www.rtp-or.org

☐ *Scouting For All*
http://www.scoutingforall.org/

☐ *Sexual Orientation and the Workplace*
http://www.nyu.edu/pages/sls/gaywork/

☐ *Snake Oil*
http://www.bbgun.com/snakeoil/

☐ *Southern Poverty Law Center*
http://www.splcenter.org

☐ *Straight But Not Narrow*
http://dislecksea.home.mindspring.com/sbnn.html

☐ *The World According to Jesse*
http://www.nando.net/sproject/jesse/helms.html

☐ *WebActive*
http://www.webactive.com

International Queers

With English the dominant language, the Web may almost seem an American product. But even the lightest sampling proves otherwise. As you tour the women's salons in the United Kingdom, hip Japanese online magazines, or Australia's burgeoning scene, you'll find that foreign sites are indeed foreign. While American pages are admired for their sense of play and sophisticated illustrations, we have a tendency to strain for entertainment. Most international pages don't put such a high value on perkiness. For example, Amsterdam's Clix.net, whose editors put out a lifestyle-magazine mix complete with celebrity interviews, stiffens the news brew with investigative reports on local politics. This isn't to say that serious topics aren't available on American pages, but they're certainly less common.

Urban Centers

And the growth, especially over the last year, has been phenomenal. Along with tons of home pages reflecting the authors' (and perhaps your) individual interests, it seems as if every major metropolitan area in the world has general pages of information, (Sydney's Lemon online), news and events calendars (Amsterdam Pink Pages) as well as weekly updates on the GLBT scene at bars and restaurants. London's *QX* magazine gives a walking tour of Soho (England's Greenwich Village), and Berlin at Night gives such detailed reports of the week's events that you feel immediately hooked into the locals' lives. (Recent reports say the dance clubs are packed with Berliners moving to everything from waltzes to *schlagers*, meaning überkitschy hits from the '70s and '80s. Can you imagine "I will survive!" sung in German?

We're Everywhere—Even Arabia

In fact, there seems a queer blossoming all over the world. South Africa now has at least ten Web pages and Portugal's queer pages reflect the national progression from very closeted scene to pride marches and proliferation of Lisbon hot spots. Even extremely homophobic countries, such as those of Arabia, now have such sites as Ahbab, a magazine-style page with features, chat rooms and recipes. (Read the report of Rev. Fred Phelps' visit to Iraq.)

Stories like this are a sobering reminder that queers are not always welcomed abroad. Arenal, a site devoted to Latin America's GLBTs, includes a links list as well as articles measuring the homophobic temperature of each country. Russian Gay Culture tells of a loosening in repressive laws that has had a resulting thaw in gay life, sadly limited to St. Petersburg and Moscow.

Beyond the Iron Curtain

Although countries that have escaped Soviet influence don't seem to be menacingly homophobic, gay life (at least gauged by Web activity) is minimal. Part of the explanation can be found at Russian/Ukrainian Club for Gay Space Werewolves. It's the home page of a Ukrainian named Victor who writes: "I've been living in London, U.K., already for two years. The reason why I'm here and not in my country is clear: there is no GAY LIFE in there! There are some gay guys but what all of us had to do is to hide our sexuality from everyone and everything: parents, "friends," employers....Was that kind of life the REAL life for me? No."

The picture from Poland is similar. As the editor of PolGay says: "This is the first attempt to construct a Web page that could be the beginning of a service for gay people in our country. We also would like to help gay people find information on what one can find in Poland and how. There are a lot of foreigners visiting this country (and this country is worth visiting!). The situation in our academic environment (in Poland one can have Internet access almost only through an educational site) is how it is—and this forces us to be careful. But there are more and more private pages of people who are out, at least on the Net." There's an address page for gay places all over Poland—organizations, bars, restaurants, news, and magazines.

Language Barrier?

Though many of the sites listed below have English versions, don't give up if only the native language is used. Very often you'll be able to decipher enough to get by since American terms are part of the global lingo. Clubs In Denmark is written in Danish, but anyone can read the country map and interpret  the message behind the image of a hunky jock raising his t-shirt while a mechanical phallus rotates on his face. As you scroll down the city-by-city club listings, you'll come across plenty of English—"jeans" or "uniform," for example, and the easily understood "motorcykledudstyr." (It's a pretty sure guess that the patrons of this bar will ride bikes or at least wear leather, ya?)

When you're Web-surfing abroad, though, expect a longish wait as your browser builds up the entire page—it's the equivalent of that pause during international calls. Just sit there, sip your coffee, and prepare your mind for the savor of a foreign affair.

Resources

The QRD has sister sites in Australia, Canada, the Netherlands, France, Germany, Israel, Slovenia, and the United Kingdom. These are all aimed toward the comprehensive reach of the mother site, with hundreds of host country documents and links on file. Each is a terrific place to begin your search of a foreign country's resources. NetQueery at PlanetOut is also an excellent reference with hundreds of links divided into the following geographic areas: Africa and the Middle East, Asia/Pacific Region, Central and South America and the Caribbean, and Europe and the former USSR.

Perhaps the largest set of international links is housed at Yahoo!, which contains indexes to 38 countries from Austria to Guam, Lithuania, Singapore, Taiwan, and the United Kingdom. The Hong Kong listing alone includes Donald's Page—"for anyone interested in Asian muscles (and brains)"—Eddy's Chinese Home, Gay Hong Kong! and L and G Utopian Hong Kong.

For addresses in Europe and Australia, check out the Ultimate Gay Pages by Hein Verkerk. He's particularly good at finding the best links to bars, restaurants, and clubs in Northern Europe. This is also his home page, so there's a more personal investment in his work. He's single (when last checked), and welcomes comments on the many links he supplies.

(Note: For more information, also see the chapters on Travel and City Guides.)

AFRICA

South Africa

- ☐ *Gaynet Cape Town*
  http://www.gaynetcapetown.co.za

- ☐ *GaySA*
  http://www.gaysouthafrica.org.za

- ☐ *GLBT Web site*
  http://www.gaysa.co.za/

- ☐ *Les Bi Gay South Africa*
  http://www.javajava.co.za/lesbigay/

☐ *Python Power*
http://www.geocities.com/WestHollywood/1282/

☐ *QOnline*
http://www.q.co.za/

☐ *Stepping Out*
http://steppingout.ru.ac.za/

☐ *University of Cape Town Rainbow Organization*
http://www.uct.ac.za/depts/src/societies/gala/

Zimbabwe

☐ *Gays and Lesbians of Zimbabwe*
http://www.icon.co.za/~stobbs/galz.htm

ASIA

China

☐ *China Gay*
http://www.gaychina.com/.

☐ *Chinese Gay Leisure*
http://www.gaychina.simplenet.com/

☐ *Gay China*
http://gaychina.simplenet.com/

☐ *Gay & Lesbian China*
http://www.gayguide.net/asia

Hong Kong

☐ *Concerned Asians and Friends*
http://home.netvigator.com/~hkmen/

- ☐ *Eddy Chinese Home*
  http://www.asiaonline.net.hk/~ekhome/

- ☐ *Gay Hong Kong!*
  http://sqzm14.ust.hk/hkgay.htm

- ☐ *Utopia*
  http://www.utopia-asia.com

Japan

- ☐ *Bear Club Japan*
  http://www.st.rim.or.jp/~lonestar/bcj

- ☐ *Butch Bar*
  http://www.barbutch.com

- ☐ *Gay Japan*
  http://www.gay-japan.com

- ☐ *Gaynet Japan*
  http://www.gayguide.net/asia/japan

- ☐ *Japan Edge*
  http://www.ces.kyutech.ac.jp/student/JapanEdge/e-index.html

- ☐ *OCCUR*
  http://www.tcp.com:8000/qrd/world/asia/japan/

- ☐ *Outrageous Tokyo Home Page*
  http://shrine.cyber.ad.jp/~darrell/outr/home/outr-home.html

- ☐ *Planet Rainbow*
  http://www.kt.rim.or.jp/~rainbow/

- ☐ *QRD Japan*
  http://www.qrd.org/qrd/world/asia/japan/

Korea (South)

☐ *Gay Korea*
http://www.chollian.net/~exzone/

☐ *Queer Korean News*
http://homepage.interaccess.com/~jasini/second.shtml

Philippines

☐ *Filipino Resources*
http://www.tribo.org/bakla/bakla.html

☐ *Kakasarian*
http://pubweb.acns.nwu.edu/~ftp/bacla.html

☐ *Philippine Gay, Bi and Lesbian Resources*
http://www.tribo.org/bakla/bakla.html

☐ *Rize Reyes*
http://www.geocities.com/westhollywood/2251/index.html

Singapore

☐ *Singapore Boy*
http://www.sgboy.com

☐ *Singapore Gay Resources and Travel Tips*
http://www2.best.com/~utopia/tipssing.htm

☐ *Singapore Room*
http://www.geocities.com/westhollywood/village/6188

Taiwan

☐ *Gays & Lesbians in Taiwan*
http://userpage.fu-berlin.de/~jensdamm/gay-tai-e.html

Thailand

☐ *DragonCastle*
http://www.dragoncastle.com/

☐ *Dreaded Ned*
http://www.dreadedned.com/

☐ *Gay Patong*
http://www.patong.com/gaypatong

☐ *Gay Phuket*
http://www.gayphuket.com

☐ *Pink Ink*
http://www.khsnet.com/pinkink/

Vietnam

☐ *Gay Viet*
http://www.gayviet.com/

☐ *Vietnamese Gay Scene*
http://www.govietnam.com/vngaytvl.html

☐ *VN-GBLF Paze*
http://www.viet.net/Gallery/vietgal/vn-gblf/

Australia

☐ *Australian Gay Bi Lesbian Information*
http://www.geko.com.au/~scotty/gblinfo.html

☐ *The Australian Gay Leather Directory*
http://www.geocities.com/WestHollywood/Heights/6771/

☐ *Australian QRD*
http://www.queer.org.au/QRD/net/

☐ *Brian's gay Australia page*
http://www.geocities.com/WestHollywood/2002/gay_oz3.html

☐ *Brother Sister*
http://www.brothersister.com.au/

☐ *Capital Q (Melbourne)*
http://www.capitalq.com.au

☐ *Cyberqueer Australia*
http://cyberqueer.rainbow.net.au/

☐ *Gay Australia-Sydney*
http://www.magna.com.au/~gismith/gayaust1.htm

☐ *Gay Maps Australia*
http://www.tma.com.au/gma.html

☐ *Gay Melbourne*
http://www.ozemail.com.au/~prees/gaymelb.html

☐ *Melbourne Star Observer*
http://www.bluestone.com.au/outrage/

☐ *Links to the Australian Gay & Lesbian Community*
http://www.tma.com.au/gaylinks.html

☐ *The Pink Board*
http://www.pinkboard.com.au/

☐ *Queer News*
http://www.ozemail.com.au/~qnews/

☐ *Queer Perth*
http://www.iinet.net.au/~lezderin/

☐ *Sydney Mardi Gras*
http://www.mardigras.com.au

☐ *Sydney Star Observer*
http://sso.rainbow.net.au/

☐ *Sydney sex venues*
http://cyberqueer.rainbow.net.au/sydney_s.html

☐ *Utopia*
http://www.best.com/~utopia/

EUROPE

Austria

☐ *HOSI*
http://www.hosiwien.gay.at/

Belgium

☐ *Liege Gay*
http://geocities.com/westhollywood/82831/

Croatia

☐ *Croatian LesBiGays on Internet*
http://www.geocities.com/WestHollywood/1824/

☐ *Gay Zagreb*
http://www.geocities.com/WestHollywood/Heights/2040/

☐ *First Croatian Drag Site*
http://www.geocities.com/WestHollywood/Village/6578/

☐ *Rainbow Croatia*
http://www.geocities.com/westhollywood/heights/8060/

Cyprus

☐ *Gay Cyprus*
http://members.aol.com/gaycyprus/index.html

Czech Republic

☐ *Amigo*
http://www.amigo.cz

☐ *About Czech Republic*
http://www.macromediasolutionslitd.com/glprague.html

☐ *SOHO (Czech Orgs)*
http://www.infima.cz/soho/

☐ *SOHO Absolut Revue*
http://www.eset.cz/soho/

Denmark

☐ *Club Octopussy*
http://www.geocities.com/westhollywood/2486/

☐ *Copenhagen Gay Homepage*
http://www.cgh.dk/gay/home.html

☐ *Copenhagen Gay Info*
http://hjem.get2net.dk/cphgayinfo/

☐ *Danish LGB*
http://www.lbl.dk/

Finland

☐ *Net-Z*
http://seta.fi/2/index.html

France

☐ *Gay France*
http://www.gayfrance.fr

☐ *Gai Pied*
http://www.gaipied.fr

☐ *Gay Guide to Paris*
http://www.imaginet.fr/~jayde/index.html

☐ *Gay Paris*
http://www.geocities.com/WestHollywood/1318

☐ *Gay PARIS Guide*
http://www.mygale.org/03/aachen

☐ *La France Gaie et Lesbienne*
http://www.france.qrd.org

Germany

☐ *Berlin*
http://www.informatik.hu-berlin.de:80/~holz/privat/

☐ *Berlin at Night*
http://www.queersonline.com/berlin.html

☐ *Gay- & Lesbian-Server (Berlin)*
http://www.vlm.net/bg

☐ *GayNet Berlin*
http://www.gaynet.de/gaynet/frameset.html

☐ *German QRD*
http://www.macman.org
http://rzstud1.rz.uni-karlsruhe.de/~uk2x/svsk/svsk.html

☐ *HUB: Gay Berlin*
http://www.informatik.hu-berlin.de/~holz/privat/

☐ *Man Base*
http://swix.ch/manbase/

☐ *German Queer Resources Directory*
http://rzstud1.rz.uni-karlsruhe.de/~uk2x/svsk/svsk.html

☐ *Queerserver (Bremen)*
http://www.uni-bremen.de/~queer/

Greece

☐ *Mykonos*
http://www.geocities.com/WestHollywood/5621/

☐ *O Pothos*
http://www.geocities.com/WestHollywood/Heights/2958/

☐ *PrideNet*
http://www.pridenet.com/greece.html

☐ *Roz Mov - Pink and Lavender Pages of Greece*
http://www.geocities.com/WestHollywood/2225/

Hungary

☐ *Gay Guide to Budapest*
http://www.gayguide.net/europe/hungary/budapest/

☐ *Gay Budapest*
http://www.gaybudapest.com/

Ireland

☐ *Gay Community News*
http://homepage.tinet.ie/~nlgf

☐ *Gay Ireland*
http://www.gay-ireland.com

☐ *Queer Ireland*
http://www.clubi.ie/queer

Italy

☐ *Orsi Italiani (Italian Bears)*
http://www.ecn.org/deviazioni/orsi/

☐ *Gaytalia*
http://www.vol.it/itf/gaytalia/index.htm

☐ *Pride*
http://www.gay.it/pride/

☐ *Queer Directory*
http://www.gay.it/pride/directory.htm

☐ *Tuscany Guide*
http://www.gay.it/pride/guida.htm

Netherlands

☐ *Cai's Gay Life*
http://www.gaycai.com/

☐ *Clix.net (Amsterdam)*
http://clix.net/clix/amsterdam/

☐ *Club Cockring*
http://www.clubcockring.com

☐ *Dutch Gay News*
http://www.xs4all.nl/~berts

- ☐ *Dutch QRD*
  http://www.xs4all.nl/~heinv/dqrd/index.html

- ☐ *Gay Amsterdam*
  http://www.gayamsterdam.com/

- ☐ *Gay Life*
  http://www.nooky.nl/gaylife/gaylife.htm

- ☐ *Gay World*
  http://www.gayworld.nl/

- ☐ *Pink Pages*
  http://www.euro.net/5thworld/pink/pink.html

- ☐ *Pride Net*
  http://www.pridenet.com/nether.html

Norway

- ☐ *BLIKK*
  http://www.glnetwork.no/BLIKK/index.html

Poland

- ☐ *Gay Poland*
  http://www.qrd.com/qrd/www/world/europe/poland/

- ☐ *Inna Strona*
  http://www.gej.net/

- ☐ *Polish Lesbians*
  http://www.geocities.com/WestHollywood/8676/

Portugal

- ☐ *Gay Portugal*
  http://gayportugal.ml.org/

☐ *ILGA Portugal*
http://www.ilga-portugal.org/

Romania

☐ *Romanian Action*
http://www.raglb.org.uk

☐ *The Gay Reality*
http://www.mediaport.org/~arthur/stichting.dacia/

☐ *Romanian Lesbigays*
http://www.geocities.com/WestHollywood/1811/

Russia

☐ *Gay Russia*
http://www.gay.ru/english

☐ *Bulletin Board*
http://www.vmt.com/gayrussia/bbs/

☐ *Russia: Living Gay in Russia*
http://www.f8.com/FP/Russia/R10a.html

☐ *Russian Queer World*
http://www.geocities.com/westhollywood/5537/

☐ *Russian Gay Life*
http://www.vmt.com/gayrussia/

☐ *Russian/Ukrainian Club For Gay Space Werewolves*
http://www.geocities.com/WestHollywood/4098/index.html

☐ *Serbia/Montenegro*
Arkadija
http://www.igc.org/neww/ceewomen/arkadija.html

☐ *Wolfy*
http://www.cea.ru/~ik/index.html

Slovakia

☐ *Slovak Gay and Lesbian Information*
http://www.gay.cz/sk

Slovenia

☐ *HaBiO*
http://www.geocities.com/WestHollywood/3417/

☐ *KeKe*
http://www.ljudmila.org/siqrd/KeKe/index.html

☐ *Lesbo*
http://www.vuk.org/lesbo

☐ *Revolver*
http://www.ljudmila.org/siqrd/Revolver/index.html

☐ *Slovene QRD*
http://www.ljudmila.org/siqrd/

☐ *Slovenia's BDSM Home*
http://www.geocities.com/WestHollywood/8294/

☐ *YAG!*
http://www.gay.cz/ganymedes/

Spain

☐ *900 ROSA*
http://aleph.pangea.org/org/cgl/rosa9e.htm

☐ *Barcelona Gay*
http://www.arsweb.com/guia/barcelona/

☐ *COGAM*
http://www.ctv.es/USERS/cogam/ihome.htm

☐ *Coordinadora Gai-Lesbiana*
http://aleph.pangea.org/org/cgl/

☐ *Gay Espana*
http://www.gayes.com

☐ *La Revista*
http://www.arrakis.es/~triduo/

Sweden

☐ *Federation for Gay and Lesbian Rights*
http://www.rfsl.se/

☐ *Gay Resources*
http://aleph.pangea.org/org/cgl/rosa9e.htm

☐ *Göteborgs gay-guide*
http://uplift.sparta.lu.se/~mirror/gbg/gbgaktiv.html

☐ *Lesbians and Gays in Sweden*
http://www.algonet.se/~lewis/

☐ *Pride*
http://www.europride98.se/start.html

☐ *QX Web Magazine*
http://www.qx.se/

Switzerland

☐ *AK Magazine*
http://www.access.ch/ak/

☐ *Pride*
http://www.regad.com/Pride_98/

☐ *Schweizer Gay Links*
http://www.gay.ch/

☐ *Swissgay.com*
http://www.swissgay.com/

☐ *T&M*
http://www.gaybar.ch/

☐ *Zurich*
http://www.access.ch/ak/zuerich/zuerich.html

Turkey

☐ *IPOTH*
http://www.angelfire.com/ca/ipoth/index.html

☐ *Istanbul Gay Guide*
http://istanbulguide.net/gay.htm

☐ *Istanbul Turkish Baths*
http://istanbulguide.net/ing/hamam.htm

☐ *Lambda*
http://www.qrd.org/www/world/europe/turkey/dergi/INDEX.HTM

United Kingdom

☐ *England Links by Gayscape*
http://www.jwpublishing.com/gayscape.ukengland.html

☐ *Belfast Queer*
http://www.geocities.com/WestHollywood/Heights/7124/

☐ *Capital Gay*
http://www.capitalgay.com

☐ *Dublin's Pink Pages*
http://abacus.oxy.edu/qrd/www/world/europe/ireland/

☐ *Freedom.co*
http://freedom.co.uk/
http://www.freedom.co.uk/gaytoz/

☐ *Gay to Z*
http://www.freedom.co.uk/gaytoz/

☐ *Gay London*
http://www.gaylondon.co.uk

☐ *Gaysites*
http://w3.win-uk.net/get/gaysites/

☐ *GayTimes & Diva*
http://www.gaytimes.co.uk/

☐ *Irish Links*
http://huizen.dds.nl/~vonb/hs-index.html

☐ *Lesbian & Gay Guide to London*
http://www.users.dircon.co.uk/~zzyzx/tourist/glguide/glguide.htm

☐ *ManBase*
http://manbase.com/english

☐ *Mr. Gay UK*
http://www.mrgayuk.co.uk/

☐ *PinkNet - Guide To Gay London*
http://www.bogo.co.uk/aceing/PinkNet/home.htm

☐ *Pink Passport*
http://www.pinkpassport.com/

☐ *Powerhouse*
http://www.powerhouse.co.uk/powerhouse/index.htm

☐ *Pride*
http://www.pride.org.uk/

☐ *QX Magazine*
http://www.qxmag.co.uk/

☐ *Scotsgay*
http://www.scotsgay.co.uk/index.html

☐ *Simon's Gay Guide to London*
http://website.lineone.net/~simon/travel.htm

☐ *UK Gay*
http://www.demon.co.uk/world/ukgay/index.html

☐ *UK Gay Guides*
http://www.gayguide.co.uk

☐ *UK Poofs*
http://uk-poofs.quipu.com/

LATIN AMERICAN

☐ *ARENAL*
http://www.indiana.edu/~arenal/Homepage.html

Argentina

☐ *Lesbian Life and Activism in Argentina*
http://www.smith.edu/~ehall/wst.html

☐ *Mundo Gay Comunicandose (MGC)*
http://www.mundogay.com

Brazil

☐ *G! Web*
http://www.geocities.com/WestHollywood/4268/

☐ *Rio de Janeiro Gay & Lesbian Guide*
http://ipanema.com/rio/gay/

Colombia

☐ *Gays, Lesbianas Y Bisexuales De Colombia Para El Mundo*
http://www.geocities.com/WestHollywood/Heights/8384/

☐ *Grupo Apoyo a la Diversidad de Orientaciones Sexuales (GADOS)*
http://www.geocities.com/WestHollywood/3554/

☐ *RIT - Colombiana*
http://www.geocities.com/WestHollywood/8459/

Mexico

☐ *Aquí Estamos*
http://www.aquiestamos.com/

☐ *DonPato's Gay Mexico*
http://www.donpato.simplenet.com/mexico/

☐ *Pride.Net*
http://www.pridenet.com/mex.html

☐ *QRD Mexico*
http://qrd.tcp.com/qrd/world/americas/mexico/

☐ *Sergay*
http://www.sergay.com.mx/sergay/index.html

☐ *World's Gay Directory*
http://www.boys2men.com/MEXICO.HTML

MIDDLE EAST

☐ *Queer Jihad*
http://www.geocities.com/westhollywood/heights/8977/

☐ *Ahbab (Arabia)*
http://www.glas.org/ahbab

☐ *Gay & Lesbian Arabic Society (GLAS)*
http://leb.net/glas/

☐ *Gay Iran*
http://welcometo/gay/iran/

☐ *Gay Arab*
http://www.gayarab.com/noframes.htm

☐ *The Homan Home Page*
http://www-pp.hobia.net/iran.homan

☐ *The Other 10% (Israel)*
http://www.ma.huji.ac.il/~dafid/asiron.html

☐ *The Pink Times (Israel)*
http://www.pinktime.co.il

☐ *Lambda Istanbul*
http://www.qrd.org/www/world/europe/turkey/

NEW ZEALAND

☐ *AKIKO*
http://nz.com/glb/

☐ *Gay New Zealand*
http://www.gaynz.com

☐ *New Zealand Pink Pages*
http://nz.com/NZ/Queer/PinkPages/

YUGOSLAVIA

☐ *Gay Croatia*
http://come.to/gay-croatia

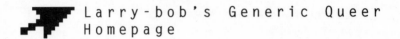

Larry-bob's Generic Queer Homepage

If there could be such a thing as a gadfly for the queer Web (and by extension all queerdom), Larry-bob would be the top candidate. Since 1996, he's been scouring the Web, writing about what he sees, tweaking the pompous and the banal, championing the unheralded and in all ways trying to raise the quality bar and make us think. The hectoring evangelism would be a little tiring if he were setting himself up as an arbiter, but he's not. Yes, he's prodigal with devastating attacks on the mindlessness of "the gay Web ghetto," but he's never mean-spirited (companies are fair targets but people are off-limits). And he's quite ingenuous, calling his reports "Rants." In fact, the irony he dispenses is liberally self-applied. His page is, after all, titled "Larry-bob's Generic Queer Homepage."

That title is the first clue to his idiosyncratic point of view, and he follows it up with the recipe that all too many Web sites follow: "Slap together some rainbow flag GIFs, pictures of naked guys, and a whole bunch of links to other gay sites with no more actual content than your own. You can probably make your own generic gay home page in less than an hour. I did."

Rants

His main objection is to home pages that are simply a links list to other links lists. "Don't you homos have anything to say? It's like an endless hall of mirrors—wander down the corridors, everything looks the rainbow-flagging same. No destinations, only pathways." As his part of the challenge he's promised to produce content—"even if it's only ranting and foaming at the mouth."

And rant he does. Whether his columns are on the power structure in gay politics, the relation of facial hair to gay identity or pose the rubicon "If God hates fags, why do fags love God?" Larry-bob is always questioning our base assumptions, pushing us past the herd mentality he sees as the great nemesis. Sometimes, as in the essay "How To Raise Your Child to be Gay," a scalding bitterness will creep in: "Make sure [your child's] toy box contains not only Legos and dollies but also toys made of latex and rubber. The child with the well-stocked toy chest always will find friends eager to play.... Of course, even though you want your child to turn out gay, you must never let on that you actually approve of homosexuality. You need to instill a certain amount of self-loathing for your child to be a normal, twisted homosexual..."

Regardless of the subject (most revolve around examples of blindly following dogma), the writing is always tight and has that sort of delayed sting as you realize the sleeping prejudice he's been pricking. And nothing is sacrosanct—not the Human Rights Campaign (which he used to call the "Human Rights Champagne Fund"), nor even coming out. "Coming-out books need to have a chapter on how to kill your parents—not because most parents deserve death—they just deserve the shock of finding such a book when snooping around in a kid's room."

Holy Titclamps!

If Larry-bob's writing doesn't interest you, then pass by his many other linked pages. If it does, follow the links on Generic to the surprisingly large world of Larry-bob. You'll come across one of the deepest, most up-to-date links lists around (Hotlist), Queer Music Explosion (the bible of queer indie rock and pop), Queer Zine Explosion (a huge list of hundreds of queer 'zines), and Holy Titclamps (Larry-bob's infamous 'zine). And there's more.

Is he a fanatic? Undoubtedly. Is he recruiting followers? Never. He's just a sort of human superreactor, turning out energy like nobody else. Drop by for a jolting charge.

☐ *Larry-bob's Generic Queer Homepage*
http://www.io.com/~larrybob/generic.html

⌐ Latino, Latina

Perhaps more than any culture within the queer rainbow, Latinos seem to bring the best of their heritage to the Web. Everyone is friendly, sensitive to other cultures and welcoming of their own. There's an easiness here, balanced by a strong sense of cultural identity.

Though the number of the Latina/o pages aren't in line with the population, the tide is turning due in large part to a younger crowd of Web masters. Confident and easygoing, they all use the word *queer* easily

Gay Latino's Queer Latina/Latino Website

and are diffident about pushing any ideological mission beyond reflecting the queer part of the authors' lives. As Dennis Medina, "El Tejanito," says on his opening page, "I hope at least something here pleases you; and, if not—*Que vaya a la chingada!*" Charmingly, he adds, "Please, don't take offense at this term; I am using it in the 'metaphorical' sense, just like Octavio Paz and Carlos Fuentes."

Gay Latino/Hispanic Web Ring

One of the richest concentrations of pages is found at the Gay Latino Web Ring. There are hundreds of pages about or for gay Latino/Hispanic men, including home pages and the pages of organizations or groups. You can browse the list and read capsule descriptions of the listing sites such as Gay Carlitos: "Just a site about my life and and some on the people in it." *Revista Adelante* is a bilingual gay and lesbian magazine with health, clubs, photos and more, and Orlando's Home Page, "a collection of my writings, experiences, and references for other gay men of color." Gay-Bi Latino Chat Room is open for everyone!! BAGGY BOY'S ZONE!! is a very cool personal Web page created by a bi-sexual young Latino who currently lives in the Los Angeles area. Paco Calderón/Fotógrafo is a Mexican gay photographer of Latin guys. The Rican Stud Home Page is a censored image collection of some of the hottest Puerto Rican papis on the Web.

Home pages

One of the best list links is maintained by QV magazine. QV stands for "Quo Vadis," a Latin term meaning, "Where are you going?" The links are divided into sections. Organizations, for example, has links to LLEGO, HoMoVISIONES and the various chapters of La Familia. The arts and entertainment section has listings for everything from art galleries to pride events to Latin Hustle, San Francisco's funniest comedy trio. (*Mas queer que tu tio Chencho!*)

La Página de Donald is an excellent home page with links reac-ing throughout the gay Latino world, both here in America and down to Mexico as well as Colombia. Another good source is Nuestro Hogar. There's a mix of fun and serious sites, from the Luis Miguel Homepage and The Macarena Home Page to Gay and Lesbian Themes in Hispanic Literature and Culture and Queer Artist Collective.

Colombia Out of the Closet

This is a safe place, a sort of intimate club for Latina/o youth to air the emotions of finding a place within society, their families, and with their queer brothers and sisters. The opening page sets the tone: "Many times we feel isolated and alone. We seek friend-ship and support from people who understand us. Therefore a place on the Web where we can go and talk or listen to others of like mind is a great help. College is stressful enough, but when you must watch your words and monitor your thoughts it makes it even more challenging." There's a great deal of empathy on these pages. And lots of reassurance. "It would be great if we could all live openly and without fear of rejection. Unfortunately we do not live in a society which is always accepting of us. Therefore it is not my intention to 'out' anyone."

Erotica

Perhaps the most interesting home page is Erotica. It's the mysterious journal of a young gay Latino in Los Angeles. Nothing is simple here, everything elusive. Even the first page is a seductive puzzle—just a totemic male figure with four arms stretching a web of chains into a rectangle around his body— there's apparently no entrance to the site. Be patient and explore the body (near the heart). To the side are the phrases: "I am somebody/*el ser gay*." By clicking on the highlighted text,

you're shown short, contemplative paragraphs, most concerned with questions of identity. The text is plain, set in vibrantly colored designs, many of which look to be infrared photographs. Together they become a diary of impressions from the days of the week—standing in a subway, not looking into a stranger's eyes, getting caught, regretting a lack of courage...always searching for what's real. He's following the advice given to those frustrated by the seemingly locked first page: There's an entrance—"you just have to be more curious."

Organizations

In the last few years many more Latin American organizations have joined the Web. Gay and Lesbian Latinos Unidos, one of the oldest, is organized around political and social issues affecting both Gays and Lesbians and Latinos and Latinas. "Unidad," the monthly newsletter, focuses on the many efforts at bettering life and laws affecting the Gay and Lesbian Latino and Latina community. It also has stories and art by gay and lesbian Latino writers and artists. National Latina/o

Lesbian, Gay, Bisexual, and Transgendered Organization (LLEGO) is another national group that promotes strengthening the community through AIDS education, local work groups, national conferences, two quarterly newsletters, and educational scholarships for GLBT Latina/os. Queers Understanding Education, Power, And Solidarity = Advancement (Q.U.E.P.A.S.=A.) has a friendly supportive site with a an online chat room and message board for queer youth. There's also information on the groups outreach work with Los Angeles' Latino/a glbt youth. Excellent links list.

Quo Vadis?

QV is one of the best Latina/o magazines. Each issue is built around a theme taken from the editorial view that knowledge and education is the key. The "Empower" issue, for example, has features, columns, and a youth section considering the benefits and costs of coming out at home, at work, and to your community. The poetry section has included "I want a tall brown man." *En La Vida*, sister publication of Chicago-based *OutLines*, is a progressive paper giving reports on local AIDS groups, alerting readers to prejudicial stereotypes and urging involvement in the political process with how-to pieces like a practical guides to the election process. *Boys & Toys*, the most popular gay magazine in Mexico, is now on the Web. It's a lifestyle mix with pictures, interviews, personals, erotic literature and articles on gay life in Mexico. La Gaiceta keeps tabs on Latin LGBT life in Latin America, Spain, and the United States. Updated on a weekly basis, its articles are reports and analyses of political and social developments. Arenal covers LGBT laws and politics in Latin America.

☐ *ARENAL*
   http://www.indiana.edu/~arenal/Homepage.html

☐ *Aqui Estamos*
   http://aquiestamos.com/

☐ *Art of Man*
   http://members.zoom.com/sanseb/

☐ *Baggy Boy Central*
http://www.baggyboy.com/

☐ *Bibliography on G&L Chicanos/as and Latino/as*
http://www.wwwvms.utexas.edu/~demedina/biblio.htm

☐ *Boricuas Gay Pride*
http://boricua.com/pride/

☐ *Boys R Us*
http://www.homestead.com/boyzrus.html

☐ *Brasil Official Attitude and the age of consent*
http://www.gw.com/lists/arenal/brasil.html

☐ *Carlito's Website*
http://members.aol.com/gtype18m

☐ *Casal Lambda*
http://www.redestb.es/lambda/

☐ *Center for AIDS Prevention Studies (CAPS)*
http://www.epibiostat.ucsf.edu/capsweb/projects/hlsindex.html

☐ *Chicana Feminist Homepage*
http://www-leland.stanford.edu/~slg/

☐ *Colombia Out of the Closet*
http://www.geocities.com/WestHollywood/Heights/1424/

☐ *David Rivera & Willie Gonzalez*
http://www.geocities.com/WestHollywood/stonewall/6243/

☐ *Dennis Medina's "El Tejanito" Home Page*
http://wwwvms.utexas.edu/~demedina/

☐ *El Cobertizo: Libreria Gay y Lesbica*
http://www.digitel.es/usuarios/personalweb/cobertizo/books.html

☐ *El Gladiador*
http://www.geocities.com/WestHollywood/9818/

☐ *En La Vida*
http://www.suba.com/~outlines/current/enlavida/

☐ *Enlaces Gay*
http://www.hispamerica.com/gr/04/links/

☐ *El Museo de GayO*
http://www.gladiador.simplenet.com/museo/index.html

☐ *Erotica*
http://www.geocities.com/WestHollywood/2472/

☐ *Exclusively Latino*
http://www.latin.webspot.net

☐ *Exhibitionist Latino Mexican Male Gallery*
http://members.tripod.com/~tutul_xiu_2/

☐ *FELIPE'S Things Latino at EgOWeB*
http://egoiste.edb.utexas.edu/cyberraza/gender.html

☐ *Fratta!*
http://members.wbs.net/homepages/f/r/a/fratta.html

☐ *Futura*
http://www.futurasf.com/

☐ *Gay Amigos*
http://www.geocities.com/WestHollywood/Village/3154/

☐ *Gay Argentina*
http://www.geocities.com/westhollywood/heights/5446/

☐ *Gay Costa Rica*
http://www.gaycostarica.com/

☐ *Gay and Lesbian Latinos Unidos*
http://members.aol.com/gllu/home.html

☐ *Gay & Lesbian Themes in Hispanic Literature & Cultures*
http://www.cc.columbia.edu/cu/libraries/events/sw25/case9.html

☐ *Gay Latino Web Ring*
http://www.webring.org/cgi-bin/webring?=latino:list

☐ *Gay Latino's Queer Latina/Latino Web site*
http://www.geocities.com/WestHollywood/Heights/6404/

☐ *Gay Mexico*
http://www.gaymexico.com.mx/

☐ *Gay Puerto Rico*
http://www.geocities.com/westhollywood/6304/

☐ *Grupo Apoyo a la Diversidad de Orientaciones Sexuales (GADOS)*
http://www.geocities.com/WestHollywood/3554/

☐ *Guía de webs personales Gay/Bi/Les*
http://come.to/guiagbl

☐ *Hermanos de Luna y Sol*
http://www.epibiostat.ucsf.edu/capsweb/projects/hlsindex.html

☐ *Homovisiones*
http://www.homovisiones.org/

☐ *Infierno (CiberGay)*
http://www.cibergay.com/

☐ *La Gaiceta*
http://www.geocities.com/WestHollywood/Heights/4500

☐ *Latin Hustle*
http://www.latinhustle.com

☐ *La página de Andreu*
http://www.gayes.com/users/u596

☐ *Latino Gay Men of New York*
http://www.members.xoom.com/lgmny/

☐ *Latino Link/Gay Chat*
http://www.latinolink.com:8003/Join

☐ *Latino Web*
http://www.latinoweb.com/index.html

☐ *LLEGO*
http://www.llego.org/

☐ *Q.U.E.P.A.S.=A. (Queers Understanding Education, Power, And Solidarity = Advancement)*
http://members.aol.com/QuePasaLA/

☐ *Queer Latina/Chicana Fiction*
http://www2.ucsc.edu/people/ktrion/jotas3.html

☐ *QV Magazine*
http://www.qvmagazine.com/menu.html

☐ *Rio de Janeiro*
http://ipanema.com/rio/gay/

☐ *Sergay*
http://www.sergay.com.mx/

Law & Legal Issues

The law can be as remote as the Latin—it's so fond of quoting, or as immediate as an empty fridge when you're running the obstacle course of qualifying for disability. Whatever your needs or interests, you'll find excellent sources online.

Subjects are as complex as S/M and the law, as simple as the list of state sodomy law and as historically mind-boggling as Disciplinary Records on Same-Gender Sexual Activity in the U.S. Navy, 1800-1861. Gay Legal Pad provides information about gay-related acts in the Congressional Record.

As you might expect, the Queer Resources Directory has the largest

and most complete collection of sources for queer law. Its a huge page with notes on the most famous cases, a state-by-state breakdown of gay rights statutes, resources for same-sex marriage, discussion of international issues, and links to sites such as National Journal of Sexual Orientation Law and the QueerLaw Digest.

The Famous Cases folder has a docket going back to 1992, including the most recent decision in Hawaii and the infamous *Bowers* v. *Hardwick* (in which the Supreme Court decided in favor of the State of Georgia's allowing law enforcement officers to break into a gay couple's home and convict them of sodomy). Among the military cases you'll find are those involving Keith Meinhold and Margarethe Cammermeyer. These files are full of curious anecdotes, such as an article detailing Bill Clinton's rather odd paranoia about the potential of same-sex dancing at the army base canteen.

Lambda Legal Defense and Education Fund features news on events across the country, from a listing of key cases, to the text of judges decisions as *Dale* v. *Boy Scouts of America* and the same-sex harassment case *Oncale* v. *Sundowner.*

There are a number of Web sites devoted to keeping people up-to-date with the latest happenings on the issue of marriage rights for same-gender couples. The most definitive (in terms of legal ramifications) is the National Freedom to Marry Coalition. The QRD also maintains a few lists of interest, such as one of companies whose nondiscrimination policies include sexual orientation, companies and organizations that provide benefits to domestic partners, states that criminalize acts between people of the same gender, ages of consent in the United States, and sodomy laws and ages of consent worldwide (matters of particular interest to travelers).

Activists

There's also a list of activist groups that use the law as a shield and weapon for civil rights, including the NGLTF, HRC, Lesbian and Gay Law Association of New York, ACLU, NOW, International Gay and Lesbian Human Rights Commission, and the Lesbian and Gay Immigration Rights Task Force. The Lambda Legal Defense and Education Fund and the International Lesbian and Gay Association also have archives of material in the organizations directory of the QRD. Each of these groups has separate legal-issues folders where you can learn more about their involvement. (Also see Canada's EGALE, which was involved in the first case on recognizing same-sex relationships to reach the country's highest court.)

You can find a huge list of articles by the national press on the subject by searching through AltaVista on "Gay Lesbian Legal." Of all the queer papers in the United States, the *Washington Blade* is by far the best, both for the depth of legal coverage and its lack of legal jargon.

HIV

One of the most personal ways in which the law affects us—particularly those of us who are HIV-positive—is through disability laws. The best source of guidance through this maze of doctors' reports and regulations is your local AIDS group. Look through Roy Radow's list of community centers at the QRD, which lists hundreds of organizations, along with their areas of expertise. Each state has an exhaustive list, whether that means the 100-plus groups in California, the six outreach groups in Alaska, or the 12 organizations in Alabama. Phone numbers are included, as well as street addresses. Most groups have the official social security disability documents, and you can also read them at various government sites and at the QRD, QIS, and other large gay collections.

Marty Howard's home page has a connection to HIV Law, a discussion list for attorneys and other advocates. The purpose of this list is to exchange information of interest to persons involved in HIV client services and HIV law and public policy advocacy.

Disabilities

For a huge list of sources on disability law, see the site called Disabilities Links. Along with groups that address specific handicaps, you'll find pointers to law sources such as LawMarks and Legal Links on the WWW. Yahoo! has a long series of links, each with further links to free advice offers on the Internet and to a variety of legal and law-related sites. America online's AIDS/HIV forum is also an excellent place to gather information; you can read messages here from people who've survived the application process. They talk about the myths, such as the false notion that once you've gone on SSI you can never work again. They also discuss the strangeness of dealing with a sense of "floating" (as one poster called life without the structure of a work schedule).

Wills

Though everyone seems nervous about wills, they are particularly important among gays and lesbians. Without recognition of same-sex marriages, how else can you guarantee that your wishes about trusteeship be honored? For an excellent guide, see About Health Care Proxies and Living Wills. Though the specific information refers to the laws in the state of New York, much of it applies to any U.S. citizen.

Military (Gay Alpha Yankee)

The three best sites dealing with homophobia in the U.S. military are Gays and Lesbians in the Military, Servicemembers Legal Defense Network and Dave's Gay Military Site. All three are solid, extremely intelligent calls to action with statistics, profiles, and examples from other militaries that have successfully integrated. Dave's is especially good if you personally are dealing with homophobia in the military. Along with articles from the major media on the topic, there are sections on Policy References and Court Cases, News Archives, Links to Other Web Resources, and a mailing list.

A Lover of Soldiers is a different animal. Although it's a sales page for Steven Zeeland's books on gay life in the army, with reviews and synopses, it's a terrifically powerful argument against homophobia on the simple grounds that an individual's sexuality exists apart from his ability to perform—that homophobia is just that, a phobia, a mind game. See also Timothy McVeigh's home page. He talks about his case with the service, his reaction to AOL's violation of his privacy, and the current situation with "don't ask, don't tell."

If you're familiar with "lawspeak," try the many university libraries. Just as gay studies are a hot topic on campus, so is the sphere of gay law, which deals with discrimination, same-sex marriage, and the "normalization" of rights. Cornell, the University of California, Berkeley, the University of Virginia, and many others have libraries filled with cases and trial briefs.

☐ *About Health Care Proxies and Living Wills*
http://www.aidsnyc.org/acqc/wills.html

☐ *ACLU*
http://www.aclu.org/issues/gay/

☐ *AIDS in the Workplace Seminar*
http://www.hsupports.org/hsupports/aiw-seminar.html

☐ *Army Discharge Review Board*
http://www.geocities.com/pentagon/1151/text22.html

☐ *Canadian HIV/AIDS Legal Network*
http://www.aidslaw.ca

☐ *Center for Lesbian and Gay Civil Rights*
http://www.center4civilrights.org/

☐ *Collected Domestic Partner Information*
http://www.cs.cmu.edu/afs/cs.cmu.edu/user/scotts/domestic-part

☐ *Coalition of HIV Legal Service Providers*
http://www.hivlegalnyc.org/home.html

☐ *Constitution of the United States*
http://www.einet.net/galaxy/Law/Constitutional.html

☐ *Dave's Gay Military Site*
http://www.gaymilitary.org/

☐ *Disabilities Links*
http://www.cirs.or /disabilities.html

☐ *Domestic Partnerships and Same Sex Marriages*
http://www.cs.cmu.edu/afs/cs.cmu.edu/user/scotts/
domestic-partners/mainpage.html

☐ *Don't Ask, Don't Tell*
   http://dont.stanford.edu/

☐ *Fair Law*
   http://ltc.law.warwick.ac.uk/

☐ *Gay Law Net*
   http://www.gaylawnet.com/

☐ *Gay Law News*
   http://www.gaylaw.com/news.html

☐ *Gay Legal Pad*
   http://www.cs.cmu.edu/afs/cs/user/dtw/www.legal.html

☐ *Gay Workplace Issues*
   http://www.nyu.edu/pages/sls/gaywork/

☐ *Gay, Lesbian & Bisexual Veterans*
   http://www.glbva.org

☐ *GLBT Disabled Veterans of America*
   http://www.geocities.com/pentagon/1151

☐ *Guide to SS Benefits and HIV*
   http://www.qrd.org/QRD/aids/guide.ss.benefit.and.hiv

☐ *HRC*
   http://www.hrcusa.org/

☐ *International Association of L&G Judges*
   http://home.att.net/~ialgj/

☐ *Keith Meinhold*
   http://www.sldn.org/km05_30_96.html

☐ *Law, Marriage: Legal Issues and Sexuality*
   http://www.halcyon.com/elf/altsex/legal.html

☐ *Lambda Legal Defense Fund*
http://www.lamdalegal.org/

☐ *Legal Aspects of Transexualism*
http://members.tripod.com/~philkirk/translaw.html

☐ *LeGal Institute*
http://www.law.cornell.edu/

☐ *LeGaL's Home Page (Lesbian and Gay Lawyers)*
http://www.users.interport.net/~le-gal/

☐ *Lesbian and Gay Law Association of Greater New York (LeGal)*
http://www.users.interport.net/~le-gal/

☐ *Lesbian & Gay Lawnotes*
http://www.qrd.org/qrd/usa/legal/lgln

☐ *Mining Co.*
http://gaylesissues.miningco.com

☐ *National Freedom to Marry Coalition*
http:/www.ftm.org/

☐ *National Gay & Lesbian Association*
http://www.nlgla.org/

☐ *National Gay & Lesbian Task Force*
http://www.ngltf.org/

☐ *National Journal of Sexual Orientation Law*
http://sunsite.unc.edu/gaylaw/

☐ *Nolo Press*
http://www.nolo.com/

☐ *NOW Gay and Lesbian Rights*
http://now.org/now/issues/lgbi/lgbi.html

☐ *Partners Task Force Home Page*
http://www.buddybuddy.com/

☐ *Queer Law*
http://abacus.oxy.edu/~ron/queerlaw.html

☐ *QRD Legal*
http://www.qrd.org/qrd/

☐ *S&M and the Law*
http://www.leatherquest.com/smlaw.htm

☐ *Same-Sex Sexual Laws*
http://www.uic.edu/orgs/lgbt/sodomy.html

☐ *Servicemembers Legal Defense Network*
http://www.sldn.org/index.html

☐ *Sodomy Laws*
http://www.sodomylaws.org/

☐ *Steven Zeeland's Military Web site*
http://www.stevenzeeland.com

☐ *Supreme Court Decisions*
http://www.law.cornell.edu/supct/

☐ *Tim McVeigh*
www.geocities.com/Pentagon/9241/INFO.HTML

Where to start? It's as if the armies of leathermen and leatherwomen around the world suddenly snapped to attention and decided to claim a large chunk of the Web as their own dungeon. Master? Slave? Novice? Today the leather community online reflects the depth and diversity of its counterpart in the 3-D world. There are clubs, picture galleries, activity announcement pages, lots of catalogs, and thousands of home pages. The gay search engines are packed with sites including even the most extreme. There's LeatherNet, with an especially useful education and mentoring section. And if you are having trouble dealing with your sexuality or fantasies, KAP (Kink Aware Professionals) has links to medical, legal, and mental help professionals with a background in leather and S/M.

However intimidating it sounds, you'll find that experienced leather lovers are the most ready to welcome newcomers. The New York Renegades, one of the largest and oldest leather clubs in the world, advises readers to tour their site and events pictures with an open mind, telling the novice there's no pressure to participate, just stand back and watch until you're ready.

Leather Edge

Perhaps the best place to start is with Leather Edge, created by the first Mr. Internet Leather. It's a beautifully designed page that works as both a personal home page and a journey into the world of leather. "People tell me, 'Take me to the edge.' I always answer 'Which one?' There's an edge form of whipping, bondage, fisting, anything. For me, edge play is about moving further and further into what turns you on. I am here only because this is where my experiences and desires have led me. Be happy where you are and find your own edge." There are sections on the philosophy of leather and practical tips as well as recommendations to various books he believes in, each with a quick appraisal. The raw meat of the page comes in stories and links to fetish sites for leather, stogies, boots, uniforms, rubber, and bears.

For a similar perspective on leather that mixes philosophy with instruction, try the GMSMA's newsletter and the home page of Mr. Internet Leather '98, Jack Rinella. Rinella's page is all about "Sane Sexuality of the Kinky Kind." Most of the articles are drawn from his own life as a 24/7 leatherman. You can read about everything from bondage to cruising to domination, fisting, raunch, and "dressing for success." There's also a personals section and information on his books, *A Handbook of Erotic Dominance* and *The Compleat Slave*.

Yes Sir, Mr. Gallagher

Joe Gallagher's Leatherpage has become one of those pages on everyone's list no matter which coast you live on, no matter how deep you are into leather. He's a friendly, incredibly connected guy (Mr. International Leather '96) and his page gives perhaps the fullest picture of a well-balanced leather life. The links list is great and there are news briefs on events around the world and links to clubs from the Berliner Truppe in Germany to Shinjuku-ku in Tokyo. And no matter where you live you can keep up with the weekly scene as reported by all the best leather world columnists from Mister Marcus in San Francisco to Daniel Premack in Baltimore.

Other well-rounded pages include those of Ms. Leather of '96 (Jill Carter), SoJourner's Paradise, The Leather Masters Association, and Mad Max. SoJourner's Paradise is the personal site of a lesbian into

B&D and S/M. She shares some information about lesbianism and her thoughts on B&D and S/M. Then there's Piglet, whose slave page introduces (obediently) the Leather Ring, a large collection of leather pages rivaled in number only by those found on the Leather Navigator. Both Navigator and the Ring are great jump sites to clubs, bookstores, catalogs and other home pages. And that's only a foretaste; there are also the giant leather libraries of stories.

Magazines & Stories

Also, check out the leather magazines like Bondagezine, Check-Mate, Cuir Underground, Leather online, In Uniform and Leather Journal for calendars of events around the US, as well as articles. The Guardian is a good place to get practical information on technique and keeping your tools in working order. For men only there's Daddy; for women-only Leatherdykes Dungeon. For some of the hottest stories go to BootJac and The Power Exchange.

Leather Navigator

One of the best of the new meeting and discussion places for leatherman is Leather Navigator, a vast multi-page space where the sex and spirit of modern day leather meet—and meet hard. Along with sections titled "Black and Blue," "Sick Puppy," and "Fresh Horses," there are photos and member profiles for getting togther for play time or at leather events such as IML. The WOOFexchange is a classifieds section where you can find partners and playmates for free and for hire. LeatherWorks, the online magazine of Leather Navigator, provides interesting coverage of leather world happenings, columnists have included Tony Mills. There are feature articles, leathersex Q&As, a calendar of events as well as club listings from around the world. One of the most popular sections of LN is The Rogue's Forum, where members write of their wildest encounters and readers write back. "Black and Blue" is the column by Phil Julian, a writer and leatherman. Here's how he explain's what the column, and Leather Navigator are all about: "If anyone ever said or iimplied to you that in order to enter this realm (this bar, this playspace, this brotherhood, this circle, this level of understanding, this kinship, this kind of love) you had to kiss their ring, and you said or implied back to them that they should kiss your ass, you are probably going to really like this column." "Play hard, play safe" is the motto.

RedRight

Further up (or down) the raunch scale is RedRight's home page. His slogan is "Double Wide, Elbow Deep." This guy is seriously into his scene and has a gallery of some of the roughest pictures on the Web depicting "handball, anal-manual stimulation, FF, elbow-riding.... If you dig around you might find a little scat too, and who knows what else?" As you might guess, this one is not for the squeamish.

As you wander around Leather online you'll find Circlet Press and XCORRIGIA; bookstore pages that offer catalogs. Boudoir Noir publicizes the magazine of the same name; it also has a free personals section, political alerts, and a useful list of links to other Web sites. The S/M, Leather, and Fetish Community Outreach page has general information plus links and safer-sex play guides.

Urban S/M

All the major metropolitan areas have a good deal of activity. Try the annotated list of clubs at Leather online for guides to Chicago, New York, San Francisco, Los Angeles, Baltimore, Denver, and Seattle. You'll find schedules of local events, links to bars, and perhaps models for your own club page. The Denver-based CODE, whose page is particularly well-done, is "a nonpolitical group of gay males into S/M, leather, and fetishes in a safe, sane, and consensual environment for educational and social contacts. The club rents and furnishes a dungeon play space in central Denver which is used by club members."

San Francisco Leather

San Francisco Leather is another excellent site with links to leather home pages, general resources, publications, clubs, smut, and fetish links as well as printable maps to bars and clubs. The Alternative Sexuality Resources page is vast, with links that connect you with newsgroups, mailing lists, the America Online Leather forum, and academic discussions on what it all means. Don't miss the Web site for San Francisco's hottest playground, The Sling (our screen will sweat) Also check out the home page list with a roster of guys like Boot Boy, Ed and his playroom, Eric the cigar-smoking leather cop, GoodPup, Jim (JockDad) Perry, and John Krieter, who's "built for abuse."

Check out Rainbow Query's listings under "Rough Trade" for sites like Cuir Underground, Fetishwerks, and The Doghouse. Houston Fister has everything you always wanted to know about fisting and handballing, plus other fetishes, contacts with other fisters, and photo gallery. Electric Leather.com has toys and videos beyond your imagination.

Conveniently, you can even submit to a test gauging whether you're truly into the scene (the 100 Point B&D-S/M Purity Test). Basically it's best to visit for indexes of categories like Cigar Studs, Spanking Resources Guide, the Gay Watersports Ring, Bootboys Page, FLAG (Fits Like AGlove), or Yossie's Handcuffs. These taste-specific pages are much more up-to-date and have links to the large indexes overlook.

☐ *'98 Mr. Internet leather (Jack Rinella)*
http://www.leatherviews.com

☐ *100 Point BD/SM Purity Test*
http://www.lungfish.com/friday/bdsm_purity.html

☐ *The Academy*
http://www.academyent.com

☐ *Aftershock (LA)*
http://www.journeyz.com/afterschock.com/

☐ *Alt.Sex Homepage BDSM*
http://www.altsex.org/bdsm/

☐ *alt.sex FAQs*
http://www.halcyon.com/elf/altsex/

☐ *American Boyz*
http://www.amboyz.com/

☐ *Arizona Power Exchange*
http://www.xroads.com/apex/.com/

☐ *Armpits*
http://www.geocities.com/westhollywood/stonewall/2141

☐ *Atlanta Eagle*
http://www.mindspring.com/~bryon/eagle.html

☐ *Baltimore Eagle*
http://www.smart.net/~leather/

☐ *Black Iris*
http://www.blackiris.com/

☐ *BlowBuddies*
http://www.blowbuddies.com

☐ *bondage boy*
http://www.guypages.com/kevin/

☐ *Big Black Boots*
http://www.boot.com

☐ *Big Boots*
http://www.bondagemaster.com

☐ *Black Rose*
http://www.br.com/

☐ *BLUF*
http://www.bluf.com

☐ *Body Modification*
http://BME.FreeQ.com

☐ *Bondagezine*
http://BME.FreeQ.com

☐ *Boot Boy's page*
http://www.bootboy.com/lead.htm

☐ *boot jaq*
http://www.skunky.org/~bootjac/

☐ *Boot Master*
http://www.geocities.com/WestHollywood/3804/indexsu3.htm

☐ *Boston Leather*
http://www.leatherboston.com/

☐ *Bound & Gagged*
http://www.boundandgagged.com/

☐ *BoundEx*
http://www.boundex.com/

☐ *Brad King*
http://www.bradking.com/

☐ *BzzzCut's's Lair*
http://www.binary9.net/bzzzcut/

☐ *Capital Leathermen (Austin, TX)*
http://www.io.com/~topman4u/capital.html

☐ *Charles Haynes Radical Sex*
http://www.fifth-mountain.com/radical_sex/

☐ *Checkmate Magazine*
   http://www.Checkmate.com/

☐ *Cigar Cop*
   http://members.aol.com/fulllthr1/cigar.html

☐ *Cigar Smoking Pig's Page*
   http://www.geocities.com/westhollywood/chelsea/7684/index.html

☐ *Circlet Press*
   http://www.circlet.com/circlet/home.html

☐ *Cole Tucker*
   http://www.Cole-Tucker.com/

☐ *Cop Wanted*
   http://www.Copwanted.com/

☐ *The Colonel*
   http://thecolonel.com

☐ *Cuffs*
   http://.cuffs.com/

☐ *Cuir Underground*
   http://www.black-rose.com/cuiru.html

☐ *Daddy's*
   http://www.wolfe.com/daddys/

☐ *Daedalus Books*
   http://www.bookport.com/htbin/publishers/daedalus/bn

☐ *Deviant's Dictionary*
   http://www.queernet.org/deviant

☐ *Dick Wad*
   http://www.dickwad.com/

☐ *Dirty Tops*
http://www.dirtytop.org/

☐ *Dog Training*
http://www.TheDogHouse.org

☐ *Drag Kings & Dyke Dads*
http://vinland.org/scamp/zgallery/dragkings/index.html

☐ *Drummer Contests*
http://www.drummercontests.com

☐ *Drummer Magazine*
http://www.drummer.com/

☐ *Dyke Uniform Cops*
http://members.aol.com/ducny/

☐ *Electric Leather*
http://www.electricleather.com/

☐ *Extreme Male Bondage*
http://www.leathersex.com/extreme

☐ *Fetishwerks*
http://www.fetishwerks.com

☐ *FFPlayer*
http://www.geocities.com/WestHollywood/1855/

☐ *Fist Fuck Gallery*
http://www.leathersex.com/fistfucking/

☐ *FLAG (Fits Like A Glove)*
http://www.lthredge.com/flag.htm

☐ *Gay Boy LACA*
http://members.tripod.com/~gblaca

☐ *Gay Lovers of Lycra*
http://phymat.bham.ac.uk/Lycra/

☐ *Gay Male S&M Activists*
http://www.gmsma.org/

☐ *Gladiator World Alliance*
http://www.vangar.com

☐ *Hanky Code*
http://www.mansco.com/hankies.htm

☐ *Homo Military Hunger*
http://members.tripod.com/~leathercub

☐ *Hot 'n Kinky Men*
http://members.aol.com/thornyc2

☐ *Houston Fister*
http://www.westom.com/fister

☐ *In Uniform Magazine*
http://www.inuniform.com/

☐ *International Mr. Leather*
http://www.IMrL.com/

☐ *International Ms. LeatherWoman*
http://www.imsl.com/

☐ *Joe Gallagher, Mr. International Leather '96*
http://www.leatherpage.com

☐ *Larry Townsend's Web Pages*
http://www.larrytownsend.com

☐ *Leather Command*
http://www.geocities..com/westhollywood/8348/

☐ *Leather Edge*
http://www.lthredge.com/

☐ *Leather Guide to SF*
http://www.wolf.nu/

☐ *Leatherfest*
http://www.leatherfest.com

☐ *Leather Jeep*
http://www.leatherjeep.com/

☐ *Leather Masters Association*
http://www.crl.com/~masters/

☐ *Leather Navigator*
http://www.leathernavigator.com/

☐ *Leather Nexus*
http://members.aol.com/nitestick/links0.htm

☐ *Leather Online Magazine*
http://www.LeatherOnline.org/

☐ *Leatherpage.com*
http://www.leatherpage.com

☐ *Leather Ring*
http://www.geocities.com/WestHollywood/3322/

☐ *Leather Web*
http://www.leatherweb.com

☐ *Living In Leather*
http://www.nla-i.com/lil.html

☐ *Lonestar Saloon*
http://www.lonestar-saloon.com

☐ *Lure (The)*
http://www.thelure.com/

☐ *Master Brent*
http://www.directnet.com/~brent/

☐ *Master & Slave Training*
http://www.leatherweb.com/butch11.htm

☐ *Men & Their Moustaches*
http://www.ozemail.com.au/~drummer/htmls/matm.html

☐ *Metropolitan Slave Magazine*
http://www.metroslave.com/

☐ *Mr Ebony Leather*
http://members.aol.com/writercain/ebony.html

☐ *Mr. Fister*
http://www.fistersdungeon.com

☐ *Mr. International Leather '96 Joe Gallagher*
http://www.nycnet.com/Gallagher/

☐ *Mr. International Leather '97*
http://www.leatherpage.com

☐ *Mr. Internet Leather Homepage*
http://members.aol.com/MrIntrLthr/

☐ *Mr. S. Leather*
http://www.mr-s-leather--fetters.com

☐ *National Leather Association*
http://www.nla-i.com/

☐ *New York Renegades*
http://www.nyrenegades.com

☐ *Peter Boots*
http://www.pobox.com/~pboots

☐ *Pig Pages / Pig Media*
http://www.pigmedia.com/

☐ *Pipe Bear Site*
http://members.aol.com/bearnpipe/pipebrs.html

☐ *Purity Test*
http://www.lungfish.com/friday/bdsm_purity.html

☐ *Randy Riddle's Cool Cat Daddy Page*
http://www.coolcatdaddy.com

☐ *RedRight's FF page*
http://www.winternet.com/~redright/redright.html

☐ *Ropeburn*
http://www.ropeburn.com/

☐ *Rough Riders*
http://www.netgsi.com~transman/roughriders.html

☐ *Safer SM*
http://alternate.com/

☐ *San Francisco Leather*
http://www.wolf.nu/

☐ *San Francisco Leather*
http://www.sanfranciscoleather.com

☐ *Scarred*
http://www.scarred.com

☐ *Skin Two*
http://www.skintwo.co.uk

☐ *Seattle S/M Resources List*
http://www.halcyon.com/elf/seattle.html

☐ *Seduction: The Cruel Woman*
http://www.gayweb.com/first_run/cruel.html

☐ *S.F. Dungeon*
http://www.sfdungeon.com/

☐ *Slakker's Leather Page*
http://www.IntNet.net/public/slakker/Home.html

☐ *Slave Den*
http://www.geocities.com/WestHollywood/5588/

☐ *S&M Board*
http://www.smboard.com/

☐ *S&M Boys*
http://www.smboys.com/

☐ *SM Gays on the Web*
http://www.powerhouse.co.uk/powerhouse/smgays/

☐ *Smokin' Dudes*
http://www.smokindudes.com

☐ *Society of Janus*
http://www.soj.org/

☐ *Stogy Pig*
http://theslingsf.com/personal.html

☐ *Stompers Bootss*
http://www.stompersboots.com

☐ *TopBear*
http://www.wizard.com/~topbear/

☐ *Total Tops*
http://www.jocks.net/tops/total.html

☐ *Tough Male*
http://www.toughmale.com

☐ *Waterboys*
http://www.waterboys.com

☐ *Wild Side*
http://www.futuresex.com

☐ *Without Restraint*
http://www.mcsp.com/smcop/welcome.html

☐ *Wolpert, Jake*
http://www.slip.net/~jwolpert

☐ *Wrestling Men*
http://members.aol.com/wrestlemen/wresmen.htm

☐ *XXX Dungeon*
http://xxxdungeon.com/

☐ *Yossie's Handcuffs*
http://www.blacksteel.com/~yossie/hcs.html

☐ *Yahoo! S&M*
http://www.yahoo.com/Society_and_Culture/Sex/BDSM

S&M Clubs

☐ *69th Precinct*
www.pridetriangle.com/69th

☐ *Defenders*
http://www.blackiris.com/~Defenders

☐ *Denver Leather Brotherhood*
www.denverleather.com

☐ *Desert Dungeons*
http://www.azds.net/dd/

☐ *FLOG*
http://www.gurlpages.com/me/moflog

☐ *Highwaymen TNT*
http://www.dcpride.org/HighwaymenTNT/

☐ *KC Pioneers*
http://www.kcpioneers.com

☐ *Leather Knights - Dallas*
http://www.flash.net/~1knights/index.html

☐ *Masters & Slaves Atlanta*
http://www.mast.org/

☐ *Military & Police Uniform Association*
http://www.members.tripod.com/~mpua/

☐ *NLA - New England*
http://www.www.circlet.com/pub/u/ctan/nlane.html

☐ *Northeast Pa. Leathermen*
http://www.nepa-leathermen.com

☐ *NY Renegades*
http://www.nyrenegades.com

☐ *Promethean Guard*
http://home.att.net/~prometheanguard/sitemai2.html

☐ *Saber MC*
http://geocities.com/westhollywood/heights/6868/

☐ *SF Phoenix Uniform Club*
http://www.wolf.nu

☐ *STARS, M.C.*
http://www.fangz.com/~starsmc/

☐ *Team Delta*
http://www.teamdelta.net

☐ *Tribe*
http://www.comnet.org/tribe

☐ *Trident - Baltimore*
http://www2.smart.net/~leather/clubs/trident/

☐ *Windy City Bondage Club's Web site*
http://www.surrenderdorothy.com/wcbc/

☐ *Zero Cop*
http://www.zerocop.com

Indexes

☐ *Bondage Reference*
http://www.queernet.org/deviant/fsbdgref.htm#Fastenings

☐ *Cigar Studs*
http://www.queernet.org/cs

☐ *Cigarmen Ring*
http://www.users.dircon.co.uk/~beartrap/ringpag1.htm

☐ *Gay Masters & Slaves Ring*
http://www.geocities.com/westhollywood/stonewall/9714/

☐ *Gay SM Ring*
http://www.geocities.com/WestHollywood/6941

☐ *Gay Watersports Ring*
http://www.aec.co.at/home/pissratte/gaywsring/

☐ *Leather Central*
http://www.leathercentral.com

☐ *Leather Ring*
http://www.geocities.com/WestHollywood/3322

☐ *Ropeburn*
http://www.ropeburn.com

☐ *Rope Web*
http://www.ropeweb.com

☐ *Rubber Fetish Site*
http://www.rubberfetish.com

☐ *Spanking Resources Guide*
http://www.viaverde.com/sex/spank.htm

Lesbian Resources

Where can women go to find a space created purely on their own, for their own, by their own? Maybe a commune in Oregon—or, if time travel were possible, Amazonia. But since we're talking about a large, comfortable place where tens of thousands of women can schmooze, sing, fondle, tease, write, and generally rock out, perhaps there is only the Web. There are sites here for political issues, health concerns, or herstory. You can find mailing lists and newsletters; visit hundreds of home pages by a kung fu dyke, music lovers, urban grrrls, farmers, or leather bikers; or explore dyke TV, poetry lists, and art—all within a lesbian context.

Lesbian Universe

If you're doubtful of the women's mastery of the Web, check out Lesbian Nation and Lesbian.com. Both are somehow able to be both large and multifaceted, as well as intimate, woman-safe spaces. Lesbian Nation has an excellent links list, diverse discussion groups and one of the best selections of articles on lesbian life around, ranging from being out at work to how potlucks began and why. The message boards are very well-attended and contain questions and answers on vacation spots for lesbians, coming out to family and friends, what to do after a divorce, and much more. There's also an incredibly complete national events calendar with info on large events like the Dinah Shore Golf Tournament and small affairs such as The Spring Lesbian Choral Ensemble at the First Presbyterian Church of Oakland.

Lesbian.com is a wonderfully ambitious, very politically aware site with a huge directory of links to activism, politics, antioppression, arts and muses, business and economy, computers, technology, family and parenting, gender, health and wellness, herstory, home and garden, literature, media, sexuality, spirituality, sports, and travel.

A Dyke's World

One of the sites you'll see listed in almost every collection is A Dyke's World by Indina Beuche. It's been around since the dark ages (1995) and every year it gets bigger and more beautiful and quirky. There are now 606 (yes that many!) pages to visit (but there's an easy-to-use navigation bar). And there's no such thing as one style or one layout here, every subarea has its own "face." There are interactive pages like The Chathouse and Message Boards with topics for women with various interests. There are home pages Indina thinks are the crème de la crème, a picture book of European women along with their thoughts, and there's a site with links you might want to check out whenever you feel "low, ill or depressed—and are in need of ideas or contacts to gain back your power. It's just a starting point to dig deeper." Lots of serious, sexy, funny stuff, including Wild Women Dreamin' Wet, Cyberdyke's Cartooncorner, Sweet Music Sisters on Stage—and lest you think Indina is naïve, there's a page called Beware Our Enemies!

Lesbian.org

Another must-see page is Lesbian.org. Its founder, Web maven Amy Goodloe, describes Lesbian.org's mission as one of "promoting lesbian visibility on the Internet," and it surely does. You can visit art exhibits such as "Love Makes a Family," join lesbian issue forums, read about writers and books, and peruse guides on coming out and learning your way around the Web (If you're curious about Mail Lists, NewsGroups or Chat, see "Finding Women on the Internet." It makes sense of them all.)

As an umbrella group, Lesbian.org hosts various groups like the June Mazer Lesbian Collection (an archive of lesbian history), the

National Lesbian Political Action Committee, the Sappho Project, the Lesbian Mother's Support Society, and many others. And Lesbian.org is a two-way street. It involves visitors with its own message board, where topics have included "New Dyke on the Net," "Coming Out Lesbian," "Lesbian Personals," "Regional Lesbians," "Lesbian Book Recommendations," and "The Lesbian Information Exchange." Of course, there are also descriptive links to other mailing lists and message boards, such as those offered on Pleiades, QWorld, and PlanetOut. If you've heard about IRC (and Lesbian.org thinks you should have), follow the advice and click over to Grrltalk: "The Grrltalk Web site features comprehensive information about how to use IRC and how to find lesbian IRC channels."

Amy's Obsession

For an example of what home pages should strive for, see Amy's Obsession. Amy is the founder of Lesbian.org and an evangelist for women on the Web. She loves books, hates malls, lives in the country with a horse and keeps a journal—where she pours out a "wordstorm" on polyamory, neediness, the joys of the road, and books. She loves books and has a section devoted to those she's read. Added to this are an impressive list of links as well as a roster of women-only forums on subjects like writing and dogs.

Web Grrls

In Web parlance, computer-savvy young dykes are, "grrrls." The growl in this new term is a little edgy, the use of "girl" is intentionally in-your-face, and if you smile as your lips wrap around the word, you should feel very much at home in most any of these technically savvy, postfeminist, community-oriented dyke spaces. They're usually created by an under-30 age group who explore their passions, whether it be sport or music, with a hip, open and modern sensibility. There is Webgrrls, Girljock, Fat Girl, Grrltalk, Grrlz Linx, CyberGrrls, and on and on. One of the best is Riotgrrl, which defines itself as about "activist music, 'zines, and other activity that builds a supportive environment for women and girls and is concerned with feminist issues such as rape, abortion rights, bulimia and anorexia, beauty standards, exclusion from popular culture, the sexism of everyday life, double standards, sexuality, self-defense, fat oppression, racism, and classism." If this definition gets your pulse going, head straight to Riot Grrl.

Links

Lesbian Life (at About.com), Oddgirl's, Amazon Online, Curvey's, Stacey's Place—each has gobs of links. Oddgirl's Lesbian Links are especially well divided into categories such as Art and Literature, Regional Directories, Shopping and Magazines. With quick-witted commentary, the author rates them using baseball metaphors. First base "includes some lesbian content, but usually it is buried deep," while a home run is "as dykey as you can get."

The sheer size of Kathy Hunsicker's Amazon Online makes it a popular bookmark for Web dykes. Go here for everything from news and magazines to sports, humor, activist organizations, health and wellness, and games. Though the links are not always lesbian-oriented, there's not a clunker in the collection.

TechnoDyke

Is there an agenda at TechnoDyke? Very much so. Their mission is to create an online community for women that expresses women as full human beings, and if you can peck at a computer, you're in as a TechnoDyke! This is a great place to get advice on surfing, E-mailing, and even finding the woman of your dreams in those not-so-scary personals. There's an astrology column, chat lines, lots of links and interesting articles such as an Interview with Debora Iyall formerly of Romeo Void, now fronting Knife In Water, an edgy pop band out of San Francisco, and there's a piece on Suzanne Westenhoefer (the Diva of Dyke Comedy) and a rant in honor of National Women's History Month—"How did we end up fearing the word 'feminist' again?"

Magazines

Although the online magazine world has a high casualty rate, there are now so many of such quality that whatever your interests you'll find a match. You're probably familiar with *Girlfriends* from the print version (the Web version has "not fit for print" interviews) but also take a look at new online-only magazines like Shescape online

and Riotgrrl. Both have a definite voice and plenty of attitude as they cover the culture scene from best books to life in the 90's. Riotgrrl has a sassy Gen X take on things.

For thoughtful, sometimes bitterly intelligent views on lesbian and feminist issues, see Melty online, Catt's Claws, MaxiMag and Double X Chromosome. Perhaps the smartest of the edgy magazines is Brillo. Very activist-oriented, it always pushes past ideology to the people it covers in the excellent profiles. The letters to the editor, tools and resources and the hit list (putting a bull's-eye on sexists) are all worth your time. Girljock, Brat Attack for leather gals, a space for lesbians 50 and over—there are Web sites for everyone.

Women Only!

The openness and inclusion of the above sites is certainly a point of strength, but there's a cost—creeps of the male kind drop by too. For a chromosomally pure environment go to the salons—as these gathering places are called— where no men are allowed past the gates. HerSalon.com has inspirational profiles of strong women in sports, media and history. LJ's Kafe for Ladies Only has chat lines covering many topics of interest— and then there's FemmeWorld: "You are now leaving Cyberspace and entering feminine Elektraspace." There is further admonition: "If you proceed you will no longer be in the 1990s. You will be in a world founded upon that quality which your world fears most and most misunderstands: innocence." Initiates are warned not to give "boys" free passes. Unless you register as a woman, you will only be able to read tantalizing conversational tidbits such as these seven separate fragments: "Bye"…"Me too"…"Talk tomorrow"…"Cheerio and enjoy the sunshine!"…"Hello all you lesbians"…"Sorry about that—Norma"… "Hello? What's up tonight?" What are they saying? Who's Norma? Exclusive and confident, these salons are some of the fastest-growing communities on the Web. Once in, you'll find resources for everything under the sun, lots of conversation, and always many links to other networking hubs.

Where the Girls Are

Personal home pages offer a similarly rich array. Three in particular are terrific starting points and touchstones for veteran Web surfers. Susan Dennis's Where the Girls Are is an immensely useful page with links to tne ADA Project, political groups, the Older Women's League, and more. Her page contains one of the largest collections of lesbian home pages. Other sites, such as WWWomen, have a big collection of home pages with short descriptions. Stacey's Lesbian Links provides not just numerous links sources, but a pointer to her personal page as well as My Other Place, the Art and Poetry of Lesbians. Dorsie's Page is a great resource for mailing lists she has started as well as others. This self-described "list-wrangler" has created PolitiDykes, Lesbian Mom's, the Owls Digest, BookWoman, Boychicks, SoberDykes, and the newly born FemmeDykes, a list for discussion of femme identity and reality.

Worldwide Sisterhood

Wherever your voyages take you, you'll find a common thread of joyful identity. The U.K. pages are more ironic and biting than the American ones; the political pages are sometimes tough calls to action (see Guerrilla Girls and Lesbian Avengers). And the devotion to the lesbian cause is amazing (Sista Power, Swade's Pages, Voxxen Worx, We Moon). But all are fertile, thought-provoking, and reach out to a constituency of sisterhood. Susan Dennis's opening remarks are typical: "When I first connected my computer to another via a telephone line back in 1980, I found a magic that still fascinates me. But I also found then and now that the population of others like me were really not like me. The majority of them are of the male persuasion. Please don't misunderstand. These males have been my friends, my confidants, my helpers and my companions and I wouldn't trade them in for anything. But I still get tickled when I meet another woman online. So I have begun a collection of home pages and other stuff of, by, and about women. Here's my collection so far."

Mail Lists, Newsgroups, Chat

For the clearest, most sensible instructions on mail lists, newsgroups, and chat, go to Amy Goodloe's page at Lesbian.org, "Finding Women on the Internet" and TechnoDyke.com.

☐ *The ADA Project: Resources for Women in Computing*
http://www.cs.yale.edu/HTML/YALE/CS/HyPlans/tap/tap.html

☐ *A Dyke's World*
http://www.dykesworld.de/

☐ *A list for lesbians 50 and over.*
http://www.helsinki.fi/~kris_ntk/lezlist/l-plus.html

☐ *The ADA Project: Resources for Women in Computing*
http://www.cs.yale.edu/HTML/YALE/CS/HyPlans/tap/tap.html

☐ *Amazon Online*
http://www.amazon.org/

☐ *Aphrodite Love Links*
http://sol.zynet.co.uk/elektra/aphrodite/

☐ *Bay Area CyberDykes*
http://www.best.com/~agoodloe/lists/bacd.html

☐ *Bitch Magazine*
http://www.bitchmag.com/

☐ *Brat Attack*
http://www.devildog.com/brat/

☐ *Butch-Femme Information Page*
http://www.concentric.net/~abigdog/Butch/butch-femme/

☐ *Butterfly's Lesbian Chat*
http://www.syncity.com/chat/

☐ *Caryl's lesbian bulletin board*
http://www.sirius.com/~caryls/bboard.html

☐ *Christian Lesbians ONLINE*
http://www.geocities.com/WestHollywood/Heights/2685/

☐ *Classic Dykes Online*
http://www.geocities.com/westhollywood/stonewall/7427/

☐ *Culture Zone*
http://www.culturezone.com/

☐ *Cybergrrl*
http://www.cybergrrl.com/

☐ *Cynical Dog Lesbian Book Salon*
http://pages.prodigy.com/cynicaldog

☐ *Domestic Violence in Lesbian Relationships*
http://www.riotgrrl.com

☐ *Drummer Girl*
http://www.drummergirl.com/

☐ *DYKE*
http://dspace.dial.pipex.com/town/square/ad454/

☐ *Dyke Action Network*
http://mosaic.echonyc.com/~dam/

☐ *Dyke London*
http://dspace.dial.pipex.com/town/square/ad454/

☐ *Dyke Net*
http://www.kaupe.com/dykenet/

☐ *Dyke Street*
http://www.demon.co.uk/world/ukgay/ukg000f.html

☐ *Dyke TV*
http://www.freespeech.org/dyketv/

☐ *A Dyke's World*
http://www.qworld.org/DykesWorld/index.html

☐ *Dyxploitation*
http://www.dyxploitation.com

☐ *Eeek Net!*
http://www.eeeek.com

☐ *Echo Lesbian Page*
http://www.echonyc.com/~lesbians

☐ *End Zone (sports)*
http://www.geocities.com/Colosseum/2526/

☐ *Euro Sappho*
http://www.helsinki.fi/~kris_ntk/esappho.html

☐ *Fabulous Netwomen*
http://www.users.interport.net/~dolphin/netwomen.html

☐ *Fat Girl*
http://www.fatgirl.com/

☐ *F2F Dungeon*
http://www.webworqs.com/f2fdungeon/

☐ *Feminist Activist Resources on the Net*
http://www.igc.apc.org/women/feminist.html

☐ *Feminists Against Censorship*
http://www.fiawol.demon.co.uk/fac/

☐ *Feminists For Free Expression*
http://www.well.com/user/freedom/

☐ *Feminists Online*
http://www.feminist.org

☐ *Femina*
http://www.femina.com/

☐ *Femme World*
http://sol.zynet.co.uk:8005/elektra/femmeworld/

☐ *Fishnet Magazine*
http://www.fishnetmag.com/

☐ *Floortje's Amazon Art (stories, art)*
http://neturl.nl/~floor/art_index.html

☐ *Forry's Brain*
http://www.best.com/~4forry/lesbian.htm

☐ *Gay Womyn*
http://www.gaywomyn.com

☐ *Geek Girl*
http://www.next.com.au/spyfood/geekgirl/

☐ *Gettogirls*
http://www.girlbar.com/

☐ *G.I.R.L.*
http://www.worldkids.net/girl/

☐ *Girl Bar*
http://www.girlbar.com/

☐ *Girl Club*
http://www.girlclub.com/

☐ *Girl Spot/Club Skirts Curtain*
http://www.girlspot.com/

☐ *Girlfriends Coffee House and Book Store*
http://www.girlscafe.com/

☐ *Girlfriends Magazine*
http://www.gfriends.com/

☐ *Girlfriends Page*
http://www.geocities.com/WestHollywood/1000/

☐ *Girljock*
http://www.tezcat.com/~ksbrooks/Gj/Gj-front.html

☐ *Girl Space*
http://www.grrlspace.com/.com

☐ *Glimpses of Our History*
http://www.swade.net/swadepages/les-hist.htm

☐ *Grrltalk*
http://www.geocities.com/WestHollywood/1123/grrl.html

☐ *Grrlz Linx*
http://www.geocities.com/WestHollywood/333/links.html

☐ *Go Grrl!*
http://www.worldweb.net/~spatrick/

☐ *Good Vibrations*
http://www.goodvibes.com/

☐ *Guerrilla Girls*
http://www.voyagerco.com/gg/gg.html

☐ *Hacker Barbe Dream Basement Apartment*
http://www.catalogue.com/mrm/barbe/barbe.html

☐ *HarCap*
http://www.geocities.com/WestHollywood/Village/9740/ (stories)

☐ *Hardcore Feminism—Reinventing Virtual Sex*
http://ernie.bgsu.edu/~lgilber/femex/

☐ *Healthgate*
http://www.healthgate.com/healthy/woman/index.shtml

☐ *Hear Us Emerging Sisters*
http://www.hues.net/

☐ *HerSalon.com*
http://www.hersalon.com

☐ *Her Site*
http://www.hersite.com

☐ *Herspace*
http://www.herspace.com/

☐ *In the Company of Women*
http://www.companyofwomen.com

☐ *Isle of Lesbos*
http://www.sappho.com/

☐ *June Mazer Lesbian Collection*
http://www.lesbian.org/mazer/index.html

☐ *Kung Fu Dykes*
http://www-unix.oit.umass.edu/~yvicious/kfd

☐ *LA Girl Guide*
http://www.girlguide.com/htm/newhome2.htm

☐ *LBJW (discussion list for lesbian and bisexual Jewish women)*
http://www.qrd.org/QRD/electronic/email/lbjw

☐ *Lesbian.com*
http://www.lesbian.com

☐ *Lesbian Battering*
http://www.forthrt.com/~chronicl/archjan6/visitdig.htm

☐ *Lesbian Disabled Veterans of America*
http://www.geocities.com/capitolhill/3726/lesbian.html

☐ *Lesbian Email Group*
http://www.geocities.com/westhollywood/chelsea/1378/main.html

☐ *Lesbian Life*
http://lesbianlife.miningco.com/people/lesbianlife/

☐ *Lesbian & Gay Aging Issues Network*
http://www.asaging.org/lgain.html

☐ *Lesbian Avengers San Francisco*
http://www.lesbian.org/sfavengers/

☐ *Lesbian Barbies*
http://gecko.desires.com/1.2/art/docs/lovegrid.html

☐ *Lesbian Chat*
http://www.instantweb.com/~sands/lchat/
http://www.geocities.com/WestHollywood/1478/lesbopg.html
http://www.spiritone.com/~sappho/leschat/

☐ *Lesbian Connections*
http://www.geocities.com/WestHollywood/5511/

☐ *Lesbian Cyberspace Biography*
http://www.echonyc.com/~lesbians/

☐ *Lesbian Directory*
http://www.scientium.com/angel

☐ *Lesbian & Gay Characters on TV*
http://home.cc.umanitoba.ca/%7Ewyatt/tv-characters.html

☐ *Lesbian Health Ring*
http://www.geocities.com/HotSprings/Spa/2466/webring.html

☐ *Lesbian History Project*
http://www-lib.usc.edu/~retter/main.html/

☐ *Lesbian Literature*
http://www.onestopcom.net/llit/

☐ *Lesbian Mailing Lists*
http://www.lesbian.org/lesbian-lists/
http://www.helsinki.fi/~kris_ntk/lezlist/lezl.html

☐ *Lesbian Message Boards*
http://www.pleiades-net.com/

☐ *Lesbian Mom's Web Page*
http://www.lesbian.org/moms/

☐ *Lesbian Mothers Support Society*
http://www.lesbian.org/lesbian-moms/

☐ *Lesbian Nation*
http://www.lesbianation.com

☐ *Lesbian.org*
http://www.lesbian.org/

☐ *Lesbian Poetry*
http://www.sappho.com/poetry/

☐ *Lesbian.org*
http://www.lesbian.org/

☐ *Lesbian Writers Guild*
http://members.aol.com/lezbnlit/lwg

☐ *LesBiGay Directory at IGC*
http://www.igc.apc.org/lbg/

☐ *The Lesbitarian (stories)*
http://www.lesbitarian.com/

☐ *#Lesbo Main Page*
http://www.geocities.com/westhollywood/1478/lesbopg.html

☐ *Leslie Feinberg's Domain: Transgendered Warrior*
http://www.transgenderwarrior.org/

☐ *Let's Talk About Sex, Babe (links)*
http://www.qworld.org/DykesWorld/Getting_hot.html

☐ *Lists of Lesbian Lists*
http://www.helsinki.fi/~kris ntk/lezlist/lezl.html

☐ *London*
http://dspace.dial.pipex.com/town/square/ad454/

☐ *Meno and More*
http://www.efn.org/~pegn/menolists.html#mollies

☐ *Museum of Menstruation*
http://www.mum.org

☐ *Nancy Drew, Girl Sleuth, Girl Wonder*
http://sunsite.unc.edu/cheryb/nancy.drew/ktitle.html

☐ *New Lesbian Chatroom*
http://www.geocities.com/WestHollywood/2225/chat_L.html

☐ *National Organization for Women - Lesbian Rights*
http://www.now.org/issues/lgbi/index.html

☐ *National Women's Music Festival*
http://a1.com/wia/nwmf/index.htm

☐ *New Hampshire Women's Festival*
http://www.nh.ultranet.com/~nhfc/

☐ *NOW*
http://www.now.org

☐ *NYC GirlScene*
http://www.girlscene.com/

☐ *Oddgirl's Lesbian Links*
http://www.sirius.com/~caryls/

☐ *On the Issues*
http://www.echonyc.com/~onissues

☐ *Owls*
http://www.teleport.com/~dorsieh/info.owls.html

☐ *Pat Califia's Homepage*
http://www.patcalifia.com/home.htm

☐ *QueerWoman.com*
http://www.queerwoman.com

☐ *Resources for the Feminist Activist*
http://www.igc.apc.org/women/feminist.html

☐ *Riot Grrl*
http://www.riotgrrl.com

☐ *Rock Grl*
http://www.rockgrl.com

☐ *Safersex-Info for Lesbians*
http://www.vub.mcgill.ca/clubs/lbgtm/info/lessafe.html

☐ *San Francisco Dyke March*
http://www.lesbian.org/sf-dykemarch/

☐ *Sappho Euro*
http://www.helsinki.fi/~kris ntk/esappho.html

☐ *Sappho U.S.*
http://www.apocalypse.org/sappho/

☐ *She Magazine*
http://www.shemag.com/

☐ *Shescape*
http://www.shescape.com/

☐ *Shades of Ebony Connections (SOEC)*
http://www.flash.net/~soec/

☐ *Shocking Lesbians*
http://desires.com/1.2/art/docs/lovegrid.html

☐ *SistahNet*
http://persephone.hampshire.edu/~sistah/

☐ *Stacy's Desert Dwelling*
http://www.goodnet.com/~stacey/desert.htm

☐ *Stacey's List of Lesbian Links*
http://www.goodnet.com/~stacey/leslinks.html

☐ *Stonebutch*
http://www.cyberramp.net/~grrlburn/sblist.htm

☐ *Susie Bright's Homepage*
http://www.susiebright.com

☐ *Techno Dyke Headquarters*
http://www.technodyke.com

☐ *Texas Lesbian Conference*
http://www.cyberramp.net/~tlcinc/

☐ *The Lesbitarian*
http://www.lesbitarian.com

☐ *Think Tank*
http://www.wonderland.com/thinktank/info.html

☐ *United Lesbians of African Heritage*
http://members.aol.com/uloah/home.html

☐ *Vancouvver Lesbian Week*
http://www.technodyke.com

☐ *Virtual Sisterhood*
http://www.igc.apc.org/vsister/vsister.html

☐ *Visibilities*
http://www.wowwomen.com/visibilities/visib_home.html

☐ *Webgrrls*
http://www.webgrrls.com/

☐ *Where the Girls Are*
http://www.eskimo.com/~susan/girls.htm

☐ *Wired Women*
http://www.wired-women.com/

☐ *Wolfe Video Home Page*
http://wolfevideo.com/

☐ *Women Folk*
http://womenfolk.com

☐ *Women Leaders Online*
http://wlo.org/

☐ *Women's Artists Archive*
http://libweb.sonoma.edu/special/waa/

☐ *Women's Golf World*
http://www.insync.net/~ldlent

☐ *Women's Sports*
http://www.womensports.com/

☐ *Womyn.org*
http://www.womyn.org

☐ *WWWomen Search*
http://wwwomen.com/

☐ *Yin*
http://www.yin.com

☐ *You Collection (toys)*
http://www.youcollection.com/catalogue.html

☐ *Young Lesbian Lovers*
http://lesbian.imco.nl/

Today, purely online 'zines like Gay Financial Network are creating a new online media genre and the online version of print magazines like *The Advocate, Girlfriends, SBC* and *XY* have a more exciting twin in the cybermirror. *Out* magazine is making a highly anticipated return to the Web and city and regional magazines like *Frontiers, QSF,* Atlanta's *Etcetera* and Denver's *Out Front* and the southeast's *Triangle* are thriving.

All this is against a much changed media context. What is different now is that "straight" online sites cover the gay issues so well that gay media's franchise on the very writers and the subjects that defined it is faltering. With the exception of the *Harvard Gay and Lesbian Review* (now *The Review*) and *Lambda Review,* many of the most respected gay writers, such as Andrew Sullivan, David Horowitz, and Frank Browning, are as likely to write for Slate, Salon or *The Nation* as *The Advocate, Out,* or *Hero,* three of the largest-circulation gay magazines.

After the murder of Matthew Shepard, Tony Award–winning playwright Tony Kushner wrote "Matthew's Passion," an attack on the lightly veiled homophobia of the far right as demonizing and therefore devaluing homosexual lives. It appeared in *The Nation,* not the gay press, and received so much comment that it spawned a discussion group in the magazine's online forum.

Interestingly, this was only one of many gay issue articles *The Nation* has run, including "Rebuilding the Gay Movement," "The Truth About Hate-Crimes Laws," and "Same-Sex Spouses in Canada".

It was Nerve.com, not a gay site, that scooped the gay lit world with an excerpt from Mark Ewart's memoir of his romance with Beat legend William Burroughs.

In response to a poaching of their core issues as well as of their high-profile writers, gay online magazines have taken different approaches to retaining market share. The largest of the national pubs, *The Advocate*, has aggressively taken advantage of Web-only qualities that free it from the constraints of monthly publication, updating news everyday, conducting on-site polling and offering frequent gay news brief E-mails. This has resulted in a much richer, more time-sensitive editorial mix than the print version, which retains a more static "lifestyle" format. Other national magazines are also using Web features to deepen their appeal. On the *Hero* site, for example, you can spruce up by reading "Look Ten Years Younger," before sending in a digital picture to the dating section at "Boyfriend Finder."

Some niche magazines are successfully cultivating an audience that remains outside heterosexual territory. The Independent Gay Forum, for example, features a generally conservative roster of writers discussing a frankly academic view of today's issues; for example, "After Equality, What?", in which it is asked, "What will we do with equality, exactly, if we get it?"

Girlfriends magazine, a national monthly for lesbians, combines celebrity authors with social issues in, for example, an article on lesbian custody cases by the acclaimed novelist Sarah Schulman.

Neither of these magazines, or other slick online productions such as *XY*, which targets gay men under 30, would have been thinkable in the previously constricted print world, both for editorial and financial reasons.

It's becoming a magazine addict's dream—and a cheap one, since no one charges. Of course there are the much-vilified ads to wade through, but there are no perfume fold-ins, and the

freedom to roam around outweighs scrolling past even the 50th
sex ad.

Word is Out

Among the smaller Web publications, you'll find some interesting
editorial variations that take advantage of Web publishing's freedom from the confines of mainstream journalism. POZ, which
serves both gays and straights, and All Worlds, for example,
don't niche its audience in any way, offering stories, features and
essays by "straight, gay, black, white, Asian, bi, trans, right-wing,
left-wing…well, you get the idea." Other magazines
are proudly narrow. Lesion Nation is a self-mocking,
terrifically acidic appeal to "educated" dykes: "If
you've come here looking for real news or social rev-
elation or even spiritual enlightenment, we suggest
you turn back now and find yourself a feel-good bad
lesbian poetry site." Circuit Noize is strictly about cel-
ebrating the gay men's party circuit in North America.

'Zines, E-'zines

Just under the slick surface of the high-profile gay and lesbian
press is the bubbling stew of underground queer publishing.
Called 'zines and E-'zines, these upstarts are small potatoes,
sometimes having a staff of one—but thanks to the miracle of
Internet distribution, they can thumb their noses at the de-
mands of advertising and still enjoy worldwide distribution. A
'zine that focuses on a particular topic, like SonomaZone does
on northern California wine country, can exist side by side with
the likes of POZ, matching graphics, editorial quality and time-
liness.

AIDS, Jocks, and Dyke Comix

'Zine titles give a foretaste of an aggressive individualism. There are
lesbian 'zines like Fat Girl, Girljock, and TeenMom, while boys have
Dick/Brain News, RiotBoy, Straight to Hell, and FAG!; Babysue mixes

the sexes. All have characteristic traits: Graphics are minimal or dazzling (there's no middle ground) and content is strenuously inappropriate for national consumption—kind of. You'll often come across experts on all sort of things. For Queer films try Intervalomete, for dyke comix, Jelli Comix; for new queer lit, there's Masque; and for gay flyers, there's Skyjack.

40+ too

Although it may seem that grrrls and Web-boys have taken over, what do you say about LEGS? It's a magazines for "40+" men. And like its kin, it hates stereotypes. Here's the editor: "Unlike so many of today's toady gay commentators, you won't get much crap about the 'good old days' from me. If they were so great they'd still be here!" The old rules just don't apply, and generalizations don't work either.

Resources

Finding Web 'zines isn't always easy or predictable though, since their mortality rate is high. Rainbow Queery and HomoRama are very good, and perhaps the best at updating the often changing URLs. But the resource of record for the 'zine scene (as has been the case for years) is Queer Zine Explosion. It's an excellent round-up of the newest 'zines, both American and European, with pithy reviews of A la brava: A Queer Latino/a Zine, Androzine, Anything That Moves: The Magazine for the Serious Bisexual...No, Really, Atomic Love, Baby Sue ,and many more. Are the titles dicey? That's just truth in advertising.

☐ *The Advocate (national)*
  http://www.advocate.com

☐ *All Worlds CyberZine! (reference)*
http://www.allworlds.com/

☐ *Alternative Family Magazine*
http://www.altfammag.com/

☐ *Ambush (New Orleans)*
http://www.ambushmag.com/

☐ *Anything That Moves (Bisexual)*
http://www.anythingthatmoves.com

☐ *A-R-K (AIDS Reality Killers)*
http://www.a-r-k.com/

☐ *Arrow (*Now *Hero,* national*)*
http://www.heromag.com

☐ *Baby Sue (Gen X)*
http://www.babysue.com/

☐ *Baltimore Alternative*
http://www.baltalt.com

☐ *Baltimore Gay Paper*
http://www.bgp.org/

☐ *Bay Area Reporter*
http://www.ebar.com

☐ *Bay Windows (Boston)*
http://www.baywindows.com/

☐ *Blair (Gen X)*
http://www.blairmag.com/

☐ *BLK Publications (Afro-Am)*
http://www.blk.com/

☐ *Brat Attack*
http://www.devildog.com/brat/

☐*Brother Sister News (Australia)*
http://www.brothersister.com.au

☐ *Brush Creek Media (national)*
http://www.brushcreek.com/

☐ *Cio (Brazil)*
http://www2.uol.com.br/mixbrasil/cio/

☐ *Circuit Noize (parties)*
http://www.circuitnoize.com

☐ *Cuir Underground (S & M)*
http://www.black-rose.com/cuiru.html

☐ *Curve*
http://www.curve.com

☐ *Dallas Voice*
http://www.dallasvoice.com

☐ *Data Lounge (cyberworld)*
http://www.datalounge.com/datalounge_info.html

☐ *Dick/Brain News*
http://www.gaywired.com/oboy

☐ *Dirty (Gen X)*
http://www.dirty.com/

☐ *Dirty Diary (Gen X)*
http://www.banjee.com

☐ *Echo*
http://www.echomag.com/

☐ *Electronic Gay & Lesbian Community Magazine*
http://www.awes.com/egcm/

☐ *Elight (youth)*
http://www.youth.org/elight/

☐ *Enqueue (film)*
http://www.enqueue.com/

☐ *Etcetera (Southeast)*
http://www.etcmag.com

☐ *Ezine Listings*
http://www.meer.net/~johnl/e-zine-list/

☐ *Fat Girl*
http://www.fatgirl.com/fatgirl/

☐ *Fear Not Drowning*
http://www.drowning.com/

☐ *Flash (deaf queer national)*
http://www.deafqueer.org/ctnmagazine/FLASH/

☐ *Flesh Contacts*
http://www.planet-sex.com.au/flesh/

☐ *Freedom (U.K.)*
http://freedom.co.uk/

☐ *Frontiers (San Francisco, Los Angeles)*
http://www.frontiersweb.com/

☐ *Gay & Lesbian OC Blade*
http://www.ocblade.com/

☐ *Gay & Lesbian Review (formerly the Harvard Gay & Lesbian Review)*
http://www.hglc.org/hglc/review.htm

☐ *Gay Forum Deutschland*
http://www.gayforum.de

☐ *GayPlace (national)*
http://www.gayplace.com/

☐ *Gay Times & Diva (London)*
http://www.gaytimes.co.uk/

☐ *Gay Today (national)*
http://gaytoday.badpuppy.com/

☐ *Gay Toronto*
http://www.gaytoronto.com

☐ *Gay Wired Times (national)*
http://www.gaywired.com/~unity

☐ *Gay Magazines (Yahoo!)*
http://www.yahoo.com/Society_and_Culture/Cultures_and_Groups/
Lesbians_Gays_and_Bisexuals/News_and_Media/

☐ *Gay Place (national)*
http://www.gayplace.com/

☐ *Geek Girl (Australia)*
http://www.geekgirl.com.au/

☐ *Genre (national)*
http://www.genremagazine.com/

☐ *Gerbil Zine (Gen X)*
http://www.multicom.org/gerbil/gerbil.html

☐ *Girlfriends (Lesbian)*
http://www.gfriends.com/

☐ *Girl Jock*
http://www.tezcat.com/~ksbrooks/Gj/Gj-front.html

☐ *Graffiti (Gen X)*
http://www.mindspring.com/~graffiti/

☐ *Gruf Magazine (unshaven faces)*
http://www.gruf.com/

☐ *The Guide (Travel)*
http://www.guidemag.com/index.html

☐ *gURL (Lesbian)*
http://www.gurl.com/

☐ *Happy Fag (Gen X)*
http://www.happyfag.com

☐ *Harvard Gay & Lesbian Review (The Review)*
http://www.hglc.org/hglc/review.htm

☐ *Hero Magazine (formerly Arrow, National)*
http://www.heromag.com/

☐ *Holy Titclamps (National)*
http://www.io.com/~larrybob/

☐ *House O'Chicks*
http://www.gayweb.com/610/610index.html

☐ *Hoss (literary)*
http://www.hossmag.com/

☐ *HX (New York)*
http://www.hx.com/

☐ *In the Family*
http://www.inthefamily.com/

☐ *Ink Pot's Zine Scene*
http://www.inkpot.com/zines/homosexual.html

☐ *Instinct*
http://www.instinctmag.com/

☐ *Lesion Nation*
http://www.lesion.com/

☐ *Lesbian News*
http://www.lesbiannews.com

☐ *Lezzie Smut*
http://prometheus.digital-rain.com/~lezzie

☐ *Libido (sensuality)*
www.sensualsource.com

☐ *Manzone*
http://www.manzone.com

☐ *Masque (literary)*
http://www.stanford.edu/group/masque

☐ *Mensual*
http://www.mensual.com

☐ *Metropolitan Slave*
http://www.metroslave.com/

☐ *New York Blade*
http://www.nyblade.com

☐ *Oasis (youth)*
http://www.oasismag.com/

☐ *Oblivion (San Francisco)*
http://www.oblivionsf.com/

☐ *Online Zines*
http://www.etext.org/Zines/

☐ *OurWorld (travel)*
http://www.ourworldmag.com

☐ *Out & About*
http://www.outandabout.com

☐ *Out* magazine
http://www.out.com

☐ *Outlines (Chicago)*
http://www.suba.com/~outlines/

☐ *Parterre Box (opera)*
http://www.anaserve.com/~parterre

☐ *Planet Q (national)*
http://planetq.com/

☐ *POZ (AIDS national)*
http://www.poz.com

☐ *QMondo*
http://www.qmondo.com

☐ *Q San Francisco*
http://www.qsanfrancisco.com/

☐ *QV Magazine (Latino)*
http://www.qvmagazine.com

☐ *Queer Nasty (Gen X)*
http://www.tripnet.com/q-nasty/

☐ *Queer Zine Explosion*
http://www.io.com/~larrybob/qze14.html

☐ *Qworld (national)*
http://www.qworld.org

☐ *QX Magazine (London)*
http://www.dircon.co.uk/qxmag/

☐ *Rex Wockner's "Quote Unquote"*
http://www.qrd.org/qrd/www/world/wockner.html

☐ *RiotBoy (Gen X)*
http://www.earthlink.net/~cbardcole

☐ *Sapphic Ink*
http://www.lesbian.org/sapphic-ink/

☐ *Sapphrodite Womyns Literary Webzine*
http://www.spiritone.com/~sappho/sapphrodite/

☐ *SBC*
http://www.sbc-online.com/

☐ *Screaming Hyena*
http://www.hares-hyenas.com.zu/screaming_hyena.htm

☐ *Scots Gay*
http://www.scotsgay.co.uk

☐ *Seattle Gay News*
http://www.sgn.org/

☐ *Shescape*
http://www.shescape.com

☐ *Skyjack (flying)*
http://www.skyjack.com

☐ *Sneer (Gen X)*
http://www.sneerzine.com

☐ *Sonoma Zone (Northern CA)*
http://www.sonomazone.com/

☐ *Southern California Gay Wired*
http://www.gaywired.com/unity/index.html

☐ *Southern Exposure Key West*
http://www.bridge.net/~exposure/

☐ *SurfGurl.com*
http://www.surfgirl.com/

☐ *TeenMom*
http://www.pform.com/teenmom/teenmom.html

☐ *Texas Triangle*
http://www.txtriangle.com/

☐ *Ten Percent*
http://www.10percent.media.ucla.edu/

☐ *Triangle (Midwesst)*
http://www.trianglemag.com/

☐ *U Report*
http://www.ureport.com/ureport

☐ *Washington Blade*
http://www.washblade.com

☐ *WebCastro "Hotlinks" (SF)*
http://www.webcastro.com/hotlinks.htm

☐ *White Crane Journal*
http://www.whitecranejournal.com

☐ *Windy City Times*
http://www.wctimes.com

☐ *XXX Fruit*
http://www.echonyc.com/~xxxfruit/

☐ *XY (Youth)*
http://www.xymag.com/

 Movies

The Internet has long been film-addicted, an incredible archive where movies of all kinds are studied, indexed, rouged up by star-fuckers, and dressed down by deconstructionists.

Today, three sites share the honors for best serving this addictive art: Bright Lights Film Journal, Cinema Q and Popcorn Q.

Cinema Q at Queer Film.com is the most Hollywood-oriented of the gay film sites. The opening page has all sorts of current news and deep listings for all the main categories (films, genres, actors) as well as Studio Briefing, which is newsy insider gossip à la *The Hollywood Reporter.* There's also a huge Net Directory with links to film sites all over the Web, including sites for films (both old and new), actors, directors, books and a great cache of miscellaneous links where you can find fringy stuff like Fur on Film,and Tattoo Films.

For the best film reviews, go to Bright Lights Film Journal. This is a highly literate mix of movie analysis, history and commentary that focuses on gay film not in a vacuum but as part of a continuum going back to the turn of the century. You'll find articles on well-known figures such as James Broughten alongside appreciations of today's innovators like the Kuchar Brothers. All the writing is informed, hip and balances a certain queeny arrogance with impeccable taste. For example, the documentary *Pierre et Gilles: Love Stories*, is "a ragged but enjoyable exercise in fan worship." The review of *Queer Kisses* opens with the question: "What is it about the sight of two men kissing that drives Americans insane?" Great, sharp stuff.

The mother lode for queer film anthropology is PopcornQ at PlanetOut. It's got excerpts and trailers of a surprisingly deep archive of films (both majors and independents) as well as interviews with actors and directors, terrific reports on queer film festivals around the world—and they're adding more all the time. It's an incredible resource. The search engine allows you to find films by themes such as activism, Asian, African, coming out, history, and class as well as by title, country where made, director, home video, or year released. There are tons of links for the novice who just wants to know what films are currently playing as well as the cineast who's hunting that hot new film from abroad.

Sure there's lots of razzle-dazzle on these pages—it's about the movies after all, but don't expect to hear the typical Hollywood tittle tattle. For example, The Queer Top Ten "is a cheeky riposte to all those dreary top ten critics' lists, where *Citizen Kane* comes out on top over and over... Here are a few of the snappiest lists from some of our best and brightest queer film critics, programmers, film and video makers." Writers include Marta Balletbó Coll (*Intrepidissima, Costa Brava*), Susana Blaustein Munoz (*Susana, Las Madres de Plaza del Mayo*), Kate Bornstein (*Crossing the Gender Divide*) and Bruce La Bruce (*No Skin Off My Ass, Super 8 1/2, Hustler White*). These guys are plugged into queer film.

Resources

Although no other sites are so extensive, there are many others with worthwhile specializations. Celluloid Cupboard: A History of Gay and Lesbian Cinema is a history of gay and lesbian cinema back to the '30s with over 300 reviews. Pink Movies is a kind of queer film free-for-all with readers' postings on all sorts of queer films. Marc Stewart's column at the Data Lounge tracks the entire industry while keeping a close eye on the gay content. The Qualia-Net Film Index has excellent lists and guides to indies, including many queer productions in sections divided into specific films, theaters, and magazines. There are lots of links to directors, actors, and specific films. CinemaQ (formerly Dave's Queer Films) is a more casual place, with classics like *Boys in the Band*, along with foreign films. Each gets a quick plot review and is rated from the rave of five stars ("You're not queer if you haven't seen this one.") to zero stars ("Yuck!"). You can find nearly 200 descriptions under gay, lesbian, transgender, or documentary, as well as actors and directors. Queer Films is shorter, but its list of mainly contemporary films has longer write-ups and some films, such as *My Own Private Idaho*, have additional links to picture galleries. Gay-themed Videos and Movies is fun place with 50 capsule reviews of recent films, lots of pictures of teen heartthrobs like Matt Damon, Ryan Phillippe, and Leonardo DiCaprio.

Lesbians in Film

Out Takes: Lesbianism in Film (formerly Killers, Rogues, Vampires and Fish) is an edgy, scholarly page. With 600+ films listed (and the author seems to have seen them all) as well as essays on subtext, this is a great place find unknown films as well as to discover unremarked aspects. But don't look for the traditional lesbian movie list. The author has a specific focus: "'Lesbian' refers to the sexual or erotic desire of one woman for another, in all the glorious myriad ways that this desire names itself." So just because Joan Crawford is butch in *Johnny Guitar*, that doesn't make her a lesbian. Instead you'll find films such as *Veronica 4 Rose*, a "documentary about teenage lesbians growing up in several diverse English cities." Or *Vera*, "a 1987 Brazilian release about a young woman who believes she is a man trapped in a woman's body."

Lesbian Flicks has very thoughtful and personal reviews. She also points out overlooked facts such as: "Forget *Philadelphia* and Tom Hanks—Shirley MacLaine had the guts to play gay decades earlier."

Film Festivals

For true film buffs, the film festivals are not to be missed. Most gay and lesbian festivals have a Web site, including those in America (New York, San Francisco, Chicago, and Austin) and abroad (Brussels, Frankfurt, Ottawa, Turin, New Zealand, London, Tokyo, Toronto). These and others are also available through Film Festivals on the WWW and PopcornQ and Bright Lights.

Some queer films are also shown at the progressive festivals like the NY Underground Film Festival. For information on all the films go to their site or to PopcornQ for an excellent report that covers not only the movies but the "cruisy" audience.

Chicago Queer Film Fest

The Chicago Lesbian and Gay International Film Festival has one of the best festival Web pages, the equivalent of a glossy brochure, containing profiles of directors, filmographies, and write-ups on an amazing history going back 15 years to its debut in 1981, which ran Ed Wood's classic *Glen or Glenda?* Other years had speakers such as Kenneth Anger introducing a retrospective of his work. In the mid-80s there was a look back at the Warhol films *The Loves of Ondine* and *Vinyl*. Other films listed in this film buff's nirvana include the early gay romance *A Very Natural Thing, You Are Not Alone, Daughters of Darkness, Teorema, Portrait of Jason* by Shirley Clarke, and *Je, Tu, Il, Elle* by Chantal Akerman.

Roll 'Em?

Seeing these films is another question. Your options include ordering the video (most of the major sites have online video ordering), or hoping that a nearby festival includes a retrospective. The best references for films currently on video are OnVideo Guide to Home Video Releases or Lesbian/Gay Film and Video by Steve Stofflet. Stofflet includes profiles of filmmakers such as Barbara Hammer, Gus Van Sant, and Gregg Araki and links to directors' home pages are promised. Once you've found your quarry, move on to Vanguard International Cinema, Wolfe Video, or Strand Releasing. They have purchase order forms, with prices ranging from $20 to $100—all of which you can order off the Web page. Wolfe Video has particularly good film reviews some its own, some drawn from outside sources. The documentary and shorts are especially deep.

The Stars!

Though you'll have to be in the know, Celebsite has profiles on a huge list of celebrities as well as links to other Web fans. Rupert Everett, for example, gets a nice long appreciative review as well as pointers to a site called Forever Everett, a "world of Rupert Everett adoration." Lots of stuff on his life in movies and his novels, along with pictures and reprints of interviews. Main page has a sexy pic of Everett lolling in chains on a beach surrounded by glinting starfish.

Old Glamour

Veronica Lake, Lauren Bacall, Franchot Tone, Lizabeth Scott, Audrey Hepburn, Alfred Hitchcock, Marlene Dietrich... If your heart flutters at the names of Hollywood gods and goddesses, spritz, gargle, then make a quick pilgrimage to the Stick's Silver Screen Siren Web site. It's a shrine to nearly one hundred fabulous dames with galleries of incredibly beautiful stills. And there's a gargantuan links list for everyone from Humphrey Bogart to Grace Kelly and the Rat Pack. See also Yahoo! and The Qualia-Net Comprehensive, Annotated, Independent Film Index.

General Film Guides

The general film indexes at Matrix, Film.com, Internet Movie Database, and Movienet all have a gay and lesbian category. The

MoviePeople Database at Hollywood online is the largest. Here you can search more than 131,000 film titles and 850,000 cast credits. To conduct a search, simply enter a person's name or movie title in the box below and hit SUBMIT. If you want to look up information on a specific film, actor, or production, just type in a search word. A search on "Hudson, Rock" (such a cute, closeted hunk) turned up 70 titles, beginning with *Fighter Squadron* from 1948. You'll also be able to cross-reference links to lesser-known filmmakers like Pat Rocco, director of *One Adventure* (1972), *We Were There* (1976), and *Mondo Rocco* (1970), featuring an early performance of Jim Bailey (as Mae West, Judy Garland, and Barbra Streisand), several erotic short films, and clips of protest marches.

Newsgroups

For newsgroups of film aficionados, see the QRD list of postings on recent movies. Posters pull quotes from every source imaginable to buttress their argument, you'll find stuff from French film magazines and Indian fanzines as well as *Entertainment Tonight*. A good deal of the talk among newsgroups is devoted to the glorious late 1950s and 1960s— an era when a certain performance or just a few lines could change us forever. For some, it was Paul Newman thrashing around the closet in *Cat on a Hot Tin Roof*, the anguish of *Sister George*, or the nasty wit of *The Boys in the Band*. Talk to anyone who went to movies back then and ask about the impact of *Some Like It Hot*'s last scene, when Jack Lemmon rips off his wig and says, "But I'm a man!" and his fiancé says, "Well, no one's perfect." A mini-Stonewall.

☐ *48th Cannes International Film Festival*
http://www.interactive8.com:80/cannes/welcome/welcome.html

☐ *Alain Delon!*
http://geocities.com/paris/leftbank/3902

☐ *All Movie Guide*
http://allmovie.com/amg/movie_Root.html

☐ *Art & Trash (videos)*
http://artandtrash.com/

☐ *ArtsEdge*
http://artsedge.kennedy-center.org/

☐ *Austin Gay & Lesbian International Film Festival*
http://www.agliff.org/

☐ *Best Boy's Film and Lit Pages*
http://www.geocities.com/westhollywood/5054/

☐ *Bike Boys, Drag Queens, and Superstars ('60s*
Underground)
http://www.lib.unc.edu/house/nonprint/gaystudiesfilm.htm

☐ *Bigstar.com (gay-lesbian)*
http://www1.bigstar.com/

☐ *Blue Diary*
http://www.butch.org/bluediary

☐ *Boston GLB Film Festival*
http://www.actwin.com/movies/GLFVF.html

☐ *Bruce La Bruce*
http://www.brucelabruce.com

☐ *Bright Lights Film Journal*
http://www.brightlightsfilm.com/

☐ *Celebrity Cocks*
http://www.wildsites.com

☐ *Celluloid Closet*
http://www.movienet.com/movienet/sonycl/celluloid/
http://www.spe.sony.com/Pictures/SonyClassics/celluloid/

☐ *Chicago Lesbian & Gay International Film Festival*
http://www.tezcat.com/~chifilm/lgff/lgff96.html

☐ *CinePad*
http://www.cinepad.com/home.html

☐ *Cinema Q*
http://www.queefilm.com

☐ *Cinema Space*
http://cinemaspace.berkeley.edu/

☐ *Cine Maven*
http://moviereviews.com/coc-roost.html

☐ *Cinevista*
http://www.gayweb.com/112/112home.html

☐ *Dave's Queer Films*
http://www.blarg.net/~dhua/films/

☐ *Dirk Bogarde*
http://www.rights.org/~deathnet/Bogarde.html

☐ *Dublin GLB Film Festival*
http://www.iftn.ie/festivals/index.html

☐ *Falcon Studios*
http://www.falconstudios.com/

☐ *Film Festivals Popcorn Q*
http://www.planetout.com/popcornq/fests/

☐ *Film Festivals Server*
http://www.filmfestivals.com/

☐ *Film.com*
http://www.film.com/film/

☐ *Filmlist*
http://www.cs.cmu.edu/afs/andrew.cmu.edu/usr/out/public/Filmlist

☐ *Film Resources at World Wide Arts Resources*
http://wwar.com/creator/film.html

☐ *Fine Line Features*
http://www.flf.com

☐ *Frameline*
http://www.frameline.org/

☐ *Gay and Lesbian Films: A Checklist*
http://www.nla.gov.au/2/film/gay.html

☐ *Gay Wired - TLA Videos*
http://www.gaywired.com/tlavideo/index.html

☐ *Gay Line Tours of Hollywood*
http://www.gaytours.com

☐ *Hollywood Jungle*
http://www.zwap.to/hollywoodjungle

☐ *Hollywood Online*
http://moviepeople.hollywood.com/

☐ *Hollywood Reporter*
http://www.hollywoodreporter.com/

☐ *Holy Homosexuality, Batman!*
http://www.eserver.org/bs/23/johnson.html

☐ *Independent Film and Video Makers Internet Resource Guide*
http://www.echonyc.com/~mvidal/Indi-Film+Video.html

☐ *Individual Queer Film Web sites (PopcornQ)*
http://www.planetout.com/popcornq/links/

☐ *International Gay Film Festival*
http://www.nz.com/nz/queer/hero/films.html

☐ *Internet Movie Database*
http://www.imdb.com/

☐ *Kubrick on the Web*
http://www.automatrix.com/~bak/kubrick/kubrick.html

☐ *Lady Chablis*
http://www.theladychablis.com

☐ *Lauren Bacall Image Gallery*
http://www.deltanet.com/users/dstickne/bacall.htm

☐ *Lesbian Flicks*
http://www.geocities.com/WestHollywood/Heights/8306

☐ *Lizabeth Scott Home Page*
http://www.deltanet.com/users/dstickne/homepage.htm

☐ *Matrix Queer Films*
http://www.queerfilm.com/matrix/

☐ *Men On Film*
http://www.rainbow.net.au/~dvs/

☐ *MIX (New York Lesbian & Gay Experimental Film/Video Festival)*
http://www.echonyc.com/~mix/

☐ *Movie Link*
http://www.moviefone.com

☐ *MovieNet*
http://www.movienet.com

☐ *Mr. Clean*
http://www.impcourt.org

☐ *New York Gay & Lesbian Film Festival*
http://www.newfestival.com/

☐ *OnVideo Guide to Home Video Releases*
http://www.gaywired.com/tlavideo/index.html

☐ *Oscars*
http://www.ampas.org/ampas/

☐ *Out Takes (formerly Killers, Rogues, Vampires and Fish)*
http://www.geocities.com/WestHollywood/6271/

☐ *Pink Flamingoes!*
http://www.flf.com/pink

☐ *Phoenix International G&L Film Festival*
http://www.azcentral.com/rep/0129lgfest.html

☐ *PopcornQ*
http://www.planetout.com/popcornq/

☐ *Pug's Linkage: The Underground Web*
http://www.pugzine.com/linkage.html

☐ *The Qualia-Net List O'Links*
http://qualia-net.com/film/links.html

☐ *Queer Asian/Pacific-Related Films*
http://www.tufts.edu/~stai/QAPA/films.html

☐ *Queer Cinema*
http://www.qcinema.com

☐ *Queer Film Festivals (PopcornQ)*
http://www.planetout.com/popcornq/links/

☐ *Queer Screen*
http://www.queerscreen.com

☐ *Reel.com*
http://www.reel.com

☐ *Roxie Cinema*
http://www.roxie.com

☐ *Seduction: The Cruel Woman*
http://www.gayweb.com/first_run/cruel.html

☐ *Silver Screen Siren Web site*
http://users.deltanet.com/users/dstickne/

☐ *Sir Ian McKellen Official Home Page*
http://www.mckellen.com

☐ *Strand Releasing*
http://www.strandrel.com

☐ *Veronica Lake Image Gallery*
http://www.deltanet.com/users/dstickne/veronica.htm

☐ *Wendy on Film*
http://members.tripod.com/~wendyonfilm/home

☐ *Wolfe Lesbian Video*
http://wolfevideo.com/

☐ *World Festival of Films*
http://vukovar.unm.edu/animafest/

 Music

Late in 1996, a poster in the rec.music newsgroup lamented his inability to find a Web page concentrating on gay music. Responses varied from shaming him for parochialism to suggesting he start his own to the queenly observation, "Don't upset yourself, honey. Cyberspace is hygienic."

Pansy Division (Lookout Records).

Today the luckless poster might get an electronic version of three sharp finger snaps and a list of URLs several pages long. Things have changed—dramatically. From an operatic duo to queer punks, choruses, protest folk, pop tunes and ecstasy-energized house, you can find artists, recording companies, and even music clips with ease. This is not to say every category of music has suddenly bloomed a crop of queers; far from it. In fact most of the out musicians you'll find are into pop or rock. But the list of Web pages goes far beyond the usual suspects of k.d. lang, Melissa Etheridge, and Freddie Mercury. The Gay & Lesbian Music Awards debuted in 1996, and things have been exploding ever since. As its Web page will tell you, the event is big time, with hosts like Harvey Fierstein and performances by Pansy Division, Disappear Fear, the Flirtations, Joey Arias, and Cris Williamson. The sponsor list is also impressive: Miller Lite Beer, American Airlines, *The Advocate*, NYC NET, Naya, and H/X. Black tie, of course.

Queer Music

One of the most interesting categories at GLAMA, and indeed all queer music is Queercore. With roots in punk, it's a sort of lavender mirror to what you hear on modern rock stations, usually hard driving and the lyrics have a *fin de siècle* irony. Pansy Division, Queercore's highest-profile band, has opened for Green Day been on MTV and in *Rolling Stone* (see Alt.Music).

Queer Music Explosion is perhaps the largest of all the queer music sites, with many links to modern rock and pop gay bands, singers, record labels, links, and documents citing all sorts of fascinating arcana. It has hundreds of reviews of bands such as Bikini Kill, James Booker, Cypher in the Snow, La Grenuda, Magnetic Fields, Pansy Division, Third Sex, and Tribe 8. There is also information here about queer music venues and tour dates. If you're interested in queer stuff from Australia, Brazil, England, Canada, France, Germany, Ireland, Italy, Japan or the United Kingdom, check out the International Queer Hotlist. Also lots of interviews. This guys knows his stuff and his asides are always interesting.

While Explosion will give you the largest, deepest take on new queer music, "straight" magazines like *Mother Jones* frequently run gay stories and often gay music stories. Check out the article "Homiesexualz—A nascent group of gay rappers want some mainstream love" for a fascinating look at how even the raucously homophobic genre of rap is slowly getting a pink tinge. "[Gay] people who weren't into hip-hop before are getting into it now," says Cazwell, [a member of the gay hip-hop group Rainbow Flava].

Queerin' Rock Music

From England, Queerin' Rock Music is by a very discerning, opinionated guy whose passion is heavy metal with a gay perspective. "If you want an instruction manual on how to be the prefect little scene queen, I recommend you piss off now." If that approach is yours, this is a must see. Along with writing album reviews he scours the rock world for news and reports on it with a vengeance. After informing us that Guns N' Roses is near death he dances on their coffin. "Slash's Snakepit pisses all over all Guns N' Roses' radio-friendly easy listening metal."

House of Diabolique

For deliriously infatuated information on queer club music, The House of Diabolique is not to be missed. From its New York home it spotlights a new dance song as well as tributes to celebrities such as Bea Arthur, Dolly Parton and Dudley from *Diff'rent Strokes*, "in commemoration of the time he was almost molested by the bicycle shop repairman." Diabolique also has a nice set of club and scene links.

Gay Discography

Gay Discography is a fascinating page, an archive of queer music from rock to jazz put together by a happily obsessive Englishman. You'll find information about such collector LPs as *AC/DC Blues*, a Stash reissue from 1977. Along with the complete listings of the artists and songs, there's lots of stuff from the liner notes, including extracts from an interview with Bessie Smith's friend Ruby Smith in which she's asked about a social club ("a buffet flat") that inspired the song "Soft Pedal Blues." Was it a gay place? Ruby Smith's answer: "Yeah a very gay place. Nothing but faggots and bull-dykers. Everyone that was in 'The Life.' "

Singers

The pages to individual singers are in some ways the most interesting. Whether put up by a fan, the record company or the artist, they can be incredibly complete and very much in the style of the artist. Vaginal Davis's page is not only as visually interesting as the artist, there's a sort of in your face pride to it all— she's in museums! The page on Phranc has a discography, reviews, biography and a gathering of quotes on her flattop: "Phranc looks a bit like Wayne Newton..."; "Fabian..."; "Grace Jones...." It ends with Phranc's own take on the debate: "It was my brother's haircut. I wanted it for myself from the time I was a little kid."

Michigan Womyn's Music Festival

Madonna

Of all the celebrities and heroes and heroines, of all the pop gods whose mention makes fans flutter, the all-time online goddess is the material girl, Madonna. At last count she had 12 home pages dedicated to her, not including the Warner Brothers record site or her own bulletin board.

There are other pop groups with more pages. U2 has a phenomenal following with 32 Web pages. Elvis has more than 50 newsgroups (which are often monitored by academics) and Frank Sinatra has his legions and a Web page. But only Madonna seems to inspire young, usually gay guys to sit at their computers gathering trivia and factoids for our enjoyment and the greater glory of their heroine.

What are these home pages like? What do they talk about? The new songs, previous record sales, costumes, and statistics of the legend. They parse lyrics for profundities and say things like, "We know her. We love her. And we will follow her anywhere."

Women's Music

Right alongside pop and queercore, women's music ranks as the most well-represented on the Web. For a taste of its most glorious expression, visit the site of the Michigan Womyn's Festival. The opening page asks you to decide if it's a performing arts festival, a political hotbed, a flirt fest, or a "female *Brigadoon* that appears each August." It seems all of these as you view the performance schedule and journals from past events. There's also information on travel and accommodations, child care and tips for first timers.

Lavender Jane Loves Women's Music

This is a wonderful, sly, and affectionate celebration of lesbian and feminist musicians, lots of them, from lesser-knowns like Azucar y to Zrazy and celebrities like Laura Nyro, Jewel, Me'Shell

Ndegéocello. You can search by the index or by genre (folk, rock, blues, soul, jazz vocals, pop alternative, and more). There are loads of pictures, thoughtful reviews, lyrics, quotes, and links to many other sites.

Women and Music is another very large site with biographies, links and sound clips (you'll need Real Audio Player 5.0) to nearly 100 women musicians. There are also interviews, not only with the artists but with members of the band and even album photographers. Also includes concert schedules, lots of links, and a discussion forum. The author is Norwegian (English translation available), so there are a lot of Europeans in the still heavily American mix ("det Patti Smith rules okey!").

Riot Grrrl

This is another great site. Concentrating on women's music you'll find links to record labels that are either woman/grrrl-powered or are woman/grrrl-positive, links to band and artist sites including Bikini Kill and Ani DiFranco, musician-related sites like the amazing Drummer Girl as well as 'zines and comics.

Publishers

Among queer music publishers, Ladyslipper, Fresh Fruit and Pop Front have excellent sites with recordings, song samples, and order forms. Ladyslipper's catalog contains more than 1,500 women's music listings and just came online this year. Though smaller, Fresh Fruit Record Store is full of independent-label artists, including Michael Callen, Romanovsky and Phillips, Lisa Koch, Grant King, Jallen Rix, and Pussy Tourette. Tourette's new album, *Who Does She Think She Is?* gets this description: "An album full of camp surprises and danceable tunes, this is Pussy's most recent and best album yet. Though most well-known for his dance tunes, we feel this glamour diva shines even brighter with his ballads. How can you resist an artist who begins a lamenting ballad with the line 'Everybody's Fucking But Me...' or opens a love song with "When I'm sitting on your face nothing can replace the way I feel about you"?

Though its page is an advertisement for its books, *Gay Music Guide* and *OutSounds*, Pop Front also gives a you a sense of what's happening. It contains a sample review of Kamchik The Singing Cowboy, and an interview: "How do you describe your music?" "It's pop with everything else thrown in. I'm a goody two-shoes with balls in drag. It's Roy Rogers in Vegas on drugs. And it's guaranteed to make you laugh or cry."

Classical & Jazz—General

Beyond the pop-rock scene, gay and lesbian music is almost totally integrated. Jazz bands and symphonic composers, pop idols and conductors are neatly plugged into appropriate positions on the large musical indexes.

Perhaps the best classical links are at the Classical Music home page and the World Wide Web Classical Music Virtual Library. These are huge compilations of pointers to hundreds of composers and their works and the symphonies, ensembles, and artists who perform them. Each contains discussion groups and mailing lists, as well as CD buying guides. And because both of their search engines are efficient workers, you don't have to wade randomly through all the riches. Various symphonies and ensembles have their own Web pages, and these (like the opera house and ballet company pages) reflect their makers. The San Francisco Symphony, for example, has an elegant home page with a design befitting its respected position. Among tasteful, free-form illustrations it lists the schedule for the upcoming season, along with short histories of the featured works and contact numbers.

Rock & Pop—General

But the energy on the Web is not among the black-tie set. Instead, it's radiating from the huge industry-backed sites that serve that gorilla of modern music—rock and roll. The first quality you'll notice on these pages is the sophisticated design. From the intentionally rough guitar logo of RockWeb to the neo-psychedelic patterns that decorate Addicted to Noise, rock pages are as illustrated as album covers.

At the top tier are Addicted to Noise, RockWeb, Internet Underground Music Archive, and the Ultimate Band List. Addicted to Noise (Vibe magazine's online edition) and RockWeb are essentially online versions of print magazines with features on current hit makers, letters columns, and lots of ads. They all have an irreverent, rock and roll outlaw sort of stance. For example, Addicted lists its interview subjects then adds that you'll also find, "...all the usual columns, reviews, sections, news and other garbage by the usual gang of idiots (to quote MAD) are in all the usual places."

Don't miss the Ultimate Band List. It's huge. You can browse the bands by name or by genre, or view the complete lists for 13 categories ranging from pop/rock/alternative to jazz/blues/R&B and dance/techno/rap. There's also an index of music mailing lists, FAQ files, and newsgroups.

No matter which of the sites you visit, you'll need to know beforehand the gay and lesbian musicians you'd like to research. Sexuality, at least in this context, is limiting rather than liberating, and no help at all when looking up a tune. The consensus confirms Mel Brooks's observation "If you take out the Jews, gays and gypsies from American culture, you're pretty much left with 'Let's Make a Deal.' "

☐ *Addicted to Noise*
  http://www.addict.com/ATN/

☐ *American Recordings*
  http://american.recordings.com/

☐ *Ani Difranco*
  http://www.columbia.edu/~marg/ani/

☐ *Broadway Cares/Equity Fights AIDS*
http://www.bcefa.org/

☐ *Mike Callen*
http://members.aol.com/sigothinc

☐ *Calliope Music*
http://www.provincetown.com/village/tobuy/calliope/calliope.html

☐ *CD Now*
http://cdnow.com/

☐ *Classical Music*
http://www.classical.net/

☐ *Classic CDs*
http://www.Futurenet.co.uk/music/

☐ *Classic Pop*
http://www.io.org/~buff/classic-pop.html

☐ *Classics World*
http://www.classicalmus.com/

☐ *Club Net SF*
http://www.club.net

☐ *Dead Can Dance*
http://www.nets.com/dcd.html

☐ *Derivative Duo*
http://www.nwlink.com

☐ *Diamanda Galas*
http://www.sundial.net/~endless/Diamanda.html

☐ *Digitopia*
http://www.digitopia.com/digitopia_info.html

☐ *Ella Fitzgerald*
http://www.geocities.com/WestHollywood/1074

☐ *Elton John*
http://ej.kylz.com/

☐ *Ferron*
http://ferronweb.com

☐ *Fresh Fruit Records*
http://www.gayweb.com/404/frshft.html

☐ *Gay & Lesbian Music Awards*
http://www.glama.com/index2.html

☐ *Gay & Lesbian Original Singers and Songwriters*
http://www.geocities.com/westhollywood/stonewall/7239/

☐ *Gay Musicians*
http://www.bostonphoenix.com/archive/in10/99/04/gay_musicians.html

☐ *Gay Rappers*
http://www.motherjones.com/newswire/homiesexualz.html

☐ *GLO Radio*
http://www.gloradio.com.

☐ *God Is Gay*
http://www.godisgay.com

☐ *Hello Betty*
http://www.hellobetty.com

☐ *Go Girls*
http://www.gogirlsmusic.com

☐ *History of Rock & Roll*
http://www.hollywood.com/rocknroll

☐ *Holly Near*
http://www.hollynear.com

☐ *HomoCore Chicago*
http://xochi.tezcat.com/~homocore/
http://www.tezcat.com/~homocore/

☐ *Hotstuff Bands*
http://www.hotstuff-nyc.com/bands.html

☐ *House of Diabolique*
http://www.walrus.com/~suave

☐ *Indigo Girls*
http://www.lifeblood.net

☐ *Internet Underground Music Archive (IUMA)*
http://www.iuma.com/

☐ *Iowar Women's Music Festival*
http://www.avalon.net/~mct/

☐ *Janis Ian*
http://www.janisian.com

☐ *Joan Armatrading*
http://www.rcavictor.com/rca/joan/index.html

☐ *Julia Fordham*
http://www.comp.vuw.ac.nz/%7Eectophil/jules/

☐ *Ladyslipper Music*
http://www.ladyslipper.org

☐ *kd lang*
http://www.kdlang.com

☐ *Lavender Jane Loves Women's Music*
http://www.geocities.com/WestHollywood/Village/1410/

☐ *Lesbian & Gay Bands of America*
http://www.gaybands.org/

☐ *Lilith Fair*
http://www.lilithl.org/

☐ *Mammoth Music Meta-List*
http://www.vibe.com/mmm/

☐ *Michael Callen*
http://members.aol.com/sigothinc

☐ *Melissa Etheridge*
http://www.ecw.ca/mle

☐ *Men Out Loud*
http://home.earthlink.net/~menoutloud/

☐ *Me'shell Ndegéocello*
http://www.meshell.com/

☐ *Michigan Womyn's Music Festival*
http://www.michfest.com

☐ *Midwest Women's Autumn Music Festival*
http://members.aol.com/autumnfest/index.htm

☐ *MTV*
http://www.mtv.com/

☐ *Mr. Lady Records & Videos*
http://www.mrlady.com

☐ *Music on the Net*
http://www.rootsworld.com/rw/

☐ *Music on the Web (Rootsworld)*
http://www.art.net/Links/musicref.html

☐ *National Women's Music Festival*
http://www.a1.com/wia/nwmf

☐ *New Bands*
http://www.hotstuff-nyc.com/

☐ *Bew Hampshire Womens Music Festival*
http://www.nh.ultranet.com/~nhfc/

☐ *OutLoud: Encyclopedia of Gay and Lesbian Music*
http://www.queermusic.com

☐ *Outcast Productions*
http://www.outcastproductions.com/

☐ *Outmusic*
http://www.outmusic.com

☐ *Pansy Division Homepage*
http://www.pansydivision.com

☐ *Phranc*
http://www.rahul.net/hrmusic/artists/part.html

☐ *Pop Front Press*
http://ourworld.compuserve.com/homepages/PopFront/

☐ *Pride Musicians*
http://www.pridemusicians.com

☐ *Queer Music*
http://www.erraticimpact.com/~lgbt/bookshop/lgbt_music.htm

☐ *Queer Music Explosion*
http://www.io.com/~larrybob/musicexp2.html

☐ *Queer Music Review*
  http://www.tiac.net/users/danam/qmusic.html

☐ *Queercore Beat*
  http://queer.qcc.org/yap/music/qcbeat.html

☐ *Queerin' the rock scene, rockin' the queer scene*
  http://wkweb4.cableinet.co.uk/peteranderson/INDEX.HTM

☐ *Riot Boy*
  http://www.geocities.com/sunsetstrip/plaza/3414/index.html

☐ *Riot Grrl*
  http://www.indieweb.com/riotgirl/
  http://www.riotgirl.com

☐ *Rock R Grl*
  http://www.rockrgrl.com/

☐ *Rock & Roll Hall of Fame*
  http://www.rockhall.com/

☐ *RockWeb*
  http://www.rockweb.com/

☐ *Small Dog Records*
  http://www.smalldog.com/

☐ *Sophie B. Hawkins*
  http://www.thecreamwillrise.com

☐ *Temptress*
  http://members.aol.com/temptress5

☐ *Trip Records*
  http://www.tripnet.com/

 News

It's hard to imagine now, but just a few years ago news of gay life came discreetly wrapped in brown paper. But nowadays, GFN.com, PlanetOut, Gay.com and *The Advocate* all offer original reports and articles. In addiction, city weeklies and special E-mail reports, like those put out by Wired Strategies (of Matthew Shepard and Stop Dr. Laura fame), are offering instant coverage and demanding a response from the straight press. Even *The New York Times*, long reluctant to give balanced coverage, now allows you to search all current and many past articles for the words "gay" or "lesbian." The on-line versions of *USA Today* and CNN now consistently report on major international and national gay stories with a pro-gay point of view. Last year, *Newsweek* did a cover article on queer families and how they are melding with their heterosexual equivalents.

Increasingly, the newly sophisticated gay news sources are finding fresher and deeper angles on the particular needs of the gay audience, whether that means finding gold-plated gay investor groups, or following the careers of gay icons like James Hormel. Gay.com and *The Advocate* have their own reporting on on finance, travel, arts and entertainment and updates from a network of gay and lesbian publications. There is also local gay-angled news coverage of the major cities.

GFN.com

Gay Financial Network is very much of the next generation. Its politically aware "community" news sits right alongside hourly reports on the stock market and a slew of topical and evergreen articles on investing and insurance, real estate, and the workplace—all written from a sharp, get-your-money's-worth sensibility. These guys are insiders who push for equality by providing tools to strengthen the readers the old-fashioned way—with savvy experience. Like the *Wall Street Journal,* its news mix is international and pivots on a group of columnists whose stories range from how our MBAs are doing in the workplace to queer-aware investment strategies and how to find tax shelters as you plan for retirement. There are also a bunch of supporting links to gay and gay-friendly companies specializing in mortgages, investing, banking, and real estate.

Gay Today

If you value skepticism in your news and expect the reporter to be open about his point of view, one of the best sources for news analysis is Gay Today. With sections on technology, health, entertainment, reviews, people and world events, this is a tabloid with professional standards—all the writers have strong views and strong personalities—and the writing is wonderful. The interviews and columns are often the strongest pieces, searching out today's activists as well as pioneers of the gay rights. Pat Robertson's 700 Club calls it "evil." Reason enough to drop by.

Rights Organizations News

The pages of activist groups such as GLAAD, HRC, and People for the American Way each keep a keen eye on gay rights, both reporting events and making the news. GLAAD's site is the most up-to-date, with daily reports on portrayals in the national as well as local media. The HRC concentrates more closely on its strategic issues, reporting on their progress (or lack of it) in more or less monthly updates; it's particularly good at interpreting the latest legal wranglings over same-sex marriage and gay rights.

People for the American Way is another lobbying group with a long-term view to bettering queer rights. Its reporting tends to concentrate more on progress bulletins. If you've forgotten which hypocrite sponsored your state's "marriage protection" law for instance, check People for the American Way's files. An excellent folder called What's Up On Capital Hill contains reports on artistic censorship, censorship in cyberspace, threats to gay and lesbian civil rights, and more.

Rex Wockner

Perhaps the most ubiquitous reporter in queer Web news is Rex Wockner (Edward R. Murrow for the '90s, as he's been called). He's an on-the-scene man, and he's got a great collection of quotes from news sources all over the world called "Quote/Unquote." Highlights of his gay news career include being in Denmark the day it became the first country to allow gay marriage, covering the first gay-pride events in Moscow and (then) Leningrad, attending the International Lesbian and Gay Association world conferences and International Conferences on AIDS, and making the first contact with emerging gay movements in eastern Europe and the third world.

Local News

Local news is best captured in the online versions of the weeklies. Of these, the *Seattle Gay News* (SGN) and *Washington Blade* are standouts. Their features, departments, columns, and excellent op-ed pages are written not to please advertisers but to report the facts and analyze events for truth. The *Blade*, for example, has broken many stories the national press is slow to find. *SGN* takes full advantage of Internet features with a customizable mailing list and a search engine enabling you to hunt through back issues for desired articles.

The largest gay and lesbian news outlet for Europe is *De Gay Krant*, based in the Netherlands. Along with continental reporting on gay rights, health concerns, and country-by-country tracking of same-sex marriage rights, local items offer the flavor of what's going on gay-wise in Belgium and the Netherlands.

AIDS/Breast Cancer

For general updates on AIDS and Breast Cancer, see the Centers for Disease Control's AIDS Daily Summary and the Cancer folder. Both are compiled from mainstream media and rely heavily on *The New York Times*, *USA Today* and the *Los Angeles Times*. Other, more cutting edge AIDS reporting can be found in *The Advocate*, *POZ*, and the many newsletters of AIDS organizations such as ARIC or GMHC. (See the chapters on AIDS and HIV, and Magazines and E-'zines for more details.)

Mail Lists

One of the most convenient methods of retrieving news is to join a mailing list. GLB News, for instance, is a digest of information and articles from around the world. Its subjects are any "news of interest to GLB folk," and its contributors include Rex Wockner's "International News" and "Quote Unquote," Australia's *Brother Sister* newspaper, the Electronic Gay Community Magazine, and Mark Proffit's Queer News Aotearoa.

☐ *A Gay Place*
http://www.gayplace.com/

☐ *Brien's Beat*
http://www.web.apc.org/~jharnick/news.html

☐ *The Daily Advocate*
http://www.advocate.com/html/news/news.html

☐ *Datalounge Daily News Feed*
http://www.datalounge.com/

☐ *Electronic Gay Community Magazine*
http://www.awes.com/egcm/

☐ *Funky Times*
http://www.realitycom.com/Funky.html

☐ *Frontiers Online News*
http://www.frontiersweb.com

☐ *Gay in America*
http://www.sfgate.com/examiner/special/gia/1996/part-1/

☐ *Gay and Lesbian International News Network (GLINN)*
http://www.glinn.com/news/gnews1.htm

☐ *Gay and Lesbian Media in the Netherlands*
http://www.xs4all.nl/~heinv/dqrd/gaymedia.html

☐ *Gay Financial News*
http://www.gfn.com

☐ *Gay News Amsterdam*
http://www.gay-news.com

☐ *Gay News Network*
http://www.gaynewsnetwork.org/

☐ *Gay News USA*
http://www.gaynewsusa.com

☐ *Gay Media Resource List*
http://www.netaxs.com/~joc/gaymedia.html

☐ *Gay Today*
http://gaytoday.badpuppy.com/

☐ *Gay Wired*
http://www.gaywired.com/

☐ *GayZette, The*
http://users.aol.com/gayzette1/index.html

☐ *GLB News*
http://www.web.apc.org/~jharnick/news.html

☐ *GLAAD*
http://www.glaad.org/

☐ *Grapevine Tribune*
http://www.drizzle.com/~ginn/index.htm

☐ *HRC*
http://www.hrcusa.com/

☐ *International News*
http://www.cs.vu.nl/~gerben/news.html

☐ *ILGA Euroletter (international news)*
http://inet.uni2.dk/~steff

☐ *La Gaiceta*
http://www.geocities.com/westhollywood/heights/4500

☐ *Mining Company*
http:// gaylesissues.miningco.com/

☐ *National Lesbian & Gay Journalists Association*
http://www.journalism.sfsu.edu/nlgja.html

☐ *News for Queers*
http://www.ece.utexas.edu/~chiu/qnews.html

☐ *Newspapers*
http://www.nando.net/epage/htdocs/links/newspapers.html

☐ *NGLTF*
http://www.ngltf.org/

☐ *People for the American Way*
http://www.pfaw.org/

☐ *PlanetOut—NewsPlanet*
http://www.planetout.com/kiosk/newsplanet/

☐ *Queer News Network*
http://plato.divanet.com/mansco/qnn.htm

☐ *Rex Wockner*
http://www.wockner-news.com
☐ *Seattle Gay News Online*
http://www.sgn.org/

☐ *USA Gay Net*
http://www.usagaynet.com/

☐ *Washington Blade*
http://www.washblade.com/

☐ *Web Active*
http://www.webactive.com/webactive/home.html

☐ *Yahoo!'s Gay & Lesbian News*
http://www.yahoo.com/Society_and_Culture/Cultures_and_Groups/
Lesbians__Gays__and_Bisexuals/News_and_Media/Newspapers/

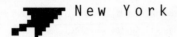 New York

New York City is the world's capital, as any native will tell you. Stonewall began there, as did the drag vogue. ACT UP was hatched in the New York hothouse, along with a hundred AIDS battalions—and where do you think the first queer punk strapped on a black boot? The Big Apple, of course. The discos are bigger, and the Village is a universal mecca (Castro, shmastro!). Everything is on a superhuman scale in Manhattan—and lest we forget its preeminence, there are hundreds of pages that give a microscopic tour of every glorious, sooty square inch.

Lesbian & Gay Community Center

Start at the Lesbian and Gay Community Center. From theater to the bar scene, AIDS organizations, films, and queer and queer-friendly places to stay, the Center has links to everything and everybody, no matter what you're looking for. You can get a schedule of the more than 200 groups meeting at the center, from ACT UP to Body Positive and the Zappalorti Society. Other local sites focus on New York's Halloween festivities, Wigstock, the Boston/New York AIDS Ride, and pride day events. There's a long list of New York–based organizations, such as Broadway Cares, GLAAD, Lambda Legal Defense and Education Fund, Lesbian and Gay Association of Lawyers, and the Times Squares ("The only square dance club in Manhattan").

New York Blade

After a few puzzling years without a gay weekly New York has now got a great one, the *New York Blade*, sister publication to the *Washington Blade*. Somehow the title, suggestive of a sharp edge, suits the subject and the paper itself is a virile expression of the city it covers—with local news, a city hall beat, and extensive coverage of the queer side of New York's cultural colossus. The paper has excellent sections on subjects like lesbian health, books and AIDS—all archived and easily retrievable. Unlike most weeklies, it is not overburdened with columns and the obits are wonderful and fitting. Last year's write-up on Wally Wallace, manager of the Mineshaft, was wonderful. Wallace "knew more about seducing men than Cleopatra and Tom of Finland combined." The bar guides are also spot-on. Here's the Clit Club for example: " A lesbian friend described Clit Club as the closest New York had to a women's pick-up joint, but one of my correspondents disagrees: 'Clit Club is a very fun place to go dancing and is definitely the "coolest" bar…[but] I've never heard of anyone picking anyone up there.' " You'll get the city's pulse.

HX Magazine

HX magazine is a weekly nightlife and entertainment magazine with feature stories, a weekly dance-music column, a weekly nightlife column, horoscopes, reviews of records, plays, and movies, and rotating departments covering books, cabaret, dance, health, the Internet, and much more. Check out the great links list for arts and culture, divas, dating, health, politics, and porn. They offer the best of New York, particularly when describing the club link sites like Mothernyc.com: "the online home for New York's premier alternative club night venue, which recently incorporated the sites for Jackie 60, Click + Drag and The House of Domination." For a quick taste of its balls-to-the-wall style, start at "Dish," (Homo and Dyke) where indefatigable reporters go to every opening, party, performance piece—all the cultural tumult that is New York.

Leather

If you're into leather and kink, go to PeterBoots's page or Leather Edge for a native's guide to upcoming events, bars, organizations, accommodations, magazines—all updated regularly and packed with links. Both give excellent characterizations of the patrons at various establishments so you always know what you're getting into fetish- and age-wise. Here's Boots's take on what he see's as a newly tamed New York night scene: "A lot has changed over the last few years. All the gay movie houses have closed. Some of the fun gay bars were closed by a city administration that doesn't like fun. Don't ask about back rooms—there haven't been any for many years.... The first pin has fallen: the Eagle has closed. There are fears about the other bars in that area with art galleries and pricey restaurants gobbling up every available space and driving up rents to ludicrous levels. Have fun in New York while you can!"

Lesbians

Girls Night Out is a terrific monthly guide to lesbian nightlife, culture and community. It's very personal without being judgmental and they're not afraid to indulge in fashion (fun with a shop-a-holic reporter) or restaurants (where you can smoke cigars or have a chocolate orgy).  Cruise up a storm, find the best books, queer and queer-friendly religious services, get your nails done, or take your kids.

Theater

What's a trip to the city without a visit to the theater? For quintessential New York, go see the home page of Broadway Cares/Equity Fights AIDS. You'll find write-ups on upcoming benefits, including the famous Easter Bonnet competition starring the companies of more than 20 shows from Broadway, off-Broadway, and touring groups. Though it's not queer, also check out Playbill for a comprehensive listing of on- and off-Broadway shows. (For more, see the Theater chapter.)

Other large links listings can be found RainbowQuery. Its NYC folder is a useful hodgepodge, with sites ranging from local media to AIDS organizations, universities, and home pages.

Fire Island (the "summer borough") has some terrific sites, everything from the links to the ferry schedule to the Web site of the legendary Pavillion disco.

History

"Over the course of gay life, a lot of bars, clubs, and night-clubs come and go. This Web site is here to document some of what I call, the gay history of New York City." Gay History of New York City is a terrific bittersweet site where the author leads you into all the neighborhoods, from the East Village to Christopher Street and the upper west side. It's a great place to visit if you've ever wandered the streets and asked yourself where a certain bar was and been curious about its history. Keller's, now closed, has a fascinating history going back to its days as a warehouse on the thriving Hudson River docks. "I share with you my history, gay history, and maybe even your history."

☐ *Act-Up*
http://www.actupny.org/

☐ *A Different Light Bookstore*
http://www.adlbooks.com/

☐ *Broadway Bound! (for women)*
http://www.companyofwomen.com/adventure.htm

☐ *Broadway Cares/Equity Fights AIDS*
http://www.bcefa.org/

☐ *Clay Irving's New York City Reference*
http://www.panix.com/clay/nyc

☐ *Cherry Grove, Fire Island*
http://www.grovehotel.com

☐ *Club Planet NYC*
http://www.clubnyc.com/

☐ *Creative Visions*
http://www.hedda.com/creative-visions/

☐ *Dirty.com*
http://www2.dirty.com/dirty/index.html

☐ *Dyke TV*
http://www.dyketv.org/

☐ *Estate Project for Artists with AIDS*
http://www.artistswithaids.org/

☐ *Fire Island*
http://www.bworks.com/fireisland/

☐ *Gay Accommodations*
http://anansi.panix.com/~dhuppert/gay/hotel/hotel.html

☐ *Gay Asian Pacific Islanders of New York*
http://www.gapa.org/

☐ *Gay Guide to NYC*
http://www.gaynyc.com/index2.html-ssi

☐ *Gay Male S/M Activists (GMSMA)*
http://www.gmsma.org/

☐ *Gay Men of African Descent*
http://www.gmad.org/

☐ *Gay Men's Health Crisis*
http://www.gmhc.org/

☐ *Gay & Lesbian Think Tank*
http://www.buzznyc.com/gaythink/

☐ *Gay Long Island*
http://www.gaylongisland.com/

☐ *GayNYC.Net*
http://www.gaynyc.net/

☐ *Girls Night Out*
http://www.totalny.com/life/girls/

☐ *Greenwich Village*
http://www.Greenwich-Village.com

☐ *Halloween in New York City*
http://www.gaycenter.org/gaynyc

☐ *Hotstuff NYC*
http://www.hotstuff-nyc.com/

☐ *House of Diabolique*
http://www.walrus.com/~suave

☐ *HX*
http://www.hx.com/

☐ *Leather Edge*
http://www.lthredge.com/

☐ *Lesbian & Gay Community Services Center*
http://www.gaycenter.org/

☐ *Lesbian Sources*
http://www.echonyc.com/~lesbians

☐ *The Lure*
http://www.thelure.com/

☐ *Metro Beat*
http://metrobeat.com:80/nyc/

☐ *Metropolitan Opera*
   http://www.metopera.org/home.html

☐ *NYC Bears*
   http://www.geocities.com/westhollywood/heights/6415/

☐ *More Gay Resources for New York City*
   http://www.gaycenter.org/gaynyc

☐ *New York City Gay History*
   http://www.angelfire.com/ny/gayhistory

☐ *New York City Opera*
   http://www.nycopera.com/index.html

☐ *New York Gay & Lesbian Film Festival*
   http://www.newfestival.com/

☐ *NYC GirlScene*
   http://www.girlscene.com/

☐ *New York Weather*
   http://www.intellicast.com/weather/lga/

☐ *New York Yellow Pages*
   http://www.niyp.com/

☐ *New York Underground Film Fest*
   http://www.metrobeat.com/~nyuff/

☐ *Papermag Girl Guide*
   http://www.papermag.com/guide/gay/girlguide.html

☐ *Peter Boots*
   http://www.pobox.com/~pboots

☐ *Playbill Online*
   http://www.playbill.com

☐ *QIS New York*
http://www.infoqueer.org/queer/qis/newyork.html

☐ *Sex Panic*
http://www.geocities.com/~sexpanicnyc/

☐ *Tom Morrissey's New York Lover*
http://www.users.interport.net/~tomorr/

☐ *Village Voice Queer Life*
http://www.villagevoice.com/choice/gl/

☐ *Vinny's Pier Murals*
http://www.vinnys.net

☐ *Welcome to Central Park*
http://mosaic.echonyc.com/~park/

 Opera

One of the most famous cartoons ever run in *Christopher Street* magazine was a drawing of two men in full leather leaning up against the bar in the old Mineshaft discussing coloratura. Everyone recognized the truth in it. Whatever the distractions, opera lovers will find each other and they'll talk and talk. Despite the ravages of the plague, they still do. Which diva is commanding the Met's new season? What's on in San Francisco, Santa Fe, Houston, or Seattle? And

Europe? There's chatter, banter, and arguments, with plenty of pulse. And opera fans have a rather nice collection of Web pages keeping track of it all.

Parterre Box

The only out opera page on the Web is the Parterre Box, and it is so out its author has tattooed Maria Callas on his chest: "It's a great way to meet guys at the gym: if they recognize the tattoo, you know they're cool. (Who wants to date a guy who has never heard of Callas, anyway?)." It's a page that is militantly in love with opera, and all "about remembering when opera was queer and dangerous and exciting, and making it that way again." The contents are, well, of operatic proportions. There's the latest gossip about repertoire, casting, and backstage dramas. Totally biased reviews of performances and recordings. And campy critiques of queer-themed operas such as *Salome* and *Un Ballo in Maschera*. If you get lost in the lingo, just turn to the "world's only illustrated dictionary of opera queen terminology." Among the links are the archived columns of "Tales of Tessi Tura." Among the lagniappe is his casting an opera version

of *Valley of the Dolls:* "Anna Moffo (Anne Wells), Teresa Stratas (Neely O'Hara), Mary Costa (Jennifer North), Sherrill Milnes (Lyon Burke), Jess Thomas (Tony Polar), Evelyn Lear (Miriam Polar),
Luigi Alva (Ted Casablanca) and Eileen Farrell as Helen Lawson." He's drunk on opera and proud of it.

Critics from the opera world rave about Parterre. "Wickedly witty. . .certainly better informed than any other opera publication in English right now."—Peter G. Davis, *New York Magazine.* "Devoted to all that is dirty, salacious, madcap, egotistical, filthy, horrendous, over-the-top, disgusting, awesome and lovable about opera.... No opera queen can live without this."—Chris Culwell, the *Bay Area Reporter.*

Opera on CD

This is a terrific site with reviews by a man who warns you straight off that his lists contain a prevalence of recordings from the '50s through the '70s because "a wealth of vocal talent was at its peak and opera recordings appeared much more frequently...." Among these his choices are refined according to a preference for "a wonderful performance in poor sound than a poor performance in wonderful sound. The clarity of digital recording makes vocal flaws and weak drama more apparent." Even if you're not in agreement with his ear, the author's views are always wonderfully knowledgeable whether he's in rapture or disgust.

General Guides

For straightforward guides, try Opera Web, Opera Stuff (excellent!), or Operabase. Of these, Opera Web is probably the largest. Its opening page is simple and direct: "This service provides information about the programs of opera companies around the world. Enjoy it." Then it gets down to business. To find a schedule, just fill in the date and city on the form. A search under March, 1997, for example, yields 28 performances at the Met, City Opera, Carnegie

Hall, and other venues about town. Opera titles, composer, director, and major roles are listed, along with phone numbers for ordering tickets.

If you want more data, such as a house seating map, return to the home page and click on History of Opera Houses. Most of the majors are given a rundown, including Amsterdam (De Nederlandse Opera), Antwerp (Flanders Opera), Brussels (La Monnaie), Budapest (Opera House), Chicago (Lyric), Cleveland (Cleveland Opera), Liège, Belgium (Opera Royal de Wallonie), London (English National Opera, the Royal Opera House), Los Angeles (Music Center Opera), Munich (Bayerische Staatsoper), Paris (La Bastille and Opera National de Paris), San Francisco (War Memorial Opera House), Sydney (Australian Opera), and Zurich (Opernhaus).

Another page gives short accounts of North American and European companies: Atlanta Opera, Opera Colorado, Dallas Opera, Huntsville Opera Theatre, Los Angeles Music Theatre Company, New York City Opera, Pacific Opera Victoria, and Pittsburgh Opera. Five European companies are also included.

For links to other opera sites, try the Lycos and Yahoo! search engines or go to the WWW Virtual Library Classical Music page. Between them, you'll be able to find old and new opera resources, as well as many libretti.

☐ *Benjamin Britten*
  http://borg.ncl.ac.uk/miscellaneous/scott/britten.html

☐ *Gilbert & Sullivan Archive*
  http://diamond.idbsu.edu/gas/GaS

☐ *Home Page of Theatre*
  http://www.cs.fsu.edu/projects/group4/theatre.html

☐ *La Scala*
  http://lascala.milano.it/

☐ *Maria Callas*
http://www.callas.it/

☐ *Metropolitan Opera*
http://www.metopera.org/home.html

☐ *Michael Black's Opera House*
http://www.stairway.bc.ca/bjorling/

☐ *Mr. Opera*
http://pages.prodigy.com/CA/mropera/mropera2.html

☐ *New York City Opera*
http://www.nycopera.com/index.html

☐ *Operabase*
http://www.operabase.com/

☐ *Opera Mailing List*
http://www.physics.su.oz.au/~neilb/operah.html

☐ *Opera News Online*
http://operanews.com

☐ *Opera on CD*
http://www.geocities.com/WestHollywood/9172/opera.html

☐ *Opera Stuff*
http://www.operastuff.com/

☐ *Opera Web*
http://www.opera.it/English/OperaWeb.html

☐ *Parterre Box*
http://www.parterre.com/

☐ *Pibweb Opera Links*
http://pibweb.it.nwu.edu/~pib/opera.htm

☐ *Virtual Opera House*
http://www.opera.co.za

☐ *Yahoo! Opera*
http://www.yahoo.com/Arts/Performing_Arts/Opera

 Personals

Online personals are (A) more polite than cruising the meat rack, (B) less expensive than print ads, (C) sexy if you can cull the bullshitters, (D) sexy because of the bullshit. Which one do you choose? The answer, of course, is...all of the above. Online personals are booming, serving up everything from kink to caring. Some cater to niche tastes, like leather daddies who like their boys smooth—after shaving. Others cast a worldwide net to broad groups whose only prerequisite is a capacity for friendship.

The advantages of digital romance are real enough. The honesty quotient, for example, is comparatively high. People do fudge bios, but less often than with print ads. Why tease readers with arias about how much you love music, gardening, or leather just to set yourself up for a fall when it's date time?

Who Are You?

The large personals sites all have a sign-up process: first you set parameters, gay or lesbian, and then you enter your personal ad, answering a menu of questions describing your sexual tastes and physical appearance, whether you're looking for long- or short-term love, and maybe something enticing about your fantasies. Before joining, it's smart to cruise through existing profiles. All the services offer this option, so you can get a feel for the system and for potential partners.

GayMatch, which runs Man-Finder and LesbianMatch, offers good advice to anyone placing a personal ad. "You want to attract some attention...be honest, but bold. Tell us who you are and why we want to contact you. Short ads don't attract much interest, so think of something exciting or different about yourself to share. Use the message area to include key words others will find of interest. If your particular interest is 'cooking,' you should include this in your message. Specific interests can often be defined by using common 'codes'...include a line in your ad that describes yourself or your interests. For example: leather, s/m, b/d, ws, tt, bndg."

One guy from Club Universe is "Rolf," who describes himself as having "moved to the States for freedom." His attitude is "enjoy today" with an "active sense of humor," and passion for "reading, films, and live poetry." Although he says he's interested in "finding a companion," there's nothing specific about sexual preferences. Sex may be the main motivation, but it's often balanced by the equal desire for E-mail pals with similar nonsexual interests.

More often though, you'll find a very up-front attitude in active gay personals sites such as BadPuppy, Catch's Place, Eye Contact, Data Lounge's Edwina, Gay.Net, Gay.com, It's Raining Men, Man Meet, and X World. Of these, Catch's Place seems the hottest, perhaps because it concentrates on a smaller geographic area and encourages correspondents to send in pictures. X World sizzles too, but after plowing through some of the ads you'll begin to wonder if the editors haven't helped hype some of the profiles. Every other guy, it seems, 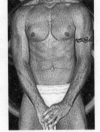 wants someone to "kiss me until I climax" and has a penis "straight as a flagpole." Hmmm.

Pay attention to the models used on the opening pages. Although nobody believes everyone you'll meet is a centerfold model, the audiences tend to sort out according to how they represent themselves. BadPuppy features mostly sexy younger guys and has a 20-something crowd. Gay.Net tends to showcase smooth-shaven

California beach types, so their personals are correspondingly youthful or youth-inclined. Though smaller, the pages with descriptive titles often yield the most successful results. Body Beautiful features twinks, Bear Depot has hairy hunks, and StudWeb seems to attract masculine guys over 30.

Pig Fest

If you like it seriously rough and raunchy, try the personals at The PigPen or the Pig Pages at Pig Media.com. The chat rooms are XXX-hot and the personal ads contain long lists of guys being very specific about what they want. The events listings cover play-dates in cities around the world, each described with its various specialities from fist-fucking to water sports and everything in between and beyond. Scat guys will want to pay particular attention to the Pig Pen profiles. There are also picture galleries and Pig Pointers (links) to pages like Gay Pig who says: "I love filthy faggots…real men who know what they want…guys who aren't afraid to expose their primitive urges. If that's you, you're in the right place."

Pig Pen is also very hot and is a popular place for travelers looking for action. Here's a sample request that came in for a weekend in Orlando: "Two FF Tops that are into many other piggy activities are in need of a pig bottom…" Aside from the personal ads, you can leave your mark on the "Graffiti Wall." But be careful, as the Web master says, "Please note that graffiti found to be truly offensive will be removed at the absolute discretion of the Web master." Don't worry, he's quite tolerant.

Friendship

If you're shy about the sexual component of personals, check out PlanetOut's People section. Along with purely sex-driven match-ups, it offers lots of less aggressive contact. In the Communities folder, for instance, you can join discussions with young people, transies, dykes, bis, queers of color, and more. There are also message boards (among the subjects are queer youth, being out at work, politics, living positive, and a general chat on the hottest sites around) and a chat line. The great thing about PNO's personals is that they will only let you join if you give them your e-mail address—a good way of ensuring that fewer creeps sneak in and spoil the fun. You can browse through the profiles yourself or let the matchmaker search for you. She's a surprisingly efficient and persistent cupid. If you don't have time to check in, she sends an E-mail alerting you of a potential match.

For Women

And what about women? Women, so many studies tell us, are much less likely to depict themselves in wild superlatives. And the stats also tell us that personals are a guy thing. In Web Personals, for instance, only a few hundred messages are from women looking for other women; there are ten times that many men on the prowl. Holland alone has hundreds of postings, while it seems only a few Dutch gals are looking for a date. Lesbians, it seems, post more on the women-only message boards.

Her Site, Lesbos.com, and the Message Board at Lesbian.org are three of the best. Lesbos opens with something you'll get used to very quickly—a warning to underage viewers and natives of certain states with hyperactive censorship and pornography laws. Just think of these warnings as foreplay—the more elaborate the cautions, the greater the payoff. As is the rule with romance novels, you can generally gauge the raunchiness of the content by the pictures on the cover. Using this measure, Lesbos is a hot place. There are lots of writhing women on the pages, and the ads are quite explicit. Her Site is more like a gay personals page with a photo gallery of hot women and a long list of detailed messages. You can also send an instant message to other women cruising the boards. Particularly useful is a matchmaking feature that cross-references your tastes with others.

Lesbian.org is at least as busy, but the sex barometer is lower. Posters open with a tag line and get a generous paragraph to detail their interests. Under "Margot takes a risk" you'll find the tentative flirtations of someone new to the online dating game:

personals

"Hello, wonderful dykes anywhere! Look, this is scary for me—
I'm very new and enjoying contact enormously on these boards,
so here is my E-mail address." Though Margot doesn't give any
personal info, it's pretty easy to gather that she's the strong, independent sort with a sense of wit. "It's no good trying to sell
me anything, this computer has cost me too much and I
dropped pesto on the keyboard yesterday which has gummed
up the more complex functions." A little unorthodox, but the
pesto bit leads you to believe she's into cooking, so she's a
gourmet, which means she's sensual...what else? Let your imagination run wild with possibilities. That's what a good personal
should do, isn't it?

□ *Aqui Estamos*
http://www.aquiestamos.com/

□ *Badpuppy*
http://www.badpuppy.com

□ *Bisexual Options*
http://www.bisexual.org/

□ *Blackmen.com*
http://www.blackmen.com

□ *Black Stripe*
http://www.blackstripe.com

□ *BLK Homie Page*
http://www.blk.com/

□ *Butch-Femme*
http://www.butch-femme.com

□ *Bust A Nut-Yeah, Squirt It!*
http://www.bust-a-nut.com/

☐ *Catch's Place*
   http://www.catchsplace.com/

☐ *Catch's Place—Latino*
   http://www.catchlatino.com/

☐ *Chub Net*
   http://www.chubnet.com

☐ *Chocolate City*
   http://www.chocolatecity.com

☐ *Circuit Noize*
   http://www.circuitnoize.com/

☐ *Cruise BBS*
   http://www.cruisebbs.com/

☐ *Cruising for Sex*
   http://cruisingforsex.com/

☐ *Edwina*
   http://www.edwina.com

☐ *Eye Contact BBS*
   http://www.eyecon.com/

☐ *Find Your Girl*
   http://www.qworld.org/cgi-bin/findgirl.p13cat=2

☐ *Gay Agenda*
   http://www.gayagenda.com

☐ *Gay.Com*
   http://www.gay.com/

☐ *G Chat*
   http://www.gchat.com

☐ *Gay Life.Com*
http://www.gaylife.com

☐ *Gay.Net*
http://www.gay.net.community/index.html

☐ *Gay Personals*
http://www.gaypersonals.com/

☐ *GayScene*
http://www.gayscene.com/

☐ *Gay Universe*
http://www.gayuniverse.com/

☐ *Gay Web*
http://www.gayweb.com/

☐ *GayM4M*
http://www.gaym4m.com/

☐ *Gay Web*
http://www.gayweb.com

☐ *Girl Talk*
http://www.girltalk.net

☐ *Girlz on Girlz*
http://www.qworld.org/womyn/grrlz.html

☐ *Hersite*
http://www.hersite.com

☐ *Hooked Magazine*
http://www.hookedmag.com/

☐ *HotChat*
http://www.hotchat.com/

☐ *Hotmen.com*
http://www.hotmen.com/

☐ *Instincts*
http://www.instincts.com/

☐ *It's Raining Men*
http://www.netland.nl/~irm/

☐ *Khushnet*
http://www.khushnet.com

☐ *Ladies' Virtual Cafe*
http://www.geocities.com/WestHollywood/2225/chat_L.html

☐ *LesbianLes.Com*
http://www.lesbianles.com

☐ *Lesbian Nation*
http://www.lesbiannation.com

☐ *Lesbian.org Message Board*
http://www.lesbian.org/

☐ *Lesbos.com*
http://www.lesbos.com/

☐ *Love Line Classifieds*
http://www.gays.com/love.htm

☐ *Male Classifieds*
http://www.maleclassifieds.com/

☐ *Manfinder*
http://www.man-finder.com/

☐ *Man Meet (SBC)*
http://www.sbc-online.com/manmet.html

☐ *ManQuest*
http://www.manquest.com/MQpersonals/

☐ *MasterVu*
http://www.mastervu.com/

☐ *Planet Amazon*
http://www.planetamazon.com/

☐ *Pig Media*
http://www.pigmedia.com/

☐ *PlanetOut*
http://www.planetout.com

☐ *Planet Q*
http://www.qplanet.com/

☐ *POZ Network*
http://www.poz.org/

☐ *QWorld*
http://www.qworld.org/

☐ *Rural Gay.com*
http://ruralgay.com/

☐ *StudWeb*
http://www.studweb.com/

☐ *Techno Dyke*
http://www.technodyke.com/

☐ *Web.com*
http://www.webcom.com/

☐ *Women's Wire*
http://www.women.com/

 Pets

Animals are important for biodiversity and all those abstract concepts, but they're wildly crucial if they're living with us. Pets are the pals we'd die for, and it's no different online. There are hundreds of pages on every species of pet, from goldfish to Siamese cats to a brown mutt named Willie whose owner would "marry him if she could." You can quiz a veterinarian, research a breed, or spend hours visiting dog/cat/fish/snake/bird home pages. There's even a cemetery where you can leave a picture and say things to ease the grieving when your pet passes over.

Pets Are Wonderful Support

Just as studies have shown that pets ameliorate loneliness, animals can provide comfort and companionship for AIDS sufferers. Pets Are Wonderful Support (PAWS) is a national group that recognized this fact years ago and has an amazingly sophisticated program to implement it.  Not only do they provide pets for free, they furnish pet food and supplies, foster home care when owners are in the hospital, and discounts for veterinary fees. And it's not just a onetime thing. If a client gets too sick to care for the pet, volunteers fill in the gaps with food delivery and veterinarian and cleanup services.

There are PAWS chapters all over the country (even in my hometown of Guerneville, Calif.). Those with Web pages have information on the others as well as lots of practical guidance on such things as zoonoses (diseases transmitted from animals to humans) and other concerns of animal lovers.

"River Wolf" is a dyke-owned and -run pet shop and general store with pet supplies and gifts for pets and pet lovers: grooming, collars, leads, and a ton of fun stuff like dog life jackets and dog-shaped lights to drape on your holiday tree or above a nighttime garden party. "Rwoof!" is a commercial page that donates a portion of its profits to PAWS It's dog-mania-here, with everything from pet supplies to "Doggie Horoscopes" and Yvonne, the "Dear Abby" of dogdom. "Hot Dog Links" is a list of sites ranging from veterinarian to breed pages and of course, there's "Dog-O-Grams," dog-themed E-postcards!

Pet Sounds

When you first hear about the Virtual Pet Cemetery, a certain skepticism may bubble up. After all, it's maintained by a group called Lava-Mind. Have no fear, though—it's legitimate, mostly. Here's their opening statement: "All of us, at one time or another, have had a pet we loved and lost. This home page is dedicated to all those given a shabby burial in the backyard or flushed down the toilet. If you wish to immortalize your beloved pet in the tombs of cyberspace for eternity, simply E-mail your epitaph."

What follows are epitaphs to pets loved and lost. Some are wry, others painfully awkward and touching. All are extraordinarily well-written mini-monuments. For example, "Touché Turtle" gets a heartfelt send off from Elder Perm Poom of the Metropolitan Community Church: "One day, I was shocked to find that Touché had dug himself into a burrow and had died. I was heartbroken.... As time went by, I adjusted to the loss of my cherished pet, until several years later when [I] discovered to my horror that desert tortoises hibernate through the winter. I'm sorry Touché...wherever you are! Please forgive me!"

☐ *Angel Animals*
http://www.angelanimals.com/

☐ *Cat Faeries*
http://www.catfaeries.com/

☐ *Cat Fanciers Home Page*
http://www.fanciers.com/

☐ *Dog Day Cafe*
http://www.dogdaycafe.com

☐ *NetVet*
http://www.netvet.wustl.edu/

☐ *PALS (Pets Are Loving Support, Guerneville, CA)*
http://www.sonic.net/~pals/

☐ *PAWS (Pets Are Wonderful Support, Maine)*
http://www.ime.net/PAWS/

☐ *Pet Planet*
http://content.gay.com/channels/home/pet.html?from=letter_000519

☐ *Planet Urine*
http://planeturine.com

☐ *River Wolf*
http://www.riverwolfgeneralstore.com/

☐ *RWOOF.com*
http://www.rwoof.com/rwoof/index.html

☐ *San Francisco PAWS (Listing of all national chapters)*
http://www.pawssf.org/chapters.html

☐ *Virtual Pet Cemetery*
http://www.mycemetery.com/my/pet_menu.html

 Politics

David M. Smith, communications director and senior strategist for the Human Rights Campaign has said, "As a constituency, we have rapidly become a fixture in American politics."

Virginia M. Apuzzo, of the National Gay and Lesbian Task Force, seconded the assessment: "What happened between 1976 and the year 2000? Two important developments. First, gay, lesbian, bisexual, and transgendered voters organized and reached out to locally elected officials who were climbing their way up the political ladder. Second, politicians learned how to count. By 1996, according to exit polls, voters who self-identified as gay, lesbian or bisexual comprised 5 person of the electorate - larger than the Latino vote (4.5 percent) or the Jewish vote (3.4 percent). And these are not automatic votes for the Democratic nominee either; in the 1998 midterm elections, fully one third of gay, lesbian, and bisexual voters supported Republicans."

As a group, gays and lesbians are one of the most cohesive and net-savvy. And the easiest, most effective method of taking part is on the Web.

The premier launchpad for queer politics is, naturally enough, Gay and Lesbian Politics: WWW and Internet Resources. This is a vast site, an index to everything from daily reports on key bills in Congress to analyses of broad historical voting patterns to links to the wealth of information like the excerpts above from the HRC and NGTLF sites. You can use the on site search engine to research your topic or scan the contents page, which is divided into subjects such as AIDS, civil rights, marriage/domestic partnership, military, parenting/family, law and legal matters, and schools and youth. The daily news is drawn from a wide sampling of sources, including various gay magazines like the Electronic Gay Community Magazine, OutNOW, the wire services, GLAAD, the ACLU, and the HRC.

There's a long list of newsgroups and mailing lists, each with pre-set forms so you can instantly log on and find out the scoop; these include ACT UP, Gay-Net, GLB News, GLBPOC, Marriage, Queer-Politics, and Queerlaw. If you're at all unsure of how to use these resources, you can jump over to GL Politics' guide for new users.

Along with an annotated list of gay and lesbian organizations, GL Politics serves up a bunch of links to homophobic sites such as the American Family Association, Christian Broadcasting Network, and Focus on the Family. In a rather amusing editorial jibe, Log Cabin Republicans are listed among the bigots.

Jesse Helms speaks

Finally, proving that for an embattled minority most things have become political, GL Politics includes links to most everything that could have a queer impact, from the full text of all congressional bills to AIDS organizations and Supreme Court decisions. A wonderful, exhaustive resource.

TurnOut

TurnOut is nearly as large and comprehensive as GL Politics and has descriptions of national rights organizations and particular issue-oriented groups that save you the trouble of losing your way among all the acronyms by which groups are so often known. This site also has a comprehensive and detailed state-by-state political breakdown. After an overview of the state, you get a report on sodomy laws, local groups, hate crimes, marriage, and civil rights along with a listing of all cities with civil rights and domestic partnership laws.

The National Gay Lobby

The NGL is a sort of nerve center for national gay political actions. It offers cheap Web hosting to political organizations alerts on various actions around the country as well as an endorsement list. Along with lots of topical articles and columns drawn from hundreds of sources it has an excellent "In the News" section that tracks breaking stories from the GLBT media and the straight media as well as archives on many topics such as the Winchell Murder, the Pope and gay marriage. The Info Kiosk has unedited press releases and announcements from GLBT and friendly organizations around the country.

QRD

Though every link and file in the Queer Resources Directory could be considered political, it does have a specific Politics folder with goodies like a page of polls by *The New York Times* and *Newsweek* as well as a lesser-known work by the American National Election Study that asks a cross section of American adults to rate several different groups and political figures using a "feeling thermometer." The results would not please the radical right, but they are reassuringly supportive of a trend toward live-and-let-live attitudes.

The full text version of the NGLTF's Fight the Right Action Kit is available here (as well as on NGLTF's site), and there are many more newsletters to be called up with a tap of your mouse. Also, following a central strategy of making our presence felt, the QRD has a complete list of governmental links so you can E-mail your representatives.

Women

Other pages with political pointers include Feminist Activist Resources and Lesbian.org, with links to more than 20 sites, including Body Politic, WHAM! (Women's Health Action Mobilization), Alert (a fact sheet on women's political progress in the U.S.), FeMiNa, League of Women Voters, IGC WomensNet, and the NOW home page.

Our Troops in D.C.

As far as national groups go, queers have come of age. We can field PACs and lobbyists with the best of them. HRC, NGLTF, National Lesbian PAC, GLVF—the list is long, and their accomplishments are distinguished. (See the chapter on Activism for more information on rights organizations.) The pages for these groups are impressively complete and detail their goals and current agenda on such issues as ENDA and hate crimes, and most have links to other political organizations. Each group wants to recruit you as a member and involved citizen. The Electronic Activist, for example, has preset forms to send E-mail to every congressperson, and the Web Alliance lists activist organizations by state (most of which are linked, so you can proceed immediately to those pages to read about what's going on in your town).

For a frill-free menu of queer political groups and other related topics, visit Lesbigay Resources on the Carleton Freenet. The ACLU Gay and Lesbian Rights page is also worth a look, for links as well as its work on free expression.

General Politics Guides

Along with advocating their agendas, you can be sure that all of these groups are closely watching the overt and covert action in Washington. Where do they tune in? CapWeb, Campaign 2000, All Things Political, Feed, and Webcorp Politics are all savvy inside-the-Beltway guides. Along with direct governmental links, you can sort out the facts, chase down rumors, and learn why a particular bill is stalled and how the latest strategy is likely to affect the outcome. Polls are sifted and compared, campaigns analyzed, issues weighed in a reality-versus-perception scale. Some offer a useful search function that allows you to enter keywords and turn up articles and lists related to your subject. If you watch Shields and Gigot on Fridays and get up Sundays for *Meet the Press*, these sites will become crucial.

For a less hyperventilating measure of liberalism, try the E-'zines listed at the Turn Left site. The Ethical Spectacle has long, thoughtful pieces; Fast Lane is a compilation of columns; Perspectives is Harvard/Radcliffe's student magazine; American Prospect offers a Jeffersonian approach; and Meanderings is an African-American journal of politics, art, and culture. Other listings include Bad Subjects, Mother Jones, and the Progressive Review.

DNC & RNC

The official party line is trotted out at the Republican National Committee and Democratic National Committee sites. The government itself is wired so that you can compare campaign promises with actual voting records, or follow bills and search them for relevant clauses. Firing off a letter of support or castigation to your representative has never been easier. Certainly the most comprehensive source of links to Congress is Thomas, the federally funded site for government online. Also check Congress.org.

But I'm Not Into Politics!

If you tend to tune out politics, the best approach is to just follow your general mindset. Sixties lefties may want to drop by WebActive which is hosted by that stalwart of liberalism, *Mother Jones* magazine. Women with a literate frame of mind will find a kindred view in The Mining Company. Party boys and girls catching the political bug get a well rounded introduction at Planet Out's Civic Forum. Webgrrls can rub shoulders at Lesbian.Org and people of color and both sexes get an excellent education on politics at SBC's site.

The Personal Is Political

Regardless of your level of interest or persuasion, from leather sites to poetry pages, you'll find calls to sign the petition for absolute freedom of expression on the Internet. They seem to think you can make a difference. It's worth a few minutes filling out a form. Yes?

☐ *ACLU Gay and Lesbian Rights*
  http://www.aclu.org/issues/gay/hmgl.html

☐ *Activist's Oasis*
  http://www.matisse.net/~kathy/activist/

☐ *Alice B. Toklas Democratic Club*
  http://alicebtoklas.org/

☐ *All Things Political*
  http://dolphin.gulf.net/Political.html

☐ *American Prospect Home Page*
  http://epn.org/prospect.html

☐ *Amnesty International Members for Gay & Lesbian Concerns*
  http://www.qrd.org/qrd/orgs/AIMLGC/

☐ *Arizona Stonewall Democrat Caucus*
  http://www.czdem.org/caucusgl/

☐ *Blue Ribbon Campaign*
  http://www.eff.org//blueribbon/activism.html

☐ *CapWeb*
  http://policy.net/capweb/congress.html

☐ *CC Watch*
  http://www4.ncsu.edu/unity/users/r/rfaggart/www/ccwatch/

☐ *Citizen's Project*
  http://citproj.ppages.com/fwjun97.htm

☐ *Congressional Voting*
  http://www.vis.org/

☐ *Congress.org*
http://congress.org/

☐ *Democratic National Committee*
http://www.democrats.org/

☐ *Democratic Leadership Council*
http://www.dlcppi.org/

☐ *Democratic National Committee*
http://www.democrats.org/

☐ *Digital Democrats*
http://democratic-party.org/

☐ *Digital Queers*
http://www.dq.org/

☐ *Directory of Human Rights Organizations*
http://www.igc.org/igc/issues/hr/

☐ *Eagle Forum*
http://www.basenet.net/~eagle/eagle.html

☐ *Electronic Frontier Foundation*
http://www.eff.org/

☐ *Einet Politics (Government)*
http://galaxy.einet.net/galaxy/Government/Politics.html

☐ *Electronic Activist*
http://www.berkshire.net/~ifas/activist/

☐ *Electronic Frontier Foundation*
http://www.eff.org/

☐ *E-mail Addresses of Congressmen & State Legislators*
http://www.berkshire.net/~ifas/activist/

☐ *Emily's List*
http://www.emilyslist.org/

☐ *Fairness & Accuracy in Reporting*
http://www.igc.apc.org/fair/

☐ *Fedworld*
http://www.fedworld.gov/

☐ *Feed*
http://www.feedmag.com/index.html

☐ *Feminist Activist Resources on the Net*
http://www.igc.apc.org/women/feminist.html

☐ *Friends of the Earth*
http://www.foe.co.uk/

☐ *Gay & Lesbian Elected Officials*
http://www.ngltf.org/cgoffic.html

☐ *Gay & Lesbian Independent Democrats*
http://members.aol.com/glidny

☐ *Gays & Lesbians for Individual LIberty*
http://glil.org/

☐ *Gay & Lesbian Politics*
http://www.indiana.edu/~glbtpol/

☐ *Gender PAC*
http://www.gpac.org/

☐ *Get Educated*
http://ernie.bgsu.edu/~ckile/poled.html

☐ *Giles Report*
http://www.webcom.com/~albany/infight.html

☐ *GLAAD*
http://www.glaad.org/glaad/

☐ *GLVF (Gay and Lesbian Victory Fund)*
http://www.qrd.org/qrd/orgs/GLVF/

☐ *GOP online*
http://republicans.vt.com/

☐ *Green Parties of America*
http://www.rahul.net/greens/

☐ *GreenPeace*
http://www.greenpeace.org/

☐ *Hands Off Washington! (Fighting antigay Ballot Measures)*
http://www.eor.com/howhtml/how.htm

☐ *Hatewatch.org*
http://www.hatewatch.org

☐ *HRC Congressional Scorecard*
http://www.hrc.org/congress/votrecrd.html

☐ *Independent Gay Forum*
http://www.indegay.org/

☐ *INFACT*
http://www.boutell.com/infact/

☐ *International Lesbian Information Service*
http://www.helsinki.fi/~kris_ntk/ilis.html

☐ *Jefferson Project*
http://www.voxpop.org/jefferson/

☐ *Jesse Helms Speaks*
http://www.nando.net/sproject/jesse/helms.html

☐ *Lambda Independent Democrats*
http://www.nycnet.com/lid

☐ *League of Women Voters*
http://www.northamerican.com/~towncenter/~politics/lwv.htm

☐ *Lesbian.org*
http://www.lesbian.org/

☐ *Lesbigay Directory at IGC*
http://www.igc.apc.org/lbg/

☐ *Lesbigay Resources from the Carleton Freenet*
http://www.ncf.carleton.ca/freeport/sigs/life/gay/les/menu

☐ *Libertarian Party*
http://www.lp.org/lp/lp.html

☐ *Liberty City L&G Democrats*
http://libertycity.org/

☐ *Log Cabin Republicans*
http://www.lcr.org/

☐ *Mother Jones*
http://www.mojones.com/motherjones.html

☐ *NGLTF Capital Gains and Losses (state by state r
view of gay-related legislation)*
http://www.ngltf.org/cgal.html

☐ *National Gay Lobby*
http://www.nationalgaylobby.org/

☐ *National Public Radio*
http://www.npr.org/

☐ *National Rifle Association*
http://www.nra.org/

☐ *Newshour With Jim Lehrer*
http://www1.pbs.org/newshour

☐ *New York Politics online*
http://www.ny-politics.com/

☐ *NGLTF*
http://www.ngltf.org/

☐ *NLPAC*
http://www.lesbian.org/nlpac/

☐ *NOW Gay & Lesbian Rights*
http://www.now.org/issues/lgbi/lgbi.html

☐ *On the Issues*
http://www.echonyc.com/~onissues

☐ *The Organized Assault on Gay Rights*
http://www.ifas.org/fw/9408/gleneyrie.html

☐ *People For The American Way*
http://www.pfaw.org/

☐ *PlanetOut*
http://www.planetout.com

☐ *Political Activism Resources*
http://www.kimsoft.com/kimpol.htm

☐ *Politics Information.com*
http://www.politicalinformation.com/

☐ *Politics Now*
http://www.politicsnow.com/

☐ *President Clinton's Pride Message*
http://www.religioustolerance.org/hom_0049.htm

☐ *QRD Politics*
http://www.qrd.org/qrd/www/qpolis.html

☐ *Reactionary Right*
http://www.webcom.com/albany/rr.html

☐ *Republican National Committee*
http://www.rnc.org/

☐ *Republican Presidential Candidate Campaign Contacts*
http://www.au.com/presidential/contacts.html

☐ *Resources for the Feminist Activist*
http://www.igc.apc.org/women/feminist.html

☐ *Slate*
http://www.slate.com/TOC/current/contents.asp

☐ *Speeches by Bill Clinton*
http://dolphin.gulf.net/Clinton.html

☐ *Stonewall Democrats (nat'l office)*
http://www.stonewalldemocrats.org/

☐ *Thomas*
http://thomas.loc.gov/

☐ *Turn Left*
http://www.turnleft.com/

☐ *TurnOut*
http://www.turnleft.com/out/

☐ *Ultimate Political Resources*
http://www.shu.edu/~kellytra/polrsc.html

☐ *UN Info Server*
http://www.undcp.org/unlinks.html

☐ *U.S. Congress-Unofficial Guide*
http://policy.net

☐ *U.S. House of Representatives*
http://www.house.gov/

☐ *Web Active*
http://www.webactive.com/

☐ *Webcorp Politics Page*
http://www.webcorp.com/politics.htm

☐ *Welcome to the Democratic Party Web Page*
http://www.webcom.com/~digitals/

☐ *Welcome to the White House*
http://www.whitehouse.gov/

☐ *White House Conference on Hate Crimes*
http://www.whitehouse.gov/Initiatives/OneAmerica/whc.html

☐ *Why Party Politics Matter*
http://www.actwin.com/hglc/frank2.htm

☐ *Wired Strategies*
http://www.wiredstrategies.com

☐ *Wired Strategies (Ex-gays Implode)*
http://www.wiredstrategies.com.exgays.html

☐ *Wired Strategies (Matthew Shepard Resources)*
  http://www.wiredstrategies.com/shepard.html

☐ *Wired Strategies (Mugged by AOL)*
  http://www.wiredstrategies.com/mugged.html

☐ *Webcorp Politics Page*
  http://www.webcorp.com/politics.htm

☐ *Yahoo!-Government:Politics*
  http://www.yahoo.com/Government/Politics/

 Pride

Since 1980, gay pride celebrations have been gathering momentum, providing an ever-larger demonstration that gays and lesbians are a vital part of society at large. From an original core of 15 city parades, the celebrations have spread to 120 cities in North America and more than 20 in Europe. Participants number over 6 million in North America alone.

Whether you'd like to march, cheer the bands, ride a float or join in the dances and celebrations leading up to the main event, the best place to learn about schedules is the Pride Events Page put up by the International Association of Lesbian/Gay Pride Coordinators (IAL/GPC). This site opens with a history of pride, and then offers

other pages explaining why attendance is important. The overwhelming reason is to "have fun with all our friends and loved ones," but there are other goals for gathering en masse. "Sodomy laws are still in effect in many countries and states. Laws protecting people against discrimination based on sexual preference are still not the rule. In most of Europe and all over the U.S. ,gay and lesbian couples suffer under discrimination." Participation is viewed as a patriotic act.

The global calendar is huge, containing hundreds of events all over the world. Subsequent pages give briefs on some of the best-attended pride celebrations. You can get the schedule and local information number for cities across America from Wichita, Kan., to Burlington, Vt.; from Nashville to Tallahassee, Fla. Some of the larger sites also receive write-ups. San Diego Pride, for example, is described as drawing people from all over Orange County, from Los Angeles to Balboa Park. An associated party at the zoo was, we are told, marred only slightly by complaints about "same-sex couples holding hands" and "women who have hair in their armpits" (oh, well).

International Pride

Information for international events is also listed. You can read about them here, and get further contact sources for festivities in Europe, Asia, Africa, Australia, and New Zealand as well as South America. Check out the "Gayzette" newsletter, with reports from recent pride events, plus links to new events. As the largest pride day of all, the weeklong celebration in Sydney, Australia, is described as hosting a mammoth parade, harbor cruises, a film festival, and much more. The annual Sleaze Ball, for example, is a dance party that attracts more than 15,000 guests. "The dress code is fetish wear, and usually the less of it the better!"

For more information, see the QRD and see the Gay and Lesbian Travel Web, which has listings of pride vacation packages to cities around the world.

☐ *The International Association of Lesbian/Gay Pride Coordinators*
http://www.interpride.org/

With so many other gay and lesbian sites on the Internet, it would seem foolhardy to saddle any single place with such an all-encompassing title as Queer Resources Directory. But in this case no one objects, since the QRD has been there from the first. It began in 1991 as an archive for Queer Nation and has grown so quickly that today more than 150,000 people download files each month, and thousands more visitors stop by to pick up useful addresses. As the community's most common and highly prized bookmark, it's the crossroads of cyberqueerdom, the central reference for every imaginable interest. (Except erotica, I should note. The QRD has no sexy stories or blue pictures, but it has everything else.)

Queer Resources Directory

And this is not just an organization of collection-mad queers. The site has a clear agenda: "It is a goal for the QRD to contain every scrap of knowledge which has been used in or is part of the struggle for full equality. We hope you are able to use this information to broaden your horizons and enrich your experience in ways you had not expected." This bunch is idealistic, yet completely cognizant of the fragility and restricted nature of queer rights. Their work is important, and they're brave enough to say so.

The home page is simple — just a list of titles for the site's main categories. Click any title and a series of related pages pops onscreen, allowing you to narrow your search to exactly what you're looking for, whether it is text or links to subjects.

These are just the main categories: Queers and their Families; Queer Youth (on campus and all over the world); Queers and Religion (religious queers); Queer Health (including safer sex and AIDS info); Electronic Resources (with links to all over the net); Queer Media (magazines, TV, movies, more); Queer Events (conferences and celebrations on a global scale); Queer Culture, History, and Origins (what makes us unique, where we've been, and where we come from); Worldwide Queer Info (from Australia to Zimbabwe, we are everywhere); Business, Legal, and Workplace (including resources on domestic partnerships and queer-friendly businesses); Politics, Political News, and Activism (fighting back with technology); and Organizations, Directories, and Newsletters (find them all here, or submit info on your organization).

Importantly, the QRD also has writings and links to people and organizations working against gays and lesbians. "Know your enemy" is one of their rallying cries. As the site notes, "This information is intended for use as counterintelligence." And it's free. Regardless of the rumors of the death of volunteerism and liberal action, the QRD is manned and womanned by a network of volunteers. "The QRD was established during the time when the Internet had a long-standing tradition of public service, and although the network has changed dramatically since then, we still consider providing free access to information our primary goal and function." Is this a plug or a review? Both. Go see it.

☐ *Queer Resources Directory*
   http://www.qrd.org/

Queer Theory & the Web

Though academic-speak, with its endless reflexives and studied jargon, is a bore, queer theory (the study of what Queer means) is a fascinating and perhaps important topic for us all. The largest collections of links to this multi-faceted subject (often confused *or* intentionally used interchangeably with queer studies) is Rainbow Query's page on QT. There you'll find everything from individual pages by lone scholars to large, link-filled sites that attempt to wrap a description around the subject. One of the best introductions is the Resources: queer theory Page. Along with links to critics, books and founders such as Judith Butler (author of *Gender Trouble*) and Michel Foucault, it includes papers (such as "Madonna—the popular embodiment of queer theory...arguably") that give a sense, if not an entirely satisfying answer, to exactly what queer theory is. Rather than a straightforward rereading of history through a queer prism, the author maintains that QT "proposes that we deliberately challenge all notions of fixed identity."

Things are Queer, an essay by Jonathan Weinberg, refines the meaning within a postmodern frame: "It is impossible to imagine queer theory existing without the identity politics of the pre- and immediate post-Stonewall era, or the later street actions of ACT UP. Queer theory is deeply indebted to feminist and African-American writings, just as lesbian and gay liberation itself was built on the model of the women's movement and on the struggle for black civil rights. In the end, I do not think it is necessary to choose between queer studies or lesbian and gay studies. We should feel free to move between them and even confuse them. Ideally, the two approaches—the queer, more theoretical and improvisational, the lesbian and gay, more dependent on the archive and biography—can go on simultaneously.

At the base of his discussions and comparisons is the acceptance of a belief that society is subject to heterosexism, that we live and breath everything from TV commercials to choosing our lovers through a thick prism of straightness.

This are jarring, uncomfortable pages, a trip through the fun house mirror. It's about us and our place in the world, beyond the bars, the discos, even beyond the queer Web, forcing us to reexamine exactly what makes us queer. And who we are.

☐ *Ethics & Morality in the G&L Community*
  http://www.mindspring.com/~siamese

☐ *Gay Gene*
  http://members.aol.com/gaygene

☐ *Gayhistory*
  http://www.gayhistory.com

☐ *Gender & Transgender Theory*
  http://www.interlog.com/bcholmes/tg.html

☐ *RainbowQuery.com - Queer Theory*
  http://www.rainbowquery.com/categories/queer_theory.html

☐ *Richard Cornwall*
  http://www.middlebury.edu/~cornwall

☐ *Rattigan Society*
  http://clients.unimatrix.com/rattigan

☐ *Queer Theory*
  http://www.theory.org.uk

☐ *Queer Web?*
  http://www.english.udel.edu/gweight/

You can see the radical religious right on television, out on the political trail, at caucuses, and at flag-draped fund-raisers—seemingly everywhere but on the endangered species list. What are they saying about us sinners? They're quite inventive, but the main message is that queers are a sign of The End.

This message is trumpeted with insidious skill on the Web. The radical right's home pages vary; some are ludicrous, a sinister parody of a *Saturday Night Live* skit. The Stormfront White Nationalist Resource Page opens with a militaristic black cross encircled by the motto "White Pride World Wide." Along with links to other fringe sites (like the militia-promoting Patriot Games), Stormfront contains a witches' brew of articles citing the Bible's support for racism and "proof" that the Oklahoma City bombing was a government plot. In descriptions of other fringe newsgroups, BBSs, and Usenet addresses, it warns readers of infiltration by "anti-racists" who "feel completely safe spewing their vitriol from behind a computer terminal."

godhatesfags.com

Fred Phelps's page is just as shocking. "My church (Westboro Baptist Church of Topeka, Kan.), engages in daily peaceful sidewalk demonstrations opposing the homosexual lifestyle of soul-damning, nation-destroying filth. We display large, colorful signs containing Bible words and sentiments, including: GOD HATES FAGS, FAGS HATE GOD, AIDS CURES

FAGS, THANK GOD FOR AIDS, FAGS BURN IN HELL, NO TEARS FOR QUEERS, SIN & SHAME NOT PRIDE, FAG=ANAL SEX=DEATH, FAG=AIDS=DEATH, GOD IS NOT MOCKED, FAGS ARE NATURE FREAKS, GOD GAVE FAGS UP, NO SPE-CIAL LAWS FOR FAGS, etc." (All the capitals are Mr. Phelps's.)

The Right (far) Side of the Web

Other radical pages are more sophisticated. They monitor the counterinsurgency of the left. The Right Side of the Web, for ex-ample, has reprinted excerpts of a review in *Wired* magazine describing it as an "online haven to all manner of dittoheads, gun nuts, and religious wackos...a kind of virtual Nuremberg rally where devotees confess undying love for goose-steppers like G. Gordon Liddy and Ollie North." After rebutting *Wired* with sarcasm, The Right Side closed their riposte with "Well, thanks for the review, *Wired*. At least you got the URL correct-ly. They must really like us there, or else we wouldn't have made NetSurf in the first place." The next item is a note about *USA Today*'s glowing assessment of Right Side.

Christian Coalition et al.

Heavily funded pages, such as Pat Robertson's Christian Coalition, blithely create a sort of parallel world where fol-lowers' lockstep views are made to seem the norm. Their polls, for instance, "verify" that only 1-2% of Americans are gay.  Then viewers are urged to call "Pat" with questions on the pressing issues of the day or to order a videotape, one of which portrays the last Stonewall March in New York as an orgy. How odd to find out what you missed thanks to the Rev. Pat.

What is the fundamental goal of these groups? Basically it mir-rors that of the Christian Broadcasting Network: "CBN's mis-sion is to prepare the United States of America, the nations of the Middle East, the Far East, South America and other nations of the world for the coming of Jesus Christ and the establishment of the kingdom of God on earth." (The full text is available on the Web page.)

This brand of extremist xenophobia has alarmed queers so much that several groups monitor and report on it all. The QRD has a special folder of articles by these watchdogs. You can read about strategies and methods for responding to homophobic rhetoric. The Reactionary Religious Right is a Web page that tracks more than 30 religious right groups. The National Gay and Lesbian Task Force has a curriculum for countering fanaticism. And independent activists have put up articles such as "How to Fight the Right Wing," an instructional essay by Stuart Norman on strategies and methods for defusing the wackos.

Though it's not specifically queer, The Institute for First Amendment Studies is worth a visit. IFAS is focused solely on the activities of the radical religious right. The page contains a wealth of information on the leaders, their agenda, copies of press releases, funding sources and lobbying efforts. Also see Interfaith Alliance. This nonprofit organization also watches the radical religious right. Its magazine, *Freedom Writer*, contains all sorts of articles documenting radical malignancies.

Conversion?

One heartening measure of the antiright movement's maturity is the development of "recovery groups" for ex-fundamentalists. Walk Away features stories by a number of former Christian fundamentalists: "The purpose of these stories is to demonstrate that other excellent, liberating choices exist—that there is life after fundamentalism."

☐ *700 Club: Christian Broadcasting Network*
  http://www.The700club.org/

☐ *Alpha*
http://www.alpha.org/

☐ *American Family Association*
http://www.afa.net

☐ *American Guardian*
http://www.thundernet.org/

☐ *American Whites*
http://www.staffnet.com/us/aw.htm

☐ *Aryan Nations*
http://www.stormfront.org/an.htm

☐ *Bob Enyart Live*
http://www.enyart.com

☐ *Buchanan Brigade*
http://www.buchanan.org/

☐ *Campus Crusade for Christ*
http://www.crusade.org/

☐ *Catholic Telecom*
http://www.cathtel.com/

☐ *Christian Coalition*
http://cc.org/

☐ *Christian Rights Party*
http://www.christiangallery.com/creator.html

☐ *Clinton's Homosexual Agenda*
http://www2.southwind.net/~vic/clint_homo.html

☐ *Colorado For Family Values*
http://www.leaderu.com/jhs/marco.html

☐ *Christian Gallery*
http://www.christiangallery.com/

☐ *Concerned Women For America*
http://www.cwfa.org/policypapers/pp_gaysuicide.html

☐ *CNG (Cyber Nationalist Group)*
http://www.crusader.net/texts/cng/

☐ *Death Penalty for Homosexuals*
http://www.paranoia.com/~wcs/homo.htm

☐ *Ellen*
http://www.anu.org/archives_ellenepisodetipoficeberg.html

☐ *Focus on the Family*
http://www.fotf.org

☐ *Gary Bauer's Family Research Council*
http://www.frc.org/

☐ *Hatewatch*
http://hatewatch.org/

☐ *Institute for First Amendment Studies*
http://www.ifas.org

☐ *The Interactive Bible*
http://www.bible.ca/bible.htm

☐ *Lunatic Right*
http://mother.qrd.org/qrd/www/RRR/lunatic.html

☐ *Nation of Europa*
http://www.demon.co.uk/natofeur/

☐ *Phelps Watch*
http://www.kaupe.com/expose.html

☐ *The Pink Swastika - Homosexuality in the Nazi Party*
http://home.earthlink.net/~lively/

☐ *Politics and Terrorism*
http://www.flinet.com/%7Epolitics

☐ *Promise Keepers*
http://www.promisekeepers.org/

☐ *The Radical Religious Right*
http://mother.qrd.org/qrd/www/RRR/rrrpage.html

☐ *The Reactionary Religious Right*
http://www.webcom.com/~albany/rr.html

☐ *Rev. Fred Phelps*
http://fileroom.aaup.uic.edu/FileRoom/documents/Cases/393phelps.

☐ *The Right Side of the Web*
http://www.townhall.com/rtside/

☐ *Skin Net*
http://ftcnet.com/%7Eskinhds

☐ *Stormfront White Nationalist Resource Page*
http://www.stormfront.org

☐ *Society to Remove All Immoral Godless Homosexual Trash*
http://www.melvig.org/mel/MELVIG.HTM

☐ *Walk Away*
http://www.berkshire.net/~ifas/wa/index.html

☐ *Who's Who of the Religious Right*
http://www.mojones.com/MOTHER_JONES/ND95/stan_guide.html

Religion & Spirituality

Even though it often seems that the religious right, whether Catholic, Christian, Muslim, or Buddhist, is successfully weeding out divergent messages, they've not muzzled the proliferation of on-line discussion sites for religious queers. There is in fact an insurgence of such forums, with reasoned, informed, and faith-based arguments for gay recognition and acknowledging our place in church history.

Catholicism

The main page for Dignity/USA contains links to all 80 of its chapters across the United States, with times of their services as well as a deep archive of articles and sermons—a faith-based history of an organization of gay, lesbian, bisexual, and transgendered Catholics and their friends. A more specific page for Catholics is A Catholic Mother Looks At The Gay Child. It's a won-

derfully informative, supportive and personal account of the give-and-take in a Catholic family as they come to a new understanding of the church and sexuality.

Michael Spire's Spiritual Information for Lesbian, Gay, and Bisexual People is both a personal exploration of the author's Catholicism and an ecumenical resource for anyone interested in researching a life of faith along other paths. Along with pointers to larger indexes, he includes his own thoughts in essays such as "An Open Letter to Gay and Lesbian Christians (and All People of Good Will)," "A Voice Crying Out in the Wilderness: An Open Letter to the People of God (On why I cannot in good conscience adhere to Catholic moral teaching regarding homosexual acts),″ and "My responses to the 'standard seven' Bible texts quoted to 'prove' that homosexuality is immoral (Or, What you always wanted to tell those fundamentalists when you didn't know what to say)."

Gay Christians

There are a number of sites devoted to queer religious organizations (like Presbyterians for Lesbian and Gay Concerns and the Metropolitan Community Church), as well as to antigay religious activities. GayChristians.Org has a supportive chat channel as well as an excellent directory of religious sites, both for and against gay and lesbian involvement. Divided into four sections, it includes documentation refuting the scriptural basis for antigay prejudice, a comprehensive list of gay and lesbian welcoming churches in the U.S., and a long list of links to "sexuality-affirming" Christian rights organizations. GayChristians, though charitable, are a forceful bunch. Here's their description heading a list of faux Christians such as the American Family Association and The 700 Club: "While often well-intended, the following sites unfortunately do more to promote prejudice—malicious and insulting assumptions about the "lifestyles" and values of gay and lesbian people of faith—than they do to promote dialogue or healing on this difficult subject for churches."

Dharma Dykes

Dharma Dykes is a private mailing list for lesbians who study and practice Buddhism in any tradition. There are no requirements in terms of length of time one has been following the path. Beginners are as welcome as those with experience. The site includes links and writings of Sarika.

Interfaith

The Interfaith Working Group has an equally well-organized outreach program to further their cause of informing the public "and providing a voice and a forum for religious organizations, congregations, and clergy who favor gay rights, reproductive freedom, and the separation of church and state." It's a diverse group of organizations and individuals who, according to its spokesman Walter Cronkite, have come together to fight the "Christian Coalition and other right wing groups and individuals who wrap themselves in the language and symbolism of religious faith."

Judaism

The first gay and lesbian Jewish organizations in the world were formed in London and Los Angeles in 1972 and New York in early 1973. By 1975, lesbian and gay Jewish organizations were also active in San Francisco, Boston, Washington, D.C., Philadelphia, and Miami.

Today, you'll find over 65 at the World Conference of Gay and Lesbian Jewish Organizations. "We mount conferences and workshops and represent the interests of lesbian and gay Jews around the world at national, continental, and global contexts." Their page gives addresses for all member organizations and has updates on the annual congress as well as the organizations application for membership in the UN and the World Jewish Congress.

"Like an Orange on a Seder Plate: Our Lesbian Haggadah is a warmly lesbian-centered page that gives you a guide to "sharing the Passover Seder together in a contemporary manner. All the rituals and symbols of Passover are explained in a way that brings the past into the present."

Johnny Abush's Jewish GLB Archives is a fascinating and huge compilation of material that Abush began after an AIDS diagnosis prompted him to reconsider his origins as a member of two persecuted minorities. Contents include profiles of gay rabbis, a newsletter and mailing lists, a guide to biographies and memoirs—as well as the light side of things on the Joke Page.

Quakers

Q-Light mailing list was created primarily for LGBT members, but it's also for people of all faiths and sexual orientations. The discussions are distinguished by the Quaker spirit, one that listens thoughtfully and gauges final truths not so much by words, but by action. Many of the postings you'll read are from those seeking clarity on their position as in a world of inimical to quiet progress.

Sources

Cristo Press promotes much the same agenda, offering free pamphlets that you can order online. Titles include "What is Abomination?" "Did God Create Adam and Steve?" "AIDS and Christianity," "Baptist and Gay," "The Ex-Gay Premise!" "Is Fundamentalist an Ugly Word?" and "What About Gay Relationships in the Bible?" Carnegie Mellon University (CMU) has a compilation of news articles on gays in religion, as does Karl's Cafe. The QRD provides a deep resource in the Queer Religion folder.

AIDS and Faith

Spirituality, naturally enough, is very much at home in the cyber-ether of the Web. A search on AIDS and Religion in AltaVista, for example, yields more than 5,000 pointers—Web pages of the major religions, along with their sadly unacknowledged peers at the Metropolitan Community of Churches and Dignity.

Surprisingly, the U.S. government funds an excellent resource. The CDC's Religion section, created with the AIDS National Interfaith Network (ANIN), lists national religious organizations providing information, assistance and referrals. You'll also find meditations, prayers, and liturgies.

Rainbow Spirituality Ring

Less doctrinal than religion but equally diverse are the various forms of spirituality. There are individual pages like Darren's Cyber Ashram as well as large pages with huge links collections such as SisterSpirit. The Rainbow Spirituality Ring is perhaps the largest collection of lesbian, gay, bisexual and LGBT-friendly spiritual groups. Pagans on the Web offers an index to hundreds of Pagan Web sites. Witches Web is exclusively for followers of the path of Wicca: "All pages contain material relating to the old religion and witchcraft." Angel Ring is a Web ring of sites throughout the WWW on the topic of angels. At the Athenian Ring you will meet "creative, poetic, philosophical, expressive, and, at times, even opinionated homesteaders, with something to share with the world."

Gay Men's Spirituality is an interesting page promoting self-discovery. "There are many paths to travel toward a healthy spiritual life, and they are as unique and varied as each individual. The paths gay men travel include psychotherapy, religion, dream study, yoga, relationships, gardening, ritual, sex, meditation, recovery groups, dancing, and much more. Either alone or by gathering with others, many gay men have opened the door to a rich and healthy spiritual life."

Yahoo!

Searching the large indexes is always recommended, but unless you want to sift through homophobic sermons, be sure to add the keywords "gay and lesbian" to "religion." You'll find many newsletters and mailing lists, and some excellent Web sites. Catholicism, Judaism, Buddhism, and Islam are all represented, but the overwhelming number of queer advocacy pages are Christian. Over and over at these sites you'll hear the basic message that God is love—they've ceded the burn-in-hell stance to their counterparts over at the Right Side of the Web and the Christian Coalition. (For info on these groups, see the chapter on the Radical Religious Right, page 442.)

☐ *A Catholic Mother Looks At Her Gay Child*
http://www.gaychild.com

☐ *Affirmations/Gay and Lesbian Mormons*
http://www.affirmation.org/~affadmin

☐ *Alternative Family Project*
http://www.queer.org/afp/

☐ *Angel Ring*
http://www.geocities.com/Athens/Acropolis/1652/

☐ *Anglicans Online*
http://www.anglican.org/

☐ *Atheism Web*
http://freethought.tamu.edu/news/atheism/

☐ *Association of Welcoming and Affirming Baptists*
http://members.aol.com/wabaptists/index.html

☐ *Avatar Search*
http://www.avatarsearch.com

☐ *Baha'i Faith*
http://oneworld.wa.com/bahai/

☐ *Balm Ministries*
http://www.geocities.com/westhollywood/8855

☐ *Beth El Binah Jewish lesbigays.*
http://www.global.org/beth.el.binah/

☐ *The Body-Religion and AIDS*
http://www.thebody.com/religion.html

☐ *Bridges Across the Divide*
http://www.bridges-across.org/

☐ *Calander of GLT Saints*
http://www.bway.net/~halsall/lgbh/lgbh-gaysts.html

☐ *CAM (Computerized AIDS Ministry)*
http://hwbbs.gbgm-umc.org/

☐ *Castro Yoga*
http://wwww.castroyoga.com/

☐ *Cathedral of Hope*
http://www.cathedralofhope.com

☐ *Christian Lesbians*
http://www.christianlesbians.com

☐ *Club Alive!*
http://www.a6164.com/fou

☐ *Christian Lesbians ONLINE*
http://www.geocities.com/WestHollywood/Heights/2685/

☐ *Congregation Beth El Binah*
http://www.global.org/beth.el.binah/

☐ *Cristo Press*
http://qrd.tcp.com/qrd/religion/judeochristian/protestantism/cristo.

☐ *Darren's Cyber Ashram*
http://www.darrenmain.com/

☐ *Dharma Dykes*
http://home.earthlink.net/~dfbailey/lzg.html

☐ *Digital Priest Confessional Booth*
http://anther.learning.cs.cmu.edu/priest.html

☐ *Dignity USA*
http://www.dignityusa.org/

☐ *EroSpirit*
http://www.gayweb.com/104/eros.html

☐ *Etz Chaim*
http://members.gnn.com/etzchaim/index.htm

☐ *Evangelical Network (resources for gays)*
http://www.xroads.com/~ten_net

☐ *Ex Ex Page*
http://members.aol.com/exexgay/index.html

☐ *First Church of Groove*
http://www.geocities.com/SoHo/1363/

☐ *Friends for Gay and Lesbian Concerns*
http://www.geocities.com/WestHollywood/2473/flgc.html

☐ *Gay Christians.Org*
http://www.gaychristians.org/

☐ *Gay Friendly Religious Links (Q-Light)*
http://world.std.com/~rice/q-light/links.html

☐ *Gay Jews Mailing List*
gopher://israel.nysernet.org:70/11/lists/gayjews

☐ *Gay Men's Spirituality*
http://www.the-park.com/barzan/main.htm

☐ *Gayla*
http://www.euronet.nl/~sniekers/html/gayla_is.htm

☐ *Interfaith Working Group*
http://www.libertynet.org/~iwg/iwg.html

☐ *Jesus in Vegas*
http://www.mediashower.com/zug/sky/xmas/

☐ *Jewish GLB Archives Online*
http://www.magic.ca/~faygelah/Index.html

☐ *Karl's Cafe*
http://www.nova.edu/Inter-Links/hytelnet/BBS/BBS046.html

☐ *L& G Jewish Resources*
   http://world.std.com/~alevin/jewishfeminist.html

☐ *LBJW (discussion list for lesbian and bisexual Jewish women)*
   http://www.qrd.org/QRD/electronic/email/lbjw

☐ *Lesbian, Bisexual, Gay, and Queer Web Pages*
   http://www.igc.apc.org/igc/www.lbg.html

☐ *LGB Catholic Handbook*
   http://www.bway.net/~halsall/lgbh.html

☐ *Like an Orange on a Seder Plate: Our Lesbian Haggadah*
   http://saltspring.com/leshag.orange

☐ *Lutherans Concerned*
   http://www.quarterbyte.com/lcna/

☐ *Metropolitan Community Churches*
   http://www.ufmcc.org/

☐ *The Oasis (LGB Episcopalian Ministry)*
   http://www.princeton.edu/~meneghin/oasis/oasis.html

☐ *Ontario Consultants for Religious Tolerance*
   http://www.religioustolerance.org/ocrt_hp.htm

☐ *OutProud, the National Coalition for Gay, Lesbian & Bisexual Youth*
   http://www.cyberspaces.com/outproud/

☐ *Pagans on the Web*
   http://www.sover.net/~jalyssia/paganweb/

☐ *Presbyterians for Lesbian and Gay Concerns*
   http://www.epp.cmu.edu/~riley/PLGC.html

☐ *Q Light Home Page*
http://world.std.com/~rice/q-light/index.html

☐ *Q Planet*
http://www.qplanet.com/spirit.html

☐ *QRD*
http://www.qrd.org/qrd/religion

☐ *Rainbow Spirituality Ring*
http://www.geocities.com/WestHollywood/3528/rainbow.html

☐ *Religion*
http://www.libertynet.org/~iwg/list.html

☐ *Religious Issues for Gays and Lesbians*
http://www.cs.cmu.edu/afs/cs.cmu.edu/user/scotts/bulgarians/

☐ *The Sisters of Perpetual Indulgence, Mother House*
http://www.thesisters.org

☐ *Walk Away*
http://www.berkshire.net/~ifas/wa/index.html

☐ *Web Ring Philosophy & Religion*
http://www.webring.org/rings_phil.html

☐ *What the Bible Really Says About Homosexuality*
http://www.ezin.net/personal/steven/homo1.htm

☐ *World Conference of Gay & Lesbian Jewish Organizations*
http://www.wcgljo.org/wcgljo/

Safer Sex

How the folks at Coalition for Positive Sexuality steer a path through safer-sex instruction without a tinge of anger at the continuing ignorance is a wonder—but they do it so well that the CPS is at the top of site-attendance lists. The page is called Just Say Yes! (*en español: Di Que Sí!*).

The language here is conversational and straightforward. "There's no preaching. No moralizing. Just the facts."The first five sections deal with questions facing today's youth: "Should I have sex? What's Safe Sex? What about Birth Control? What if I'm gay? What about Pregnancy? What if I get a disease?" The answers are exactly how every sane adult hopes he sounds when giving advice: measured, honest, willing to admit that there are some things we don't know, and yet always reinforcing that having sex is an individual choice.

There are many other sections. The glossary is very good, defining consent (consensual sex), coming, oral sex, transgender and many more. The best part (or the most frightening, if you thought everyone was informed) is Let's Talk!, a forum for teens to talk about sex with each other. Resident sexperts answer questions by E-mail.

The FAQs are especially good. In answer to those questioning their sexuality, the authors write in part: "Most people do define themselves as lesbian, gay, bisexual, or straight; but ultimately people are more complicated and interesting than these categories. It's up to you to figure out how you want to identify yourself (as bisexual, lesbian, gay, straight, or whatever). Keep in mind that there are as many sexualities as people out there, and there's one that is uniquely yours. Enjoy it!" And they're quite clear about the "sinful" aspect of their page. "We respect the fact that your beliefs about sexuality may differ from ours, but we aren't here to debate with anyone. Our mission is to provide information."

The links list, which is very high quality, is broken down into categories; Activism; AIDS; Birth Control; Gay, Lesbian, Bi, and Transgender; Gay, Lesbian, and Bi Youth; Sex and Sexuality; Sex and Business; STDs; Violence/Harassment/Abuse; and Women's Healthcare.

For Adults

The primary audience at Just Say Yes is youth, but there are some terrific adult-oriented pages, such as Toronto's Safer SM Education Project. Nothing is out of bounds here, as the S/M community discusses how to prevent infection. Topic headings include Earning Your Stripes (whipping), Psychology of S/M, Bound and Determined (restraints and bondage), Better Homes and Dungeons (playroom construction), and Get the Point (piercing).

Sex-positive guidelines. Go yourself and then send your ostrich friends.

☐ *Blowfish*
http://www.blowfish.com/

☐ *Boy2Boy*
http://www.boy2boy/.org/

☐ *Coalition for Positive Sexuality*
http://www.positive.org/

☐ *Focus International*
http://www.sex-help.com/

☐ *G.L.A.R.E (Gay Liberationist Association for Rights Everywhere)*
http://www.unca.edu/glare

☐ *Gay Men Fighting Aids (GMFA)*
http://www.demon.co.uk/gmfa/Safe

☐ *Good Vibrations*
http://www.goodvibes.com

☐ *Hot Sex Safely*
http://weber.u.washington.edu/~sfpse/safesex.html

☐ *Just Say Yes*
http://www.positive.org/cps/Home/index.html

☐ *Lesbian Safer Sex*
http://www.safersex.org/

☐ *Playware*
http://www.playware.com/

☐ *Queer InfoServer-AIDS & HIV*
http://www.infoqueer.org/queer/qis/health.html

☐ *Queer Resources Directory*
http://abacus.oxy.edu/QRD/aids/

☐ *Safe Magic for Gay Men*
http://www.safersex.org/ssex/safemagic.html

☐ *Safer Sex Page*
http://www.safersex.org/

☐ *Safer SM Education Project*
http://alternate.com

☐ *Safe Sex Discussion*
http://www.halcyon.com/elf/altsex/

☐ *WET Formulas International*
http://www.wetlubes.com

☐ *Yahoo! Resources*
http://www.yahoo.com/Society_and_Culture/Sex/

San Francisco

Can you imagine *The New York Times* showcasing a gay section in its online home page? Or *The Dallas Morning News*? The *San Francisco Examiner* does, with subpages on community books and transsexual resources to boot. And that is the magical differ-

ence in San Franciscan life—gays and lesbians are interwoven culturally as nowhere else. With Silicon Valley just down the road and a bevy of local universities giving students free access to the Web, the Bay Area has more online sites per capita than any other part of the country. And they love visitors.

The first stop, both for locals and visitors is the *B.A.R.* It's the city's GLBT paper of record and has been since the 1970s. Whatever's got the city excited, whether politically or arts-wise, it's bound to be reported there. The columns are often very good, covering San Francisco's lively books scene, leather, and lesbian life as well as AIDS news and celebrity gossip (local and global). The massive personals section is probably the largest of any in the world—endless pages for every persuasion.

GayGlobal San Francisco

This is a slick new page that is coming close to its aim of being a comprehensive guide to the entire San Francisco region. It's a directory of accommodations, bars, clubs, community organizations, businesses, events… not only in San Francisco but in the adjoining cites, even up to San Francisco's answer to P-Town and Fire Island, the Russian River.

One of its strong points is its excellent write-ups. On Tranny Shack for example: "San Francisco's defining cabaret. I imagine when we look back at this decade and bitterly reminisce about our youth, we'll recall the glamorous/tragic nights at the Shack— at least the nights we didn't black out. ... The midnight show showcases all walks of drag queens and kings, trannies, go-go's, genderfuckers, and beyond. ... The weekly crowd is a regular variety pack, but you can always count on a host of beautiful guys hanging out and watching the show."

WebCastro

The WebCastro site does The gay mecca proud. It's a wonderful, long and interesting page that gets better every year. Like a magazine, it has articles (check out the deep history pages on how the Castro became the Castro, and on Harvey Milk), an events calendar, book reviews, poetry, chat lines, travel tips, and gay and gay-friendly accommodations. The illustrated essays on current exhibitions are especially good, as are the recommendations for those new to town.

Guys

The two best guides to gay San Francisco are SOMA Boy and Wolf's Guide to Leather San Francisco. Both are home pages by two guys who seem to know every bar in town and are able to describe the scene so you feel you've been there. Wolf concentrates on the leather world with comments and characterizations on new and long-running bars, sex clubs, and restaurants. He even includes street maps! The calendar is meticulous, running out months in advance. New this year is a free mini-guide. Just send him the dates you'll be in town, mention what you're looking for, and he'll E-mail you a list of suggestions. Check out his biography—he's very tall, works out, and flags black and blue on the left.

SOMA Boy

This is huge site concentrating on the area of San Francisco known as SOMA (South of Market). That's the leather/bear area, but the author of these pages likes "skinny, long-haired boys, shaved or really close-cropped heads, unkempt, scruffy, or flat-out sloppy appearance." He's funny, acerbic, and gives an opinionated tour of all San Francisco. From snarls at the Castro ("A great social experiment has now become an upscale gay theme park.") to raves about SOMA, he's always got a point. About North Beach, the Italian section and famed home to the beats he says, "Allen Ginsberg is dead and the Hungry I is a strip joint now."

If there's one thing he's very positive about, it's sex. He's got the lowdown on what's going on in the bars, sex clubs and back alleys. Also check out the tips on eating, sleeping and shopping, where "ties are neither required nor tolerated."

Girlz

Amazon Online, has a very good links list to San Francisco and the surrounding area. You'll find what's going on in the bars, restaurants, theater, sports, and cafés. And it's definitely written by locals. The large guides always seem to miss great places like Mama Bear's, the famous women's bookstore and café in Berkeley or CoCo Club, a women's speakeasy. There's also a heads-up on where all the hottest women are gathering: The Box, Junk Women, or the G-Spot, "a lesbian institution in San Francisco, whose motto is 'If you can't find it, you can't come.' " Also listed are floating clubs appearing once a month, like Club Q, DIVA, Club Salsa, Avalon, and more.

University Guides

The jewel in the San Francisco Area's online crown is the Queer InfoServer (QIS) from just across the bay in Berkeley at the University of California. It's a giant resource of all things queer with special San Francisco links connecting you to the Castro, pride day schedules, and the film festival, among many other cultural events. Other universities in the area include Stanford and UC San Francisco; both have sites that are chock full of pages giving you a taste of the city, from its bars and restaurants to symphonies, politics, and health organizations.

Stanford Queer Guide to San Francisco is a city companion with listings for events, bookstores, cafés, movies, theater, and nightclubs as well as area organizations. As Wanda, a Stanford graduate, says, "Before Queer Guide, I didn't really think in terms of having a life...now I'm a member of 73 organizations, go dancing every night, have nine girlfriends, and roller blade every Sunday in Golden Gate Park."

Magazines

Since last year San Francisco's city magazines have come online big time. There's *Lavender Pages* and *Frontiers Newsmagazine San Francisco Edition*. *Q San Francisco* has the best online presence, with good articles on restaurants, bars, theater and a very explicit guide to sex at the beach. Monthly departments cover the arts, books, health, and cyberqueerness. Its reviews of bars and restaurants are divided into districts, such as the Haight and the Castro. The Lavender Pages (Fabulous Pages), Gay San Francisco is a commercial site with information for both locals and visitors on restaurants, hotels and bed-and-breakfasts, stores, and other services.

Bars & Sex clubs

You might think that everyone in this net-mad town is a Web wanderer, and a growing number of bars now have Web pages. One Web pioneer, the Lonestar Saloon (a bear bar on Folsom Street), has a doozy of a site. It loads quickly and it has a beautiful design—stars in all sorts of colors and renditions. And though its normal clientele are intimidatingly big and burly men, the opening page is so friendly it makes you want to drop by the real place. Along with a calendar of events and a huge links list to bear clubs around the world, there's a recipe page for what can only be described as comfort food. Check it out.

Daddy's is a leather bar in the Castro whose page has a different sort of spin; the editor addresses you as "boy." Harvey's (at the corner of Castro and 18th Street) is a bar/restaurant named for Harvey Milk, who was a regular at the same location when it was the Elephant Walk. The page enshrines the old days in a showcase of treasured memorabilia that includes a portrait of San Francisco's first Empress, a glittering kimono worn by the pop star Sylvester, and a tiny Speedo autographed by Olympic diving champ Greg Louganis.

BlowBuddies

When a sex club has as handsome a page as BlowBuddies does, you know it's well-run and hot as hell. The photographs are terrific and many have been digitized for that extra kick—some of the dicks jiggle provocatively. Water sports, underwear, leather, naked—whatever your taste, there's a night for you and a good portion of the San Francisco guys.

Home Pages

On top of all these resources, there are many home pages with long, lovingly maintained lists of links. Of these pages (also check Rainbow Query under San Francisco), the one with the most information on San Francisco is JimboLand. It's got a hot links section, along with a few quirky favorites—like a calendar of Celtic music and medieval literature readings. JimboLand even has a search engine you can use to hunt for area activities and pastimes.

For general links to San Francisco sites go to Yahoo!'s San Francisco page or Z San Francisco (a straight but hip resource magazine) and the home page of the *San Francisco Examiner*, the city's afternoon daily newspaper. Among its featured articles is the now-famous series "Gay in America"; you can read the original version or the sequel, which revisits the people profiled in this award-winning piece on gay life. At least 14 of the original 93 have died of AIDS. Others have gone on to have babies, found a church, work in the Clinton White House, run for judge and generally live their lives as normal citizens of "Baghdad by the Bay."

☐ *A Different Light Bookstore*
http://www.adlbooks.com/

☐ *Alta Plaza Restaurant and Bar*
http://www.altaplaza.com/

☐ *Amazon Online*
http://www.amazon.org/

☐ *Asian Pacific-Islanders*
http://members.tripod.com/~nomsgjaded/index.html

☐ *Bears of San Francisco*
http://www.bosf.org/

☐ *Black Iris Home Page (Leather)*
http://www.blackiris.com/

☐ *BlowBuddies*
http://www.blowbuddies.com/main.shtml

☐ *Cafe Du Nord*
http://www.cafedunord.com/

☐ *Carl's Men On The Street*
http://www.sfcarl.com

☐ *The Castro*
http://www.kqed.org/fromkqed/tv/hood/

☐ *Castro Online*
http://www.castroonline

☐ *The Castro Sweep*
http://hometown.aol.com/sfpdriot/sweep.html

☐ *Cockettes*
http://www.cockettes.com

☐ *Community United Against Violence*
http://www.xq.com/cuav/index.html

☐ *Daddy's*
http://www.wolfe.com/daddys/

☐ *ExoticEdge Men4Men*
http://www.exoticedge.com/

☐ *Fife's Resort (Russian River)*
http://www.fifes.com/

☐ *Folsom Street Fair*
http://www.folsomstreetfair.com/

☐ *Frontiersweb Online News Magazine*
http://www.frontiersweb.com/

☐ *Futura*
http://www.futurasf.com

☐ *Gauntlet*
http://www.gauntlet.com/

☐ *Gay Global San Francisco*
http://www.gayglobalsf.com/

☐ *Gay Nude Beaches*
http://qsanfrancisco.com/qsf/96may/travel.html

☐ *Gay San Francisco*
http://www.gaysf.com/

☐ *Gay SF B&B's*
http://www.sfbayguardian.com/GuardianGuides/Inside
Guide/96_02/022196ingay.html

☐ *Girl Spot/Club Skirts Curtain*
http://www.girlspot.com/

☐ *Gus Presents (Dance parties in SF)*
http://www.guspresents.com/events.html

☐ *Harvey Milk Institute*
http://www.harveymilk.org/

☐ *Harvey's*
http://www.harveysbar.com/

☐ *The Hole in the Wall*
http://www.gaysf.com/sites/bars/hole/hole.html-ssi

☐ *How Castro St. became The Castro*
http://www.q-net.com/htdocs/df96a001.htm

☐ *Imperial Court*
http://www.impcourt.org/

☐ *Jimboland*
http://www.jimboland.com

☐ *Josie's Cabaret and Juice Joint*
http://www.citysearch7.com/E/V/SFOCA/0000/48/10/

☐ *Kweer.com*
http://www.kweer.com

☐ *Lavender Pages/Fabulous*
http://www.lavenderpages.com/

☐ *Leather-SF*
http://www.leather-sf.com/

☐ *Lesbian Avengers of SF*
http://www.lesbian.org/sfavengers

☐ *LGBT Community Center*
http://www.sfgaycenter.org/

☐ *Lone Star Saloon*
http://www.lonestar-saloon.com/

☐ *Master Eric's Dungeon*
http://www.geocities.com/WestHollywood/Heights/6119/

☐ *OutNow!*
http://www.outnow.com/

☐ *Paul's Bay Area Weather Page*
http://www.wco.com/~paulg/weather.html

☐ *Planet SOMA*
http://www.planetsoma.com

☐ *Phoenix Uniform Club of San Francisco*
http://www.SFPhoenixUniformClub.org/

☐ *Project Open Hand*
http://www.openhand.org/

☐ *QSF Magazine*
http://www.qsanfrancisco.com/

☐ *Q San Francisco*
http://www.qsanfrancisco.com/

☐ *Queer Guide to the SF Bay Area (Stanford)*
http://www-leland.stanford.edu/group/QR/guide.html

☐ *Queer InfoServer (Berkeley)*
http://www.infoqueer.org/queer/qis/

☐ *Queer Things to do in San Francisco*
http://www.io.com/~larrybob/sanfran.html

☐ *San Francisco AIDS Foundation*
http://www.sfaf.org/

☐ *San Francisco Examiner*
http://www.examiner.com/

☐ *San Francisco Gay Men's Chorus*
http://www.sfgmc.org/

☐ *San Francisco's Gay Pride Parade*
http://www.sf-pride.org/

☐ *San Francisco's Gay Tourist Information Center*
http://www.gaysf.com/

☐ *San Francisco International Film Festival*
http://www.sfiff.org/

☐ *San Francisco Lesbian Gay Bisexual Transgender
Pride*
http://www.sf-pride.org/

☐ *Sisters of Perpetual Indulgence, Inc.*
http://thesisters.org/

☐ *SF Dyke March*
http://www.lesbian.org/sf-dykemarch/index.html

☐ *San Francisco Eagle*
http://www.sfeagle.com/

☐ *SF 69er's home page*
http://www.geocities.com/WestHollywood/9369/

☐ *Slot*
http://www.backdoor.com/hall/home.html

☐ *South Bay Queer & Asian*
http://members.aol.com/SBQA/index.html

☐ *SO WHAT!*
http://www.microweb.com/phantom/sowhat/index.htm

☐ *Stanford University. Guide to SF*
http://www-leland.stanford.edu/group/QR/qg94.html

☐ *STUDS BBS and STUDSNet*
http://www.creative.net/studs/

☐ *Top Grrl*
http://www.sirius.com/~topgrrl

☐ *Uncle Donald's Castro Street*
http://www.backdoor.com/castro/

☐ *WebCastro*
http://www.webcastro.com/hotlinks.htm

☐ *Wolf's Guide to Leather SF*
http://www.wolf.nu/

☐ *WOW (Way Out West)*
http://www.gaysf.com/sites/shopping/wow/wow.htm

☐ *Yahoo!'s San Francisco Gay Guides*
http://sfbay.yahoo.com/Community/Cultures_and_Groups/
Lesbian__Gay_and_Bisexual/Travel/

☐ *Z San Francisco*
http://www.zpub.com/sf/

Russian River (North of SF)

☐ *Concierge Services*
http://www.rreservations.com

☐ *Fab (dance club)*
http://www.fabpresents.com

☐ *Fern Grove Cottages*
http://www.ferngrove.com

☐ *Fife's Resort*
http://www.fifes.com/

☐ *Gay Russian River.com*
http://www.gayrussianriver.com/

☐ *Highland's Resort*
http://www.highlandsresort.com

☐ *River Wolf Pet Shop & General Store*
http://www.riverwolfgeneralstore.com/

☐ *Russian River Eagle*
http://www.russianrivereagle.com/

☐ *RRR (Russian River Resort)*
http://www.russianriverresort.com

☐ *Willows Resort*
http://www.willowsresort.com/

 Seniors

Although the techno gap allowing seniors access to the Web remains wide, the talent and skills of this age group are quickly remedying the situation. Last year alone has seen at least a trebling in the number and depth of organizations reaching out to seniors' special needs. Groups like the Prime Timers, GLARP (Gay and Lesbian Association of Retiring Persons), LGAIN (Lesbian and Gay Aging Issues Network), and Pride Senior Network are leading the way, providing networks to deal with issues from finding gay-friendly retirement communities to making sure that the legal and medical systems respect gay and lesbian bonds.

GLARP

Perhaps the highest-profile organization is Gay and Lesbian Association of Retiring Persons. Calling itself "AARP with an attitude and an agenda," GLARP's Web page is excellent, giving a statement on the group's vision, biographies of its directors, a rundown on benefits and services as well as a newsletter of recent developments. Among its goals are discounted services for

Gay and Lesbian Association of Retiring Persons

health, legal, financial, travel, and insurance issues. Like AARP, it expects to use the economic clout of this very attractive "silent minority" to offer members discounts.

Unlike AARP, its focus is on gays and lesbians, specifically the development of retirement communities. "Our ultimate goal is to raise money to develop gay and lesbian retirement communities and retirement resorts. We need independent living centers, assisted living centers, and skilled nursing centers. We expect the baby boomers of tomorrow to create a need 20 times that of today. Yet we keep asking, 'Where are the gay and lesbian retirement centers of today?' We think gay-owned, gay-run communities will be more attractive to our aging community—Isn't it about time?"

Though not activist politically (they will leave political lobbying to existing LGB organizations), GLARP is aggressively straight-forward in confronting our communities' special needs, from dealing with legal areas of heirship and proxies to addressing the question of whether gays and lesbians will want separate retirement communities.

Fine Wine

Fine Wine is a cybercommunity of lesbian and bi women over 40 that was formed in 1995 to serve its members' social and informational needs. You'll find discussions on every sort of topic, from the intensely personal (coming out to family and children) to practical questions of finding lesbian-friendly health services. Though based in Chicago (where members meet at various functions), Fine Wine also meets weekly on Sundays, Tuesdays, and Thursdays at 9 P.M. Eastern Time in the OnQWomen's Conference Room at Keyword: WS on AOL. You can also subscribe to the "Fine Wine" newsletter.

LGAIN

Lesbian and Gay Aging Issues Network is an information group that works on a variety of issues. Its goals include dispelling stereotypes and myths about older lesbians and gay men, encouraging research that explores the experiences of older lesbians and gay men, providing links between providers and agencies in health care, long-term care and human services, and working with existing lesbian and gay community organizations to develop programs responsive to seniors, needs.

LGAIN is part of the American Society on Aging, the country's largest professional membership association in aging and related fields. Its major vehicle for information dissemination and exchange is its quarterly publication, OUTWord, a source of information about lesbian and gay aging issues.

Pride Senior Network

PSN is a New York area–based network whose main goal is to inform members of services for older gays and lesbian in a number of areas. *The Networker* newsletter features articles on health (getting the most out of managed care), fitness (guidelines for later life nutrition, exercise,

and strength), retirement (what locations and facilities have gay and lesbian communities? What is the cost?), legal protection (what documents will protect me, my estate, my partner, and special friends?), travel (appropriate tours, accommodations, and best values), and stories (glimpses into the lives and careers of admired older lesbians and gay men).

Prime Timers

One of the oldest and most vibrant organizations serving seniors and their admirers, Prime Timers was founded in 1987 by men who found gay culture to be nearly exclusively centered on youth. The organization has grown to over 40 chapters worldwide located throughout North America and Europe.

Today its diverse membership includes gay and bisexual men of all ages from varied backgrounds who enjoy community with "volunteerism, politics, gay issues, arts, entertainment, and every other facet of healthy living." Some are fathers and caregivers, others are active in business, and others are retired. Some are always on the go and some enjoy the quiet company of others at home. But one thing is true of all Prime Timers: They enjoy the opportunities and friendships that develop with other Prime Timers throughout the world.

- ☐ *Ben Boxer's Silverfox Clubhouse*
  http://www.maturemen.org/

- ☐ *Classic Dykes Online*
  http://www.geocities.com/classicdykes

- ☐ *Cafmos*
  http://www.members.aol.com/caffmos

- ☐ *Fine Wine*
  http://www.glbt.com/finewine/index.html

- ☐ *Gay and Lesbian Association of Retiring Persons, Inc. (GLARP)*
  http://www.gaylesbianretiring.org/

- ☐ *Lesbian and Gay Aging Issues Network*
  http://www.asaging.org/networks/lgain/lgainbro.html

- ☐ *Gay Men 40+*
  http://www.gaymen40plus.com

- ☐ *L-Plus (A list for lesbians 50 and over)*
  http://www.helsinki.fi/~kris_ntk/lezlist/l-plus.html

- ☐ *Lesbian & Gay Aging Network (LGAIN)*
  http://www.asaging.org/lgain

- ☐ *Living Easy*
  http://www.livingeasy.com

- ☐ *Mature Friends*
  http://www.gayscape.com/maturefriends

- ☐ *Owls*
  http://www.teleport.com/~dorsieh/info.owls.html

☐ *Pride Senior Network*
http://www.pridesenior.org/

☐*Prime Timers Association Worldwide*
http://www.primetimers.org/

☐ *Prime Timers, Edmonton*
http://www.cglbrd.com/entries/24.html

☐ *Prime Timers, Portland Metro*
http://www.teleport.com/~haggerty/pmpt.

☐ *Prime Timers Austin*
http://members.aol.com/jrdavistx/primetimers.

☐ *Prime Timers of Baltimore/Washington*
http://wsrv.clas.virginia.edu/~mab2b/pti.html

☐ *Prime Timers of Dallas-Fort Worth*
http://www.primetimers-dfw.org/

☐ *Prime Timers of Las Vegas*
http://www.geocities.com/WestHollywood/Heights/5178/

☐ *Prime Timers of the Desert*
http://members.tripod.com/~PrimeTimer/index.html

☐ *Prime Timers Toronto*
http://www.geocities.com/WestHollywood/2519/

☐ *PrimeTimers Chicago*
http://www.primetimers.org/Chicago!

☐ *Sage*
http://www.sageusa.org/

☐ *Third Age*
http://www.thirdage.com/

 Sex

Since the chill on porn lifted with the Supreme Court's order on free speech, sex sites on the Web have exploded. You've still got places that sound like something out of a John Waters movie, but the large sites serve up raunch with a flair that eclipses the old-style walk down a foul cyberalley. Chisel.com, HunkHunter, Hotmen, HisWeb, Men On the Net, Sexyboyz—all these and many others are terrifically sophisticated, both in the computer graphics and presentation of sex. You'll be offered everything from still pictures to "live" sex shows, chat lines, and videos. Some even have articles and an editor's page so you can defend your time online by using Dad's excuse that he only read Playboy for the articles. Men on the Net is a virtual sex emporium with tons of pictures, stories and a shopping mall with sexy stuff. Luxe costs though. Every sight worth returning to has a door charge—you've got to prove you're an adult with either a credit card or license from one of the numerous adult checks. (These average about $17 per year.)

The hottest sites are, of course, competitive. Check out the awards a page has won. If the kudos come from Adam's All Male Review, Gay XX Top 30 or Sexplosion, the play is often among younger guys. HotMen.Com, Babylon Hot 20, SexyBoyz, Tight Site and Evil Body bestow gold dick trophies to the more masculine sites where the men are unquestionably grown-ups—i.e., some have hair!

Hunk Hunter

Hunk Hunter has perhaps more awards than anyone else. It's a huge site. You can tell guys what to do and they will perform for you right on your screen. There are chat lines, personals, stories, newsgroups, and pay-per-view listings. The links list is nearly overwhelming, weighing in at 4,500. It's easier to just visit their top rated sites and check out the "Hunks of the Week."

For a more traditional mix of photo galleries try SexyBoyz. There are big dick shots, hot butts, leather and bears, restroom pics and, of course, celebrity photos. You can also shop for toys, videos, and condoms.

Most of the sex pages contain a links list for further browsing. 'Net-Stallions' has annotated lists divided into two categories—sex sights as well as purely photo galleries. Tight Sights and StudsWeb are good and GaySeek, which serves a younger crowd, has one of the hottest, most updated anywhere. Along with a weekly file of new listings, there's a man of the da, and top 25 gold sites followed by top 15 platinum sites. Each has a good description. For the leather crowd there's Absolutely Male with exclusive models at work in sections like "Private Label," "Hairy Chested," "Men In Leather," and "Real Men." Gay Garage of XTC has a good selection of uniform links.

Fetish & Kink

Though there have always been a few lone warriors ready to tour you around fringe sextivities, it seems as if every kink now has a army of supporters. There's Soccer Kit Fetish and Qbacker's Gridiron for sports sex. For discipline army-style try Strictop's Male Spanking or M/M Corporal Punishment. Boot Camp Report puts grunts through their paces and Cum Bunny has 50 shooters. Then there's the guys who  work farther down at BootJaq, Boots and More, Bootman's Closet, Boots and Shoes. Steve's Fetish Pages has smelly sneakers. SkinsDeep has unlaundered socks pics.

Most of these concentrate on a single fetish, but others diversify. Squaddie John, for example is an S/M squaddie skinhead biker and his page reflects a multitude of interests from wrestling to horse- and pony-training fantasies, confinement, boots, hiking—all sorts of tough stuff.

Up for bedtime stories? Try the Gay Cafe, CynTil8ing Stories, Kyle Stone's Back Room, the Nifty Erotic Stories Archive, Bill's S/M Erotica Archive, or Fucker Tales. The Gay Cafe has the largest selection; its categories include bestiality, bisexuality, gay male, lesbian, and transsexual. If you know of any good tales, send them in. (They're on the lookout for stories with slave themes.)

Off-Web Porn

When the Web itself doesn't seem quite the satisfying outlet, it still provides experts on what else is available. See GayPlace magazine's Porn Column for the best reviews of new porn videos, books and live events. The author is a witty insider who's got the scoop on new releases from all the major studios. Cruising for Sex is an incredible site indexing sexy spots all over the nation, from truck stops to bookstores, sex clubs, and library stalls. Much more than a stripped-down list of addresses, he'll quite often devote an entire paragraph to a single spot. Here's just part of a single write-up: "There is a good old fashioned truck fuel stop (Amoco) at the Union exit (#45) on I 20/59 about 30 miles west of Tuscaloosa, Alabama. The tearoom upstairs is for truckers and has three stalls. There are two glory holes in the first stall and one very large glory hole between the last two showers. Also a peephole to the three urinals next to the first stall. If you like graffiti and uncut men, this stop is a must! These holes have been there for more than ten years and I recommend this exit for those traveling west or south on I-20/59." Amazing. Also, don't miss the "guided tours"—essays on road trips and bathhouses across the United States.

Pointers?

For those of you needing practical advice and definitions on exactly what you're reading about (or doing), go to Patrick's

"How To" Sex Guide or the Altsex page. Start off with the columns: Contessa Noire answers questions on sexual conduct, and Alan Wexelblat teaches a crash course in polyamory. If you're confused by the terms, read on. Altsex gives graphic descriptions of multiple-person loving, along with all sorts of other practices. The S/M Bondage and Discipline explanation is particularly good.

Lesbian Sex

Lesbian lust on the Web is less pictorial and more literary than gay sex, but it's still very much alive and in tune with what makes women hot. Lesbian Sacred Sexuality has very beautiful, evocative art, and you find reams of sexy stories at Lesbian Stories. And at least once you should drop by the online address of the most famous lesbian sex magazine, *On Our Backs*. It's got a long listing of "best of" stories.

Two terrific guides to all that's available are Mining Co.'s "Lesbian Erotica" and DykesWorld. Lesbian Erotica is an annotated index with a handful of quality sites and DykesWorld is, as its name implies, an entire territory with over 200 lesbian sites. Two of the sites, created by Indina Beuche are Wild Women Dreamin' Wet (stories) and Let's Talk Sex, Babe(an annotated page of links to various sites including House of Chicks).

What you'll find on many of these pages is a warning to men (especially straight men!) to stay out! Swade's Erotica (stories), for example, opens with this admonition to het men: "Why not go buy a copy of Penthouse and be happy with the male version of what lesbians are: one-dimensional vaginas and breasts that are rescued from their lesbianism by some penis! Sheesh!" Like Swade's, Harcap has a steamy collection of heroines in no need of rescuing. Here's an excerpt from the story "Caramel Couch" by Claire Cappelletti: "Cupping her furry bush in my hand I could already feel the dampness beginning to settle among the curly tips of her hair. She grabbed my ass and spread my cheeks as I bent my lips to her breasts. We fell backward onto the couch, kissing and grinding our hips..."

☐ *A Woman's Touch (toys)*
http://www.a-womans-touch.com

☐ *Ali Matteau*
http://www.alimatteau.com

☐ *alt.sex*
http://ww.altsex.org/altsex-home.html

☐ *Artemis Oakgrove's Fiction*
http://www.pw2.netcom.com/~oakgrove/fiction.html.com

☐ *Aslan Leather*
http://www.ASLANLeather.com

☐ *Bad Attitude Mag (S/M)*
http://www.lifestyle.com/lesbian/

☐ *Kuma Erotica*
http://www.www.kuma2.net

☐ *Blowfish Catalogue (toys)*
http://www.blowfish.com/catalogue/

☐ *Brat Attack (leather)*
http://www.devildog.com/brat/

☐ *Dyke Daddy*
http://www.dreamwater.com/dykedaddies

☐ *Dyke Porn*
http://adult.iamproud.com/~dyke/

☐ *Dykes World (Indina Beuche)*
http://www.dykesworld.de/

☐ *Eve's Garden*
   http://www.evesgarden.com/

☐ *Fishnet Magazine*
   http://www.fishnetmag.com/

☐ *Girl Club*
   http;/www.girlclub.com/

☐ *Good Vibrations*
   http://www.goodvibes.com/

☐ *Grand Opening (toys)*
   http://www.grandopening.com

☐ *HarCap (stories)*
   http://www.geocities.com/WestHollywood/Village/9740/

☐ *Lesbian Erotica (Mining Co.)*
   http://lesbianerotica.miningco.com/mlibrary.htm

☐ *Lesbian Sacred Sexuality*
   http://www.wildheartsranch.com/

☐ *Lesbian Stories*
   http://www.nifty.org/

☐ *Naughty Lesbian Sex*
   http://www.girls-nextdoor.com/index2.html

☐ *On Our Backs*
   http://www.girlfriendsmag.com/onourbacks

☐ *Pat Califia's Homepage*
   http://www.patcalifia.com/home.htm

☐ *Seduction: Cruel Woman*
   http://www.gayweb.com/first_run/cruel.html

☐ *Stormy Leather*
http://www.stormyleather.com

☐ *Susie Bright's Homepage*
http://www.susiebright.com/

☐ *Swat Paddles*
http://www.sbpaddleco.com/htms/paddles.htm

☐ *Underwear Page*
http://www.users.skynet.be/tup

☐ *Vixen Creations*
http://www.tenderbuttons.com/vixen

☐ *Web by Women for Women (Feminist sexuality)*
http://www.io.com/~wwwomen/

☐ *Womyn's Ware*
http://www.womynsware.com

☐ *Young Lesbian Lovers*
http://lesbian.imco.n.'

☐ *Welcome to the F.l.S.T.*
http://members.aol.com/FISTWomen/

☐ *Well Sexy Woman (safe sex)*
http://www.gayweb.com/wolfevideo/sexy.html

☐ *Wild Women Dreamin' Wet*
http://www.dykesworld.de/

For Men

☐ *69th Precinct (cops!)*
http://www.geocities.com/westhollywood/6249/

☐ *Adam's All-Male Review*
http://www.adamsxxx.com/top100/

☐ *A Few Good Men*
http://www.afewgoodmen.com.com

☐ *All Gay All Hardcore*
http://www.sexjunky.com/gay

☐ *All Kink's "Vintage Jockstraps"*
http://members.aol.com/allkink/index.html

☐ *Alpha Gay Links*
http://www.alphagay.com/

☐ *Altsex*
http://www.altsex.org/

☐ *Alternate Sources Home Page*
http://alternate.com

☐ *alt.sex.bondage FAQ*
http://www.cis.ohio-state.edu/hypertext/faq/usenet/alt-sex/

☐ *Any One For Sex?*
http://www.gayzzzsites.com/anyoneforsex

☐ *Arm Pits*
http://www.geocities.com/westhollywood/stonewall/2141/

☐ *Armed Forces Insignia Overview*
http://www.defenslink.mil/news/nov1999/n1122/n1122199_9911224.ht
ml

☐ *Backdoor*
http://www.backdoor.com/

☐ *BadPuppy*
http://badpuppy.com/

☐ *Beefy Boys*
http://www.beefyboys.com

☐ *Berkeley Steamworks*
http://www.locker--rooms.com/berkberkhome.html

☐ *Bibble (stories)*
http://www.bibble.org/

☐ *Big Cocks*
http://www.boytoboy.com/asbigastheyget

☐ *Big Dicks*
http://www.male.com/hclub/horsemen.shtml

☐ *Blokes For You*
http://www.blokes4u.com

☐ *Bootsplus*
http://www.bootsplus.com/btlnks.htm

☐ *Boudoir Noir Online*
http://www.boudoir-noir.com/index.html

☐ *Buzz Link (index)*
http://www.buzzlink.com/adult/

☐ *Cap'n Smut Awards*
http://www.smutlinks.com/

☐ *Catch's Place*
http://www.catchsplace.com/

☐ *Chisel*
http://ad.chisel.com/

☐ *Cocks Anonymous*
http://www.unitedgaysites2.com/cocksanonymous

☐ *Cuir Underground*
http://www.black-rose.com/cuiru.html

☐ *Cruising for Sex*
http://www.cruisingforsex.com/

☐ *CynTil8Ing Stories*
http://members.aol.com/cyntil8ing/

☐ *Dade Art (erotica)*
http://www.blackiris.com/dadeart/

☐ *The Deviant's Dictionary*
http://www.queernet.org/deviant/

☐ *Dick of the Day*
http://www.DickOfTheDay.com

☐ *Dick Zone*
http://www.dickzone.com

☐ *Dirty Mind*
http://www.dirtymind.com/

☐ *Domxxx-Gay and Kinky*
http://www.domxxx.com/gaysex.html

☐ *ErectMale*
http://erectmale.com

☐ *Eroscan Index (Index)*
http://www.eroscan.com

☐ *Erotic Penis Enlargement*
http://www.metco.com/

☐ *Evil Body (index plus)*
http://www.evilbody.com/

☐ *Extreme Gay*
http://www.extreme-gay.com

☐ *F2F Dungeon*
http://www.webworqs.com/f2dungeon/

☐ *Falcon Studios*
http://falconstudios.com

☐ *Fetish Network*
http://www.tfnbbs.com/tfnhome.htm

☐ *Foreskin Restoration Sites*
http://www.4skin.com

☐ *Foot Buddies*
http://www.footbuddies.com/

☐ *Foreskin Gallery*
http://www.grahampg.demon.co.uk/

☐ *Fucker Tales*
http://www.bway.net/~supine/x.html

☐ *FuzzButt's*
http://www.fuzzbutt.com/

☐ *Gay Bondage*
http://www.gaybondage.com

☐ *Gay Cafe*
http://gaycafe.com/nifty/gay/

☐ *Gay Fisting*
http://www.fisters.dircon.couk

☐ *Gay Guys*
   http://www.gay.sexhound.net/paulfrance

☐ *Gay Haven*
   http://www.gayhaven.com

☐ *Gay Sex Live*
   http://www.gaysexlive.com/

☐ *GaySights Sex Directory*
   http://www.diode.com/gs/

☐ *Gay Spanking*
   http://www.gayspanking.com/

☐ *Gay 1000 (index)*
   http://www.hitbox.com/wc/home.gay.html

☐ *Gay Warehouse (Index)*
   http://www.serve.com/p-jay/warehouse/

☐ *Gay XX Top 30*
   http://www.freesexypics.com/gay/

☐ *Hairy Chest Page*
   http://www3.creative.net/~hcp

☐ *Hairy Page*
   http://www.geocities.com/WestHollywood/3083/hairy.html

☐ *Hein's Ultimate Gay Links*
   http://www.xs4all.nl/~heinv/heindoc/gayhttp1.html

☐ *His Web*
   http://www.hisweb.com/

☐ *Hotshots*
   http://www.execworld.com/cgi-bin/hotshots.pl?setid=rainbow

☐ *Hotstuds*
http://www.hotstuds.com/

☐ *HunkHunter's*
http://www.hunkhunter.com/personal.html

☐ *Iron Men*
http://www.creative.net/~adworx/

☐ *Jackin World (masturbation)*
http://www.jackinworld.com

☐ *Jock Boys*
http://www.jockboys.com/

☐ *Jock Straps*
http://www.jockstraps.com

☐ *Kyle Stone's Backroom*
http://www.sff.net/people/soles/index.htp

☐ *Larry Townsend*
http://www.larrytownsend.com

☐ *Leather Club*
http://www.arrakis.es/~global

☐ *Male Celebrities Totally Nude*
http://www.malecelebrities.com

☐ *Male Feet*
http://www.rvisions.com/malefeet

☐ *Men on the Net*
http://www.menonthenet.com/

☐ *Military Guys*
http://www.militaryguys.com/

☐ *Military & Police Uniform Assoc.*
http://members.tripod.com/~mpua/

☐ *Muscle Boys*
http://www.muscleboys.com

☐ *Nifty Erotic Stories Archive*
http://library.gaycafe.com/nifty/

☐ *Patrick's "How To" Sex Guide*
http://www.creative.net/~jetlag/sexguide/

☐ *Penis Enlargement*
http://www.metco.com/enlarge.html

☐ *Pierced Parts*
http://www.xxxtrailertrash.com/pmp/pmpmc.html

☐ *Rad Video XXX*
http://www.radvideo.com/mjvideo.html

☐ *Radical Sex*
http://www.fifth-mountain.com/radical_sex/

☐ *Ray Dragon's Wyrm Hole*
http://www.wyrm.com/

☐ *Rimming*
http://www.dreamlands.net/freepage/rimming

☐ *Rough Buddies*
http://home6.swipnet.se/~w-69238/index.htm

☐ *Sexy Boyz*
http://www.sexyboyz.com/

☐ *Sludgemaster*
http://www.sludgemaster.com/

☐ *SMAQ (Sex, Men, & Queers, index)*
http://www.smaq.com/

☐ *Smooth Buddies (shaving)*
http://www.io.com/~mboy/

☐ *Smut*
http://www.hysteric.com/smut/

☐ *Spanking Page*
http://www.express.ca/bas/

☐ *Spanking Home Page*
http://www.dircon.co.uk/cpenn/INDEX.HTM

☐ *Tight Site (index)*
http://www.freegay.com/

☐ *Trittster's Place (underwear)*
http://www.geocities.com/~tritt/undie.html

☐ *Uniform/leather site*
http://www.teleport.com/~uniform

☐ *Well Hung*
http://www.well.hung.net

☐ *Wet Levis*
http://www.downtownmale.com/wetlevis

☐ *Wolfie's Dungeon*
http://www.geocities.com.WestHollywood/1925/

☐ *XS4Skin Gallery*
http://www.grahampg.demon.co.uk/

☐ *Yossie's Handcuffs*
http://www.blacksteel.com/~yossie/hcs.html

Adult Check Sites

☐ *Adult Check*
http://www.adultcheck.com/cgi-bin/apply.cgi?4486

☐ *ManCheck*
http://www.mancheck.com

☐ *UnitedGayAdultSites*
http://www.unitedgayadultsites.com/signup/signup.cgi?1938847

☐ *ManSights*
http://www.mansights.com/join.cfm?site=ms176

 Sports

Not all of those jocks you went to high school with were straight! Some were bent, as the Australians say, and they've grown up and created a startlingly wide network of gay and lesbian sports groups online. Boxing, cycling, figure skating, hockey, martial arts, outdoor adventuring, rowing, running, scuba, skiing, softball, swimming, tennis, volleyball, wrestling—each sport has a group of aficionados who've come together, sometimes in compassion, often just for love of the sport.

LGB Sports

For a comprehensive list of nearly all queer sports club activities, go to the Gay Games page. There's a good search engine enabling you to click on over a hundred sports and get info on team schedules, club info, and event dates. A search on track and field for instance, gives you a short description of all the clubs and their links. There's information on upcoming games as wells as an archive of past games that has pictures as well as links to Uncle Donald's history of how the games started. It's an amazing account of the opening ceremony: "Mayor Dianne Feinstein was conveniently in Hawaii...and that left Doris Ward as acting Mayor. Before she spoke the crowd started chanting 'Say it...Say it.' She got right to it and said, 'I'd like to welcome you all to the first Gay Olympics!!!' There was a loud collective roar from the stands and from the playing field where the athletes were on their feet, cheering."

There's a subscription to the official newsletter, a list of detailed results from previous Gay Games (the times to beat) and an address to which you can send your tax-deductible check. There's also a preliminary rundown of the slew of parties and ceremonies planned to be held and an index of the official sports involved.

Clubs & Teams

All of the online organization sites give schedules, sign-up sheets, and a general introduction to the club's goals and character. Without exception they welcome everyone as spectator or player and tend to have rather lighthearted names like the Pink Pongs or the Rainbow Hoops.

Out Sports

This is a great page by a couple of jocks who keep one eye on the scoreboard and one on the sexy guys on the field. There's the Week in Review, a rundown of the weeks highlights in College and Pro sports; articles (a high school linebacker in Massachusetts comes out and the world doesn't end) and interviews (gay ex-jocks talk about life in the sports closet). And naturally there's a chat room called the Clubhouse. "Whether you're looking to find somebody to talk about Jason Sehorn's abs, the upcoming baseball season, or looking to find a guy to shoot hoops or, dare we say it, date, you can find him here."

Gay & Lesbian Sports (Los Angeles)

One of the largest club pages you'll find. The Gay and Lesbian Sports Alliance of Greater Los Angeles was formed in August 1991 to promote recreational and competitive sports within the community. The Alliance does not organize any sports, but instead acts as a source of information for who's playing what, when and where. The Alliance operates a 24-hour hotline (310-515-3337) for people to get information on about 30 sports. Some (swimming, bowling, running and tennis, for example) are very well-established while others (gymnastics, roller hockey) are in the formative stages

GirlJock

"There's nothing quite so intimate as sweating together, breathing hard, in a public place. There's nothing quite so satisfying as a hot shower, sauna, and terry towel rub afterward. And food tastes better when you are a girljock. Haven't you noticed?" That's an excerpt from Girl Jock, by Amy Cheney, the author of this excellent Net 'zine for dykes in athletics. It's a very hot page' the opening image has included a nude Brandi Chastain, the first lady of California soccer. You'll find articles on other girl jocks who've taken it off (and pictures) as well as comics and the dos and don'ts of dating a teammate. And check out the long girl jocks resources, which include the Frances Willard Society (Where women sportswriters get together), National Association for Girls, Women in Sport, and Sportsforwomen.com.

Frontrunners

The Frontrunners' club page has a calendar of events, a forum, and a bunch of links as well as a wonderful page on the club's history that puts today's queer sports achievements in perspective: "In the early '70s, there were only a handful of gay organizations: the gay pool, bowling and softball leagues, Gay Rap, and the royal courts, to name a few. There were few gay activities that

were not centered around the bars. There were no gay hiking clubs, track, swimming, skiing, wrestling, bicycling, or tennis clubs, bands, choruses, theater groups. For many, the Lavender U Joggers was their first gay group they had joined. For more than a few, it was their first experience knowing and being around other gays. Although many exchanged their full names, many others revealed only first names— there was no membership list." Today Front Runners is an international organization with chapters around the world. (And it is named for the novel.)

IGLOO

Of all the gay and lesbian sports organizations online, one of the best organized is the International Gay and Lesbian Outdoor Organization (IGLOO). If you love the outdoors, hiking, cross-country skiing, diving, mountaineering, or anything else that puts you in strenuous contact with nature, go see this page. But don't look for competitive sports; IGLOO is about noncompetitive activities. And they don't organize tours per se. Members pay for and organize trips on their own, using IGLOO as a meeting and advice center. Sure it's loose and idealistic, but thousands of its members prefer this independent approach to that of a rigidly structured tour.

Chiltern Mountain Club

Chiltern Mountain Club is not a part of IGLOO, but the philosophy is similar and it's a good example of queer sports pages on the Net. Essentially the home page reaches out to new members by identifying what the group is about and offering subscriptions to the monthly newsletter. You'll learn that Chiltern is one of the world's largest volunteer gay and lesbian outdoor organizations with activities such as hiking, biking, canoeing, kayaking, tennis, skating, rock climbing, cross-country and downhill skiing, snow shoeing, backpacking, camping, and sailing. If you enjoy outdoor sports, this is a must-see.

Around the World

Gay Sports has vast databases, enabling you to search by sport, country and month for queer events in 20 countries, from Australia to the United States. Though the U.S. is certainly sports-mad, it may come as a surprise that European queers are on average much more team oriented. Check out Gay Sports' links to The Gay Integration through Sports and Activities Holland (GISAH) foundation and many other gay/Lesbian sports groups in Europe.

The professional sports world has taken to the online world with a vengeance. Major magazines such as *Sports Illustrated* have sites, as do ABC and other networks. ESPNET SportsZone (ESPN's page) is particularly timely and detailed with daily updates from sports events around the world. Some of the features and columns are fee-based. For the most current club listings on the Web, see the LGB Sports page, Yahoo!, NetQueery, or the QRD.

- ☐ *Adventure Group*
  http://www.adventuregroup.org/

- ☐ *Adventuring*
  http://adventureing.org/cgi-bin/main.idc

- ☐ *Arizona Gay Rodeo Assoc.*
  http://www.agra-phx.com/

- ☐ *Aspen G & L Ski Weekend*
  http://www.rof.net/yp/skiweek

- ☐ *Billy Bean*
  http://members.tripod.com/~homeo/billybean.html

- ☐ *Boxing For Everyone*
  http://www.girlbox.com

- ☐ *Chiltern Mountain Club*
  http://www.chiltern.org/chiltern/

- ☐ *ESPN's Women's College Basketball*
  http://espn.go.com/ncw

- ☐ *Federation of Gay Games*
  http://www.gaygames.com/
- ☐ *Female Muscle*
  http://www.femalemuscle.com/

- ☐ *Frontrunners*
  http://www.frontrunners.org/

☐ *Gay Bowling*
http://www.igbo.org/

☐ *Gay Football (soccer)*
http://www.iglfa.org/

☐ *Gay Games 2002*
http://www.gaygamesVI.org.au/index2.html

☐ *Gay Games*
http://www.gaygames.org/

☐ *Gay & Lesbian Rowing*
http://www.geocities.com/TheTropics/1257/

☐ *Gay & Lesbian Tennis Alliance*
http://members.aol.com/gaytenis/index.htm

☐ *Gay & Lesbian Sport*
http://www.gaysport.cjb.net

☐ *Gay & Lesbian Sports (Los Angeles)*
http://www.webcom.com/bkm/sa.html

☐ *Gay Golf*
http://www.gaygolf.com

☐ *Gay Martial Arts*
http://members.aol.com/iaglmado/iaglma.html

☐ *Gay Muscle*
http://www.gaymuscle.org/

☐ *Gay Scuba*
http://www.gayscuba.com

☐ *Gay Sport*
http://www.gaysport.org/

☐ *Gay Sports Fan Central*
http://www.geocities.com/colosseum/mound/6659/

☐ *Girl Jock*
http://www.girljock.com

☐ *Gladiators World Alliance*
http://www.vangar.com

☐ *International Gay Bowling Organization*
http://www.igbo.org/

☐ *International G & L Aquatics*
http://www.kwic.net/igla.html

☐ *International Association of Gay & Lesbian Martial Artists*
http://members.aol.com/IAGLMAdo/IAGLMA.html/

☐ *International G & L Outdoor Organization(IGLOO)*
http://www.chiltern.org/chiltern/igloo.html

☐ *International Gay Rodeo Association*
http://www.igra.com/

☐ *National Women's Basketball League*
http://www.nwbl.com/

☐ *Out Sports*
http://www.outsports.com

☐ *Sports Jam USA*
http://www.sportsjamusa.com

☐ *Turkish Oil Wrestlers*
http://www.grecco.com/

Square Dancing

Brush off your Stetson, spit shine your boots, and get ready to do-se-do. There is a huge gay and lesbian square and western dance culture out there, full of friendly guys and gals ready to give you a twirl. There's DoSeDo.com and International Association of Gay & Lesbian Western Dance Clubs, as well as the International Association of Gay Square Dance Clubs.

IAGSDC is a no-nonsense, link-filled page has the latest on square dancing around the world. You can contact member clubs listed by state or province. Foreign club addresses are also listed here for Australia (New South Wales), and Canada (Alberta, British Columbia, Ontario). Most listings include schedules, newsletters, and descriptions of the club activities and skill levels. And don't miss events such as "fly-ins," like the one where a Chicago club recently hosted more than 1,200 guests from around the nation.

Recipes & Etiquette

Along with the general information, the IAGSDC page has a cookbook called *Square Dish* with lots of aptly named recipes for hungry hoofers. You'll also find plenty of advice on dance-floor etiquette. A favorite is written by the quite properly named F. William Chickering. You just know his belt buckle sparkles and his shirt never puckers. His Guide to Excruciatingly Correct Square Dance Behavior is full of somewhat starchy but nevertheless useful advice. Among the rules are many no-no's (such as eating garlic and not bathing before a

dance), as well as emergency behavior if a dancer is hurt
(form a circle and raise your hands around the injured party).
Who says this isn't a contact sport?

Diablo Dancers

Many of the clubs listed have E-mail. Others, such as the Diablo
Dancers, have a full-fledged Web page—nothing too fancy, just
loads of information about upcoming dates, club history, and member breakdowns along sex and skill lines. (Most clubs seem to divide equally among men and women, and nearly all welcome newcomers as well as experts.) Like many of the clubs, the Diablo
Dancers host biannual dances, called hoedowns, of course.

Square dance clubs emphasize a friendly community spirit. If that
seems "square," you're in the wrong pasture. These clubs are about
coordinated team dancing with a strong traditionalist flavor.

☐ *Diablo Dancers*
http://www.diablo-dancers.org/

☐ *Dosado.com*
http://www.dosado.com

☐ *International Association of Gay Square
Dance Clubs*
http://www.iagsdc.org/

☐ *International Association of Gay & Lesbian Western
Dance Clubs*
http://www.iaglwdc.org/

⬛ Stonewall

"Homo Nest Raided, Queen Bees Are Stinging Mad." That was the headline from the July 6, 1969, issue of the *New York Daily News*. To read from other contemporary accounts, no one would have predicted the tidal wave of gay liberation that began that night, but it's become a rallying cry for all of us. And now there are dozens of online sites that tell the story, both as it happened and as it continues to reverberate through gay culture.

Perhaps the best place to start is an article by Robert Amsel that appeared in *The Advocate*. The writer was there, and he tells an intreresting story, giving context of the time and trying to sort through the myth and inspiration that came of those riots (and yes he does say they were riots). "The Stonewall myth, beatified, has inspired gay protest movements throughout America and the  world. But considering the miles this legend has covered, perhaps a retread job, or at least a realignment, is in order."

The QRD's Stonewall folder is also filled with articles and memorabilia. You can read the full text of the "Homo Nest" article, the keynote address for Stonewall 25, and many other related pieces. One of the best is an excerpt from the late Arthur Bell's book, *Dancing the Gay Lib Blues: A Year in the Homosexual Liberation Movement*.

For another eyewitness account, take a moment to read the QRD's copy of the entire 5,000-word article from the *Village Voice*'s account. "New York's Tactical Police Force (TPF) arrived on the scene. They were helmeted and carried clubs but were unprepared for the guerrilla warfare that awaited them. These streets were gay territory.... Two TPF men chased a gay guy down a side street. Before long a large group was running. A man at the head of the group suddenly held out his arms and yelled, 'Stop!' The group stopped and he called out, 'There are two pigs and how many of us?' A moment of meaningful silence. The two cops had also stopped, were looking at one another and then at the crowd. The group leader grinned. 'Get the bastards!' About face. The cops were now running at full gallop, a lynch mob on their heels. 'Catch 'em! Fuck 'em!' "

Also worth seeing is Rainbow Confusion's authorized site. It's packed with pictures from Stonewall 25. Although the images are small and collaged, just click once to bring up a full-size version (50 to 120K), from the Stonewall 25 March for Lesbian, Gay, Bisexual, and Transgender Rights.

GLAAD's chronology of the Gay and Lesbian Movement in the U.S. is a concise history with links and a collection of articles. Stonewall and Beyond is an illustrated exhibit created to commemorate the 15th anniversary. Featured here are clippings from the local New York City press reporting the "melee" in 1969, along with firsthand accounts about that night published in later years, and photographs and pamphlets with excerpts from coverage by *The New York Times*, the *New York Post*, and the *Village Voice* as well as books on the subject.

☐ *After Stonewall*
   http://www.afterstonewall.com

☐ *Coming Out Twice*
   http://www.geocities.com/westhollywood/stonewall/4161/comeout.html

☐ *Lambda: History of a Symbol*
   http://www.cs.cmu.edu/afs/cs.cmu.edu/user/scotts/bulgarians/lambda

☐ *GLAAD*
   http://www.glaad.org/

☐ *Lesbian and Gay History Month*
   http://www.glaad.org/glaad/history-month/

☐ *Martin Duberman Papers*
   http://www.nypl.org/research/chss/spe/rbk/faids/duberman.html

☐ *Pre-Stonewall*
   http://www.gayweb.com/first_run/queen.html

☐ *Queer Teen Life in the 50's*
   http://www.conterra.com/jsears/writjew.htm

☐ *Stonewall and Beyond*
   http://www.columbia.edu/cu/libraries/events/sw25

☐ *Stonewall South*
   http://www.conterra.com/jsears/stone.htm

☐ *Stonewall, The Start of a Revolution*
   http://www.geocities.com/westhollywood/village/1122/main.html

☐ *Stonewall Revisited*
   http://www.stonewallrevisted.com

☐ *Stonewall 25 Information (QRD)*
   http://qrd.tcp.com/qrd/www/Stonewall25.html

☐ *Stonewall 25 Perspectives*
   http://www.actwin.com/stonewall/index.html

☐ *Stonewall Inn Raid*
   http://www.yak.net/ian/stonewall.html

 Television

Television and the Web are technological cousins, so it's only logical that they should be fond of each other. Overly fond, some might say. The online world tracks the tube like a lover. Want to discuss queer on-air kisses in episodes of *Roseanne*, *Ellen*, *Babylon 5*, or find out about other moments of amour that ended on the cutting-room floor? How about signing a petition demanding that *Star Trek Voyager* include a gay or lesbian character? Organized tube-o-philes can set the VCR a week ahead for upcoming gay and lesbian shows. Or you can join the legions of *Xena* followers. There are lots of quirky indulgences as well as pages like GLAAD where the serious side of gay and lesbian portrayals really hits home.

Gay TV

Whatever your desires, Michael Biocco's Gay Televison page gives just what its title suggests, a breakdown of weekly gay television. Reruns of movies like *Philadelphia* and *An Early Frost* as well as shows with gay characters like *Friends* take up the bulk of the schedule, but there are some surprises, particularly when reruns of series from the '70s get a showing: Billy Crystal in *Soap*, for example, or that unforgettable scene in *Dynasty* when Moldavians murder Lance's on-again, off-again lover.

News and Views

The *Washington Blade*'s "On The Air" has an excellent column on Gay TV news with lots of behind-the-scenes background and interviews with producers, and network honchos as well as the stars.

PopcornQ's Television section is one of the most up-to-date and discerning surveys of queer television. It pays particular attention to the many local gay cable shows like *Dyke TV, Gay Entertainment,* and others. You get upcoming schedules and notes on why a particular show is interesting whether it's an subtly made old movie like *In the Glitter Palace* or another Jerry Springer screamfest. There are also pointers to related sites such as the HRC and GLAAD pages on what *Ellen* meant and where we go from here.

GLBT Characters to 1961

The perfect companion page is David Anthony Wyatt's List of Gay/Lesbian/Bisexual Television Characters. This is a scholar's page giving a calendar of upcoming shows as well as a chronicle back to 1961 of hundreds of widely-syndicated entertainment shows in the U.S., U.K. and Australia. "For the purposes of this list, a character is described as 'recurring' if he or she has appeared in at least three episodes." A meticulous researcher, Wyatt includes a reference to Web sites as well as articles on the subject from *The New York Times* to *Out* and GLAAD.

The detailing is incredible. Among his research he documents the number of gay characters by decade of debut: 1961-1970 (1), 1971-1980 (50), 1981-1990 (84 characters documented), 1991-present (199 characters documented to date). He also includes insider notes on how gay storylines were and were not included: *Star Trek: The Next Generation* (science fiction) Syndicated 1987-1994. Dr. Crusher's orderly in an unproduced first season script, Ensign Freeman, was supposed to be gay. A 1991 promise by series creator Gene Roddenberry to introduce minor regular gay characters during the 1991-92 season was reneged on by Paramount after Roddenberry's death. Two other episodes touched on orientation identity issues: "The Outcast" (1992) ("heterosexual" of the gender neutral J'naii people de-oriented by psychotherapy) and "The Host" (1991) (Trill object of affections of female crew member changes hosts and therefore outward gender). *Star Trek: Deep Space Nine,* in the episode "Rejoined," also used the Trill host-symbiot construct to portray love between two Trills, now both female."

Gay Trek

Up until recently, the largest gay television site was for gay trekkies. The Gay and Lesbian Star Trek Home Page was home to the USS Harvey Milk (trek clubs and organizations around the world usually refer to themselves as ships), the Gay and Lesbian Star Trek Association, the Planet Stonewall Gay and Lesbian Science Fiction Association, and the Gay and Lesbian Star Trek Voyager Visibility Project.

Though *Next Generation* went off air, there are still trekkies out there,saving much of their ire for series producer Rick Berman who, contrary to creator Gene Roddenberry's original vision, refused to allow gay characters on screen; though, as this page makes clear, the writers had developed them in the story line.

To gauge how seriously this page was taken, read the responses by the producers and actors to the petition to include a gay character. Patrick Stewart is all for it, James Doohan is "unclear on the concept," and Majel Barrett's answer is "disappointing." With its letters, petition campaign, surveys, and chat rooms, this page still has an enormous audience. Beam on over.

The clearinghouse for gay TV talk is the QRD. You can find hundreds of postings here (future gay TV and movies, gay soap opera…), along with links to commentators like the Tinseltown Queer and the Smithers' Sexuality Page. In the latter, Dave Hall tracks every possible lead as to whether or not Smithers on *The Simpsons* is gay. "Whether be it gay, burnsexual, or a sycophantic side-kick, Smithers' sexual preference is often debated on alt.tv.simpsons. Although it is unlikely the writers will ever give us a true confession, the following is a list of Smithers' innuendoes." Along with citations from the script, Hall has quotes from various times when the writers and producers were asked if in fact Smithers was in love with Burns.

The largest links to gay sites concerning every aspect of television is at Yahoo! with 23 categories ranging from actors and ac-

tresses to links with producers, networks, and Usenet groups. The Actors and Actresses heading alone
has 161 links. The links on shows is
amazing. You'll find Web pages of
Ellen, of course, along with *All My*

*Children, Babylon 5, Friends, Melrose Place, My So-Called
Life, NYPD Blues, Roseanne, The Simpsons, The Tick,* and
Xena: Warrior Princess.

☐ *Anne Heche Fan Page*
   http://www.wiltschko.org/heche/heche.htm

☐ *Cable Positive*
   http://www.cablepositive.com/

☐ *CelebSite: Anne Heche*
   http://www.celebsite.com/

☐ *Channel 4*
   http://www.channel4.co.uk/

☐ *Coming Out Under Fire*
   http://www.itvs.org/ITVS/programs/Coming_Out_UF/index.html

☐ *Dharma & Greg*
   http://abc.go.com/primetime/dharma_and_greg/dg_home.html

☐ *David Wyatt's List of Gay/Lesbian/Bisexual
   Television Characters*
   http://home.cc.umanitoba.ca/~wyatt/tv-characters.html

☐ *Dyke TV*
   http://www.dyketv.org

☐ *Electric City Network*
   http://members.aol.com/cheaptv/index.html

☐ *Gay Comedy*
http://www.hanksite.com/gaycomedy

☐ *GayDaze Soap Opera*
http://gaydaze.com

☐ *Gay & Lesbian Star Trek Home Page*
http://www.gaytrek.com/

☐ *Gay & Lesbian Television (AU)*
http://www.queervision.com.au/

☐ *Gay & Lesbian Television (Biocco)*
http://www.jersey.net/~not2/gaytv.htm

☐ *Gay Media Resource List*
http://www.netaxs.com/~joc/gaymedia.html

☐ *Gay News Network*
http://www.gaynewsnetwork.org

☐ *Gay Star Trek*
http://www.webpan.com/dsinclair/trek.html

☐ *Gay Trek*
http://www.gaytrek.com/gaytrek

☐ *Gay TV at ITVS*
http://wwwaj1.com/gaytv/gtvdoorglweb.html

☐ *Gay TV: The Best Clips*
http://www.jersey.net/~not2/

☐ *Gaylaxians*
http://www.gaylaxians.org/index.html

☐ *Gays on the Tube*
http://www.advocate.com/html/issuelinks/gaytube1.html

☐ *GLAAD TV Scoreboard on the World Wide Web*
http://www.glaad.org/glaad/scoreboard.html

☐ *Hedda Lettuce*
http://www.hedda.com

☐ *Home of Anne Heche & Ellen DeGeneres*
http://www.geocities.com/WestHollywood/Heights/4333/

☐ *I Ain't Famous, But I am Gay!*
http://www.geocities.com/westhollywood/heights/3622

☐ *In the Life*
http://www.inthelifetv.org/

☐ *Internet Movie Database at the World Wide Web URL*
http://us.imdb.com/

☐ *Lambda TV*
http://www.tde.com/~lambdacom

☐ *Loskene's Tholian Web*
http://www.loskene.com/

☐ *Nicholas Snow's Notes From Hollywood*
http://www.gaywired.com/nicholas

☐ *On the Air Gay TV (The Washington Blade)*
http://www.washblade.com/point/ontheair.htm

☐ *Popcorn Q Queer Television*
http://www.planetout.com/popcornq/queertv/

☐ *Queer Resources Directory*
http://www.qrd.org/qrd/

☐ *Rainbow Television Network*
http://www.rainbowtv.co.uk

☐ *Rox Quarry*
http://www.rox.com/quarry/

☐ *Smithers' Sexuality*
http://www.snpp.com/family/smithers.sexuality.html

☐ *Steven Capsutos Queer Characters on TV*
http://wanda.pond.com/~stevecap/lecture.com

☐ *Subtextopedia: Guide to Xena Subtext*
http://subtext.simplenet.com

☐ *Tales of the City*
http://www.talesofthecity.com/

☐ *Veronica's Closet*
http://www.nbc.com/tvcentral/shows/veronicacloset/

☐ *Will & Grace*
http://www.nbc.com/tvcentral/shows/willandgrace/

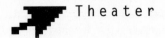 Theater

Is there anything more exciting than sitting in a theater as the house lights dim and a 40-foot curtain goes up? Not much. And the Web, particularly since 1996, has organized a feast to feed opening-night cravings. There's a banquet of stage talk, from practical information on what's playing where (both on Broadway and around the world), to arcane talk for true aficionados (like the Stephen Sondheim Page).

Queer Theater

Though the gay-meter veers deep in the pink zone while visiting theater sites, your first stop should be the Gay Comedy—Queer Performance—Lesbian Comedy site (formerly Gorilla Blue). It's a great page, a fan's page, where the author offers "a polite nod to all who have had the nerve to get up on a stage and put themselves on the line...and a rousing ovation to those who succeed in doing it well." Even if you're not a live-performance buff, you'll be happily overwhelmed at how many gay and lesbian performers are doing their stuff on the stage, on television, and in clubs. However he feels about what he's seen, the writing is sharp and fiercely intelligent. Here's an example of his style: "Some points seem obvious: Comics can say things that political activists can't. The best comedy of this century has been created by oppressed groups. The stuff gay and lesbian comics are saying in the '90s is a tribute to the material of Jewish and black comics in earlier decades. The rest is a matter of taste, opinion, and sense of humor." There's also a bunch of links to various venues, like Josie's Juice Joint (San Francisco), and performance artists like Frank Aqueno, Justin Chin, Tom Ammiano, and Karen Ripley.

Theatrical Groups

In the last year, more of the gay clubs and theater groups are putting up a Web page. Theater Rhinoceros's page is one of the best. You get a sense of who they are by reading the explanation for their name, "a horned animal which is mild and peace-loving unless provoked." There's a schedule of current and upcoming plays as well as an photo-studded archive of the company's 20-year history producing and developing dramatic works by lesbian and gay playwrights.

Big Mess Theater has a wonderful page (animations!) with all sorts of information on the troop, as well as a reviews page. Of the hit

play *Naked Cocktail*, The Philadelphia Enquirer-said, "the show opens with Fifi Flaubert, a seriously dragged-around drag chanteuse. After we are introduced to Fifi, we meet DiStefano as the singer's violent (and shockingly well-hung) boyfriend, Randy Hanes, and finally Christophe as Ralph the Drunk, who emcees, sort of, to let us know what we're in for, in his words, 'a story about losers, misfits...world domination and giant insects.' "

Geigel's Favorite Theater

Among the comprehensive theater sites, Joe Geigel's Favorite Theater has become a mecca. It's got everything. First come the links to other resource sites, including ArtsNet and ArtsUSA. Then comes a list of general resources, such as text archives and Tony Award FAQs. The people section has links to the who's who of Broadway, from playwrights to performers and producers. Next is a collection of sites with reviews and ticketing information, concentrating on large professional theaters on Broadway and Off Broadway as well as London's West End. Then more than 50 companies are listed (with links) along with other resources for producers, actors, composers, and playwrights. Finally we come to what must be Mr. Geigel's true love, the Broadway plays and musicals. He's listed all the show home pages, from *Forever Plaid* to *Sunset Boulevard* and old favorites from *Pippen* to *Jesus Christ*

Superstar. Running shows have all scheduling information, ticket prices, and ordering numbers.

Show Tunes

One of Geigel's recommendations is Better Living Through Show-tunes. As you can guess from the title, the author is a missionary for the subject. His page is a wonderfully complete guide to musicals on CD, including rare recordings and new ones in production. Check out his best-of-year lists. This is indeed "a home for everyone who can't wait for the next batch of Broadway musicals."

Theater Central

Theater Central is another huge draw for buffs, with more than 1,000 visitors daily. It's less Broadway-oriented than Geigel's site and includes more information on amateur and scholastic productions. Also, it's only minimally enhanced for Netscape, so those of you with other browsers won't be frustrated. Actors, directors, and those in the business can find a wealth of information here, ranging from magazines and newsgroups to tips on contracts, vendors, associations, and educational facilities. If you're planning a visit to New York, don't miss Keith Prowse's New York Theater page. Like Geigel, he gives plenty of ticketing information and insider news.

Playbill

One of the rituals of theatergoing is reading *Playbill,* and now you can do it on the Web. The Playbill site contains an index of articles and a useful search engine so you can easily find out about your favorite actor. And for those of you who collect records, there's an exhaustive index of cast recordings, both currently available and soon to be released. Find such rare gems as *Mata Hari,* the 1966 flop musical with that chart topper, "I'm Saving Myself for a Soldier." Other worthwhile sites are the Home Page of Theatre, whose playwrights' section is the deepest source of fact and lore on authors from Sam Shepard to Shakespeare. ArtsUSA provides a forum on all the arts, including theater—engaging members in discussions about the NEA, public broadcasting, and other policy matters. Playbill is particularly good at monthly updates on AIDS events, regularly listing Broadway Cares benefits in New York and fund-raisers such as a reading of Quilt-themed playlettes during its tenth anniversary in San Francisco.

☐ *About Face Theatre Collective*
http://aboutface.base.org

☐ *African-American Lesbigaytrans Performance*
http://www.uic.edu/orgs/arealread/

☐ *ArtsUSA*
http://www.artsusa.org/

☐ *B-Girlz*
http://www.interlog.com/~antenna/b-girlz

☐ *Broadway Cares/Equity Fights AIDS*
http://www.bcefa.org/

☐ *Catalogue of Lesbian Plays, Musicals, One-Acts, and Monologues*
http://www.monitor.net/~carolyn/

☐ *Crude-rom.com*
http://www.crude-rom.com

☐ *Current Art Fag*
http://www.capitalxtra.on/ca/queercapital/cx/cx68/arts/cx_68html

☐ *Diversionary Theatre*
http://www.diversionary.org/

☐ *Execution of Justice*
http://www.randy.com/executionofjustice/

☐ *Gay Comedy*
http://www.hanksite.com/gaycomdy/

☐ *GorillaBlue*
http://www.hanksite.com/gaycomdy/

☐ *Home Page of Theatre*
http://www.cs.fsu.edu/projects/group4/theatre.html

☐ *Joe Geigel's Favorite Theatre-Related Resources*
http://www.jogle.com

☐ *Keith Prowse New York Theatre*
http://www.keithprowse.com/

☐ *Musicals*
http://www.yahoo.com/Arts/Performing_Arts/Theater/Musicals

☐ *One in Ten Theatre Company*
http://www.azstarnet.com/~jdbanks/1in10.htm

☐ *Performing Arts Online*
http://www.performingarts.net/links/theatre.htm

☐ *Playbill online*
http://www.playbill.com/

☐ *Queer Cafe (Pussy Cat Theatre)*
http://www.pussycattheatreco.com/queer.htm

☐ *Queer Lives in the Theater*
http://gwis2.circ.gwu.edu/~rmb/doorway.html

☐ *Queer Stage List*
http://ausqrd.queer.org/au/qrd/net/lists/queerstge.html

☐ *Rent Homepage*
http://www.siteforrent.com/index.html

☐ *Sir Ian McKellen*
http://www.mckellen.com

☐ *Stephen Sondheim Stage*
http://www.sondheim.com/

☐ *Theatre Central*
http://www.theatre-central.com/

☐ *Theatre Reviews*
http://www.freetown.com/picadilly/westminister/1079/razzle.html

☐ *Theatre Rhinoceros*
http://www.therhino.org/

☐ *Tony Awards*
http://www.tonys.org/

☐ *Village Voice OBIE Awards*
http://www.villagevoice.com/obies

☐ *Wings Theatre*
http://www.brainlink.com:80/~cjeffer/

☐ *Yahoo!-Arts:Drama*
http://www.yahoo.com/Arts/Drama/

Transsexual/Transgender/ Drag

How many ways are there to be a girl, boy, man, woman? Personality, chemistry, and behavior are all entwined in an answer that can be as searching as Leslie Feinberg's work as a transgender warrior. Or it can be as light and flirty as Club Kid's nail lacquer tips. Whether curious for yourself, your friends, or your family, the entire spectrum of gender play is on the Web.

What do TV, TS, and gender dysphoria mean? What's the difference between a transvestite and a cross-dresser? You might begin at the venerable Transgender Forum. TG has samples from its newsletter, a photo gallery, community information, personals, and chat lines. Among the links are those to sites for M2F or F2M transsexualism, intersex, TG Activism and TG Support. Anna's Transgender and Transsexual links is a huge compilation of over 250 links that cover questions on how to deal with family, how to pass, surgery, workplace issues, your rights under the law and many more. There are also pointers to TG fiction, FAQs, newsgroups, mail lists, and organizations in the U.S. and around the world. Transgendered Resources has listings of national clubs and professionals providing support and surgical services. Global Transgender Ring has pages from all points on the globe including Australia, Scotland, Italy, Germany, Japan, China, and Poland.

TG Guide

Another large site is TG Guide, with an exhaustive list of re-sources. The articles constitute one of the largest gender li-braries on the Web: everything from Zen and the Art of Post Op-erative Maintenance to differences between the male and female brain, childhood influences on sexual identity and a comparison of TVs, M2Fs, TSs and male homosexuals. There's also an excellent message board. Just write in a question on hair (too much or too little), hormones, being out at work—whatever. It's a lively place and most questions get three or more answers within a day. There are lots of fascinating tidbits scattered throughout the site. You'll find, for instance, the CIA report on transsexuals. Contrary to expectation, "Findings in this report suggest a need to rethink criteria for evaluating a number of forms of atypical sexual behavior, some of which may be unrelated to security risk."

Home Pages

Home pages most often target cross-dressing men with tips and advice for passing. Veronica Vera's Academy is one of the best. She's an evangelist of sorts and a wonderful talker. Vera tells how she and the academy have been uplifted on the broad shoulders of a sea of grateful men in skirts. "From the time I created Miss Vera's Finishing School for Boys Who Want to Be Girls, the world's first male-to-female cross-dressing academy, my princess phone began to ring off the hook…. Most callers asked me if the school was for real. Could I actually help them to 'pass' as female? When I answered 'yes,' it was as if someone had confirmed the existence of Santa Claus, or as I prefer to think of myself, Cinderfella's fairy godmother."

Club Kid is another very readable page for cross-dressing party girls. She's playful and loves working with his image. "The kind of drag I do is what I call sexy vampire drag. It's a little bit of Jayne Mansfield, a hint of Elvira, a scoop of Fran Drescher, and a handful of Minnie Mouse." And if you like to hit the party circuit, she's got advice galore on the latest music, the best make-up and, of course, how to rule the dance floor.

Drag

Writer, performer, drag queen extraordinaire, Hedda Lettuce has a home page featuring—herself! It's a tour de force of drag queen wit, outrageous and sparkling with downtown glamour. In an interview with *POZ* magazine she dishes the dirt, talks of her media empire, and answers questions on work (waiting on people goes against drag queen karma), disses bad drag (facial hair is a no-no and heels are a must). She's a "sexist pig when it comes to drag...Hedda Hitler."

The Issues

Amid the talk of wigs and sequins on the Web, there's conversation on gender as a window on our culture and its most basic structures. For an international roundup of what's happening see, GLNN's TransGender News. You'll find headlines and abstracts followed by full text articles. Genderqueers online is an always-interesting mail list for people "who bend even the boundaries of transgenderism, who identify as many genders, or no gender, or third-gendered." But it's not a pointy-headed place. The moderator, Raphael Carter, tells of a little joke s/he often plays as people watch her to see which bathroom she'll go into. "I pause by the entrances to the bathrooms, pull a coin out of my pocket, and flip it....I look down at the coin with an expression of dismay, mutter aloud, 'Oh, God, not again'—and walk into the bathroom I was going to use anyway."

Bornstein and Feinberg

Two of the highest-profile leaders in today's transgender liberation movement are Kate Bornstein and Leslie Feinberg. Both have their own pages and appear in quite a few of the articles you'll find. In an interview with Bornstein by Shannon Bell, Bornstein takes on one of the most troubling questions for the queer community. "Yes there is a lesbian and gay movement, yes there is a transgendered movement. What do these movements have in common? They fuck with gender roles. Nothing else do they have in common."

Feinberg's page is a good introduction to this disarmingly gentle revolutionary. She talks of her books and her lover and has snippets from speeches, and video clips from events. Along with hotlinks to other organizations and political struggles. And the forums on her books *Stone Butch Blues* and *Transgender Warriors* offer a unique talk with the author herself.

Tranny Shack

You can read about publicly advertised drag balls in the 1920s—and perhaps even remember them—but today there is a club that's become the new mecca of drag, the supernova of genderfuck. It's a late night club in San Francisco that's tilting the center of performance drag to the West Coast with a cast of talented performers like Heklina and Pippi Lovestocking. Check out the Web site for stills of the stars: more pink zebra stripes and makeup than is legal in a shimmying, singing, dancing version of what is termed "Techno Dolly Parton."—just an elegantly rancid foretaste of the "Psycho Tranny Show."

Wigstock

"Peace, love and hairspray" are the watchwords for Wigstock, the infamous, ever-outrageous drag fest. The festival has been the subject of a full-length documentary, *Wigstock: The Movie*. it has been profiled on CNN, BBC Television, MTV News, and in *Vanity Fair*, *Newsweek* and even *Screw* magazine. The event has featured almost every queen in New York City and some of the music industry's hippest stars including RuPaul, Deborah Harry, Deee-lite, Cindy Wilson of the B-52's, Crystal Waters, and John Cameron Mitchell of *Hedwig and the*

Angry Inch. Check out the Web site for the next event. And as Lady Bunny says, "Have a very good hair day!"

QRD, Rainbow Queery

Other sources of info are the QRD and Rainbow Queery. Each maintains a large folder on "our trans cousins." There are articles and newsletters from a cross section of media, ranging from *Mother Jones* magazine to the *San Francisco Chronicle.* Titles include "Sex Change Ends Inner Conflict," "Graduation Speaker Vetoed," and "A Transgender Diary."

Books

For offscreen reading, go to the International Foundation of Gender Expression (IFGE) Internet Bookshop and cruise the book stacks for works such as *Men Are From Mars, Women Are From Venus; Art and Illusion: A Guide to Crossdressing, Vol. 1, Face and Hair; Gender Outlaw;* and *The Apartheid of Sex: A Manifesto on the Freedom of Gender.*

☐ *A B Gender*
   http://www.abgender.com

☐ *Above & Beyond*
   http://www.abmall.com/cb/tg/res.html

☐ *Alcina's Lair*
   http://www.alcina.net

☐ *Androgyny RAQ (rarely asked questions)*
   http://www.chaparraltree.com/raq/

☐ *Anna's Transgender and Transsexual links*
   http://www.geocities.com/WestHollywood/4114/

☐ *Bay Area Transgender Resources*
   http://www.transgender.org/tg/people/jff/tgrg.html

☐ *Boychicks*
http://www.e-zines.com/boychicks/

☐ *Butch-Femme*
http://www.butch-femme.com

☐ *Caroline's Listings Page*
http://www.geocities.com/westhollywood/heights/4346/america.html

☐ *ClubKid*
http://www.cris.com/~Kalina/Vamp/ClubKid.html

☐ *Cocktailin' to Hell*
http://members.tripod.com/seanbne/

☐ *Clara's Extra-Gender World*
http://www.geocities.com/devikuanyin/ingles.html

☐ *Cross Dress On the UnderNet*
http://crossdress.tvheaven.com/

☐ *Cross Dressers Online (CDS Bookstand)*
http://www.cdspub.com/

☐ *Cross Dressers Web Ring*
http://www.webring.org/cgi-bin/webring?ring=cdwr;list

☐ *Drag Queen City*
http://www.dqc.tsx.org/

☐ *Drag Queen Make-Over*
http://www.abmall.com/grae/

☐ *Eunuchs In Literature*
http://www.angelfire.com/ri/tucker/gender/eunuchs5.html

☐ *Female to Male International*
http://www.ftm-intl.org/

☐ *F2M, Transgendered, Interesexed, Androgynous, and Sexuality Links:*
http://www.netgsi.com/~listwrangler/translinks.html

☐ *Gender Mall*
http://www.abmall.com/cb/tg/res.html

☐ *Genderqueers Online*
http://come.to/sphere

☐ *Gladys Kravitz, Queen of Karaoke*
http://www.gladyskravitz.com/

☐ *Global Transgender Ring*
http://www.webcoves.com/tgring.html

☐ *Hedda Lettuce*
http://www.hedda.com/index2.html

☐ *Holly Woodlawn*
http://www.hollywoodlawn.com/

☐ *IFGE Home Page*
http://www.transgender.org/tg/ifge/

☐ *Ingersoll Gender Center Home Page*
http://www.halcyon.com/ingersol/iiihome.html

☐ *Intersex Society of North America*
http://www.isna.org/

☐ *Kate Bornstein (by Shannon Bell)*
http://www.ctheory.com/./a-kate_bornstein.html

☐ *Leslie Feinberg (Transgender Warrior)*
http://www.transgenderwarrior.org/

☐ *Madkats*
http://www.madkats.com/

☐ *Miss Kitty's Longbranch Saloon*
http://www.angelfire.com/ga/beverlyann1

☐ *Patty's Place*
http://www.igc.net/~lost/

☐ *The Plaid*
http://www.wintermute.co.uk/users/snuffles/The_Plaid/

☐ *Queer Resources Directory*
http://www.qrd.org/qrd/

☐ *Rainbow Query: Transgender*
http://www.rainbowquery.com/categories/transgender.html

☐ *Renaissance Education Association*
http://www.ren.org/

☐ *Sphere*
http://www.bombdiggity.com/shrapnel/sphere.html

☐ *Susan's Place of Transgender Resources*
http://www.susans.org/

☐ *TG Community Info*
http://members.aol.com/onqgwen/index.html

☐ *TG Directory*
http://weber.u.washington.edu/~sfpse/l/transgen/transg2.txt

☐ *TG (TransGender) Forum*
http://www.tgforum.com/content1.html

☐ *TG Guide*
http://www.tgguide.com/index.html

☐ *TG Support Groups*
http://www.tgfmall.com/info/wwgrp.html

☐ *Transsexual Menace*
http://www.echonyc.com/~degrey/Menace.html
http://www.apocalypse.org/pub/tsmenace

☐ *Transgender Forum*
http://www.transgender.org/

☐ *Transgender Ring*
http://www.echonyc.com/~degrey/LCove/tgring.html

☐ *TRANSGENDER WARRIOR (Leslie Feinberg)*
http://www.transgenderwarrior.org/

☐ *Transgendered Community at Temenos*
http://www.temenos.net/trans

☐ *TV/TS Forum*
http://www.tgforum.com/content1.html

☐ *Vanessa Kaye's Transgender Resource Page*
http://www.3dcom.com/couples/framehtml

☐ *Velvet Underground Chat*
http://www.jupiter.beseen.com/chat/rooms/e/131/

☐ *Veronica Vera's Academy*
http://www.missvera.com

☐ *Wigstock*
http://www.wigstock-nu/

☐ *What is Inter-gendered?*
http://www.donnas-hideout.org/intergen.html

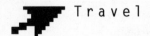 Travel

Is it okay to bring a friend back to your hotel room in Turkey? Israel? Moscow? Where's the hottest cruise party, an ultra-luxe B&B, queer mountaineers? Whether you're planning an exotic journey or a randy hour at the truck stop, the Web is the place to find answers.

Actually, you don't even need to have any preset plans—but it's prudent to check that the travel agency is a member of IGTLA (International Gay and Lesbian Travel Association). You can browse the site directory of more than 1,200 IGTA member agencies by region, type of service, or business names.

International Gay & Lesbian Travel Association

Most if not all IGTLA members offer more detailed information elsewhere, either on the large travel sites or on their own pages. For example, Gay and Lesbian Travel Web hosts such well-known travel companies as Advance Damron Travel, Olivia, Vicki Skinner's Doin' It Right, Home Suite HOM, and Destination Discovery. Cruise operators in particular are very generous with photographs. RSVP has so many seductive sun and sea photos it takes a long time to load.

 Another excellent resource is Out and About, whose page contains a compilation of cruise lines, pride events and a selection of reviews. Check out the piece on gay Russia, the report on Key West guest houses, or the ratings guide of how mainstream travel companies stack up on the queer-friendly scale. There's also practi-

cal advice for HIV-positive vacationers and a queer-friendly ratings guide of car rental companies.

Word on the Street

The most compelling reason to visit the multisite travel pages is to read reviews on a potential destination. GayWired Travel has wonderful travel columns, among them an excellent piece on Cuba. "Augusto was late, and all eyes seemed to be on this foreigner standing alone in the obviously well-acquainted crowd outside Yara. When Augusto did arrive, I was introduced as "pan caliente" (hot bread) and then, following perfunctory introductions, whisked into a taxi and off to a party in a private house deep in the suburbs of Havana. We paid out ten pesos (50 cents U.S.) to enter, and descended into the back garden and a scene from the inferno set to disco with some salsa thrown in...."

Over the Rainbow's travel reports are most often written by natives. On Israel, for example, we're told that although sodomy laws were repealed several years ago and public acceptance seems high, few "Israelis live openly gay lives, and the closet is still the accepted norm." It goes on to report that Tel Aviv is the most open city.

Gay-Web

Although you'll only find Gay-Web (note the dash!) at its own site, it's one of the most sophisticated travel agencies on the Web and its 30 years in the business shows up in a particularly interesting array of tour options ranging from a visit to Germany for Oktoberfest to a llama trail ride for lesbians to deluxe international cruises. You can book plane and housing right from your screen. Make sure and check out the weekly air fare and cruise packages—even last-minute travelers can find some great bargains.

What is most impressive about Gay-Web is the huge folder of 300 travel articles on Asia, Australia, North and South America, the

Caribbean, Europe, and Africa. Much more than brochure hype, the author gives suggestions on all sorts of real-world considerations like reasonable bed-and-breakfasts, what to see, and what to avoid.

GayScene.com

GayScene.com has come a long way in the past few years, enlarging its collection of over 3,000 links from around the world and winning the Rainbow, FunkyDiva, and Freedom awards.

Once in, you'll see why it's so popular. Rather than slogging though all the sites, you can either click on a country or just type in SWEDEN, for example. And though the pages have lots of ads, once you determine a destination there are reports by natives with addresses, hours, descriptions of the crowd—all the stuff you'd tell a visitor to your own neighborhood.

XXX Guide

This is a sort of little black book for gay travelers. Instead of winking at sex opportunities, it has extremely detailed rundowns on action at the baths and public meeting places. The fabled saunas in Turkey, Berlin, Rome—they're all here at their steamiest.

City and Regional Press

Aside from specifically travel-oriented sites, it's always a good idea to visit local magazines and E-'zines. Tulsa Family News is a terrifically well-written guide to what's going on around town and SonomaZone covers the wine country in Northern California with an editorial slant that's two parts *New Yorker*, one part '60s *Esquire*, and a sprinkle of Swiftian satire. Once read, you'll know it like a neighbor.

Community Sites

Especially since 1996, general interest community sites have added travel sections. GayWired, GayWeb, The Mining Company, The Rainbow Mall, and PlanetOut each have extensive selections. The Mining Company always has some of the best reporting available, and their travel section is especially good. Along with the gay scene at many world capitals, you get the inside story on shopping, museums, sight seeing, exchange rate tips, and more. Their links list is of equal quality. One recommendation for example, is The Gay Times Guide to London, a local's acerbic impression of every bar and restaurant in town, covering nightlife in an obsessive sometimes hilariously jaundiced eye. PlanetOut has perhaps the largest assortment of gay travel links. Some are multidestination travel agencies, while others are advertisements for local businesses. For example, the Manto Bar on Mykonos promises the epitome of chic in one of the world's oldest gay playgrounds and The Old Mill Bed and Breakfast conjures a bucolic rest and cure beside a mountain stream.

Rentals & Adventure

One of the best ways to save money and get a true taste of another culture is to stay with locals. For information on an international network of people who open their homes to travelers, go to Lesbian and Gay Hospitality Exchange International. For bed-and-breakfasts, visit Gay B&Bs or see the list at the Rainbow Destinations site. If you're up for adventure, try Adventuring IGLOO (International Gay and Lesbian Outdoor Organization), with member clubs in many U.S. and international cities. This nonprofit organization functions as an open forum, allowing anyone with an itch for adventure to fulfill their dreams. What do they do? "You name it: day hikes; short, weekend and week-long cycling tours; camping; cabin trips; skydiving; rafting, sailing and canoeing; skiing and ice skating"—anything out of doors.

QRD

As always, the QRD comes through with hundreds of files, ranging from a PWA travel kit to a letter from Hilton on "sexual orientation policy" to a press release for a book of sexy Spanish phrases like "I just broke up with my boyfriend" and "Take the handcuffs off!" See also the chapters on City Guides and International Queers.

☐ *Above and Beyond Tours*
http://www.abovebeyondtours.com

☐ *Adventuring*
http://adventureing.org/cgi-bin/main.idc

☐ *Alternative Travel*
http://www.a-1travel.com/altntive.htm

☐ *All About Destinations*
http://www.aadintl.com/

☐ *Australian Gay & Lesbian Tourism Association*
http://aglta.asn.au/index.htm

☐ *Broadway Bound! (New York theater for women)*
http://www.companyofwomen.com/adventure.htm

☐ *California Men's Gathering*
http://www.webcom.com/cmg/

☐ *Capitain Barb's Lesbian Cruises*
http://www.captainbarb.com

☐ *City.Net*
http://www.city.net/

☐ *Crete Spiritual Traveling*
http://www.gaycrete.com

☐ *Cruising With Pride Cruises & Resorts*
http://www.cruisingwithpride.com

☐ *Damron Guide*
http://www.damron.com/

☐ *European Railways*
http://rail.rz.uni-karlsruhe.de/rail/english.html

☐ *Ferrari Guides*
http://www.q-net.com/qnet.htm

☐ *Gay Airline & Travel Club*
http://members.tripod.com/~gatc

☐ *Gay Bed & Breakfasts*
http://www.serve.com/schultz/gbbg/main/shtml

☐ *Gay Berlin*
http://www.datacom.de/~ron/gay/

☐ *Gay Global Network*
http://gayguide.net/

☐ *Gay Hotels*
http://www.gayhotelnetwork.com/

☐ *Gay Inn's Online*
http://www.gayinnsonline.com/

☐ *Gay, Lesbian & Fat-friendly Tours*
http://www.camelottravels.com/

☐ *Gay & Lesbian Home Exchange*
http://www.homearoundtheworld.com/

☐ *Gay and Lesbian Travel Association*
http://www.gtla.com/

☐ *Gay and Lesbian Travel Web*
http://www.gaytravel.com/

☐ *Gay Day at Disney World*
http://www.gayday.com/

☐ *Gay Explorer*
http://gay-travel.gayexplorer.com

☐ *Gay Fun Tours*
http://www.gayfuntours.com

☐ *Gay-Travel*
http://www.gay-travel.com/

☐ *Gay Mart (travel books)*
http://www.gaymart.com/shopbook/2item/i004584.html

☐ *GayWeb Travel*
http://www.gaywired.com/travel.htm

☐ *GayWired Travel*
http://www.gaywired.com/unity/index.html

☐ *GLINN/Travel (news reports)*
http://www.glinn.com/news/travel1.htm

☐ *The Guide*
http://www.guidemag.com/

☐ *HIV+ Travelers*
http://www.overtherainbow.com/

☐ *International Gay Travel Association*
http://www.igta.org/

☐ *Leather Travel*
http://www.loop.com/~leatherman/

☐ *Mantos Bar on Mykonos*
http://www.otenet.gr/pierros/Manto1.html

☐ *Mining Co. Travel*
http://gaylesissues.miningco.com/msub22.htm

☐ *Olivia Cruise & Resorts*
http://www.a-1travel.com/altntive.htm

☐ *Our World Travel*
http://www.rainbow-mall.com/igta/ourworld/index.html

☐ *Out in America (Bad Puppy)*
http://badpuppy.com/

☐ *Out & About*
http://www.outandabout.com/

☐ *Over The Rainbow*
http://www.overtherainbow.com/

☐ *PlanetOut*
http://www.planetout.com/

☐ *Pride Infonet*
http://www.pridetravel.com/

☐ *Purple Roofs*
http://www.mongooseontheloose.com/purpleroofs/index.html

☐ *Queernet*
http://queernet.org/

☐ *Queer Resources Directory*
http://www.qrd.org/qrd/

☐ *Rainbow Mall*
http://www.rainbow-mall.com/

☐ *RSVP Cruises*
http://www.rsvp.net/

☐ *Sydney Mardi Gras*
http://www.mardigras.com.au/

☐ *TimeOUT*
http://www.timeout.co.uk/

☐ *U.S. State Department Travel Advisories*
gopher://gopher.stolaf.edu:70/77/.index/US-State-Department-

☐ *Venture Out*
http://www.venture-out.com

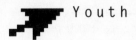 Youth

Though the topic of gay and lesbian youth was long considered off-limits for fear of fomenting wacko accusations of recruiting, the statistics on suicide and a general recognition that homosexuality is genetic rather than behavioral has lifted the lid on youth-oriented groups, particularly on the Web. The Rainbow Query, QRD and Yahoo! all have long lists of sites, as do a few university servers. The largest index of all is at Queer America. With more than 3,700 entries, it's a huge database of youth resources that includes information on community centers, support organizations, PFLAG chapters, and more. These can be great places to meet friends, get questions answered, or find support.

One of the best is the appropriately named YouthResources.com. It's a comprehensive page geared toward education with articles on the current state of LGBT student life, news from schools around the country, and an advice column for kids and teachers as well as a long links list to related topics such as scholarships, hate crimes and AIDS. This is a frequently updated site with revolving themes, such as a

recent feature on LGBT Youth and Disabilities. One of the highlights is its moderated forums set up in tandem with feminist-campus.org. These discussions provide a useful and welcoming place to set up an virtual 'LGBT student office where topics have included starting a campus group, how to deal with violence, access to scholarships, and spirituality among queer youth.

The one feature that marks each of these pages is tenderness. Even the staunchest activist seems to realize that although kids are looking for answers, the most effective counselor is one who listens. For a jolting reminder of just how exposed kids can be, consider the suicide statistics for queer youths. Or take a look at Scoutingforall.com. This page, perhaps more than any other, marks the change in attitude not only toward gay youths, but gays in society. Rather than hide, founder Steve Cozza and his associates have put together a wonderful page of resources, news and testimonials of former and current Scout members. There's an incredible determination everywhere on this page and a reminder that neither the Girl Scouts of the United States or Camp Fire Boys and Girls discriminate against gay, lesbian, bisexual, and transgendered youth and adults

Out! Proud!

What isn't on this site? There are book recommendations, profiles of gay and lesbian role models for kids, resources to make schools safer, brochures on sexual orientation from clinical treatises by doctors and psychiatrists to plainspoken definitions of sexual terms, news of interest and a survey that gives a sometimes heartening sometimes heartbreaking impression of queer kids today. The links list is vast and of use (as is the entire site) to "queer and questioning youth" as well as queer and straight parents. You'll find PFLAG's excellent self-check list on things to think about before coming out to parents. Also suicide studies and a pointer to the White Ribbon Campaign. And more.

Gender, Sex, and Sexuality

One site that makes everyone's list is Youth.org, which seeks to help youth sort fact from fiction. Its purpose "is not to advocate homosexuality, bisexuality, heterosexuality, or any gender identity." Instead, its "mission is to support people that are trying to accept themselves for who they are." To do so, the site's creator offers some no-nonsense guidelines on gender identity, roles, and sexual orientation. There are also articles on AIDS, safer sex, the rainbow flag, and monogamy.

The Cool Page for Queer Teens!

The Cool Page is a nonpatronizing effort to educate kids in a straightforward manner. The first story asks the question "Just who am I anyway?" And there are others answering fundamental questions every teen has: "How do you know if you're gay, straight, bisexual, transgender, or what?" "I think I may be gay or lesbian—now what do I do?" By walking kids through the potential consequences of coming out and getting them to think about things in a logical manner, it makes the process of becoming one's true self seems much less hazardous. There are also guides to smooth the rough times, such as what to do when you've been outed unexpectedly or are having trouble at home or in school. A resource list includes chat lines, various youth organizations (including PFLAG), and a list of books, magazines, and videos.

Youth Assistance Organization

YAO was created to help self-identifying gay, lesbian, bisexual, and questioning youths. Its mission is to "provide young people with a safe space online to be themselves." Along with a resource list, this page has a message board where teens log questions about every conceivable topic, including that age-old fear that they are "the only one." With commendable ease, the authors walk that fine line of being both personal and objective.

Magazines by Youth, for Youth

Though the above organizations offer a wealth of information, it is with the youth magazines that teens themselves seem most involved. ELight! and Oasis are two of the best and both concentrate on giving kids a place to talk with one another by asking questions telling stories of school life, family life, dealing with school problems, self-image—anything that's on their minds. Elight! has a more literary feel with poetry and essays on first experiences, coming out, and perceptions from the closet.

Oasis ("Because it's a desert out there!") is less formal. Though following a magazine format with features, and departments, everything is written by kids. Nicely, the authors photograph always appears with the columns on coming out to friends, first crush, choosing a college, or dealing with belonging to an anti-homosexual church.

GirlZone, Gay Goth, Young Gay Men

There are also a number of sites geared to a more particular audience. GirlZone is a mail list for bi/lesbian females under 18 years of age. Gay Goth Network provides a place for young gay teenagers devoted to the Gothic culture. Out and Out Racing is the place for gay kids into motorcycles. Young Gay Men Talking has conversations about coming out, sex, and HIV and AIDS. "Being gay is not a way of life, it's a part of life."

Home Pages

If you're looking for a less structured atmosphere, try the home pages. Tiger and Bear's Teen Shack is a surprisingly well-done home page with resources, penpal gallery and message board for teens, their families and friends. Aaron and Eric's Gay Youth Site has a list of favorite sites and impressions of the author's hometown and at the movies. Teenage Girl Diaries is exactly that—a personal diary on the Web.

☐ *Aaron & Eric's Gay Youth Site*
  http://www.usinternet.com/users/aehappel/youthsite/

☐ *Advocate's for Youth*
  http://www.advocatesforyouth.org

☐ *Alternative Kids (coming out)*
  http://www.afn.org/~afn63843/

☐ *All Together.Com*
  http://www.alltogether.com

☐ *The Art Project*
http://www.youthresource.com/gallery/

☐ *AVERT AIDS Education and Research Trust*
http://www.avert.org/

☐ *Be Yourself*
http://www.outproud.org/html/brochures/brochure_be_yourself.html

☐ *Blair*
http://www.blairmag.com

☐ *Child Welfare Services for Lesbian, Gay and Bisexu-al Youth*
http://www.casmt.on.ca/lgby1.html

☐ *Coming Out to Your Parents (PFLAG)*
http://libertynet.org/~pflag/brochure.html

☐ *Cool Web Page for Queer Babes and Dudes*
http://www.pe.net/~bidstrup/cool.htm

☐ *Creating Safe Schools*
http://members.tripod.com/~twood/guide.html

☐ *Children of Lesbians and Gays Everywhere (CLAGE)*
http://www.colage.org/

☐ *The Coming Out of a Lesbian's Mother (coming out)*
http://www.angelfire.com/co/lesmom/index.html

☐ *ELight!*
http://www.youth.org/elight

☐ *Fruit Loopz*
http://www.interlog.com/~tclgby/soy/fruitloopz/home.html

☐ *Gay and Lesbian Organization of spiRitual Youth (GLORY)*
http://www.toronto.anglican.ca/MoosWeb/glory/

☐ *Gay Bisexual Youth Suicide Studies*
http://www.virtualcity.com/youthsuicide/

☐ *Gay Goth Network*
http://www.glasnost.com/gaygoth/index.htm

☐ *Gay Prom*
http://www.gayprom.org/

☐ *GLBT Youth Resource Directory*
http://members.aol.com/ouryouth/index.html

☐ *GLSEN*
http://www.glsn.org

☐ *Hotlines for Youth*
http://www.geocities.com/WestHollywood/2680/hotlines.html

☐ *incite! (youth activism)*
http://www.incite.org/

☐ *Lesbian & Gay Youth & Coming Out*
http://www.ncf.carleton.ca:12345/freeport/sigs/life/gay/out/menu

☐ *Lesbian, Gay and Bisexual Students' Bill of Educational Rights*
http://gaylesissues.miningco.com/library/content/blstuds.htm

☐ *LYRIC (Lavender Youth Recreation & Information Center)*
http://thecity.sfsu.edu/~lyric/

☐ *Oasis Magazine*
http://www.oasismag.com/survey/

☐ *OutProud*
  http://www.outproud.org/

☐ *Person Project*
  http://www.youthorg.loco/personproject/

☐ *Pride USA*
  http://www.studentalliance.org/Prideusa.htmd

☐ *Qstreet (youth jobs postings)*
  http://www.qstreet.com/gayjobs/index.html

☐ *Queer America*
  http://www.queeramerica.org/

☐ *Queer Youth Resource Directory*
  http://www.qrd.org/qrd/youth/

☐ *Rainbow Youth Links*
  http://www.youthweb.com/rainbow/

☐ *Rainbow World*
  http://www.geocities.com/WestHollywood/7207/

☐ *Resource Page for Parents of Gays, Lesbians, Bisexuals, Transgenders*
  http://www.pe.net/~bidstrup/parents.htm

☐ *Scouting For All*
  http://www.scoutingforall.org/

☐ *Some Teens Are...*
  http://www.geocities.com/WestHollywood/3514/

☐ *Speak Out*
  http://www.youthresource.com/speakout/

☐ *Squarepegs*
http://arts.ucsc.edu/squarepegs/home.index.html

☐ *Teenage Girl Diaries*
http://www.bway.net/~teengirl/

☐ *Temenos*
http://temenos.net

☐ *When a Son Says He's Gay*
http://www.parentsoup.com/library/dkl050.html

☐ *White Ribbon Campaign*
http://www.whiteribbon.org/

☐ *Yazone*
http://www.yazone.com//

☐ *Youth Assistance Organization*
http://www.youth.org/

☐ *Youth Gay/Lesbian Issues at the Mining Co.*
http://gaylesissues.miningco.com/

☐ *Youth Guard*
http://www.youth-guard.org/

☐ *Youth Resource*
http://www.youthresource.com/